THE WORLD OF
BUSINESS

THE WORLD OF
BUSINESS

GERALD H. GRAHAM
Wichita State University

ADDISON-WESLEY PUBLISHING COMPANY

Reading, Massachusetts

Menlo Park, California

Don Mills, Ontario

Wokingham, England

Amsterdam

Sydney

Singapore

Tokyo

Mexico City

Bogotá

Santiago

San Juan

Janis Jackson Hill *Acquisitions Editor*

Kristin Belanger *Art Editor*

Hugh Crawford *Manufacturing Supervisor*

Robert Hartwell Fiske *Development Editor*

Hannus Design Associates *Cover Designer*

Lorraine Hodsdon *Design Coordinator*

Intergraphics *Illustrator*

Martha K. Morong *Production Manager*

Margaret Pinette *Production Editor*

Sheila Pulver *Copy Editor*

Margaret Ong Tsao *Text Designer*

Karen Watson *Title Page, Part Opener, and Chapter Opener Artist*

Eric Wurzbacher *Photo Researcher*

Library of Congress Cataloging in Publication Data

Graham, Gerald H.
  The world of business.

  Includes index.
  1. Business.   2. United States — Commerce.
3. Business enterprises — United States.   I. Title.
HF5351.G658 1985   650   84-273
ISBN 0-201-11440-2

ABCDEFGHIJ-DO-898765

PREFACE

In the early 1980s, for the first time in history, three books about business appeared on the best-seller lists at the same time: *In Search of Excellence, Megatrends,* and *The One Minute Manager.* Periodicals about business practices have never been more popular than they are today. Government and community leaders are looking more than ever before to business for answers. Students, also picking up this theme, are enrolling in business courses in record numbers.

With the increasing popularity of business courses, colleges and their instructors and textbook writers and their publishers must assume a greater responsibility for providing the best business education possible. Since the Introduction to Business class is usually the first business course for most college students, it is critical that we do a good job in this area. Of course, the classroom instructor is the most vital ingredient among the total influences on students' learning experiences. A textbook, and the many supplementary materials that accompany it, are simply tools in the hands of a good instructor. Still, the text is an important feature, one that can make the instructor's job easier or more difficult.

All of society is demanding higher quality from businesses and other institutions. No longer can we sell products or services (texts included) simply by providing "balloons and suckers" to would-be purchasers. Like the business world, authors, to be successful, must create texts of outstanding quality. With *The World of Business*, we have responded to this challenge by producing a text for the 1980s, one that carries students to broader and deeper learning experiences.

COMPLETE COVERAGE

"The most complete coverage of any intro to business text on the market," is the way reviewers describe this text. As some critics have pointed out, many introductory texts provide information that is "a mile wide and an inch deep." That is, there is a little information about a lot of different topics but not much about any particular topic. But today's business students are more demanding, wanting solid concepts and comprehensive coverage of relevant topics.

Comprehensive coverage does not, however, mean "dry and dull." After reading the manuscript, one student said, "I found the text to be lively as well as informative." We hope that we have created a comprehensive, yet easy-to-read text. At least, that was our goal.

REAL-WORLD EXAMPLES

Research from communication experiments stresses the importance of tangible, practical examples for increasing interest and learning. After presenting concepts, the text frequently shows several cogent examples to reinforce student learning of the concept. In one of the marketing chapters, after discussing the concept of "pioneering advertising," the text illustrates how Coca-Cola used Hollywood-type hype successfully to launch its Diet Coke. And after presenting "listed securities," in a finance chapter, the text records that Braniff Airlines stock set a record in trades while the company was still in bankruptcy.

Theories of business practices are very important, but nothing happens in a vacuum. Primarily through the use of actual examples, the text shows how businesses translate the theory into practice. For instance, the computer chapter describes electronic mail and then shows how Franson and Associates, a public relations agency, uses electronic mail in their business. Another section shows how Chrysler uses 30 robots, equipped with computer-chip brains, to weld 100 new cars an hour in its Delaware assembly plant. Whenever there is an opportunity, the text describes real-world businesses applying the concepts.

STRONG ISSUES EMPHASIS

The World of Business recognizes the dynamics of the business environment and attempts to capture the ever-changing nature of business by discussing critical, unresolved issues, such as: Should employers be allowed to use lie detector tests? Should insurance rates be the same for men and women? What overall impact will the increasing use of robots have on our economy?

Today's highly competitive business world increasingly demands business people equipped to think clearly about issues and make well-reasoned decisions. Throughout this book, students are presented with current business issues and

asked to take a stand. The "Crossfire" inserts are such a feature; they carefully delineate the pros and cons of issues and can easily be used to generate classroom discussion, mock debates, or student projects.

BACKGROUND FOR THE TEXT

Like most authors, I surveyed the topics considered important for an introduction to business text. And I have used the material in teaching more than 1200 introduction to business students in the last few years. Using the concept of "close to the customer," I've relied heavily on student feedback to tell us what to include and how to present the material. Current business periodicals were examined to get the latest trends and applications of the concepts. I would like to acknowledge the supportive role my publisher played in helping me develop the most effective teaching and learning package for instructors and students. I am greatly indebted to Robert Fiske, developmental editor at Addison-Wesley, for his many original ideas.

STIMULATING PEDAGOGY

The World of Business contains a number of outstanding pedagogical devices that are designed to aid the students' enjoyment in and understanding of the material.

- *Design.* The four-color design of this text is unlike any competing text. The artistic part- and chapter-opener collages, the wealth of photos, the art program, and the magazine-like layout all make this as pleasing a book to look at as it is to read.

- *Writing style.* Great pains have been taken to ensure the readability of this text. An occasional use of humor (quite aside from the *Funny Business* cartoons) also serves to stimulate the students' interest in the book.

- *Realistic examples.* As already mentioned, there is an abundance of up-to-date business examples throughout the text.

- *Part outlines and chapter learning objectives.* These two pedagogical devices help the students grasp the material even before it's presented.

- *Features.* "Business Bulletin" features provide extended real-world illustrations of numerous business areas. "Taking Stock" features assess the current status of specific businesses or various aspects of the business environment. "Crossfire" features present both sides of controversial issues.

- *Enrichment chapters.* There are five supplemental chapters in the text that allow the instructor to tailor the book to student and course needs. Enrichment Chapters A and B are unique to introduction to business books. The five chapters are: A, "Corporate Culture"; B, "Strategic Marketing"; C, "The Uses of Statistical Methods"; D, "Careers in Business"; E, "The Future of Business."

- *Funny Business.* A sprinkling of cartoons occasionally lightens the mood by entertaining the students.

- *End-of-chapter material.* This includes the summary, a synopsis of chapter highlights; "Mind Your Business," a chapter self-quiz for the students (with answers at the back of the book); key terms, bold-faced in the text and listed (with page-number reference) at the end of the chapter; review questions, a chapter test that the instructor may want to assign; and cases, two per chapter, enhance the students' understanding of concepts presented in the chapter.

- *Careerscope.* Following each of the book's six parts is a section on career planning. All six parts have a short vocational aptitude quiz to help the students assess their personality, interests, and values. These quizzes were devised by professional career counselors, Thomas Harrington and Arthur O'Shea of Career Planning Associates, Inc., of Needham, Massachusetts. The "Careerscopes" at the end of Parts II through V also contain a list of job descriptions applicable to the four business areas discussed in the text.

- *Glossary.* Finally, a glossary defines all key terms used in the text. A chapter-number reference accompanies each key term.

COMPREHENSIVE INSTRUCTIONAL/ LEARNING PACKAGE

Accompanying *The World of Business* is a complete, thoroughly integrated package of resource materials designed to assist the instructor in course preparation and management. The components of this instructional package, available to adopters in an attractive resource box, are the following:

- *Course Planner and Film Guide.* This resource is designed to explain the organization and use of the complete text package. A matrix illustrates the interrelationships of the components. Alternative approaches to assigning the text for quarter, semester, or short courses; general strategies for course planning, grading, and administration; and projects and resources are discussed. The extensive Film Guide lists and summarizes films with information on securing and using them in class.

- *Instructor's Resource Manual.* Detailed lecture outlines are presented for each chapter supplemented by teaching strategies for explaining concepts and enrichments materials that summarize recent business events. Student projects and activities; answers to end-of-chapter review questions and cases; and achievement texts, midterms, and final exams are provided.

- *Test Item File and TESTGEN.* Over 2000 test items—multiple choice and true-false—are available. Answers to all questions are key-referenced to chapter and page in the text and identify either factual or applied questions. Test items are available in printed form as well as through TESTGEN, a free computerized testing program available to adopters.

- *Transparencies.* A set of 120 transparencies, mostly original art not appearing in the text, will be available free to adopters. Business documents are included as transparencies.

- *The Career Decision-Making System (CDM).* The CDM is a comprehensive, easily interpreted measure of vocational interests, combining three important elements of effective career counseling — interests, abilities, and values — with extensive interpretive information about 283 occupations that employ the vast majority of the work force. This instrument was developed by Thomas Harrington and Arthur J. O'Shea, professional career counselors, who also prepared the vocational aptitude quizzes appearing in the "Careerscope" sections that follow each part of the textbook. The "Careerscopes," combined with the CDM, offer a well integrated approach to career planning.

■ *Businesswise Library.* To enhance your classroom lectures, the Addison-Wesley Businesswise Library offers you a number of timely Addison-Wesley books spanning a variety of business topics: *Theory Z, The Hundred Best Companies to Work for in America,* and *Corporate Cultures,* to name a few. This library is available to adopters.

■ *Student Activity Guide.* This useful study aid offers a detailed review of each chapter plus extensive self tests. The innovative aspects of the guide are the numerous involvement exercises that require students to apply information learned from the text to realistic, managerial situations. The exercises can be completed by students on an individual as well as group basis. Features such as "Critics Corner," "Problem Line," "From the Mailroom," "You Are the Manager," and "It's Your Opinion" ask students to assume the role of a manager and make decisions.

■ *Bu$iness Sen$e: A Decision-Making Simulation.* A microcomputer simulation specifically designed for this course accompanies the text. Students form companies and make decisions in a competitive environment simulating a business situation. Playing the game gives students a better understanding of the relationship between production and operations management, marketing and finance. The Student Manual explains how to play, supplies worksheets, and provides a case study of the actual industry being simulated. The Instructor's Manual gives numerous options for integrating the simulation into the course.

ACKNOWLEDGMENTS

Many reviewers aided us in the preparation of this text. In recognition and appreciation of their willingness to work with us, we list here their names and affiliations:

Doug Anderson, Marion Technical College

Patti N. Andrews, Boston University

Carol Asplund, College of Lake County

Alec Beaudoin, Triton College

John Beem, College of DuPage

Karen Bessey, Merced College

W. C. Bessey, Golden Gate University

Frank A. Blackwood, Anne Arundel Community College

Robert Boatsman, Seattle Community College

Marvin Burnett, St. Louis Community College at Florissant Valley

William A. Clarey, Bradley University

James Cockrell, Chemeketa Community College

Phyllis Graff Culp, Kansas City Community College

Harris D. Dean, Lansing Community College

Wayne Decker, Memphis State University

Don Freeman, Pikes Peak Community College

Robert W. Harris, Mercer County Community College

Laurence Harvey, DeAnza College

A. C. Hawthorne, Central Piedmont Community College

David Hearn, Jefferson State Junior College

Larry E. Heldreth, Danville Community College

Ron Herrick, Mesa Community College

William Jedlicka, William Rainy Harper College

Tom Johnson, William Rainy Harper College

Gerald W. Jones, Spokane Community College

Elvin E. Kellermeyer, Southwest Texas State University

Francis S. King, Westchester Community College

George Leonard, St. Petersburg Junior College

Chad T. Lewis, Everett Community College

John W. Lloyd, Monroe Community College

Andrew Lonyo, Macomb County Community College

Esther Lowery, Connors State College

James Meszaros, County College of Morris

John Miller, Chabot College

Robert W. Mitchel, Orange Coast College

Bill Motz, Lansing Community College

Bonnie D. Phillips, Casper College

Joseph Platts, Miami-Dade Community College

Paul Plescia, American River College

Kathryn J. Ready, University of Wisconsin/LaCrosse

Edward Rinetti, Los Angeles City College

Robert Rizzo, Indian River Community College

William L. Roach, Washburn University

Gene Schneider, Austin Community College

Dennis Shannon, Belleville Area College

Jack Shapiro, Loop College

Leon Singleton, Santa Monica College

Donald A. Smith, Los Angeles Pierce College

Robert N. Sullivan, Eastern Illinois University

Ray Tewell, American River College

Charles E. Tychsen, Northern Virginia Community College

Pablo Ulloa, Jr., El Paso Community College

Robert Vaughn, Lakeland Community College

Keith Weidkamp, Sierra College

Edward Welsh, Phoenix College

Ralph Wilcox, Kirkwood Community College

Paul Williams, Mott Community College

Ira Wilkser, Lamar University

Martin J. Wise, Harrisburg Area Community College

Heidi Wortzel, Northeastern University

Thomas W. Zimmerer, Clemson University

Wichita, Kansas   G. H. G.
November 1984

Gerald H. Graham holds the R. P. Clinton Distinguished Professor of Management Chair at Wichita State University and was recently awarded the Wichita State University Regents' "Excellence in Teaching" award.

The author has more than 20 years of teaching experience at the university level and has taught an introduction to business course during 10 of those years. He received his doctoral degree in business from Louisiana State University. Prior to coming to Wichita State, Dr. Graham taught at Northeast Louisiana University and Nicholls State College, also in Louisiana. He currently teaches in the business area with specific emphasis on introduction to business, management principles, and organizational behavior. Dr. Graham has published dozens of research articles in management and human behavior, which have appeared in such journals as *The Academy of Management Journal*, *Personnel Journal*, and *Personnel Administrator*. He has authored textbooks in management and human relations.

Over the past 15 years, Dr. Graham has conducted management development workshops for more than 75,000 participants from major corporations, such as: American Express, Chase Manhattan Bank, Standard Oil, AT&T, IBM, Bank of America, McDonald's, Wendy's, and Xerox. He has also been a consultant to many other national business organizations and thereby has first-hand experiences with their application of business concepts in their operations. Recently, Dr. Graham has been actively involved in developing and teaching training courses via teleconferencing for managers throughout the country.

Dr. Graham is president of the National Association for Management, which publishes training materials for industry. One of his publications is a monthly *Applied Management Newsletter* that is distributed throughout the United States and other nations to thousands of business managers. He also writes a twice-monthly, nationally syndicated "Management File" column for the Knight-Ridder newspaper chain.

CONTENTS

PART III ■ THE MARKETING OF BUSINESS

PART V ■ DATA PROCESSING IN BUSINESS

1

FOUNDATIONS OF OUR PRIVATE ENTERPRISE SYSTEM

Welcome to the world of business! You could not have picked a more exciting time to study the private enterprise system of the United States. For years, we were content with the fact that our economic system was the strongest and most powerful in the world. And, no doubt, many people took it for granted. In fact, during part of the 1960s and 1970s, some Americans maligned business, blaming our economic system for many of the country's problems.

However, things have changed. We have suddenly awakened to discover that our economy no longer dominates the world in the way that it once did. For instance, some automated factories in Japan can build a car in 9 hours flat; it takes American workers about 31 hours to build a car. In the early 1980s, Japan became the number 1 car producer in the world, exceeding our production by almost 50%. Tokyo, not New York, is the largest city in the world. The economies of many nations, including South Korea, Taiwan, Saudi Arabia, Kuwait, and Japan, are growing at more rapid rates than the U.S. economy. Other nations have greater supplies of global riches than we do; Asia and Australia have far more oil, Russia has more iron ore, Asia and Australia produce more grain, Latin America and Africa have more forests.

How have our nation and private enterprise system reacted to these realizations? Very positively. We still have the largest economy in the world, producing twice as much as our closest rival, the Soviet Union. But we are no longer a sleeping giant. Innovation and change inspire our private enterprise system once again. The evidence is everywhere. Computers are changing everything. "The most dramatic economic change in the next 50 years," according to the editors of *U.S. News & World Report,* "will be the renewal of the private sector as it departs from its manufacturing base and advances further in to the 'Information Age.'" Soon 80% of our employees will be working to provide services and information to society. Robots are taking over many menial tasks. Our large companies are entering into partner-

ships with large companies of other nations. And in just 10 years, our businesses, working with government, and perhaps other nations, will have a permanent, manned space station in earth orbit. Shortly after, we will see large-scale commercial manufacturing in space. Yes, this is an exciting time to study business.

But what exactly do we mean by business? In our study we define **business** as any organization—from the largest computer corporation to the corner grocery store—that engages in the creation or sale of goods and services with the goal of earning a profit. The composite of all business firms and their relationships (to one another, the public, and society at large) makes up our **business system.**

We refer to our business system as a private enterprise system. By **private enterprise** (sometimes called **free enterprise**) we mean a system that encourages private choices of individuals and private ownership and operation of businesses. This chapter briefly discusses the evolution of our private enterprise system, defines its components and characteristics, and analyzes just how well the system is doing.

EVOLUTION OF OUR PRIVATE ENTERPRISE SYSTEM

Although it had its beginnings in simple bartering, our current private enterprise system has evolved into an exceedingly complex and dynamic system. In the following pages, we will trace the history of our system and consider the beginning of business, mercantilism, the Industrial Revolution, the consumer era, and the current age of technology.

The Beginning of Business

Cave dwellers engaged in warfare to capture goods and satisfy their needs, but people later learned that the exchange of goods and services was more efficient (and less lethal) than war. The early Greeks and Syrians became especially accomplished in business by founding and developing **trade,** the exchange of goods or services, between countries. They produced fine fabrics and exchanged them for silver and copper from Spain and tin from Britain. Early traders became ship builders and profited from the commerce between countries. By the eleventh century, trade became a source of great wealth. **Barter,** as this process is also called, is still with us in the twentieth century. Though not a common occurrence, it is by no means unheard of for a doctor's or dentist's services to be ''paid for'' with, perhaps, an original oil painting or an automobile engine tune-up. Recently, in 1983, American Airlines traded eight 747s for fifteen DC-10s from Pan American World Airways. Likewise, some nations barter billions of dollars worth of products with each other.

Mercantilism

Most large European nations developed mercantile policies by the fifteenth century. Under **mercantilism,** these countries established, and controlled, colonies to increase their own wealth. By forcing the colonies to buy products at inflated prices and by capturing their natural resources the European nations prospered. The United States became a colony of Britain in just this way.

Mercantilism provided much of the foundation of American business.

Jamestown, for example, provided England with a wealth of raw materials such as tobacco, indigo, ginger, and cotton. At the same time, the colonists were forced to purchase England's surplus goods, such as sugar and tea. Eventually rebelling against

the strict rule that controlled their trade, the colonies began trading illegally with other countries and refusing to buy English goods at inflated prices. The Boston Tea Party, where the colonists dumped 342 chests of tea into the harbor, is a famous example of colonial rebellion. Although mercantilism lost its power and popularity by the early 1800s, it provided much of the foundation of American business. It gave a healthy beginning to production and trade and strengthened the settler's desire for independence and private ownership of property.

Industrial Revolution

The **Industrial Revolution,** which was characterized by the substitution of hand tools for power-driven machines, began in England around 1760 and came to the United States some thirty or forty years later. In this country, Alexander Hamilton set the groundwork for expansions in production by encouraging government actions to benefit factories. Eli Whitney's cotton gin (1793) increased the availability of cotton which, along with tobacco, became a valued commodity. What's more, Whitney contracted with the government to deliver 10,000 muskets for the

Established in 1913 by Henry Ford, this movable assembly line could turn out a finished Model T every ten seconds.

BEGINNING OF BUSINESS	MERCANTILISM	INDUSTRIAL REVOLUTION	CONSUMER AGE	AGE OF TECHNOLOGY
Trade Merchant marines	Colonial system Restricted trade	Enterprise Invention Productivity Natural resources	Consumer orientation Advertising Prosperity Capital	Computers Electronics Data processing

Figure 1.1
Evolution of our private enterprise system.

sum of $134,000 (which at today's prices would probably make it the first million-dollar contract). His concept of interchangeable parts that could be manufactured and assembled by unskilled workers was not only the beginning of mass production, but also the division of labor — the foundation of the factory system.

Other inventions that spurred industry were the steam engine, the steamboat, the telegraph, and the coast-to-coast railroad networks that were completed in 1869. Henry Ford established the first movable assembly line in 1913. This period was also influenced by dynamic business leaders — called **entrepreneurs** — who initiated, organized, and managed resources and workers, reaching record levels of production.

Electronic banking and shopping directly from the home are available to subscribers of this videotex service.

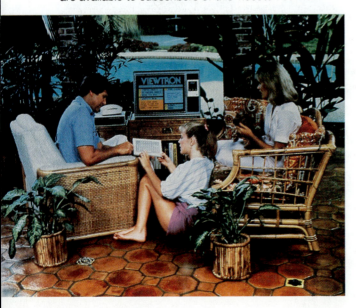

These pioneers included Carnegie (steel), Morgan (banking), Rockefeller (oil), Mellon (aluminum), Ford (automobiles), McCormick (farm equipment), Singer (sewing machines), and Edison (power). This combination of enterprise, invention, natural resources, and productivity quickly made the United States the industrial leader of the world and provided Americans with the highest standard of living.

Consumer Era

With the success of the Industrial Revolution came an adequate supply of products. The next challenge was to sell them. Before the **consumer era,** which began around 1870, the production of goods was determined largely by basic need. There was little regard for color, style, or consumer preference, Ford cars, for example, were available in any color you'd like — as long as it was black. Though stimulated by the prosperous years following World War I and, even more so, following World War II, the consumer era went into full swing when manufacturers became more concerned about the tastes and desires of their customers.

The emergence of General Motors did a lot to spark the flame of the consumer era. With its first cars, GM advertised style and variety. It made a special effort to satisfy consumer needs. Not only did Ford respond in kind, but manufacturers and sellers of most products quickly followed their example. Department stores emerged and began catering to the desires of customers. Montgomery Ward began in 1872. In 1887, Alvah Roebuck, a watchmaker, answered an ad in the *Chicago Daily News* and was hired by Richard Sears. This was the beginning of Sears and Roebuck, one of the most famous partnerships in the business world. The first 5 and 10 cent store was opened by F. W. Woolworth in 1879.

Another feature of the consumer era was the **advertising boom.** Before this time, there was little advertising. Once sellers learned that they could expand their markets and quickly increase sales and profits through advertising, it became a new way of life. Needless to say, it is still with us today and as healthy as ever.

Financial conditions also contributed to the consumer era. Before 1910, banks loaned money mostly to factories and businesses. Even home mortgages were rare. When the Federal Reserve Bank was established in 1913, consumer credit became available for purchases of consumer goods. With healthy supplies of money, products, and advertising, the consumer era thrived.

Age of Technology

Many consider the most recent development in our private enterprise system to be the **age of technology.** While technology was certainly a part of the Industrial Revolution (with its inventions and improvements in productivity), today's business world uses technology to a much greater degree. The age of technology is characterized by the rapid proliferation of electronics in the form of computers, business machines, and household products. Electronic goods of every kind have found their way into America's homes. Electronic technology has revolutionized methods of doing business, both in the factory and in the office. Computers of one sort or another are found in automobiles, stereos, voting booths, video games, and yes, even college testing programs.

BUSINESS BULLETIN

An Example of Evolution in Our Business System

To illustrate the evolution of our business system, let's take a look at agriculture and see how it has changed over the years.

In earlier times, more than 90% of the U.S. population were involved in agriculture. We needed this effort to provide enough food to eat. Still, few nations produce all the food they need or want. As early as 100 A.D., farmers in Italy and France were able to trade their crops through merchant marines for, say, rice from China or olives from Greece.

Mercantilism greatly affected the colonial farmers of the United States. England in essence said to the colonies, ''Grow what we need, and we will pay you what we want to for your crops.'' But the Industrial Revolution, introducing massive machinery and time-saving tools, had probably the greatest impact upon our farming industry. Advanced technology allowed farmers to produce two and three times their previous crop yields.

During the consumer era, farmers were able to produce more and different kinds of crops. Consumers then concerned themselves with agricultural products beyond what they needed to stay alive. Believing there were consumers who desired beer and cigarettes, some farmers plowed under their cotton crops to grow hops and tobacco.

In this advanced technological age, farmers use modern, productive equipment to plant, harvest, process, and transport their crops. Because of the efficiency of today's technology, fewer and fewer farmers are producing more and more food. In fact, less than 10% of our population currently work on the farm, though for all practical purposes, we have the ability to produce enough food to feed the entire world.

OUR PRIVATE ENTERPRISE SYSTEM AT WORK

The qualities of our private enterprise system are the subject of frequent debates among scholars, politicians, business leaders, students, and citizens. Almost every political election, at every level, focuses on issues that affect how our economic system works. Let's take a closer look at the much-discussed characteristics of our system and the factors of production associated with it.

Characteristics of Our Private Enterprise System

In Chapter 2, we shall discuss three economic systems (capitalism, socialism, and communism) with regard to ownership, choice, competition, and profit. Here, we consider each of these qualities as it pertains to our business system.

Ownership and risk. In colonial America, feelings about individual property ownership were so strong that it was protected in the Constitution. Article 5 of the Bill of Rights states that no individual can be deprived of property without due process of law, and no private property can be taken for public use unless individual owners are paid a fair price. Later, the Fourteenth Amendment strengthened this trend by promising the right of private property to all citizens. Thus, our modern business system relies heavily on the right of private property, but we have come to accept more government ownership.

Federal, state, and city governments own parks, lakes, roadways, schools, highway systems, and military bases. Additionally, the government owns some large enterprises, such as the Tennessee Valley Authority (TVA) utility company. Today, the federal government owns one-third of all the land. This amounts to an area the size of all the states east of the Mississippi River plus Louisiana and Texas, a total of 742 million acres.

Freedom of choice. In our society, individuals can choose to be mechanics, or morticians, or salespeople, scientists, teachers, or tailors, clerks, or welders, or witches. *The Dictionary of Occupational Titles* lists 40,000 different jobs in more than 600 major job groupings. Businesses have almost unlimited freedom to choose a type of business activity, and customers can select from dozens of different product brands, hundreds of automobile models, and thousands of food items.

Our government does limit freedom of choice.

On the other hand, our government does limit freedom of choice. It prevents some mergers in the interest of competition; some states own and control liquor stores; there are several restrictions on cigarette advertising; employers with federal contracts have to follow affirmative action guidelines in hiring; there are many restrictions on pricing; and during some periods, the government imposes rigid price and wage controls.

In our business system, we also have the right to conduct business activities with little restriction. The government does, however, levy some restrictions. Monopolies are limited, and some states have passed laws forbidding pyramid schemes because many unsuspecting people were losing money. While these laws are opposed to the true spirit of capitalism (see Chapter 2), they have been passed to protect the citizens of the country. Most of us have come to accept and even respect these laws.

Our system also offers the freedom to invest our money as we choose. As long as an individual legally acquires capital, the choices of investment are broad. Some restrictions do apply. A person may not invest in illegal activities, such as importing illegal drugs. To sign a contract, one must be of sound mind and at least 18 years of age. To invest

TABLE 1.1 ■ USES OF FEDERALLY OWNED LAND

Predominate Use	Square Miles
Bureau of Land Management	500,000
National Forests	298,437
National Wildlife Refuges	135,937
National Parks and Monuments	115,625
Other (including Indian reservations and military properties)	184,375

Source: General Services Administration.

FUNNY BUSINESS

Drawing by Wm. Hamilton;
© 1976 The New Yorker Magazine, Inc.

"How little we really own, Tom, when you consider all there is to own."

by forming a corporation or business requires a license and other approvals. Still, the freedom to invest is probably as great as in any other country.

Markets and competition. Competition was evident in early America, and it is deeply ingrained within our life-style today. We teach competition effectively: Athletic teams compete for victory, churches compete for attendance, students compete for grades, and businesses compete for profits. For our purposes, let us define **competition** as the rivalry between two or more businesses striving for the same customer, market, or resources.

We are quick to praise the benefits of our competitive system. It stimulates development, advancement, and efficiency. To succeed, businesses seek an advantage over their competitors by developing and distributing their products and services more effectively. We give less attention to the potential problems of competition. In efforts to outdo others, managers sometimes resort to cheating, fraud, misleading advertising, and price fixing. For this reason, we have passed many laws to regulate competition. The government does reduce competition by supporting monopolies in utilities, transportation, and communication, and by regulating their prices through commissions.

Contrary to the spirit of true capitalism, the government also has many restrictions with regard to pricing—a most critical aspect of competition. Grocery chains are limited in the degree to which they can take losses in "price leaders." Utilities, such as the phone companies and power companies, must get government approval before raising prices. During the energy crisis, there were numerous restrictions on the prices that could be charged for gasoline. Even a governmental agency like the post office needs approval before raising postage rates. On the other hand, the 1980s has produced many government actions that have deregulated some industries in an effort to stimulate competition.

Economists use the term "competition" in a specialized way. "Pure competition" or "perfect competition" exists when no one seller produces enough of a product to influence the price in the market. Pure competition, in reality, is very limited; but it does occur in some agricultural commodity markets. In wheat, for example, no one farmer produces enough wheat to influence the market price.

More commonly, "imperfect competition" exists when a firm produces a product or service that the consumer considers to be in some way different from other similar products or services. Most companies, through product design and advertising, try to make their product unique, or at least appear to be unique. This allows them some control over the price. Home computer manufacturers, for example, compete more on style, image, and other minor differences than on the basis of price.

The young cable television industry is a highly competitive business, sprung from recent deregulation measures, new technologies, and market demands.

Profits and incentives. Ford Motor Company reported a record $1.87 billion profit in 1983. Chairman Philip Caldwell said that, after three straight years of losses, Ford had become, "profitable at home and abroad." He also added, "Many more good years lie ahead." The 1983 profits broke the previous Ford record of $1.67 billion set in 1977. General Motors also reported a huge profit for 1983, $3.73 billion in fact. The two auto makers, by themselves, earned $5.6 billion for the year, topping the industry record of 5.18 billion in 1977.

Profit, the return received on business activity after all costs and operating expenses have been deducted, is vital to our business system today. Most businesses state that profit is one of their most important objectives, and all recognize that they need profit to survive. Profit, therefore, becomes a driving mixture for businesses to provide goods and services to consumers.

But there is another view. In the 1800s, when many businesses grew very large and some leaders used bribes, price fixing, and other unethical means to reduce competition, many citizens thought businesses were making excess profits at the expense of their employees and customers. The huge profits of oil companies in 1979–1981 created quite a stir. The companies said they needed the increases in profits to promote the risky business of finding oil. But customers, who

Figure 1.2
Profit trends for selected industries:
(a) Corporate profits before and after inflation; (b) earnings of major industries. *Source: U.S. Department of Commerce.*

Billions of dollars

Profits after taxes
"Real" profits

(a)

	4th Quarter, 1983	Percentage Change from Year Ago	4th-Quarter Profits as Percentage of Sales 1982	1983
Aircraft, missiles	$ 451 mil.	Up 32%	3.1%	3.7%
Airlines	$ 112 mil.	Up 15%	3.8%	3.6%
Banks	$2,205 mil.	Up 7%	*	*
Broadcasting	$ 79 mil.	Up 29%	13.3%	13.9%
Brokerage firms	$ 45 mil.	Down 80%	8.5%	1.8%
Building materials	$ 332 mil.	Up 170%	1.8%	4.3%
Chemicals	$ 380 mil.	Up 108%	2.2%	4.1%
Computers, office goods	$2,828 mil.	Up 30%	9.1%	10.1%
Drugs	$ 761 mil.	Up 13%	12.6%	13.1%
Electric utilities	$1,873 mil.	Up 14%	10.4%	11.2%
Food, beverages	$ 573 mil.	Up 37%	4.0%	4.3%
Gas utilities	$ 67 mil.	Down 9%	4.9%	4.9%
Health care, supplies	$ 179 mil.	Up 13%	6.8%	6.9%
Leisure time	$ 25 mil.	Down 19%	8.5%	5.9%
Machinery, electrical	$ 958 mil.	Up 21%	6.0%	7.0%
Machinery, other	$ 10 mil.	*	*	0.3%
Motor vehicles	$ 118 mil.	Up 28%	3.6%	4.4%
Nonferrous metals	$ 206 mil.	*	*	4.9%
Paper	$ 288 mil.	Up 473%	1.0%	4.7%
Petroleum	$5,370 mil.	Up 4%	4.8%	5.2%
Printing, publishing	$ 239 mil.	Up 21%	8.5%	9.2%
Railroads	$ 404 mil.	Down 5%	6.8%	5.2%
Restaurants, lodging	$ 102 mil.	Up 17%	8.1%	8.2%
Retail food stores	$ 43 mil.	Down 1%	1.5%	1.4%
Rubber	$ 41 mil.	Up 239%	1.7%	4.7%
Savings and loans	$ 43 mil.	Up 52%	*	*
Steel	−$ 135 mil.	*	*	*
Telephones	$ 735 mil.	Down 54%	8.9%	3.9%
Textiles, apparel	$ 121 mil.	Up 64%	3.0%	4.4%

(b)

were asked to lower their thermostats and drive smaller, more fuel-efficient cars, viewed the oil executives as crooks. Most people felt that big business was taking advantage of a scarce resource and charging excessive prices. Most Americans want fewer restrictions, but will call for them under extreme conditions. Figure 1.2 shows profits for selected major industries.

The purpose of the progressive tax structure is to reallocate income from the wealthy to the less wealthy.

Under pure capitalism, profits determine who will have wealth. In recent times, our government has taken a larger role in allocation by attempting to distribute wealth through such plans as taxation, social security, and welfare programs. The purpose of the progressive tax structure is to reallocate income from the wealthy to the less wealthy by increasing the rate of tax as earnings increase. Social security contributions transfer income to benefit older and less privileged persons. Welfare programs such as food stamps, rent supplements, and housing aid are other means of redistributing income. While these practices have moved us from our earlier free enterprise practices, the world still considers us to be the epitome of a free enterprise nation.

Factors of Production

Factors of production are the elements necessary to produce goods and services; they include (1) natural resources, (2) labor, (3) capital, and (4) management.

Natural resources. In addition to land, we consider oil, coal, gravel, water, and natural gas to be examples of **natural resources.** Natural resources also include items we produce from the land such as cotton, corn, lumber, and hay. As the bases of production, natural resources are used to make other things. Unfortunately, nations eventually deplete their natural resources. As all of us know, we use millions of barrels of oil every day, yet it takes thousands of years for nature to create oil. Motivated by our creative technology that re-

quires us to use oil in hundreds of products, our demand has been greater than our resources. Since we and other nations have a tendency to use our natural resources avariciously, we will probably continue wrangling over shortages.

Labor. **Labor** is the physical and mental effort of people. Factory workers, farmers, doctors, lawyers, and writers are only a few examples of laborers. Although our supply of natural resources is limited, labor expands with the population, but not directly. Certain segments of the population—the very young, the very old, and the handicapped—may not be a part of the labor force. In 1984 there were more than 100 million persons in the labor force. Two specific changes have been occurring within the labor force in the past few decades. First, the labor force has more years of formal education. In 1964, workers averaged 12.2 years of formal education. By 1980, that figure was 12.6. It is expected to be even higher in 1985 when eight out of every ten adults will have completed high school. Second, productivity per person-hour has virtually levelled off. It has been increasing only 2 to 3% during the last 5 years compared to 6 to 8% in earlier years. In 1981, it actually decreased. This compares to increases of 10 to 15% in Japan and Germany. At first, these two trends appear to be contradictory. But the combined desire for higher education and dissatisfaction with highly specialized jobs has resulted in worker apathy and inefficiency in many jobs.

Labor is obtained by wages. If the cost of labor increases the price of a product too much, the demand for the product will fall. In these cases, workers may lose their jobs. What better example exists than the problems facing U.S. auto workers in 1982? Their unions actually gave up increased wages and benefits so that the factories could stay open and workers could keep their jobs.

Capital. The monetary value of machinery, equipment, buildings, and tools, as well as cash investment and reserves, represents **capital.** Capital is essential to all business activity. It is required to start a business as well as to run it. In fact, a common reason for business failure is inadequate capital. The major sources of capital to companies are investors, lenders, and retained earnings. People invest in companies in the hope of earning a reasonable return on their investment; we loan for

High-risk ventures like exploring for oil—a natural resource, one factor of production—bring into play the three other factors: an experienced management, substantial capital investment, and a skilled labor force.

the promise of repayment plus interest; and managers hold onto some of their profits for the purpose of using them to make even greater profits. With technological advances, capital requirements are increasing rapidly. Since most of the capital in the United States is privately owned, firms continuously seek ways to attract capital.

Management. The management skill of successfully utilizing the first three factors of production is called **entrepreneurship.** Entrepreneurs are the people who unite natural resources, labor, and capital within a business to produce and sell goods and services. These entrepreneur-

managers face both opportunities and risks. If they are successful, they are well paid; but a failure may result in the loss of money put up by investors as well as the loss of a job. As a successful entrepreneur-manager put it, "I have been very successful. Last year, I made over a million dollars. But there were times when I thought we were going to lose the whole thing."

Likewise, each factor of production presents additional risks. Natural resources may become scarce or be available at too high a cost; environmentalists may make it difficult to get certain resources. Labor is a constant source of worry. Not only do entrepreneur-managers have to find and

TAKING STOCK

Success and Failure in
Computer Manufacturing

Why does one firm succeed mightily and another have less success? For many different reasons, of course. The stories of Three Rivers Corp. and Apollo Computer Inc. provide a vivid contrast in operations and in degree of success.

The firms are similar in that both build supermicrocomputers, and both had emerged as industry leaders in the late 1970s. But in 1983, Apollo's stock had a market value of $365 million and its sales approached $100 million. By contrast, Three Rivers' sales totaled about $10 million, the same as in 1982; what's more, their top management team had just resigned under pressure.

Three differences in strategies apparently account for the success of Apollo: (1) financing methods, (2) marketing strategy, and (3) delivery.

1. Three Rivers' early financing consisted primarily of a quick $5 million investment from two Schlumberger executives. This dried up other financing because venture capitalists were not willing to put up money for additional needs, nor were the original investors willing to ante up more. As one venture capitalist said, "Three Rivers went to amateur investors without staying power." Apollo, however, put togther a very elegant financing scheme, getting venture from The First National Bank of Boston and four other top venture capital firms. Their contacts led to other investment contacts as well as to early customers.

2. The differences in marketing strategies were quite pronounced. Apollo targeted a 50–50 split in sales between end users of their computers and original equipment manufacturers (OEMs). Contact with the end users kept them close to applications, and the OEMs provided a base for long-term purchasing power. Apollo also signed more than 100 companies to write software programs for their computer, making their product more desirable to the end user. Three Rivers was very inconsistent in its marketing. With no well-defined strategy, they were very late to sign software vendors. And they concentrated mostly on sales to OEMs; but there were so many hardware vendors, the OEMs were quite selective and bought only a few computers at the time.

3. Finally, Apollo worked hard to have computers ready when the orders began to roll in; and when they shipped their machines to the users, they worked. There were many reliability problems in Three Rivers' product, and they got behind in shipping their orders. Customers who had prepaid their order were understandably furious about late shipments.

In this comparison, two firms with good technical products performed quite differently, clearly demonstrating that success depends on good management as well as on resources, labor, and capital.

Source: G. Thomas Gibson, "Two Startups, One Winner," Venture, August, 1983, pp. 96–98.

develop the proper skills in the work force, they have to worry about labor unions, strikes, turnover, and pressures for higher pay. Capital is a scarce commodity. Companies must attract enough capital to meet the needs of the business at the right time and at a reasonable cost. The entrepreneur–manager is also an element of risk, for he or she must make crucial decisions. Too many wrong choices could mean failure of the business.

HOW WELL IS OUR SYSTEM DOING?

The United States has always taken pride in its stance as the world's symbol of private enterprise opportunity. Yet, there is some question as to how well our system is working, especially in light of the recessions of the 1970s and early 1980s. Let's look at some hard facts about our economy's performance.

In Satisfying Economic Needs

The 1970s delivered two recessions and the sharpest inflation rates in decades. The early 1980s produced the greatest economic downturn since the Great Depression. Yet, in almost every way, we are better off today than ever before.

The buying power of the average person is almost twice as much today as it was 30 years ago.

Buying power is the money we have left to spend after taxes and after accounting for inflation. Since the hardening experience of World War II, buying power has increased 94%. This means that the average person is able to buy almost twice as much today as 30 years ago. We have also had increases in the number of people who own their own homes, frequency of foreign travel, average life span, and proportion of families owning more than one car. In addition, we are wealthier and better educated than ever before. For heads of families, age 25 or older, who had finished college, the median family income in 1982 was $35,778. For those who had finished high school, the figure

was $23,837. Figure 1.3 illustrates these improvements.

"But," you might ask, "are we happy?" A recent Gallup poll showed that 57% of citizens expressed "a high level of satisfaction" with life in the United States. Gallup pollsters also took samplings in nine democratic countries in the Western world. Citizens of the United States and Denmark showed more satisfaction with their general lot in life than people in other countries.

In Providing Methods of Production

Productivity rate, the increase or decrease in goods and services produced in an hour of work, measures the effectiveness of our methods of production. **Output** is the annual production per person, adjusted for inflation.

As Figure 1.4 shows, our productivity rates declined the past 10 years. During this time, our productivity growth has trailed that of Japan, France, and Germany. In three years, the productivity rate was negative; and in 1982, it was zero. However, experts are now predicting that annual growth rates in output could run as high as 3.0% a year for the rest of the decade.

Several reasons caused the earlier decline in productivity rates. First, we allowed our plants and equipment to run down because we did not invest enough to keep them modern. Second, many companies did not spend enough in research and development, and they were not able to come forth with new innovations in products and services. Third, some experts believed that management did not do enough to motivate employees effectively. Incentives that management had traditionally relied on — higher pay, bonuses, fringe benefits, and the like — did not seem to work so well during the 1970s and early 1980s. Employees coming into the work force today are more interested in job challenge, advancement, and fulfilling work.

Experts are more optimistic about future productivity growth rates for several reasons. The Economic Recovery Act of 1981 encourages businesses to invest more capital by offering them faster depreciation write-offs. As a result, capital per worker is expected to increase into the 1990s. This will encourage the introduction of more and better technology, especially robots and computers, into the workplace. The government hit commerce and industry with a wave of federal regulations during the 1970s. Now, most people believe that the cost of these regulations has been largely absorbed. Further, the trend has swung toward deregulation, and this is expected to boost productivity even more. Companies have increased their research and development spending, bringing forth a wave of innovations in methods and in products. Finally, stimulated by foreign competition and economic troubles of the early 1980s, a new cooperation has emerged between workers and management. Now, joint labor–management productivity teams are trying to get workers to identify more closely with company goals.

In short, we may still be hard pressed to catch up to the productivity increases of some other nations, especially Japan, but the situation looks better for the remainder of the 1980s.

Figure 1.3
Improvements in our economic need satisfaction. *Source: Compiled from data from U.S. Department of Commerce, Labor, and Health, Education and Welfare; the Federal Reserve Board; the Motor Vehicle Manufacturers Association.*

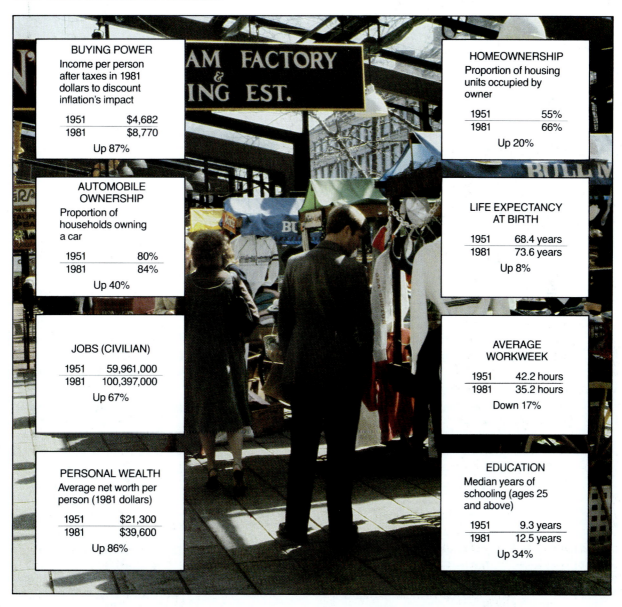

BUYING POWER
Income per person after taxes in 1981 dollars to discount inflation's impact

| 1951 | $4,682 |
| 1981 | $8,770 |

Up 87%

AUTOMOBILE OWNERSHIP
Proportion of households owning a car

| 1951 | 80% |
| 1981 | 84% |

Up 40%

JOBS (CIVILIAN)

| 1951 | 59,961,000 |
| 1981 | 100,397,000 |

Up 67%

PERSONAL WEALTH
Average net worth per person (1981 dollars)

| 1951 | $21,300 |
| 1981 | $39,600 |

Up 86%

HOMEOWNERSHIP
Proportion of housing units occupied by owner

| 1951 | 55% |
| 1981 | 66% |

Up 20%

LIFE EXPECTANCY AT BIRTH

| 1951 | 68.4 years |
| 1981 | 73.6 years |

Up 8%

AVERAGE WORKWEEK

| 1951 | 42.2 hours |
| 1981 | 35.2 hours |

Down 17%

EDUCATION
Median years of schooling (ages 25 and above)

| 1951 | 9.3 years |
| 1981 | 12.5 years |

Up 34%

Percentage of change in output per hour
(nonfarm businesses)

Figure 1.4
Decline in U.S. productivity. *Source: U.S. Department of Labor.*

Year

In Distributing Wealth

Critics might give our system bad marks for the way that we distribute wealth. They would say that we have too many people at the extremes—too many that have accumulated too much wealth and too many that have accumulated too little. The poor and disadvantaged, experts say, account for many of our criminal and social problems. However, proponents point out that we need accumulations of wealth, for that is where much of our investment and growth capital comes from. They also add that accumulation of wealth is the reward for being successful in a capitalistic economy in providing goods and services that others need. Finally, even though we have people who are poor and disadvantaged, this group in our economy is far better off than the poor and disadvantaged in other economies.

There is also evidence that more and more people are entering the wealthy class. There are about 638,000 millionaires in the United States, or 1 out of every 360 Americans. And almost 6000 people make a million dollars or more per year. This is up from only 33 in 1920. Sure, a million dollars today is worth only about $200,000 in 1920 dollars, but there are 167 times as many people making a million dollars annually today as there were in 1920.

In Providing Growth

In the past, our economic system has provided an excellent growth record. However, because of the decline in productivity and output rates, our overall growth rate has also slowed.

Seven nations met at the annual economic summit in 1983. A comparison of economic growth in six important indicators for the years 1972–1982 ranked the United States third, behind Japan and West Germany. Figure 1.5 totals these

Figure 1.5
A comparison of economic growth.
Changes in six important indicators of economic growth from 1977 to 1982. *Source: U.S. News & World Report, June 6, 1983.*

Output: Production per Person, Adjusted for Inflation

1. Japan	Up	19.4%
2. Italy	Up	12.1%
3. France	Up	8.2%
4. West Germany	Up	8.0%
5. Great Britain	Up	2.8%
6. United States	Up	2.0%
7. Canada	Up	1.3%

Currency: Change in Value

1. Japan	Up	17.0%
2. United States	Up	12.8%
3. Great Britain	Up	11.5%
4. West Germany	Up	10.0%
5. Canada	Down	9.6%
6. France	Down	16.0%
7. Italy	Down	28.6%

Jobs: Persons Employed

1. Canada	Up	9.5%
2. United States	Up	8.0%
3. Japan	Up	5.5%
4. Italy	Up	3.2%
5. West Germany	Up	0.3%
6. France	Down	0.4%
7. Great Britain	Down	5.3%

Exports: Amount per Person

1. West Germany	Up	24.5%
2. Japan	Up	20.2%
3. France	Up	16.5%
4. Italy	Up	14.6%
5. United States	Up	9.4%
6. Great Britain	Up	8.1%
7. Canada	Up	7.4%

Prices: Cost of Living

1. Japan	Up	25.1%
2. West Germany	Up	25.9%
3. United States	Up	59.3%
4. Canada	Up	63.2%
5. France	Up	73.6%
6. Great Britain	Up	76.0%
7. Italy	Up	115.3%

Industrial Production: Output of Factories and Mines

1. Japan	Up	27.7%
2. Italy	Up	9.6%
3. West Germany	Up	3.3%
4. France	Up	2.0%
5. United States	Up	0.3%
6. Canada	Down	2.0%
7. Great Britain	Down	2.9%

On the basis of 7 points for first place, 6 for second place, and down to 1 for seventh place:

1. Japan	39
2. W. Germany	29
3. U.S.	25
4. Italy	22
5. France	21
6. Canada	18
7. Britain	14

An Industrial Policy? Free Enterprise versus Government Intervention

In recent years, we have seen our nation fall behind Japan, Germany, and some other European countries in economic performance. Because of this, many people are calling for an industrial policy (IP) to help the United States maintain its competitive position in the world. Generally, an IP is an overall, conscious government policy to aid industrial development and growth. Government assistance may come in several forms, for example, subsidies, tariffs, cheap loans, export aid, tax breaks, and research support. The intent would be to identify future growth areas, called "sunrise industries," and help them grow as a part of our overall strategy.

Arguments for an IP

There are many arguments for an IP. Some of the major ones are:

1. A national, coordinated IP will help make the United States more competitive, thereby reducing the odds that we will become a second-rate economic power.
2. Japan and other nations have had success with their IPs.
3. The government currently helps many industries, but there is no thought-out, coordinated plan of assistance. For example, the government now spends five times more on research for commercial fishing than for steel.
4. The government has always aided some industries, so we should quit pretending that we are pure free enterprise.
5. Ad hoc attempts to help industries, such as guaranteed loans to Lockheed, Chrysler, and New York City, are too often politically motivated bail outs; they do not replace a centralized plan.

figures. Since 1975, our growth rate has continued to be sluggish; it looks as though moderate growth will continue into the foreseeable future.

In explaining moderate growth, an economist from the Brookings Institute lists some probable causes: (1) more inexperienced workers in the labor force — more previously unemployed women, more younger workers, (2) the end of the migration from farms to the cities, (3) inflation and high interest rates that scared off some necessary investment and expansion, and (4) the need for more investment to meet the high cost of safety and pollution standards.

Other experts point out that the news may not be as bad as it appears. Many view the 1970s as a period when things did not improve much; still, personal income, after adjusting for inflation, increased 28%; gross national product, after infla-

tion, rose 33%; and the number of workers in the civilian labor force increased 28%.

In Providing Methods of Economic Activity

While our methods of economic activity have been excellent in the past, the 1970s produced some problems in this area as well. Two recessions in the 1970s produced high interest rates — as high as 21% for a period, and unemployment — more than 9% in 1982. It looks as though the high inflation rates — more than 10% for much of the 1970s — have finally been conquered. Now the goal throughout the 1980s will be to stimulate additional growth and increase employment. In late 1983, economists were concerned about eco-

Arguments against an IP

Some of the major arguments against an IP are:

1. An IP is clearly a method of government intervention that reduces the forces that make a private enterprise economy effective.
2. An IP will create additional governmental bureaucratic layers that make for inefficiency.
3. Historically, the bigger the role of the government, the more messed-up things become. For example, the government heavily subsidized both the railroads and interurban transportation, both of which have suffered under heavy regulations.
4. Subsidizing industry increases the cost to the taxpayer; it does not increase the ability of firms to compete.
5. Conditions are not the same as they are in Japan, and success with an IP there does not mean it is the thing for us to do.

How do you feel about government involvement in business via an industrial policy? (Check the following statement that best describes your position.)

___ A. An IP would be very helpful to the United States.

___ B. An IP would be somewhat helpful to the United States.

___ C. An IP would be somewhat harmful to the United States.

___ D. An IP would be very harmful to the United States.

List three reasons for your position.

A. _____

B. _____

C. _____

nomic growth and increased employment during the last half of the decade.

SUMMARY

The private enterprise system stresses private ownership of business and individual choices in business activities. It is close to the free enterprise system, which gives total power to individuals without government intervention. A business is an organization that engages in the production and sale of goods and services with the goal of making a profit. The business system is the composite of all businesses and their relationships.

Early forms of business included trade and mercantilism. The Industrial Revolution, which was characterized by the replacement of hand tools with power-driven machines, has provided the greatest boom to business and industry. During the consumer era, businesses started to emphasize the tastes and desires of the consumer. The advertising boom took place during this era. The modern age of technology utilizes electronics and computers in business and household products.

Our free enterprise system stresses a limited role of government in business activities. While it is not totally capitalistic, our system encourages a maximum (though not total) role of individual choice within business. It strives for the highest levels of competition, profit, and private ownership. Resources used to produce goods and services are natural resources, labor, capital, and entrepreneurship and are called the factors of production.

In viewing how well our business system is doing, we decided that it provided us with the highest standard of living at one time. Recently, problems with recession, interest rates, unemployment, and decreased productivity have issued challenges to our system.

MIND YOUR BUSINESS

Instructions. Indicate whether you think the following statements are true (T) or false (F).

____ 1. On the average, business profits amount to 25% of their total sales.

____ 2. The real backing of the U.S. dollar is gold.

____ 3. Higher wages is the major cause for an increase in the standard of living.

____ 4. About two-thirds of all civilian workers belong to unions.

____ 5. There are more corporations than individually owned businesses in the United States.

____ 6. The major purpose of the stock market is to increase company profits.

____ 7. The federal government owns less than 5% of all the land in the United States.

____ 8. Fringe benefits such as vacations, insurance, retirement, and sick leave average about 20% of our paychecks.

____ 9. Most of the money spent on advertising goes for television ads.

____ 10. When you buy a company's bonds, you become part of the company.

____ 11. Spending by governments at the federal, state, and local levels is equal to about 20% of the total gross national product.

____ 12. Over the past 25 years, prices have increased more than wages.

____ 13. When the dollar gains value in foreign markets, the cost of living in the United States goes up.

____ 14. It is impossible for a company with a union to fire an employee.

____ 15. There is clear evidence that advertising causes the prices of goods to be higher.

See answers at the back of the book.

KEY TERMS

business, 6

business system, 6

private enterprise system, 6

free enterprise system, 6

trade, 7

barter, 7

mercantilism, 7

Industrial Revolution, 7

entrepreneurs, 8

consumer era, 8

advertising boom, 9

age of technology, 9

competition, 11

profit, 12

factors of production, 13

natural resources, 13

labor, 13

capital, 13

entrepreneurship, 14

buying power, 16

productivity rate, 16

output, 16

REVIEW QUESTIONS

1. What was the first business activity? What was business like before mercantilism?

2. What is the difference between business and the business system?

3. What is the difference between the private enterprise system and the free enterprise system?

4. What is the difference between barter and trade?

5. Describe mercantilism and its effects upon our modern business system.

6. What were the characteristics of the Industrial Revolution? Where did it begin? What are some of the events that occurred in the United States during that period?

7. Describe each era within the evolution of our private enterprise system.

8. What prevents our business system from being pure capitalism? Explain.

9. Why was private ownership of property so important to the American colonists? What steps did they take to ensure the private ownership of property?

10. What is competition and what role does it play in our business system? What is profit and what is its relationship to competition? Explain in detail the strengths and weaknesses of our private enterprise system. What are its current challenges?

CASES

Case 1.1: How Are Economic Indicators Related?

Recently, a U.S. congressman said that most of our economic problems were caused by the fact that Americans were just not willing to work as hard as people did in the past. He cited statistics showing high job turnover, changes in attitudes of younger employees, and scant increases in productivity rates. He commented that inflation was too high because we wanted to buy too many things that we did not need, and because we made too many demands on the government. "Everyone," he said, "was looking for a handout, from the largest corporations to the smallest business, as well as most of the individuals in the country." "In short," he said, "we were spoiled, pampered, and expected too much without having to work for it."

Questions

1. How do you feel about these statements? _____ generally agree? _____ generally disagree?

2. Why did you answer as you did? List reasons.

Case 1.2: Potential Entrepreneur

Mari Tallinger is a college student with a strong desire to work for a while and then get into a position, either with a large company or on her own, to operate as an entrepreneur. She feels that she has the capability to put together the ingredients necessary to make a business function. However, at this point in her education, she feels a desire for a great deal more information and she has come to you for advice.

Questions

1. What do you think about a college student who has the desire to be an entrepreneur?

2. Make an extensive list of the types of things Mari would have to know to operate effectively as a business entrepreneur.

After studying this chapter, you will be able to:

- List the goals of an economic system.

- Describe four characteristics that differentiate between economic systems.

- Describe and list the main differences between the three major economic systems of the world: capitalism, socialism, and communism.

- List and interpret ten key indicators of economic activity.

- Describe economic growth cycles.

BUSINESS AND
ECONOMIC
SYSTEMS

here is only one free lunch in economics,'' according to Treasury Department economist Ronald Hoffman, ''—an increase in efficiency.'' And that is just what businesses have been doing. Battered by foreign competition and mounting customer complaints, businesses have worked hard to improve quality and efficiency. In November 1983, production at B. F. Goodrich Tire Company was a full 36% higher than in 1975. Goodrich and other companies have adapted to the pressures within our economic system by eliminating waste, improving scheduling, slimming product lines, and using technology more effectively. And that is the way our economic system is supposed to operate, by providing incentives to reduce waste and be more efficient.

WHAT ARE THE GOALS OF AN ECONOMIC SYSTEM?

Though **economic systems** may differ substantially, they generally have similar goals (see Fig. 2.1):

- To satisfy the economic needs of people.
- To provide methods of producing goods and services.
- To distribute wealth.
- To stimulate growth.
- To create economic activity.

Satisfying Economic Needs

If you were to make a list of the things you have used today, what would you mention? Food? Clothes? Transportation? Stereo? Books? Have you ever stopped to think where these came from and how they got to you? Although we tend to take most of our daily necessities and pleasures for

**Figure 2.1
The goals of an economic system.**

Economic systems such as:

COMMUNISM   SOCIALISM   CAPITALISM

have goals to:

Satisfy needs | Provide production | Distribute wealth | Stimulate growth | Create economic activity granted, our economic system is usually working overtime to deliver them. The primary goal of an economic system is to satisfy the economic needs of its people. When we are left wanting, we tend to blame **economics;** but when our stomachs are filled, we often forget to credit the system.

Providing the Methods of Production

To satisfy economic needs, an economic system must establish methods for producing goods and services. Sometimes these methods emerge naturally and spontaneously, while at other times, the economic policies of a country attempt to cause certain productions. For instance, although Japan has almost no natural resources relating to steel production, they do have the ability to manufacture automobiles quite efficiently. Japan's economic system assumed the economic responsibility for trading with other countries to acquire much-needed steel so they could produce automobiles. They did this so successfully that they became the number 1 producer of automobiles in the world.

Distributing Wealth

Through economic incentive and reward systems, an economic system tries to provide ways of distributing wealth to its people. As a political candidate recently said, "One of the greatest problems that any economic system has is to distribute the wealth of the country fairly." Different nations handle wealth distribution in various ways. In Mexico, there are both extremely wealthy and extremely poor citizens. Finland, however, has few affluent citizens and very few that are poor.

Stimulating Growth

Economics strives to provide growth in our production and distribution of goods and services. Most countries need growth to continue to satisfy the economic needs of their expanding populations. The economic system spurs growth by identifying needs and finding ways to meet them. Before the end of World War II, the German government decided that more automobiles were needed. To stimulate growth in the automobile industry, the government built factories and man-

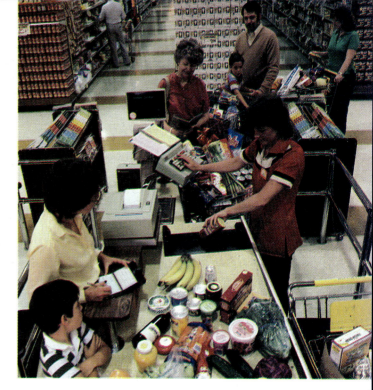

Providing and delivering goods and services to consumers is a primary goal of any economic system.

ufactured the Volkswagen, which means "car of the people."

Establishing Methods of Economic Activity

An economic system develops methods, rules, and procedures by which it operates. Businesses then must follow these regulations. As corporations in the United States began to grow very large, there seemed to be a need for an efficient method of investing in and owning them. So our government developed a system of laws for owning and investing in businesses. One of the results is today's stock exchanges where people buy and sell millions of shares of stocks daily.

WHAT ARE THE CHARACTERISTICS OF AN ECONOMIC SYSTEM?

Although the goals of differing economic systems may be similar, characteristics of systems vary greatly. We can differentiate between economic

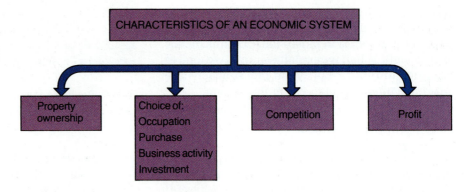

Figure 2.2
Characteristics of an economic system.

Diagram: CHARACTERISTICS OF AN ECONOMIC SYSTEM — Property ownership; Choice of: Occupation, Purchase, Business activity, Investment; Competition; Profit

systems by looking at how they treat (1) property ownership, (2) freedom of choice, (3) competition, and (4) profit.

Property Ownership

To most readers, individual ownership of property is taken for granted. We buy homes, cars, records, and fishing equipment which we own in our own names. However, this is not the case in all economic systems. In a country without individual ownership, a worker may work in a state-owned factory and live in a state-owned house.

Freedom of Choice

Different economic systems also provide varying degrees of freedom of choice. Citizens of some countries might actually be told where to work, what type of work to do, and they may have few choices regarding goods and services. Likewise, citizens may not have the opportunity to invest in a business, sign a contract, or choose where to take a vacation. While freedoms of working, purchasing, and investing seem basic to us, some systems do not provide such liberties.

Competition

Competition plays a different role in economic systems. Some economic systems, such as ours, stimulate competition in many areas, especially sales of products and services. Yet other countries do not encourage, or even allow, competition. A state-owned factory, for example, might hire workers at a state-determined wage; and the people may buy a product or service at a state-determined price.

Profit

Each system develops policies concerning profits. Will profit be allowed? If so, how much? Some countries operate businesses where the concepts of profits do not really exist. Proceeds from business sales go for the costs of production. If there is an excess, it goes to the state.

There is some correlation among these characteristics within an economic system. A system that encourages private ownership will also encourage freedom, competition, and profit. And systems that discourage one of these factors will also discourage the others. These characteristics are diagrammed in Fig. 2.2.

ECONOMIC PHILOSOPHIES

In the world today, three major economic philosophies exist: capitalism, socialism, and communism. We will see how each of these systems treats property ownership, freedom of choice, competition, and profit. (See Table 2.1 for a capsule comparison of these three economic systems.)

Capitalism

Adam Smith, a Scottish economist, described the foundations of **capitalism** in his book, *The Wealth of Nations.* Ironically, he published the book in 1776 — the same year the American colonies stated their feelings in the Declaration of Independence. Smith argued for a policy of **laissez-faire,** meaning that the government should keep its hands off all business activities, letting them function without regulation or restriction. He believed that businesses competing among themselves would produce the most efficient product at the best price. He likened the competition between firms to that of an "invisible hand" that would encourage firms to set prices at their lowest feasible point and thus reward the most efficient. As a store owner explained, "We have to operate as efficiently as we can to keep our costs low. If our costs are not low, we cannot keep our prices low; and if our prices are not low, our competitors will take our customers." If profits become too high in a particular industry, competitors will move in, driving the prices down. Efficient producers with the lowest prices gain the rewards of high sales and increased profits, and inefficient firms would be eliminated.

Though the economic system of the United

States is a good example of capitalism, it is

not purely capitalistic.

While the economic system of the United States may be a good example of capitalism, it is not purely capitalistic. In this section, we present the idea of capitalism.

Property ownership. Maximum ownership of private property is basic to capitalism. It stresses that an individual, with profit as an incentive, will manage the property with maximum efficiency and greatest results. Governments, with their detached motivation and bureaucracy, cannot utilize property with the same zeal and productivity as an individual who stands to gain from the profitable management of property. Consider the situations where one family owns its home and another rents from either a landlord or a government. The first family will care for and improve its home because it will benefit from the increased value when it decides to sell. The second family, because of lack of motivation, may let the property fall into a state of disrepair because only the owner will benefit from its efforts. Under this concept, if all families owned their own

TABLE 2.1 ■ A COMPARISON OF CAPITALISM, SOCIALISM, AND COMMUNISM

Concepts	Capitalist Theory	Socialist Theory	Communist Theory
Property ownership	Privately owned, capital invested by owners.	Mixture of private and public ownership, basic industries owned by state (steel, transportation, utilities, etc.), individuals may own other businesses.	Common ownership through the state which owns all productive capacity.
Freedom of choice	Wide range of choices, workers free to select occupations, consumers face many choices at the marketplace.	Limited range of choices, workers select occupations but state planning influences employment, consumers have some variety in purchases.	Very limited choices, state determines your occupation and where you will work, consumer items are standard.
Competition	Unrestricted competition, owners assume risk of gains and losses, determine prices and wages.	Regulated competition, wages highly regulated by state, citizens assume risks of state-owned companies with losses coming from taxes, private companies may be pressured by state to produce certain things.	No competition, planned economy, state owns markets, state assumes risks, losses reduce living standards, state planning is enforced by law.
Profit	Highly desirable, reward for risk and efficiency, profits and wages are in relation to willingness and ability to contribute.	Profits within boundaries, stresses nonmonetary incentives, privileges and prestige.	No profits, try to get people to produce out of loyalty to the state, medals, state recognition, and fear of legal punishments.

Deregulation and the Airlines

In 1978, the U.S. government ordered an end to government control of airline fares and rates. This allowed carriers to invade each other's markets and compete by offering lower rates. Many fare wars developed, in which bargains and discounts were offered to passengers.

Reacting to these new freedoms, Braniff expanded its routes significantly. However, the airline was unable to attract enough customers at the rates needed to cover its costs, and in the summer of 1982, Braniff declared bankruptcy.

Since 1978, many other airlines have also lost money. In fact, the airline industry did not show a profit between 1979 and 1983. Pan American lost more than $485 million in 1982, more than any U.S. airline in history. After staggering along for several months, Continental Airlines sent shudders through the industry when it became the second major airline to file for bankruptcy within 16 months. Eastern Airlines, apparently on the brink also, threatened to file for bankruptcy before getting their union to agree to a pay cut.

Although adjustments to deregulation, after decades of highly regulated routes and fares, was no doubt the cause of many problems, the airlines also faced other obstacles. The economy was in a recession during the early 1980s, interest rates were high, fuel costs were high, and air traffic controllers had a strike. Any one of these events would have been enough to create shock waves; combined, they created havoc in a once-predictable industry. The accompanying diagram shows the profit picture of airlines since 1975. Experts predicted that other airlines would also suffer bankruptcy, and everyone agreed that it could be many years before the industry stabilized.

Operating income of U.S. scheduled airlines. *Source: Air Transport Association.*

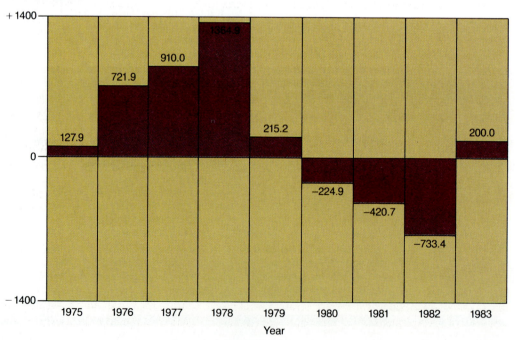

Millions of dollars

Year	Operating income
1975	127.9
1976	721.9
1977	910.0
1978	1364.9
1979	215.2
1980	−224.9
1981	−420.7
1982	−733.4
1983	200.0

homes, all homes would be better cared for and increase in value much faster than properties owned by the state. For another example, consider farmers who own their own land. They will likely be motivated to work hard because they could benefit directly from their labor. If the state owned the land and paid them standard salaries, the assumption is (and the evidence suggests) that they would be less motivated.

Freedom of choice. Freedom of choice means that individuals can make their own decisions. Believing that freedom of choice increases motivation and productivity, capitalists stress freedoms when choosing occupations, purchases, professions, schools, and the like. Within a capitalist system, a high school senior has the freedom to decide whether or not to go on to college. Because of incentives of higher pay, better working conditions, and more prestige, many students choose to become better educated. The result is more doctors, engineers, and business professionals, which benefit the society as a whole. The front end sacrifice of school, study, and less wealth is made for future goals of wealth, status, and a higher standard of living. In a capitalist system, these choices are made by individuals, whereas in a communistic society, they are made by the state according to need.

Competition. The capitalist system encourages maximum competition within all business activities. Capitalists believe that increased competition results in better products, greater efficiency, and superior service. Again, the theory is that the rewards gained by outperforming the competition will motivate individuals to greater achievements and benefit the overall society as a result. If competition becomes too great, some businesses will fail, and those people and resources will be directed by the "invisible hand" to enter other industries that are less competitive and more profitable. In a capitalist system, competition is regulated by the choice of individuals rather than restrictions by the state.

For example, if a firm is having difficulty in competing in the minicomputer market, it may choose either to improve its strategies or to switch its resources to another, less competitive industry. If it wants to become more competitive, it must find a way of producing better computers at a lower price. Capitalists view competition to be ad-

A corporate-sponsored careers seminar for students provides information on the wide range of occupational choices available — a characteristic feature of capitalist economies.

vantageous to the society because it creates more effective methods, superior products, and lower prices. A minicomputer produced by a communistic system may be more expensive and less efficient, but, because there is no competition, it continues to be produced and be the only model available. Smith would say that because of lack of competition, the society suffers by having to use an inferior product.

Profit. After a company pays all its costs and expenses, what remains is profit — the difference between the total income received and total expenditures of operating the business. Under capitalism, we identify winners by the amount of their profits. Because of the incentive of profits, capitalists believe that individuals will work harder and produce more, and that this will thereby benefit the overall society.

Socialism

Socialism is a broad term used almost interchangeably with communism until after the Russian Revolution. The system favors use of property for public welfare and challenges the sanctity of private property. Socialism developed during the Industrial Revolution as an alternative to help poor people who had no choice other than poverty. In socialist countries, governments own and operate much of the property, but there is also individual ownership. Socialist theory stresses limited freedoms of choice, regulated competition, and less emphasis on profits. The United Kingdom, West Germany, Finland, and Norway are some of the best-known examples of socialist countries. In their functioning and characteristics, they are somewhere between the communist and capitalistic countries.

Property ownership. In many socialistic countries, the government owns the basic industries, such as banking, large manufacturing, and mining. Socialists feel that the state can operate these large industries more efficiently than individuals can. However, there is private ownership of smaller companies and shops.

Freedom of choice. The socialist system stresses that a country's resources ought to be allocated according to some master plan that will best serve the needs of the majority. Yet consumers do have some freedom of choice with purchases, and workers can choose among several occupations. However, the state has means of encouraging employees to enter occupations of the greatest need. Investments and business activities are conducted by individuals but are limited and carefully restricted by the state.

Competition. While competition exists within the socialist framework, it is limited and highly regulated by the government. Many of the larger industries are completely owned and controlled by the state, allowing no competition in the key segments of the economy.

BUSINESS BULLETIN

On Adam Smith

Adam Smith, a bachelor with no recorded love affairs, lived the life of the stereotypical absent-minded professor. At social gatherings he might relegate himself to a corner for long periods smiling and talking to himself. In the classroom, he would stutter and stammer for 15 to 20 minutes before getting warmed up for the lecture. One night he awoke from his sleep and walked more than 15 miles in his nightgown, intellectually massaging a theory, before he realized what he was doing. Indeed, few businessmen sought the advice of the quiet, intense scholar on such matters as prices, wages, and profits. Yet his writings, salted with just the right amount of deadpan wit, came alive, breathing his views of the necessity of political and economic liberty. Smith's book *The Wealth of Nations* went through five editions in his lifetime at a price equivalent to $65 per copy, and it still sells several thousand copies annually. Smith's insatiably curious, broad-ranging intellect speculated on the intellectual underpinnings of many aspects of society:

ON COLLEGE RULES: The discipline of colleges and universities is . . . contrived not for the benefit of the students, but for the interest, or more properly speaking, for the ease of the masters.

ON WORK AND LEISURE: Great labor, either of mind or body, continued for several days together . . . requires to be relieved by some indulgence sometimes of ease only, but sometimes too of dissipation and diversion.

ON LOTTERIES: The world neither ever saw, nor ever will see, a perfectly fair lottery . . . because the undertaker would make nothing by it.

ON HAPPINESS: What can be added to the happiness of a man who is in health, who is out of debt, and has a clear conscience?

ON HUMAN EQUALITY: The difference between the most dissimilar characters, between a philosopher and a common street porter, for example, seems to arise not so much from nature, as from habit, custom, and education.

Source: "The Revolutionary of Economy," *Time,* July 14, 1975, pp. 54–55.

```
                    ┌─────────────────┐
                    │  PURE CAPITALISM │
                    └─────────────────┘
```

| Totally private ownership of property | Maximum choice of: Occupation Purchases Investment Business Activities | Unrestricted competition | Major emphasis on profit |

**Figure 2.3
Characteristics of pure
capitalism.**

Profit. Profits exist in socialist economies, but they do not carry the importance of capitalist profit. The guiding force of socialism is a carefully planned system that regulates, rather than controls, the production and distribution of goods; however, privately owned businesses do make a profit.

Communism

The basics of communist theory were set forth by **Karl Marx,** a German economist who lived from 1818 to 1883. His major tenets were presented in a work entitled *Das Kapital,* first published in 1867. He predicted that there would be a class struggle and the laboring classes would overthrow the capitalists. Marx believed that the state should own everything. **Communism** stresses centralized management of all production and distribution. It is quite willing to sacrifice freedom for production, distribution, and production efficiency. The best-known examples of communist economics are Russia, Communist China, and Poland.

Property ownership. Communism practices common ownership by all. There is no private property; everything belongs to everyone in the state. Farmers do not own their land, laborers do not own their tools, and doctors do not own their offices. The central government owns all property. The will of the state is of utmost importance. The state not only owns all the factories and businesses but also the homes that people live in. According to Marx and his followers, individuals will be better off if they suppress their desires for individual accumulations of wealth.

Freedom of choice. Communism gives the central government the strongest possible role in all aspects of business and economics. The central party sets the goals and operates the distribution of goods. Individuals have limited choices. The central government carefully plans the careers of its citizens by selecting them for and guiding them into particular jobs. They have little choice regarding the type of work they will do or for whom they will work. Likewise, customers face limited choices in the marketplace: In the extreme, there is only one type of each item that the government deems necessary. This is because the state dictates the type, style, quality, and amount of goods to be produced. Investments and business activities are not conducted by individuals.

The purchase of certain equipment—such as this British Airways Concorde airliner—is often demanded by the government in socialist economies.

Competition. There is little need for competition in a communist society, especially within the business world. The state allocates resources according to its judgment of who is needful of what goods.The government asks individuals to contribute to the production of goods and services according to their abilities. In short, the planners allocate goods according to who needs them, and they demand contributions according to individual capabilities.

Profit. The communist philosophy, through central planning, eliminates the necessity of profits. Goods and services resulting from workers' efforts benefit the state rather than individuals. Individuals' compensation comes from the government as it perceives their needs. All financial resources are managed by the state rather than by business. All proceeds go to the government and are utilized in other forms of business that are managed, owned, and controlled by the state. In this way, communists believe that people will work harder and accomplish more than when there is the potential handsome profit which is basic to the capitalistic system. For example, all grocery store owners in Russia may receive the same compensation regardless of the amount of business or the efficiency of their operations. A capitalist grocer, however, would strive to buy at a lower price, advertise to attract more customers, and carry products that better fulfill the needs of customers in order to realize a greater profit.

INDICATORS OF ECONOMIC ACTIVITY

Now that we understand the goals and characteristics of various economic systems, we can add to our knowledge of economics by discussing some indicators of economic activity and by looking at how our economy tends to go through growth cycles.

Key Economic Indicators

Economists try to identify major changes in our economy that serve as key indicators of how well the economy is doing. Since our economy is so complex, we often look at several indicators of

> **By comparing the key economic indicators with previous periods, we can tell whether our economy is growing or declining.**

economic activity. Some of the key indicators are expressed as indexes, and others are expressed in actual dollar amounts. By comparing current indicators with previous periods, we can tell whether our economy is growing or declining. Many of the more popular key indicators are as follows.

Gross national product. **Gross national product,** or **GNP,** is a measure of the dollar value of the economy's output of goods and services. GNP tells us the value of business activities and is usually presented for a period of a year. For example, the GNP for the United States in 1983 was more than $3 trillion, meaning that business activities produced goods and services worth that amount for the year. The percentage increase (or decrease) in GNP from one period to the next indicates growth or decline. **Real gross national product** is the measure of GNP that removes price changes. If, for example, from one year to the next, GNP rose 5% while prices increased 4%, real GNP would only increase 1%. Figure 2.4 shows the changes in real GNP for 1982, 1983, and 1984.

Consumer price index (inflation). The **consumer price index (CPI)** is an average of the prices of goods and services and is published regularly by the Department of Labor. The number used in the CPI expresses a percentage change over the established costs of a previous year — the current base year is 1967; however, 1977 will soon become the base year. The base year merely represents a year that the Bureau of Labor Statistics chooses to use as a benchmark. For example, the estimated index for the United States in 1983 was 309. That means a sample of goods and services purchased in 1967 would cost 309% more in 1983. **Inflation** simply means "increase in price"; therefore, the increase in the consumer price index is a measure of inflation.

Inflation concerns us because it means that we have to spend more money to buy the same amount of goods and services. Suppose that you

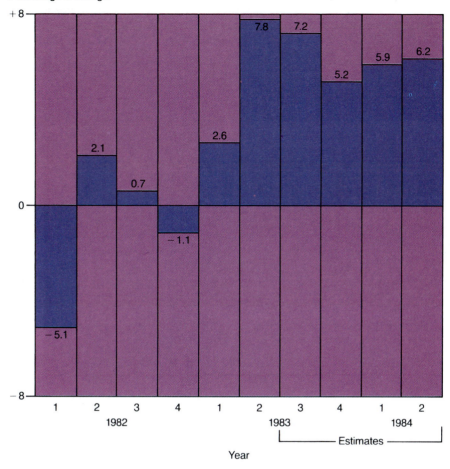

Percentage of change

**Figure 2.4
Changes in gross national product, 1982 – 1984.**
Source: Department of Commerce.

rent an apartment for $300 per month. After one year, when the lease expires, the landlord increases the rent to $330 per month. This is the same as cutting your income by $30 per month because you have to pay that much more for the same product. While the **inflation rate** caused extreme concern in the early 1970s and during the first part of the 1980s, the mid-1980s indicated that the rate was once again down to a reasonable level. Figure 2.5 shows the increase in prices for selected items during a 5-year period, and Fig. 2.6 shows the average increase in consumer prices from 1973 to 1983.

Unemployment rate. The **unemployment rate** is the percentage of employable persons looking for work that are not employed. During the early 1980s, the employment rate climbed to more than 10%. Historically, this was an excep-

tionally high rate, and it caused hardships for many people in our society. By early 1984, the rate had reduced to 8%, and it was expected to fall slowly during the next few years.

Unemployment causes more trouble in some groups and in some regions of the country than in others. The highest rate of unemployed persons is typically among blacks and especially among black teenagers. Table 2.2 shows the unemployment rate by category and industry for 1982 and the first half of 1983. Figure 2.7 shows swings in the unemployment rate since 1969.

People's incomes. People's incomes represents the total amount of income for all the people in the United States, after taxes. This figure reveals the total amount of money that people are making from all sources, and it suggests their ability to buy products and services and to invest. The figure

Percentage of change

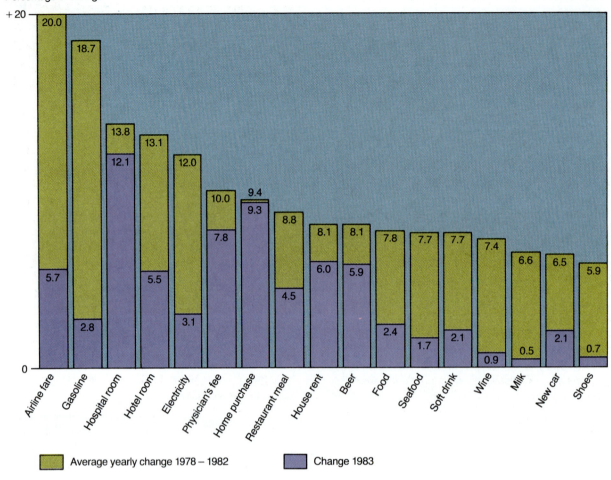

Average yearly change 1978 – 1982   Change 1983

Figure 2.5
How inflation in the cost of consumer items has slowed. *Source: Bureau of Labor Statistics.*

Figure 2.6
Average annual increase in consumer prices, 1973 – 1983. *Source: Bureau of Labor Statistics.*

Percentage of change

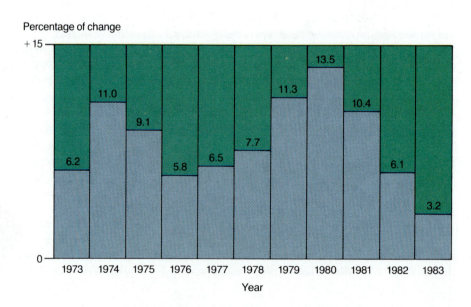

Year

amounted to approximately $2.3 trillion in mid-1983.

Retail sales. Retail sales is the total volume of sales by retail outlets. An increase in retail sales is a healthy sign because it means that more people have confidence in the economy. Also, the increase in retail sales allows retail outlets to buy more inventory, hire more people, and perhaps expand their facilities.

Producer prices, finished goods. This is the price of finished goods at the wholesale level, that is, before the costs of transportation and retailer costs and profits are added to the final price. This price is similar to the consumer price index except it represents wholesale rather than retail prices. Movement of producer price index is important because if it goes up (or down) consumer prices are likely to go up (or down) in the near future.

Corporate profits. Corporate profits is the after-tax profit made by all corporations. Higher profits suggest economic growth because the profits can be used for expansion, increasing employment, and greater distribution of profits to stockholders.

TABLE 2.2 ■ UNEMPLOYMENT RATE BY CATEGORY AND INDUSTRY

	December, 1982 (%)	June, 1983 (%)
By Category		
Adult men	10.1	9.0
Adult women	9.2	8.6
Whites	9.7	8.6
Blacks	20.8	20.6
Hispanics	15.3	14.0
White teenagers	21.6	20.0
Black teenagers	49.5	50.6
By Industry		
Construction	22.0	18.1
Farm employees	16.5	17.0
Manufacturing	14.8	11.5
Trade	11.0	10.2
Transportation	8.0	7.8
Finance	7.9	7.2
Government	5.1	5.1

Source: Department of Labor.

Figure 2.7
Highs and lows in unemployment rate, 1969–1982. *Source: Department of Labor.*

Percentage of change

Since new home building represents both employment in several major industries and a general consumer confidence, the number of housing starts serves as a key economic indicator.

Auto production. Auto production measures the total number of cars produced for a period of time. Because auto production is such a large segment of our economy, it influences many other factors. For example, an increase in auto production increases employment significantly, but it also increases the need for many products such as steel, rubber, glass, and the like. Literally thou-

sands of companies derive their livelihood from the auto industry.

Home building. Home building figures register the number of private housing starts per year. Similar to auto production, home building is a key indicator because so many other aspects of our economy depend upon it. An increase in home building suggests that people are able and willing to purchase additional homes. In mid-1983, the annual rate of housing starts was running at about 1.7 million units per year, one of the highest levels in recent years.

Interest rates. Interest rates, the amount paid to borrow money, also indicate economic movement. Higher rates slow economic growth because people will borrow less, therefore curtailing expansion. Likewise, lower interest rates spur economic growth because people are willing to borrow more for expansion and growth. Interest rates affect the consumer also; when rates are lower, the consumer typically uses more credit to increase consumption. Interest rates, as an indicator, are a little complicated because there is no single rate that reflects the cost of money. The

BUSINESS BULLETIN

What Key Economic Indicators Are Doing

In mid-1983, the ten key economic indicators discussed in the text showed the following measurements. (You might want to get a comparison by looking up current measures to see how the indicators have changed since mid-1983. The indicators are published regularly by government sources, and you can also find them in many periodicals such as *Business week, U.S. News & World Report,* and the like.)

Key Indicator	Mid–1983	Current
Gross national product (billion 1972 dollars)	$1,477.26	_____
Consumer price index (1967 = 100)	296.9	_____
Unemployment rate	10.2%	_____
Peoples' incomes (billion per year after taxes)	$2,286.5	_____
Retail sales (billion per year)	$1,156.6	_____
Producer prices, finished goods (1967 = 100)	286.0	_____
Corporate profits (billion per year after taxes)	$124.0	_____
Auto production (cars per quarter)	1,800,000.	_____
Home building (private starts per year)	1,632,000.	_____
Interest rates (prime rate)	10.5%	_____

BULLETIN

How Reliable Are Economic Indicators?

"In a narrow sense, the statistics are doing the job, but they do not capture the trends as well as they did 5 years ago," says Stephen S. Roach, senior economist at Morgan Stanley & Co. Some critics have always doubted some aspects of our economic indicators, but our economy is now changing at a dizzying pace. Newer industries, the so-called high-tech firms, come and go quickly. And our indicators tend to read activities in the older, more mature industries.

Economists believe that the indicators may be OK for short-term analysis; but if used for long-term policy making, indicators could lead us far astray. If the government intervenes too much in the economy, many economists contend, the mistakes in the data are multiplied.

Look at an example of an out-of-date classification. Decisions about major industry groups were made in the 1930s. Thus, the leather and tobacco industries, which between them account for only 0.4% of total output, are both listed as major industries. Yet, the computer industry, which did not even exist in the 1930s, is not represented accurately in industry figures. The accompanying table is an estimate by *Business Week* of indicator accuracy.

How 15 Key Economic Indicators Rate

On the mark	Understate activity	Unreliable
Employment	Real gross national product	Money supply (weekly M1*)
Consumer price index	Industrial production	Retail sales
Housing starts	Personal income	Inventories
Auto sales	Savings rate	Durable goods orders
Weekly unemployment claims	Capacity utilization	
	Productivity	

* Currency and checking accounts.

Source: "Why Economic Indicators Are Often Wrong," *Business Week*, Oct. 17, 1983, p. 168.

prime rate is the rate that banks will loan to their best customers. New treasury bills, which come due every six months, give an indication of short-term interest rates, whereas the rate for corporate bonds provides a more long-term view of rates. In mid-1983, these rates were as follows: prime rate = 10.5%, new treasury bills = 9.02%, and corporate bonds = 11.34%.

Business Cycles

Economic systems have fluctuations in the degree of business activity, called **business cycles**—periods of growth and declines. **Booms** are periods of prosperity with increased production,

employment, profits, and consumption. By contrast, hard times, called **recessions,** occur when the same functions decrease. **Depressions** are periods of severe recession where economic conditions are much worse compared to other periods. These conditions are relative, however. A developing country such as India could be experiencing a boom period under the same conditions in which Japan would be having a depression. Modern business cycles tend to swing through five stages: recovery, heating up, holding the boom, cooling off, and recession.

Stage 1: *Recovery.* The recession is over and business starts picking up. There is a lot of idle capacity and companies are hungry for orders. Many people, unemployed during the recession, are eager to get back to work.

Stage 2: *Heating up.* People gain confidence and are willing to spend more. Companies are getting more orders and are willing to expand and hire more workers. Retailers foresee the

need for more products. Profits are increasing, encouraging businesses to expand and invest even more. The recession is over, and people are looking ahead with optimism.

Stage 3: *Holding the boom.* Because of the increased pace of the economy, problems begin to occur. Factories exceed capacity and can-

CROSS FIRE

SUPPLY-SIDE ECONOMICS?

When President Reagan entered office, the economy was in a recession. He and his advisors suggested a new approach to stimulating economic growth which became known as **supply-side economics** because it tended to stimulate the production of goods and services, as opposed to the more traditional attempts to stimulate demand for products and services. Arguments ensued over which was the best way to spur an economy that was in a recession.

A comparison of the supply versus the demand orientations is as follows:

Supply-Side Economics	Demand Stimulation
1. Economy is in a recsssion. Cut taxes on individuals and corporations; also provide other economic incentives for firms to produce more goods and services. Reduce government spending.	1. Economy is in a recession. Increase government spending and cut individual taxes to put more money in consumers' pockets
2. Firms are able to retain more profits which they are able to invest. Investment and expansion creates jobs and, along with individual tax cuts, stimulates consumer buying. These incentives also encourage individuals to work harder and produce goods and services at a cheaper cost.	2. The increased amount of money in consumers' pockets stimulates them to spend more for goods and services.
3. The expansion by businesses combined with increased effort of employees increases output of industry and provides more money for consumer spending.	3. Increased spending and demands of consumers stimulates firms to expand, produce more, and hire more employees.

4. *Desired result by both approaches:*
Economic growth—increased employment, greater consumption, business expansion, inflation held in check, interest rates low, increased tax receipts due to increased profits and incomes.

Which of these two approaches do you think is most effective for stimulating an economy in a recession?

____A. Supply-side   ____B. Demand stimulation

List three reasons for your selection.

A. _____

B. _____

C. _____

GNP growth rate

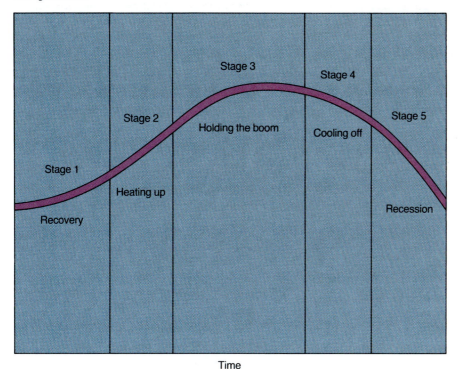

Stage 3
Stage 4

Stage 2
Holding the boom

Cooling off
Stage 5

Stage 1

Heating up

Recession

Recovery

Time

**Figure 2.8
The business cycle.**

not keep up with the new demand. Shortages develop, prices soar. Demand for credit increases, as do interest rates. Unions strive for higher wages to keep up with higher prices. Consumers have caught up with their demands and increase their spending at slower rates. Merchants have more goods in inventory, so they start to order less. The stage is set for a cooling of the economy.

Stage 4. *Cooling off.* Producers cut their production and lay off some workers. Consumers tighten their belts even more as their income lessens. Prices and interest rates are still high. Confidence drops and the economy moves toward recession.

Stage 5. *Recession.* Businesses cut costs and work their inventories down, and consumers strive to pay their debts. Many companies go bankrupt and some plants close. The government looks for ways to make more money available so that companies can invest and consumers can buy more. Interest rates are lowered and government spending usually increases. Eventually, we will overcome this slowdown, but exactly when is uncertain. If

the recession is severe and lengthy, it becomes a depression. Figure 2.8 illustrates this business cycle.

SUMMARY

An economic system is made up of citizens, businesses, and governments that work together to provide laws and guidelines for business activity. Each economic system has five main goals: satisfying economic needs, providing production, distributing wealth, providing growth, and creating economic activity. Each economic system can be characterized by its views concerning property ownership, freedom of choice, competition, and profit.

There are three major economic systems or philosophies: communism, socialism, and capitalism. There are few, if any, countries that are purely communistic or capitalistic. Communism was founded by Karl Marx, who believed that the state should own everything, that people should have almost no choice in commerce, and that all business activity should benefit the state. Socialism is a blend between communism and capitalism and places somewhat equal emphasis upon the individual and the state with regard to co-ownership and control. Capitalism, founded by Adam Smith, stresses that the individual is paramount and should have total control over all business and economic activities. Smith's doctrine of laissez-faire states that government should not interfere with commerce. His concept of the invisible hand maintains that, if left to its own functions, business will naturally operate within reasonable, acceptable boundaries.

Key economic indicators offer suggestions on how our economy is doing. The ten key indicators discussed in this chapter include GNP, consumer price index, unemployment rate, people's incomes, retail sales, producer prices, corporate profits, auto production, home building, and interest rates.

Business cycles are the fluctuations in the level of business activity where booms are times of prosperity and recessions are the downswings. A depression is a severe recession.

MIND YOUR BUSINESS

Instructions. Match the following descriptions with the proper economic philosophy by placing the appropriate letter in the blank at the left.

A = capitalism   B = communism   C = socialism

___ 1. State owns the sources of production.

___ 2. Elected government slowly takes control of nation's key industries.

___ 3. Government uses taxing power to redistribute the wealth.

___ 4. Private individuals own land and businesses.

___ 5. Consumers in the marketplace largely determine at what prices goods will be sold.

___ 6. Central planners set production quotas.

___ 7. A government can regulate businesses through laws.

___ 8. Government sets wages of employees.

___ 9. Strong unions bargain with management for wages.

___ 10. Employees and management in individual firms determine wages.

See answers at the back of the book.

KEY TERMS

economic system, 26
economics, 27
Adam Smith, 28
capitalism, 28
laissez-faire, 28
socialism, 31
Karl Marx, 33
communism, 33
gross national product (GNP), 34
real gross national product, 34
consumer price index (CPI), 34
inflation, 34
inflation rate, 35
unemployment rate, 35
interest rate, 38
business cycles, 39
boom, 39
recession, 39
depression, 39
supply-side economics, 40

REVIEW QUESTIONS

1. What is economics? What is an economic system, and how does it function?

2. What are the five major goals of an economic system? Can you give an example of each?

3. What are the three main economic philosophies or systems? What are the differences between them? Who were the founders of communism and capitalism?

4. Who coined the terms "laissez-faire" and "invisible hand"? What do they mean and which system are they a part of?

5. If you were to begin a business, which economic system would you prefer? Why?

6. What reasons would Karl Marx and Adam Smith give for our current economic problems? Would they agree?

7. What are key economic indicators? Identify the ten indicators discussed in this chapter.

8. What does the consumer price index measure, and how is that measurement expressed?

9. What is the difference between inflation and the inflation rate?

10. What is a business cycle? Is our country currently in a business cycle and if so, which one? What is the difference between a boom, recession, and depression? At which stage of the business cycle are economic times the best?

CASES

Case 2.1: Is the United States Going the Way of Britain?

Nobel Prize-winning economist Milton Friedman says, "If we continue down the road that Britain has been following, we shall have much higher inflation than we have yet had; we shall see a larger and larger part of our freedom taken over by the government; our vaunted productivity will go down." Others agree with him, but we still see support for the government taking a larger part in our lives.

If the United States becomes more socialized, we will see some or all of the following happening:

■ Government will own and run many of the coal mines, steel mills, and railroads.

■ Most sick people's medical and hospital bills will be paid for by the government.

■ Much more housing would be subsidized.

■ Taxes would go up.

Questions

1. Do you think any of these are likely to happen within the next 5 years?

2. Which would you like to see happen, if any? Which would you argue against?

3. What are the arguments for moving in this direction? Against?

Case 2.2: The Role of Profits

In a talk given to a college class in business, a business leader was asked, "What is the major purpose of your business?" The leader responded, "Profits, the bottom line! That's where it is. If you don't have profits, you don't have anything. You can't grow, you can't expand, you can't progress, you can't even survive."

In response, a student commented, "Yes, but you really seem to be involved in growth and expansion, and you are using your profits for that purpose. Are you really interested in the profits, or only what they can do for you?"

In answering, the businesswoman admitted that she really liked the excitement of growth and expansion—the contest of the game of winning by outdoing competitors. In her words, "It is true profits are the score; they tell you how well you are doing relative to others. I enjoy the game of competition; I just like to win. That's why I like the profits to keep growing."

In further discussion, other students asked what she thought about government regulation, well-being of consumers and employees, and government ownership of property and businesses. In sum, she thought that government should get out of business altogether and should own nothing, and that consumers and workers never had it so good.

Questions

1. Do you find yourself agreeing or disagreeing with the viewpoints of the businesswoman? Why?

2. If you had been a student in the class, what questions would you have asked?

3. If you were in business, how would you have answered these questions?

After completing this chapter, you will be able to:

■ List the arguments for and against businesses becoming involved in social responsibilities.

■ Define consumerism.

■ List the major points of the Consumer Bill of Rights.

■ Describe the current state of our pollution problems.

■ Provide current data on discrimination and identify business and government responses.

■ Describe the four major sources of ethics in our society.

■ Comment on ethical behavior in business.

■ Describe the energy situation in America.

BUSINESS AND

SOCIETY

Pollsters frequently check the attitudes of Americans toward their major institutions. The institution of "big business" has often been ranked at, or near, the unenviable bottom of the heap — below the military, television, organized labor, and Congress. There is today, however, a burgeoning interest in and newfound respect for the field. As evidence, witness the unprecedented success of popular books on business. During 1983, nonfiction bestsellers were *In Search of Excellence*, *The One Minute Manager*, and *Megatrends*. These three books were also the bestsellers on campuses from coast to coast. Late in 1983, *In Search of Excellence* climbed to number 1 on the Chronicle of Higher Education's campus reading list, making it the first business book to top the list since it was started 13 years ago. When books like these can capture such a large reading audience, we can be fairly sure that a change in attitude is taking place.

Nevertheless, as we've said, big business does often suffer from a bad image. What do you suppose — in this land-rich, career-oriented, and pension-assured society of ours — accounts for this attitude? As one executive commented, "I just cannot understand it. We provide good products, we pay people good wages, give them comfortable jobs, pay enormous taxes, and help with community projects. Yet the public's opinion sours on us." Many business owners and executives share this frustration.

There are three possible explanations why people do not have more confidence in business. First, historically, societies have not viewed business in a positive light. Religions taught against the evils of materialism and usury. Business was a low occupation in Greece. Napoleon slurred the British as "a nation of shopkeepers." No doubt, some of these jaded attitudes are still with us today. Second, some businesses are very big, and people have a tendency to distrust bigness. Some business leaders accuse the media of stirring public anger by spotlighting big business's problems, while failing to mention its contributions. Third,

people in business do make mistakes. Business owners and leaders got their values from our society, which sometimes places too much emphasis on materialism, greed, and intense competition. This chapter presents arguments for and against the involvement of business in social concerns (see Figure 3.1) and outlines what is happening in consumerism, the environment, discrimination, ethics, and energy.

THE SOCIAL RESPONSIBILITY OF BUSINESS

Social responsibility means that decision makers consider the impact of their actions on society's welfare by evaluating the expected social impacts as well as the firm's profits. This contrasts with the traditional role in which they considered only the profits of their business activity. Social responsibility suggests that such narrow interest undermines the overall benefits to society.

Today, social concerns of business are fixtures in the programs of most business schools; novels, movies, and plays reflect the issue; and social concerns are commonly discussed in boardrooms, planning meetings, business flights, shop floors, legislative committees, and production lines. Business leaders cannot escape taking a position on the social responsibilities of their firms.

Arguments for Social Responsibility

Advocates of social concern believe that business should take an active role in improving society and solving social problems. They believe that businesses, by working to improve the overall society, can often improve their operation and profits in the long run.

Society grants businesses the right to exist. One of the strongest arguments for the social concern of business is the premise that society grants organizations the right to exist. Cultural norms — sometimes expressed through legal means — allow businesses to form and function; actions of individuals in society enable them to flourish. Business leaders should not forget that their right to exist carries an obligation to serve society's

goals. Business organizations should serve society rather than society serving business. It is the moral duty of all units of society — including business — to strive for a better world. As overall conditions improve, all the components of society will benefit accordingly.

Social responsibility contributes to business profits. In many cases, a company will make greater profits in the long run if it considers benefits to society. Since cultural norms permit organizations to exist, profits are earned only within cultural limits. When enough people believe a business no longer serves society's best interests, they may pressure the firm into its grave by boycotting its goods or services, influencing officials against it, condemning it in the media, or patronizing other firms.

Social concern can also benefit short-run profits because of current public expectations. Because the public now expects business to benefit society, a firm that maintains a good record will find it easier to hire better employees and win more customers. In the early 1970s, Caesar Chavez and the United Farm Workers called a strike

Figure 3.1
Issues of social responsibility.

A company's daycare center for its employees' children is one example of how business resources can be used in a socially beneficial manner.

against the Gallo wine company because of alleged abuses in the compensation and working conditions of employees. After much publicity, it was estimated that as many as 20% of consumers boycotted the purchase of Gallo wine. After several years, Gallo came to terms with the farm workers and the boycott was officially cancelled. Sales of Gallo wine improved dramatically. It could be argued that if Gallo had originally invested more in the benefits of its employees, both short-run and long-run profits would have been much better. Also, it is hard to establish just how much the company was hurt by the bad publicity. Possibly, as many as 5 to 10% of consumers still prefer to give their business to other companies as a matter of principle.

Businesses have resources. Another argument for business involvement in social concerns is that businesses have personnel and capital resources. Businesses, the argument continues, also have years of experience in organizing human, technical, and monetary resources to solve seemingly uncontrollable problems. In this day, when we view government bureaucracy as too big, too costly, and too inefficient, there may be strong reasons for business to do more.

Experience shows, for example, that federally sponsored day-care center programs tend to be quite costly. By contrast, several companies that hire a large number of mothers of young children have established and managed their own company-operated centers. Some of these company-operated centers cost only about 20% as much as

the typical, federally sponsored center. Companies offer these centers because they can attract highly motivated and happier employees as a result.

Businesses can avoid government interference. Businesses can forestall additional government regulations by voluntarily serving some social needs. From management's view, government regulations are undesirable because they limit freedom. Keeping up with social demands may be a small cost to retain flexibility, restrain government growth, and advance both company and society interests. For instance, equal opportunity in hiring and training employees is a major concern of government and society. If a business takes the initiative, provides the necessary programs, and gives more opportunities to the disadvantaged, it may avoid future restrictions levied by government in the way of quotas and hiring requirements.

Arguments against Social Responsibility

Critics of business participation in social responsibility also have valid points to make. Like the pro side, the cons range from philosophical views to everyday pragmatic considerations.

Businesses require profits. Classical economists argue that business can best fulfill its social responsibilities by maximizing profits through increased efficiency and reduced costs. They believe that business is more socially responsible when trying for the highest possible return to the investors. When the total system operates more effectively, Adam Smith's "invisible hand" disperses improvement throughout. Milton Friedman, a classical economist, says, "There is one and only one social responsibility of business — to use its resources and engage in activities designed to increase its profits so long as it stays within the rules of the game, which is to say, engages in open and free competition, without deception or fraud." Overall, these economists say, if businesses would focus only on its goal of providing goods and services more effectively, the resulting economic advantages would naturally help improve social conditions. If businesses become too involved in providing social benefits, the cost will be a diminished overall economy.

Consumers pay. Critics are quick to add that social benefits provided by business do not come free. Ultimately, consumers pay through higher prices for consumer goods. The private enterprise system motivates managers to operate as efficiently as possible to produce the greatest amount of goods using the fewest resources. If they have to expend part of their income on social needs, managers simply have to charge higher prices, causing this social burden to be borne by consumers. As in the example of day-care centers, the cost in terms of monies spent and employee time expended will be recovered by the higher cost of goods and services provided by the company. Just as government involvement results in higher taxes, company efforts result in higher prices and, possibly, lower profits.

Fear of business domination. Some people fear that business money for social causes will result in solutions that reflect business values. Each institution, such as business, religion, military, government, or education, has values that it imposes upon the society as a whole. If any of these institutions becomes too powerful in its influence, it could negatively affect society. Some social scientists believe that business already has enough social power and that further influence could threaten the balances within our society. They argue that if business becomes too powerful, it might control and dictate to other institutions such as religion and government.

Agencies already exist. Many critics of the business resource argument say that the government has spent billions of dollars on social agencies and programs to solve social problems. Perhaps implying that the government has spent too much on these issues, critics say that it is wasteful duplication for businesses to try to solve the problems. In fact, under the Reagan administration, there were attempts to slow the rate of growth of these government agencies and, in some cases, actually cut back on budget allocations. Still, this argument maintains that, since the agencies exist, let them take responsibility for the problems.

The Reality of Social Responsibility

The case against business's social responsibility is weakened in the face of severe social problems, an oversimplistic concept of profit maximization,

and the force of society's demands. Concerned citizens feel that social problems threaten our culture's supporting foundation. If the system that guards against social problems fails, our entire enterprise system may be in jeopardy.

Peter Drucker, a noted management consultant, observes, ''Under any circumstances, we are moving in the direction of demanding that our institutions take responsibility beyond their own performance and beyond their own contribution. We will demand this not only of business enterprise but of all other institutions as well — the university and the hospital, the government agency and the school.'' Management simply cannot ignore these pressures.

CONSUMERISM

The public demand for more protection of buyer's rights is called **consumerism**. Every day, about 230 million people in our country spend more than $3 billion. We are satisfied with a lot of things: product availability, variety of goods and services, opportunities to work, and a high standard of living. But as consumers deal with business, some serious problems occur. Here are just a few complaints from the files of a consumer protection agency: ''A repair person worked on my refrigerator on and off for two years and never got it working properly.'' ''I had my hair colored in a beauty shop; the color was awful, my hair went flat and my scalp burned for a week, and there was nothing I could do but let it grow out.'' ''A washing machine repair person gave me an estimate of $25, but charged $110 for the job.'' ''They were especially nice to me when I applied for the loan, but when I got a little behind in payments, they called me three or four nights a week, threatened to take my furniture and get me fired.''

In a recent year, consumers filed more than one million complaints with the Better Business Bureaus around the country.

''When I bought the coffee maker they said 'satisfaction guaranteed,' but I have been trying to return it for three weeks and the company refuses to give me my money back.'' In a recent year, consumers filed more than one million complaints

TABLE 3.1 ■ THE TEN MOST COMMON CONSUMER COMPLAINTS

Category	Percentage of Complaints
Autos	23
Consumer credit	16
Recreation goods, activities	6
Books, magazines	6
Medical supplies, services	4
Housewares	3
Debt-collection services	3
Appliances	2
Home furnishings	2
Other goods, services	35

Source: The Federal Trade Commission.

with the 143 Better Business Bureaus around the country. **Better Business Bureaus** are nonprofit organizations that businesses organize to monitor and control unethical and illegal practices; most deal with poor service. The ten most common complaints in 1981 appear in Table 3.1.

Consumer Rights

Worried about consumer's rights, President John F. Kennedy established a **Consumer Advisory Council** in 1962. One of the Council's actions included a **Consumer's Bill of Rights** which included:

Safety. When we purchase a product or service, we have a right to expect it to be safe. Because of this, laws have been passed to keep dyes and other chemicals out of foods, to require the warning "may be injurious to your health" to be printed on cigarette and saccharine packages, and to force the recall of automobiles with defective brakes and dangerously located fuel tanks. Perhaps some of the most visible aspects of consumer safety are the recent laws requiring drug manufacturers to be more precise in describing uses and negative side effects of drugs.

Information. We have a right to expect the information given us about products and services to be accurate. The Federal Trade Commission (FTC) oversees advertising to make sure that it is true. In recent years, the FTC has: pressured toy manufacturers to stop showing ads that made toys do things that children at home could not duplicate, prohibited the STP Oil Corporation from saying that its oil treatment prevented friction and engine breakdowns when it did not, ordered Warner-Lambert to admit lying about the effects of Listerine mouthwash against colds and sore throats, and made firms cease claiming that their products were better than competitors', without proof.

Choice. Our society believes that we should have a right to choose from several products and brands. Competition is healthy in our private enterprise system. We encourage several different producers to make similar products under different labels. In 1890, the government passed the Sherman Antitrust Act to prevent monopolies. Today, the FTC and the Justice Department work to prevent companies from restraining competition.

Hearing. Consumers have a right to be heard; thus companies should establish ways to respond to consumer complaints. Surveys show that as many as 70% of customers will return products to retailers in a given year.

Consumer Protection

Because of the interest in consumer welfare, the federal and state governments have created agencies and councils to watch out for consumers' interests. There are several nongovernment agencies that also help. Better Business Bureaus and Chambers of Commerce exist in most cities, and they often hear complaints from customers. These groups may bring a complaint to the attention of the seller, or keep a record so that when others ask about a business's reputation, they can provide the correct information. Several newspapers, radio, and television stations publicize consumers' complaints so that public opinion will act as a pressure to correct problems. The **Consumer Union**, another nongovernment organization, tests and rates products. Results are published in a respected monthly magazine called *Consumer Reports*.

Most states and many cities have consumer agencies that help consumers with reasonable complaints. Most cities operate small claims courts where you can bring lawsuits for small

VDT Safety

Debates abound over the safety of video display terminals (VDTs). Since the early 1970s workers have realized that frequent use of VDTs may cause eye strain and back aches. But now, growing numbers of women who regularly operate VDTs are becoming increasingly concerned that working on them could cause miscarriages, birth defects, or difficulties in conception. Though no conclusive evidence exists that VDTs pose such a hazard, recent reports of pregnancy problems among VDT operators in the United States and Canada are beginning to create widespread fear.

Because of this, researchers at the National Institute of Occupational Safety and Health (NIOSH) are now studying whether VDTs are the cause of these problems. It is known that VDTs do emit tiny amounts of X-ray and microwave radio-frequency radiation, but these emissions are extremely low. NIOSH will look at nearly 4000 women workers — half will use VDTs and half will not — over three years. NIOSH hopes to release its findings by 1987.

What's more, some state legislatures, in response to growing public concern, are beginning to consider rules to limit workers' exposure to VDTs. In at least five states, proposed legislation would allow pregnant workers to transfer from work requiring a VDT. Canada and Sweden are also examining the effects of radiation emitted by VDTs.

The organization for office workers, 9to5, is pushing for legislation to regulate the manufacture of the keyboard and terminal combinations. Critics of the organization say 9to5 is just trying to drum up support and publicity for the union. However, Karen R. Nussbaum, executive director of 9to5, says their toll-free "VDT risks" hotline gets 100 calls a day. "Over the next five years," she predicts, "we'll see serious legislation passed in several states."

Although the radiation hazards of personal computers are still controversial, other physical discomforts are not. This ad illustrates one company's response.

Source: "Pregnancy and VDT Workers: Pressure Leads to a Quest for Hard Facts," *Business Week*, April 23, 1984, pp. 80–82.

amounts (usually under $500) without having to hire a lawyer. You simply fill out a form, appear in court, and present your evidence. The court then decides what should be done.

Businesses have responded to these activities by being more sensitive to consumer complaints. Most larger businesses have created customer service departments whose primary objective is to respond to problems and maintain positive customer relations. Usually, if there is a doubt regarding a customer complaint, most companies decide in favor of the customer. One large department store recently returned money to a customer for a pair of shoes she'd bought there that she said hurt her feet. Since the department manager was not familiar with the style, he researched his files and found that the shoes had been discontinued in 1939.

ENVIRONMENTALISM

Just what is the cost of a dead sea gull? At an oil conference, an economist put the estimate between $1 and $10. "I don't think anyone," he said, "would say they have a value of more than $10 a bird." To this, the environmentalists reacted with pained disbelief. One naturalist commented that economists "know the price of everything and the value of nothing."* In light of the many world problems, such a reaction over one sea gull may seem to be out of place. But it demonstrates the attention we have begun to place on our environment. It also illustrates the conflicts. We need to drill for offshore oil, but who pays when the wells leak and cover our beaches? We need cheaper energy, but do the highly efficient nuclear power plants exact too great a price in terms of safety and pollution of the environment? Chemicals in the streams and air are unsafe, but who pays to clean them up? **Environmentalism** is the movement that tries to protect our resources and our health by keeping the environment clean and safe.

How Serious Is Pollution?

Pollution of the environment has been an issue for centuries, but for the first time, many fear pollution to be a real danger to human survival. Within the past 15 years, we have become aware of many

---

From 1971 through 1982, chemical spills killed 287 persons and injured 7638 people in 126,622 separate incidents.

dangers. Although air in many major cities is cleaner than it was before the passage of the Clean Air Act in 1970, the Environmental Protection Agency reported in early 1983 that 111 of the nation's 3000 counties (50 million people) failed to meet federal air pollution standards. From 1971 through 1982, chemical spills killed 287 persons and injured 7638 people in 126,622 separate incidents. About one-third of the country's streams and shorelines remain polluted. Many streams and lakes, once sparkling and pure, are now off limits to swimmers; fishermen cannot eat their catch; and water must be purified to be drinkable. Toxic waste disposal has everyone fearful, and acid rain takes the joy out of fresh rainfall. Acid rain is formed when chemicals from burning coal, oil, or gasoline get into the air and mix with rain. The mixture forms a weak sulfuric acid, nitric acid, or nitrous acid. Almost 10,000 lakes in the eastern half of the United States have suffered some acid rain damage, according to the National Wildlife Federation. Once acid rain destroys a lake, there is virtually no way to restore it. Many citizens are subjected to between 50 and 90 decibels of noise pollution; and solid waste threatens to bury us. As the pollution problems have become better known, public sensitivity has increased. In a public opinion survey of environmental and economic issues sponsored by the Continental Group, Inc., 77% of the respondents put a high priority on a clean environment. In July, 1983, William Ruckelshaus, administrator of the Environmental Protection Agency said, "We're just fooling ourselves if we think Americans will let Congress or any administration ease up in any way if it seriously jeopardizes public health or the environment."*

Business and Government Response

There is little doubt that businesses have been a major contributor to our pollution problems; but until recently, accountability had been nil. For in-

---

* *The Wall Street Journal,* September 2, 1975, p. 1.

* "We Must Restore Our Credibility," *U.S. News & World Report,* July 11, 1983, p. 50.

stance, many years ago, Pittsburgh was covered by blankets of steel mill smoke. To complaints, officials responded, "Smoke means jobs." Thirty years ago, the Ford Motor Company, responding to a Los Angeles County official complaining of soot, stated, "The Ford engineering staff, although mindful that automobile engines produce gases, feels that these waste vapors are dissipated in the atmosphere quickly and do not present an air pollution problem." Although environmental decisions today are still controversial, our attitude has changed drastically from these early days. We no longer think of pollution as merely a nuisance; it menaces the survival of many people. Over the years, government and business programs have begun to tackle environmental problems.

Programs. Perhaps the greatest impact upon environmental protection has been made by the **Environmental Protection Agency (EPA),** which formulates and interprets environmental laws. The EPA has assessed penalties against polluters and prompted a number of laws, including the **National Environmental Quality Act of 1970** which regulates air pollution and the **Clean**

The Dioxin Controversy

In 1983, Times Beach, Missouri, moved — all 2500 residents. The federal government bought most of their 800 homes and 30 businesses. Cost to the government was $36.7 million.

People were moving away because a very toxic substance, known as dioxin, was found in their community. Dioxin, a highly toxic by-product of certain chemical-making processes, is considered dangerous by some experts at one point per billion. Levels many times higher than this were found in people's driveways and yards. The chemical was apparently in waste oil used to spray for dust control on roads in Missouri and in other parts of the country.

Dioxin is not just one chemical; actually, the label refes to any of seventy-five different chemicals in eight different chemical families. One of the most widely known uses of the substance was in Agent Orange, a defoliant used in the Vietnam War. It is also the by-product in many insecticides, herbicides, wood preservatives, coolants, and copy paper.

Even though dioxin has caused quite a scare around the country, the American Medical Association (AMA) claims that the news media have blown the issue completely out of proportion. Their resolution said in part that the "lives and well-being" of people living in areas contaminated by dioxin "have been unnecessarily and ignorantly damaged by this hysterical malreporting."* Doctors, representing the AMA, report that dioxin has been around a long time, yet it has not produced any documented deaths or anything of a serious medical nature. Chemical companies also maintain that fears are exaggerated.

Still, researchers report links between dioxin and many health problems with research animals in the laboratory. And some doctors say that persons exposed to dioxin are much more susceptible to heart attacks, liver problems, and soft-tissue cancer. Finally, more than 16,000 Vietnam veterans have filed disability claims attributing many ailments to the dioxin in Agent Orange. Experts on both sides agree that more study is needed to pinpoint the effect of dioxin on human health.

* "AMA says Dioxin no Imminent Threat," *The Boston Globe,* Associated Press, June 23, 1983.

TABLE 3.2 ■ MAJOR FEDERAL ENVIRONMENTAL LEGISLATION

1899 Refuse Act

Made it unlawful to dump refuse into navigable waters without a permit. A 1966 court decision made all industrial wastes subject to this act.

1947 Federal Insecticide, Fungicide and Rodenticide Act

Enacted to protect farmers from fraudulent claims of salespersons. Required registration of poisons.

1955 Federal Water Pollution Control Act

Set standards for treatment of municipal water waste before discharge. Revisions to this act were passed in 1965 and 1967.

1963 Clean Air Act

Assisted local and state governments in establishing control programs and coordinated research.

1965 Clean Air Act Amendments

Authorized establishment of federal standards for automobile exhaust emissions, beginning with 1968 models.

1965 Solid Waste Disposal Act

Provided assistance to local and state governments for control programs and authorized research in this area.

1965 Water Quality Act

Authorized the setting of standards for discharges into waters.

1967 Air Quality Act

Established air quality regions, with acceptable regional pollution levels. Required local and state governments to implement approved control programs or be subject to federal controls.

1967 Federal Insecticide, Fungicide and Rodenticide Amendments

Provided for licensing of pesticide users. (Further authority granted through 1972 revision.)

1970 National Environmental Quality Act

Established Council for Environmental Quality for the purpose of coordinating all federal pollution control programs. Authorized the establishment of the Environmental Protection Agency to implement CEQ policies on a case-by-case basis.

1970 Clean Air Act Amendments

Authorized the Environmental Protection Agency to set national air pollution standards. Restricted the discharge of six major pollutants into the lower atmosphere. Automobile manufacturers were required to reduce nitrogen oxide, hydrocarbon and carbon monoxide emissions by 90% (in addition to the 1965 requirements) during the 1970s. Set aircraft emission standards. Required states to meet deadline for complying with EPA standards. Authorized legal action by private citizens to require EPA to carry out approved standards against undiscovered offenders.

1970 Resource Recovery Act

Authorized government assistance for the construction of pilot recycling plants. Authorized the development of control programs on national level.

1970 Water Quality and Improvement Act

Required local and state governments to carry out standards under compliance deadlines.

1972 Federal Water Pollution Control Act Amendments

Set national water quality goal of restoring polluted water to swimmable, fishable waters by 1983.

1972 Noise Control Act

Required EPA to establish noise standards for products determined to be major sources of noise. Required EPA to advise the Federal Aviation Administration on acceptable standards for aircraft noise.

1972 Pesticide Control Act

Required that all pesticides used in interstate commerce be approved and certified as effective for their stated purposes. Required certification that they were harmless to humans, animal life, animal feed, and crops.

1974 Clean Water Act

Originally called the Safe Water Drinking Act, this law set (for the first time) federal standards for water suppliers serving more than twenty-five people, having more than fifteen service connections, or operating more than sixty days a year.

1975 Federal Environmental Pesticide Control Act Amendments

Established 1977 as the deadline for registration, classification, and licensing of approximately 50,000 pesticides. This deadline was not met.

1976 Resource Conservation and Recovery Act

Encouraged conservation and the recovery of resources. Put hazardous waste under government control. Disallowed the opening of new dumping sites. Required that all existing open dumps be closed or upgraded to sanitary landfills by 1983. Set standards for providing technical, financial and marketing assistance to encourage solid waste management.

1977 Clean Air Act Amendments

Changed deadline for automobile emission requirements from 1975 and 1978 to 1980–1981.

1977 Amendments to Clean Water Act

Revised list of toxic pollutants and set new policies for review. Required that pollutants be monitored "by best available technology" that is economically feasible.

1977 Federal Water Pollution Control Act Amendments

Authorized extension of the 1972 regulations.

Water Act of 1974 which controls water pollution. In 1980, Congress created a Superfund to deal with toxic waste dumps. The Superfund, containing $1.6 billion in 1983, was being used to help clean up chemical dumps in alleys, backyards, and other places. Additionally, the **Solid Wastes Disposal Act** exercises some control over disposal of solid wastes, and the **Federal Occupational Safety and Health Act** regulates noise levels for manufacturers in interstate commerce. (See Table 3.2 for a list of major federal environmental legislation.) The government has also used financial incentives, zoning restrictions, research grants, and denial of government contracts to enforce pollution control measures.

Prompted by society's concern and Congress's prompting, businesses are now investing billions of dollars to reduce and prevent pollution. In fact, in 1983, government and business's pollution control expenditures amounted to $50 billion a year — $220 for every person in the country. For a power plant, capital costs for pollution control may run as high as 25%. For most other plants, it ranges between 1 and 10%. For example, Mobil Oil engineers have designed many refinery units to minimize emission of mist, sulfur dioxide, petroleum vapor, and other chemical compounds. Georgia Pacific installed a system that recycles and removes all pollutants. Dow pledged, "No plant will be built if there is any waste effluent or air pollution." Another approach by businesses is to design and produce products that improve pollution control. Examples include automobiles that are less polluting, detergents that dissipate more quickly, and recyclable cans and bottles. See Table 3.3 for a listing of the costs of fighting pollution in the 1980s.

Achievements and future problems. Environmentalists show many achievements in their attacks on pollution. Some of them are as follows:

- In the eighteen worst cities, violations of carbon monoxide standards have dropped 66% since 1975.
- Private industry has invested about $60 billion to control air pollution during the past 10 years.
- Smoggy days have dropped 36% during the last decade in the twenty-two cities with the worst smog.

TABLE 3.3 ■ ESTIMATED COSTS OF FIGHTING POLLUTION IN THE 1980s

Air pollution	$393 billion
Water pollution	$228 billion
Solid waste pollution	$ 22 billion
Land reclamation	$ 19 billion
Noise	$ 11 billion
Toxic substances	$ 11 billion
Drinking water	$ 4 billion
Pesticides	$ 2 billion
Total cost (1980–1989)	$690 billion

Source: Environmental Protection Agency.

- Since 1975, sulfur dioxide emissions — from burning coal, oil, and other fossil fuels — have been cut by 5 million tons a year.
- Automobile-produced carbon monoxide is 40% lower than a decade ago.
- The Great Lakes cleanup campaign in the late 1970s has produced increased fish and other marine life once again.

While we appear to be slowly winning the battle against air and water pollution, chemical and radioactive wastes are emerging to provide new threats. Our factories produce between 40 to 60 million tons of contaminated wastes per year. Service stations, dry cleaners, and other small businesses add to this, making the total about a ton a year per person.

Although some firms practice controlled disposal of hazardous chemical wastes, improper disposal and pollution have emerged as major environmental concerns of the 1980s.

CROSS FIRE

Should Pollution Laws Be Tighter or Looser?

The debate over the government's role in fighting pollution is ongoing. In an interview with Gaylord Nelson, Chairman of the Wilderness Society, reported in *U.S. News & World Report,* Nelson makes the following points for not loosening pollution laws.

- Our society cannot last long if we do not fully implement the laws passed by Congress over the past few years.
- Although it is costly to prevent and clean up pollution, cleanup measures save society billions of dollars. In the long run, antipollution measures are cheaper than pollution costs.
- We will not be at a disadvantage in international markets by spending more on pollution control because other countries are going to have to do the same thing.
- If the federal government's role is reduced, you would have fifty states, each with different standards — an unmanageable mess.

A. Alan Hill, chairman of the Council on Environmental Quality, makes the following points for reducing the federal government's role in environmental protection:

- We are already spending a lot of money on pollution control — $50 billion annually. This is much more than the gross domestic product of 141 nations that report such expenditures.
- According to statistics, lower spending levels will not endanger the environment.
- Laws protecting public health should be given top priority.
- Since people throughout the nation demand a clean environment, giving more power to the states would not worsen the problems.
- Experience by 3M, Eastman Kodak, and other companies has shown that pollution control measures can be cost effective; thus, it is reasonable to expect industry to do more voluntarily in the area.

How do you stand? Do you think the federal government should be more or less involved in controlling pollution?

___ A. Much more involved   ___ C. Somewhat less involved
___ B. Somewhat more involved   ___ D. Much less involved

Give three justifications for your position.

A. _____
B. _____
C. _____

Source: "Should Pollution Laws Be Loosened?" *U.S. News & World Report,* April 4, 1983, pp. 51–52.

DISCRIMINATION

Discrimination is unequal treatment of people based on race, sex, religion, age, or national origin. Measurable discriminations against minorities and the disadvantaged, including women, blacks, Mexican-Americans, Indian-Americans, and other ethnic groups, have revealed blatant injustices within our society. These groups have difficulty gaining access to many of the opportunities within business. Furthermore, they are discouraged from pursuing their traditional cultures.

Although law and adjustments are being made in some areas, the actual figures show that discrimination is still widespread. The number of women in the work force is at the highest peak ever, more than 44 million, and that number is expected to top 54 million by 1990. In 1950, only 30% of the total work force consisted of women. The number will be 45% by 1990 (see Figure 3.2). In spite of the influx of women into the work force, a wide disparity in pay exists between jobs dominated by men and those held by women. According to U.S. Department of Commerce, women still earn only 59¢ for each dollar earned by men.

Business Reaction to Discrimination Pressures

As the dire need has become more evident, businesses have tried to deal with discrimination in several ways. Federal and local governments have been active in providing pressures that encourage the support of business in overcoming discrimination.

Although the media have publicized the Reagan administration's hostility toward enforcement of affirmative action laws, two-thirds of the executives in a 1982 Harris poll reported that government pressure for salary equity is as strong as ever.[*]

Hiring and promotion. The **Civil Rights Act of 1964** prevents employment discrimination based on race, religion, national origin, or sex. The federal government appointed the **Equal Employment Opportunity Commission (EEOC)**, a

---

[*] "How Executives See Women in Management," *Business Week*, June 28, 1982, p. 10.

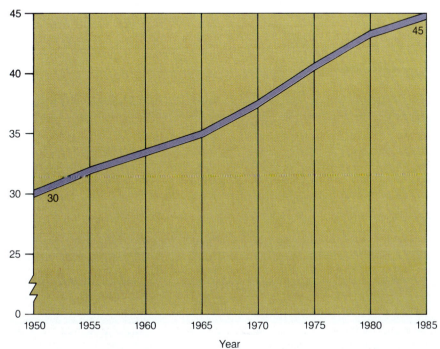

Figure 3.2 Growing percentage of women in the work force. *Source: Department of Labor Statistics.*

More Women in Management

In 1982, about 28% of all managers and administrators were women. This is up from 18% ten years earlier. Though this is a substantial increase, speculation exists that the percentages of women in top and middle level management is lower than it should be. Perhaps because the competition is getting keener, some women wonder if men—holders of nearly all the top jobs, as they are—will instinctively favor other men. Patricia McGrath, a graduate of the Harvard Business School, laments that "in big corporations it's not as easy to promote a woman as a man." Nevertheless, there are women who fervently aspire to becoming their company's CEO (chief executive officer), gaining directorships, or being picked for a plum governmental post. The accompanying chart pictures the growth in percentage of women bosses.

Female managers and administrators
(millions)

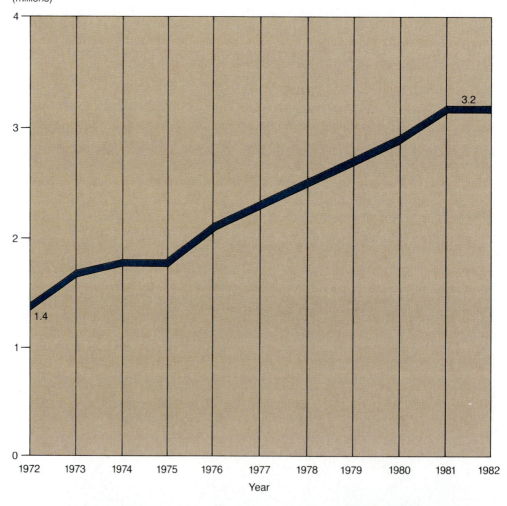

Source: "Women as Bosses: The Problems They Face," *U.S. News & World Report,* July 11, 1983, pp. 56–57, and "How Harvard's Women MBAs Are Managing," *Fortune,* July 11, 1983, pp. 58–72.

federal agency, to enforce the act. Title VII of the Civil Rights Act, strengthened by several executive orders, requires an **Affirmative Action Program** as follows:

> Every company that has 40 or more employees and government contracts of $50,000 or more must develop a detailed plan that identifies weaknesses in hiring and promoting minorities and women, and a specific plan, along with dates, for correcting them.

In 1973, the EEOC won a landmark discrimination settlement against AT&T which required them to pay $15 million in back pay and $23 million a year in raises for discrimination in job assignments, pay, and promotions. However, there is some concern that this requirement places to heavy a burden on small businesses, and in 1983 there were efforts to relax requirements for some small firms.

Even in the face of President Reagan's budget-cutting efforts, the EEOC budget was increased to $150 million for 1983, up $6 million from the year before. About 2800 of the commission's 3100 employees operate in the investigative area. Companies found guilty of job discrimination may be prevented from bidding on government contracts. Also, courts may force a guilty employer to hire an individual, provide back pay, or take other corrective actions.

Prompted by these pressures, companies have become more sensitive in hiring and promoting. While some must try to meet the minimum requirements of hiring and promotion without regard to sex or race, other companies vigorously publicize their openings to minority groups. And some companies give priority to minorities and women, even though doing so makes them susceptible to the charge of reverse discrimination.

According to activity in the EEOC, unlawful job discrimination (including age, racial, and sex discrimination) continues to be a problem in our society (see Figure 3.3). Clarence Thomas, chairman of the Equal Employment Opportunity Commission, says, "It's fair to say that job discrimination is still very, very serious, although it is not nearly as blatant and obvious as it was 20 years ago."

Training programs. Offering a job does not always solve the problem, especially for the underqualified. Again, with some government prompting and assistance, businesses have offered training programs to help train disadvantaged people to perform at required skill levels. In 1984, the Job Training Partnership Act provided federal funds in an effort to unite public and private sectors into a job-producing partnership. Businesses who hire the unemployed and provide on-the-job training receive some reimbursement for their costs and may receive special tax credits. Small business owner John Ringler says the program is very helpful. In his case, government funds pay about 40% of the salary of an employee, allowing him to hire two people instead of one.

Minority enterprise support. Minority enterprises are businesses owned by blacks, Spanish-speaking Americans, native Americans, Orientals, and other minority groups. For instance, as a result of the 1971 settlement, enacted by Congress, of the land claims of Alaska's 80,000 Eskimos, Indians, and Aleuts, the natives of Alaska are establishing business empires. The natives were granted 44 million acres to help them enter the

FUNNY BUSINESS

Source: Stockworth by permission of Sterling & Selesnick, Inc. and The New York Times Syndication Sales Corp.

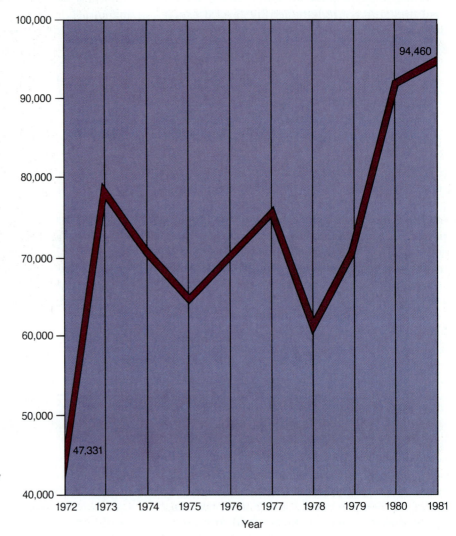

**Figure 3.3
Charges found to have
merit by the EEOC
(1972–1981).** *Source:
Equal Employment Opportunity
Commission.*

capitalist mainstream, and $962.5 million was in-
cluded to establish 203 village businesses and 12
giant regional corporations (see Figure 3.4). In addition to this and other government-sponsored
programs, a number of companies help minority-
owned businesses by specifically awarding contracts to them and agreeing to finance some developmental projects. For instance, Southland
Corporation, the operator of 7-Eleven convenience stores, pledged a 5-year commitment to
raise the level of minority participation in the corporation to 23% by 1988. The percentage goal applies to all levels in the organization, including
managers, professionals, technicians, sales
workers, office personnel, and clerks. In addition,
Southland pledged to expand its college intern

program to include at least 23% minorities; use
minority vendors for 23% of its outside purchases;
and increase usage of minority companies it does
business with in accounting, advertising, banking,
insurance, legal services, and real estate.

Corporate charity. Studies show that many
companies have voluntarily increased their donations to aid minority causes. These efforts, often
not related directly to their businesses, aid in education, drug programs, playing centers, day-care
centers, hospitals, career development programs,
and help for the elderly.

The United Way is one of the most visibly successful programs where companies and individuals work together to aid the disadvantaged. Com-

panies provide skilled managers to help run the campaigns, and company employees collect and encourage donations from other employees. Many companies match the contributions of their employees. That is, if employees raise $5000 among themselves, the company will contribute another $5000.

Another example of corporate charity to minority groups is Xerox Corporation's recent $6 million gift of talking computers for blind students at various colleges across the country. Two hundred Kurzweil Reading Machines, which convert any kind of printed material into actual spoken English, will be used by an estimated 4600 of the 6000 currently enrolled U.S. college students who have severe visual impairments.

Corporations, needless to say, do not contribute exclusively to minority groups and concerns. Many instances of corporate philanthropy could be listed, but let us mention merely a few:

- IBM recently contributed $40 million in computer-aided manufacturing equipment to twenty universities.

These Native American salmon fishermen are shareholders in their own company, one of many established through Congressional action in 1971.

BUSINESS BULLETIN

The Discrimination Case of Christine Craft

In the summer of 1983, Christine Craft sued her former employer, Metromedia, Inc., for sex discrimination. Craft had been hired as a television anchorwoman by Metromedia to do newscasts.

After a few months on the job, Craft's supervisor demoted her because, as the supervisor said, ". . . audience reaction to her was very negative." The reaction was based on surveys that the station had taken of its viewing audience. An expert witness testified that the survey's findings were based on unscientific data. He commented that the sample of the audience was not a true representation of the station's total audience, and he said that the survey asked questions that were not normally asked about male newscasters.

However, Craft maintained that she was demoted because the news director told her she was, ". . . too old, unattractive, and not deferential enough to men." The news director denied saying this to Craft.

Craft's suit claimed sex discrimination. The federal jury of four men and two women agreed. They recommended awarding $500,000 to Craft— $375,000 for actual damages plus $125,000 in punitive damages. Although Metromedia appealed the decision and got some changes, the courts agreed substantially with Craft's position.

Source: "Jury Awards Craft $500,000 in Suit Against TV Station," Associated Press, *The Wichita Eagle Beacon,* August 9, 1983, p. 1.

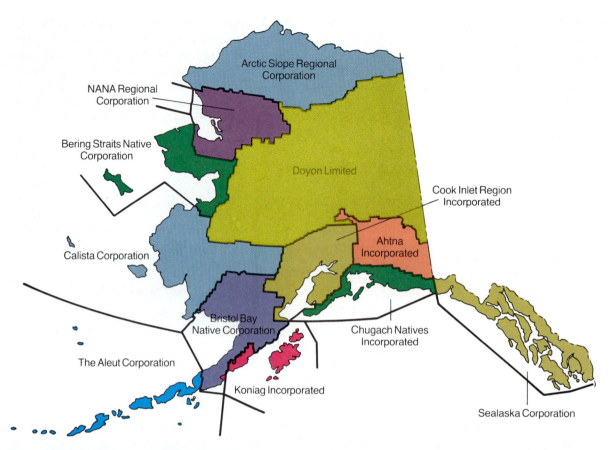

Figure 3.4
The Alaska regional native corporations.

- Wang Laboratories contributed $4 million to the Metropolitan Center in Boston.
- Mainpro, a $2.8 million maker of lubricants and maintenance products, each month gives each of its fifty employees a $24 check to be used for any philanthropic purpose.

ETHICS AND WHITE COLLAR CRIME

Ethics are principles of right or good behaviors. They involve moral values as to what conduct is proper. And business ethics involve other moral values in our society. As one businesswoman said, "Many of our moral decisions are borderline; some people view a certain practice as being unethical, while others think it to be totally proper." Many influences in our society determine which behavior is ethical.

Sources of Ethics

While each individual develops a code of what is ethical, we are influenced by laws, cultural attitudes, professional codes, and individual values.

Influence of law on ethics. Many ethical standards are defined by laws. But the law does not cover all unethical conduct; it merely tries to prevent serious violations. Many laws, especially new ones, are unclear. Since humans make laws, some of them are not perfect and others are later found to be unconstitutional. Still, most authorities agree

Recent surveys by the Cable Channel News indicate that as many as 40% of the population cheated on their income tax returns.

that abiding by the law defines a minimum guide for ethical behavior. For example, the law states that each citizen must be honest in filing tax returns, yet recent surveys done by the Cable Channel News indicate that as many as 40% of the population cheated on their income tax returns. Also, the law states that employees should not steal from their employers, yet many workers see nothing wrong with taking office supplies home for personal use.

Cultural values and ethics. Values are accepted standards of behavior within a given society. All societies develop broad-based values that are generally accepted by most of its members. Communities of people usually share common views. Often, these views affect the values and conduct of businesses in local areas. For example, many communities believe that stores should not sell alcoholic beverages on Sunday. And, in fact, citizens may exert pressure for passages of laws that prohibit doing so. Stores in other areas may remain closed on Sunday mornings, not because of laws, but out of respect for the community's values.

Professional codes and ethics. Many national associations have ethics committees that develop standards for their communities. The purpose is to use group behavior to encourage ethical practices that build goodwill and trust. A good example would be the code of ethics published and enforced by the National Board of Realtors in Fig. 3.5.

Individual values and ethics. Although we may all grow up in the same society, there is a broad range in the values we adopt. Individual values vary with background, family, religion, and environment. Some people think it is all right to mislead customers in order to get a sale. Others may choose to lose the sale rather than misrepresent the product in any way. In one survey of business people, 19% said they had quit a company for ethical reasons. Sometimes a company may try to influence an employee to act against personal values. In the same survey, 87% said it was wrong to compromise personal values even if the success of the company was at stake. While individual values vary, most people agree that it is wrong to lie, cheat, steal, and purposefully misrepresent.

How Ethical Is Business Behavior?

Are business practices becoming more unethical? There is no easy answer. Bribery, profit gouging, price fixing, embezzlement, monopolizing, and other illegal practices cost consumers more than $40 billion a year in higher prices and taxes. A spokesperson for the U.S. Chamber of Commerce says that the extent of bribes, kickbacks, and payoffs is "pervasive." These unethical activities might involve anyone from the janitor to the chairman of the board. A recent study of 3000 executives by the American Management Association found that most employees felt pressure from their companies to compromise their personal values. Another study by the Opinion Research Corporation of 531 top and middle mangers reported that 48% felt that it would be all right to pay bribes to foreign officials if that were an accepted way of doing business in that country. The famous

Figure 3.5
Excerpts from the code of ethics of the National Association of Realtors.
Source: The National Association of Realtors.

Article 1. The Realtor should keep himself informed as to events affecting real estate in his community, the state, and nation so that he may be able to contribute responsibly to public thinking on such matters.

Article 4. The Realtor should seek no unfair advantage over his fellow-Realtors and should conduct his business so as to avoid controversies with his fellow-Realtors.

Article 8. The Realtor shall not accept compensation from more than one party, even if permitted by law, without the full knowledge of all parties to the transaction.

Article 9. The Realtor shall avoid exaggeration, misrepresentation, or concealment of pertinent facts. He has an affir-mative obligation to discover adverse factors which a reasonably competent and diligent investigation would disclose.

Article 10. The Realtor shall provide equal professional services to all persons regardless of race, creed, sex, or country of national origin. The Realtor shall not be a party to any plan or agreement to discriminate against a person or persons on the basis of race, creed, sex, or country of national origin.

Article 17. The Realtor shall not engage in activities that constitute the unauthorized practice of law and shall recommend that legal counsel be obtained when the interest of either party requires it.

Watergate caper and the recent ABSCAM scandal, with their resulting public outrage, have increased investigations into the ethical practices of business. To date, almost 450 firms have admitted to secret payments or bribes, both within the United States and to other countries.

Can society thrive without some minimum standards of honesty and ethics? We think not. Since business depends on society's survival, a certain level of honest dealing is necessary. The capitalist system glorifies pursuit of self-interest, but business people understand as never before that they cannot be successful without the trust of others. Bad-mouthing competitors is sometimes considered a valid business strategy, but as Kirk Hanson, a business administration professor at Stanford University, says "There is a growing appreciation for the fact that businesses owe some kind of obligation to competitors and customers. They are realizing they are vulnerable [to each other's] innuendo."

Some business people feel that it is simply good business to be ethical. Ethical behavior stimulates others to be more cooperative and prevents angry behavior by competitors, peer companies, and government agencies. Customers like to trade with honest companies, employees value fair bosses, and investors feel more secure with law-abiding companies. Further, the recent interest in corporate culture (see Enrichment Chapter A) and the realization that successful companies are the ones with good values have helped spotlight corporate ethics still more.

Since the Watergate incident, more than 300 business ethics courses have been added to the curriculums of the nation's colleges and universities. What is more, business ethics is showing up in more sales training classes, boardrooms, and company policy statements. As an indication of the emphasis that some companies have begun to place on ethical behavior, Chemical Bank in New York now includes ethics in a new management training program, and Conoco Inc. publishes an in-house booklet on moral standards.

New ethics issues are always emerging. As some experts see things now, the most important ethics issues during the next decade will be:*

The rights of workers. Do companies owe anything to laid-off workers? Do they owe them training or new jobs? What about the effect of automation on the work force, or company responsibility to the families of working women, or sexual harassment on the job, or minority hiring? The whole issue of hiring and the quality of work life is having, and will continue to have, an immense impact on workers' rights.

The rights of citizens in other countries. Kenneth Goodpaster, a professor at Harvard Business School, believes "there is a globalization of business." Companies will likely have to "look at their values from a transcultural" point of view in order to help ensure their success in the marketplace.

The rights of companies and the public as technology advances. With the change to a society based on information come concerns about the right to privacy. Along with this, there is an increasing concern about people stealing trade secrets and copyrighted material. With the burgeoning field of computers and information processing comes computer crime and the need for computer laws.

The rights of the environment. Only today are we beginning to experience the effects of acid rain and toxic waste dumping. Who has responsibility for cleaning up wastes that were disposed of a decade or two ago? Dow Corning Corporation, a manufacturer of silicones, says in its code of ethics that "Dow Corning will be responsible for the impact of its technology upon the environment."

ENERGY

With only 6% of the world's population, Americans consume over 30% of the world's total energy. And our consumption rate has been rising rapidly during the last few years. In the United States, an average person uses as much energy in a few days — driving a car, mowing the lawn, mixing a cake, cleaning the rug, cooling and heating homes, and enjoying leisure — as most individuals in other countries use in a year.

This hydroelectric facility at a Massachusetts dam and the geothermal steam plant in Utah represent options to meet future energy needs with renewable, regionally distinct, resources.

Where Do We Get Energy?

Energy is the capacity for the action or the ability to do work. Of course, we use physical energy when we run, walk, lift, stand, or even sit. But we have such great demands for energy that it is impossible to satisfy all of our energy needs with physical effort. We can't very well propel a jet-liner across the ocean with human energy, can we? Energy comes from many sources, most of which are becoming increasingly expensive.

Oil. Oil is our greatest source of energy, and we are hugely dependent on it. By 1990, we will be using more than 20 million barrels a day, or more than 7 billion barrels annually. Because the United States is not capable of producing all the oil it uses, half of our needs must be imported. (See Figure 3.6 for a graphic of the world's known oil reserves.)

Indeed, our known and proven reserves within the United States amount to only about 28 billion barrels, enough for about 4 more years at our current rate of consumption. If we rely on so much foreign oil, we leave ourselves open for political blackmail and price gouging. And we are trying to become less dependent. We built a pipeline from Alaska, but by 1985, it is expected to supply only about one eighth of the oil we need. Politicians talk about energy savings plans, but oil is so central to our economy, it is hard to reduce our consumption sharply.

Coal. Within our boundaries, we have one of the world's oldest energy sources: coal. And we have a lot of it, about one fifth of the globe's supply. If we mined and used all of it, we could run all our machines and gadgets — to meet all of our energy

Middle East 58%
Soviet Union 15%
Africa 9%
Latin America 6%
United States 4%
Western Europe 4%
Asia 3%
Canada 1%

Figure 3.6
The world's supply of known oil reserves.
Source: American Petroleum Institute, Canadian Petroleum Association, Oil & Gas Journal.

needs—for the next 200 or 300 years. But, although we have the resources, there are problems with using it. It defaces the land when mined and pollutes the air when burned. The EPA (Environmental Protection Agency) and the Clean Air Act of 1970 regulate the burning of coal. Scientists can turn coal into natural gas, which burns cleaner, yet the cost is too great.

Natural gas. As far back as 1950, natural gas supplied about 17% of our energy demands. By 1980, it supplied almost 25% of our energy needs. It has been a less expensive form of energy and we have a lot of gas wells. The Federal Trade Commission has regulated natural gas prices in order to keep them low. In fact, prices have been kept so low that there has been little incentive to undertake the costly exploration of new supplies. In 1981, legislation was passed to deregulate gas prices, allowing gas companies to charge higher prices. This, some experts argue, will provide the push for more discovery and production.

Atomic energy. Nuclear power, which is generated from atomic reactors, is surely the most controversial energy source. Advocates insist that it is the only reasonable and practical source of energy for the future. And they argue that utility companies will have to start expanding their capacities by the mid-1980s to meet expected demands in the 1990s.

Others strongly oppose atomic energy because of the safety hazards in processing it and storing its waste. The Three Mile Island mishap in 1979 was an eye-opener for many people. They realized, perhaps for the first time, that something could go seriously wrong.

We currently generate 12% of our electrical energy from atomic power. But this may grow to 18% over the next 2 years when 33 more reactors begin their operations. Still, because of the heated emotions involved, the nuclear controversy will probably continue for some time.

Other energy sources. Several other possible energy sources for the future include synthetic oil, fusion atomic energy, solar energy, and wind energy. All sources of energy have pluses and minuses, as Table 3.4 indicates.

BUSINESS BULLETIN

Dim Future for Nuclear Plants

On April 20, 1983, the Supreme Court ruled that states may outlaw nuclear plants not yet under construction. The decision upheld California's 1976 moratorium on building new nuclear plants until there was an acceptable method for handling nuclear waste. Several other states have similar moratoriums and others are sure to follow.

Still, according to a Washington think tank, the American Enterprise Institute, business and government leaders have a strong preference for nuclear power. Yet, the American public apparently does not feel the same way, and, in this case, public opinion prevails.

The much-publicized Three Mile Island (TMI) incident is still very much an issue. The problem at TMI occurred in 1979, and cleanup operations began in 1982. Cost of the cleanup is a staggering $1 billion, and experts feel that it will take 4 years to achieve the cleanup.

Currently, 80 nuclear plants are operating, and another 57 are still under construction. The court ruling affects neither the operating plants nor those under construction. But the future for nuclear construction appears dim, considering public desires. As an official of the Nuclear Regulatory Commission said, "A utility executive would be crazy to commit his company to a nuclear power plant in the current political and regulatory climate."

Source: "Nuclear Industry Takes It on the Chin Again," *U.S. News & World Report*, May 2, 1983, p. 8.

TABLE 3.4 ■ SOURCES OF ENERGY

Energy Source	Advantages	Disavantages
Foreign oil	Plentiful, accessible, safe.	Political dependence, high cost, lack of control, outflow of dollars, political problems, transporting cost.
Coal	Plentiful, cost effective, wide usage.	Polluting, defacing in mining, transporting cost, water needed for processing.
Natural gas	Limited, cost effective, clean, efficient, wide usage.	Limited resource, transporting cost, safety hazards.
Atomic energy, fission	Cost effective, plentiful, efficient, accessible, wide usage.	Safety hazards, storage of wastes, polluting, capital investment, political problems, nuclear threats.
Atomic energy, fusion	Plentiful, efficient, clean, unlimited energy with more technology, accessible, wide usage.	Safety hazards, more technology required, capital investment, political problems, nuclear threats.
Solar	Clean, plentiful, safe, accessible.	Limited usage, original cost, not efficient, more technology.
Wind	Clean, plentiful at times, safe, accessible.	Not consistent, limited usage, not efficient, noise and visual pollution.
Synthetic oil	Clean, plentiful, safe, accessible.	Cost, limited usage, more technology required, capital investment, limited usage.

Source: Lester Thurow, *Zero-Sum Society*, New York: Penguin Books, 1980.

What Can Business Do?

No doubt, there is a serious energy shortage facing us. We either need greater, more efficient supplies or we need to consume less energy. Business is responding to both sides of the equation.

Finding new resources. A lot of firms are exploring for new sources of energy. They are discovering new oil, coal, and gas reserves. There are numerous projects underway to advance our technologies for converting coal into gas, sun into energy, synthetics into oil, and wind into power. As in the past, when a need exists, business rises to the challenge of fulfilling that need.

Conserving energy. A lot of energy, as much as half, is actually wasted. We lose some by transmitting it. Electricity may travel thousands of miles from its source to the consumer, resulting in a loss of energy. In research and development departments throughout the country, companies are finding new ways to conserve, produce, and transmit energy. And companies are trying to conserve by lowering their thermostats in the winter and using less air conditioning in the summer. Some large companies are using less energy

now than they did 8 years ago. In the manufacture of products, businesses now take energy usage into design considerations. Government encourages consumers to use less energy by such measures as the 55 mile per hour speed limit and gas mileage requirements for new cars.

Attentive energy audits of industrial processes led to reduced energy needs for this steel manufacturer.

There are many solutions to the energy problem, but some choices will have to be made, and some sacrifices will have to be endured. We may choose to conserve, depend on foreign sources, risk safety, harm the environment, tolerate noisy windmills, or install solar receptors. For each choice, there are benefits and resulting costs.

SUMMARY

In recent years, society has applied increased pressure for businesses to become more socially responsible. The major arguments for social responsibility are: (1) Society grants businesses the right to exist, (2) social responsibility contributes to business profits, (3) businesses have resources, and (4) businesses can avoid government interference. Arguments against business participation in social problems are: (1) Businesses require profits, (2) consumers pay, (3) there is fear of business domination, and (4) agencies already exist. Consumerism requires that businesses act in the interest of consumer protection and consumer rights.

In the past, business has been a major polluter of the environment. Although the environment is a continuing concern, environmentalists, working together with business, are preventing some future pollution and cleaning up past mistakes.

Discrimination against employees because of race, religion, sex, age, and national origin continues to be a problem in our society. Business and government agencies are working together in an effort to combat discrimination and provide more equality for the future.

White collar crime continues to be a social ill. Business is working to establish more rules of conduct and educate employees in ethical values.

Because of the severity of the energy crisis, business has become involved in finding new sources of energy, as well as conserving present resources. The energy shortage can be overcome, but some sacrifices will have to be made.

MIND YOUR BUSINESS

Instructions. Business's relationship to social problems provokes many arguments and emotions. To get an idea of where you stand on the major socially related issues, respond to the following questions by using a scale from 7 to 1 to record the intensity of your feelings.

Very strongly   Very strongly
   agree   7 6 5 4 3 2 1   disagree

____ 1. Businesses should contribute time, money, and expertise to solve social problems.

____ 2. Government and business should protect and ensure the rights of consumers.

____ 3. It is the responsibility of government and business to clean up the environment, regardless of the economic cost.

____ 4. Businesses and government should make more effort to ensure that discrimination at work and in the marketplace is eliminated.

____ 5. The ethical behavior of businesses should be improved.

____ 6. We should try to solve future energy problems by government-induced rationing methods, as well as by searching for new energy sources.

See answers at the back of the book.

KEY TERMS

REVIEW QUESTIONS

1. Define social responsibility. Give an example.
2. List and explain each of the arguments for business becoming more involved in social problems.
3. List and explain the arguments against business becoming more involved in social problems.
4. What is consumerism?
5. What are the provisions of the Consumer's Bill of Rights?
6. Discuss the means by which consumers are protected.
7. What is discrimination?
8. Discuss the ways in which businesses are reacting to discrimination pressures.
9. What is environmentalism?
10. What has the government done to fight environmental problems?
11. What have businesses done to help with environmental problems?
12. Define ethics. What are the major influences of ethics?
13. What are our major sources of energy? What can businesses do to help with the energy problem?

CASES

Case 3.1: Are Businesses Doing Enough to Hire Minorities?

Many women and blacks complain that they are not getting good jobs in business and government. And companies complain that they cannot find enough professional and skilled women and minority workers to meet their affirmative action goals. Business leaders say they are working hard, but competition for hiring women and minorities has increased intensely.

There has been, according to government statistics, a steady but slow gain for women and minorities in higher-paying jobs. But feminist and civil rights leaders do not believe the statements of business leaders that "we just cannot find enough qualified minority and women workers." One industry leader says, "We cannot find enough engineers period, much less women and minority engineers." He makes his point by stating that only about 800 of the 40,000 engineering graduates in a recent year were black.

Labor experts say that businesses are not hiring enough women and minorities for three reasons: (1) Some professions, such as engineering, traditionally attract only a few women and minorities, (2) some businesses do nothing more than skim off the top women and minority professionals, and (3) other businesses simply do not look hard enough.

Questions

1. Whose arguments do you tend to agree with?
   ___ A. Women and minorities
   ___ B. Business executives
2. Why?

Case 3.2: What Can Our Company Do?

A citizens' group in a medium-sized industrial city planned a discussion between city officials and industry representatives. The topic of the discussion concerned industry's responsibilities to the city. The city was having trouble with unemployment, discrimination in employment, traffic congestion, air pollution, pollution in a nearby stream, a rising crime rate, and a deteriorating tax base.

Mr. Appleby is a top official in one of the chemical companies that uses city resources. He is respected by both government and industry as a sincere, concerned citizen. Like many business leaders, he has devoted a considerable amount of time to civic projects. His company has been quite profitable over the years but has spent little money attempting to curb the pollutants it discharges into the river. At the preliminary presentation by representatives of the citizens' committee, Appleby appeared concerned about the problems faced by the city. Upon closer questioning, he seemed somewhat frustrated and curtly responded, "But what can our company do?"

Questions

1. Prepare a position paper for Mr. Appleby, outlining the reasons for and against his company's participation in city problems.
2. What specific actions should the city take to enlist the support of the industrial community?
3. What specific actions do you recommend that Mr. Appleby's company take?

After completing this chapter, you will be able to:

■ Define proprietorship and list the advantages and disadvantages of this form of ownership.

■ Define partnership and list the advantages and disadvantages of this form of ownership.

■ Understand partnership modifications that we call joint ventures, limited partnerships, and business trusts.

■ Define corporation and list its major characteristics.

■ List the procedures for creating a corporation.

■ Understand the rights and responsibilities of owners of corporations.

■ List the advantages and disadvantages of the corporate form of ownership.

■ Describe the major forms of business combinations.

4

FORMS OF
BUSINESS
OWNERSHIP

Businesses that produce Snickers® candy bars and Estee Lauder® cosmetics are both owned by families. When the board of directors of these firms meet, they might start with kissing and hugging among brothers, sisters, cousins, and other relatives. Economists predict that family owned businesses account for about 50% of the gross national product, and they constitute more than 12 million of the approximately 14 million businesses in the United States.

Stroh Brewery Company, also family owned, persuaded its twenty-seven family members to take a lower dividend so they could borrow funds to buy Joseph Schlitz Brewing Company. Peter Stroh says that family sacrifice is one of the major reasons they are successful. Leonard A. Lauder, president of Estee Lauder, says their family name is on every package. This produces a drive to succeed with a high-quality product.

Although most large companies are corporations, many started as sole proprietorships or partnerships. Some companies have a few owners, as in the case of the family-owned businesses mentioned; others have thousands of owners. As we shall see in this chapter, owners face several alternatives when deciding upon a form of ownership, and each form has advantages and disadvantages.

SOLE PROPRIETORSHIPS

A **sole proprietorship** is a form of business that is owned by only one person. Its simplicity makes it by far the most common form of business. Proprietorships in the United States total about 10.9 million companies, or about 78% of our 14 million businesses. However, proprietorships do only about 10% of the total business sales. Most are quite small; their average profits are not much more than $25,000.

Over half of the proprietorships are farms, and many others are part-time, operating out of the owner's spare room, basement, or panel truck. They are also popular in service businesses, such as laundromats, beauty parlors, newsstands, drugstores, liquor stores, repair shops, nightclubs, restaurants, and plumbing services.

Advantages of Proprietorships

Most advantages of single-owned companies stem from their simplicity and relative freedom.

Ease of starting and stopping. In many cases, an individual can form a proprietorship without permission from the city, state, or federal governments, although in some cases, a license is required. Doctors and lawyers usually need state

Convenience shops offering quick-turnover items are a common type of business owned—and often operated—by a single proprietor.

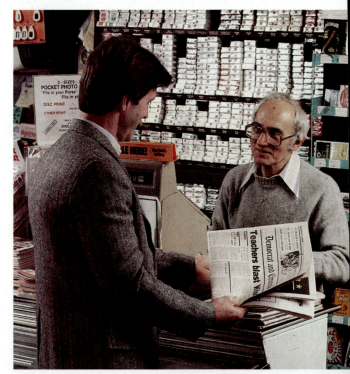

approval to practice. Other businesses, such as restaurants, liquor stores, and bars, may require a special license. But the dream of owning a business is still quite accessible, even today. The new owner can just put up a shingle, rent a building, have stationery printed, and open for business. The company is just as easy to dismantle. The owner merely settles outstanding accounts and agreements and closes the door.

Wide range of freedom. There is no body of law directed at proprietorships: no special tax laws, no unique liability laws, and no ownership agreements. The individual's business activities are not distinguished from personal activities; thus, for all practical purposes, the owner enjoys all rights as an individual citizen in running the business. A versatile owner can expand, apply for a loan, offer new services, alter prices, sell on credit, or engage in a variety of other business activities simply by deciding to do it.

Greater motivation. Single-owned companies appeal to the old-time values of independence and hard work. All the rewards of success and the frustrations of failure rest squarely on the shoulders of the owner. More than in any other form of ownership, the owners can see the results of their work. This motivates many owners to work long hours and endure extreme hardships in order to accomplish the goal of personal success and independence.

Almost unlimited secrecy. Proprietorships do not have to make public reports, and they have no boards or committees with which they have to share information. The owner can make all the decisions and does not have to tell anyone. The only time this prime secrecy might be threatened is during a tax audit. Otherwise, the proprietor can be as secret as he or she wants. This privacy makes it very difficult for competitors to uncover the strategies of a proprietor.

Tax advantages. There are no special taxes on a proprietorship; the owner simply pays personal income tax on profits. However, the tax advantage may not be as great as it was once thought to be. For one thing, small corporations may, in most states, choose to be taxed as a proprietorship. Thus, the proprietorship may have no tax advantage. Second, many owners of smaller corpora-

tions take the income out in personal salaries. Although the owners must pay personal income tax on their salaries, it is a nontaxable expense to the company.

Disadvantages of Proprietorships

Like the advantages, most disadvantages of a proprietorship stem from its simplicity.

Unlimited liability. Unlimited liability means that the owner's personal wealth may be used to pay off debts and obligations of the business when the business is unable to do so. Without doubt, this is the most stunning disadvantage. Thousands of small businesses fail each year, and the owners lose many of their personal assets and some of their pride in the process.

Size and capital limitations. Usually, it is hard for an individual owner to acquire the capital necessary for rapid growth. Even if the owner is wealthy, it would be hard to raise the several million dollars needed to develop a new product, expand a new plant, or hire salespeople nationwide. As a small business owner commented, "It is hard for me to spend $40,000 or $50,000 on some risky new idea. The slightest credit squeeze or drop in sales may create a new crisis for the business."

Limited management and employee skills. Since the business usually operates on limited capital, the owner provides most if not all of the management skill. Often, one manager, the owner, makes all decisions on marketing, pricing, financing, taxes, hiring, buying, advertising, and the like. It is hard for one person to have expertise in all these areas, yet the proprietorship must compete with corporations that may have specialists or even departments making these decisions. In a proprietorship, there is little or no opportunity for advancement, pay is usually low, and the fringe benefit package meager. For these reasons, employees are quite often relatives, friends, or individuals with limited skills.

Noncontinuous life. A business that is entirely dependent on the energies and resources of one owner is highly unstable. Sickness or a serious accident to the owner might prove fatal to the business; death of the owner is a legal end to the business. Further, proprietorships are difficult to sell because survival is so dependent upon the owner's reputation. The company may be passed on to a relative upon the owner's death, but when this occurs, a new business is formed. Finally, limited resources render most small proprietorships vulnerable to swings in the economy. About one in five new proprietorships goes out of business during the first year of operation, and only one in ten survives five years or more.

PARTNERSHIPS

A partnership, sometimes referred to as a **general partnership,** is a business with two or more owners and is slightly more complex than a proprietorship. A few partnerships number more than one hundred owners, but more than 80% have only two. A partnership does not necessarily require a written contract, but it is most advisable. Most states require a written contract when real property is transferred to the name of the partnership or when the agreement lasts longer than a year. The **partnership agreement,** sometimes called *articles of co-partnership,* varies from state to state, but usually includes: (1) the name of the company and identity of the owners, (2) arrangements for contributing finances, skills, and management to the company, (3) means for dividing income, (4) method for one or more partners to withdraw, and (5) steps for dissolving the agreement.

We can classify partners according to whether or not they are active in management and known to the public. A **silent partner** takes no active part in management but is known to the public. Usually this occurs when a company takes a well-known personality as a partner for the use of a famous name. In reverse, a **secret partner** actively participates in management but is unknown to the public. A combination of a silent and secret partner is a **dormant** or **sleeping partner.** This owner is not active in management and is not known to the public; he or she merely invests in the business. Last, a **nominal partner** allows, or even encourages, the public to think that he or she is a partner, but is not an owner at all. This rarely occurs because the courts have maintained that this pretender can be held liable in the same sense as a general partner.

Historically, partnerships date back to Roman law, as early as the eleventh century. They are

Partnerships are not only few in number, but their total number decreases each year. One million partnerships exist in the United States, and they account for only 4% of total sales.

almost as old as proprietorships, but they are less common. Their greatest area of concentration is in wholesale and retail trade and professional services such as accounting, medicine, law, and insurance. Partnerships are not only few in number, but their total number decreases each year. One million partnerships exist in the United States, and they account for only 4% of total sales. An analysis of the advantages and disadvantages of partnerships indicates why they have such a small impact on our total business system.

Advantages of Partnerships

The partnership is an extension of a proprietorship, and its advantages overcome some of the major shortcomings of individually owned companies.

More specialized management.   A logical reason for two or more persons to own a business is to combine skills and judgment. Two or three people can bring different but complementary skills to an association. One partner might be a specialist in manufacturing, another in marketing, and a third partner might be an accountant. Medical doctors and lawyers often form a partnership so that they can pool their resources and hire specialists to manage the internal affairs of their respective practices. Another seemingly ideal strategy is when one partner is a creative risk taker and the other is a logical, conservative decision maker. Their combined judgment often leads to better decisions than would have been made individually.

Greater source of capital.   Partners have the advantage of combined capital resources. The partnership can draw upon the savings of all partners, and their combined personal wealth makes borrowing easier. Many partnerships form

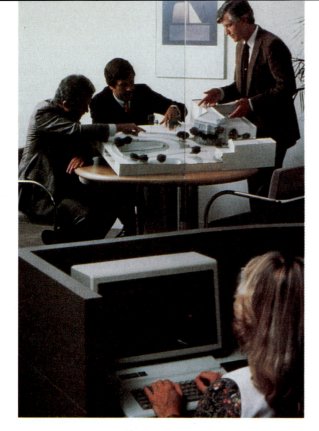

Architectural firms are often partnerships, combining the specialized skills of several professionals to attract and serve clients.

when an individual with an idea or skill lacks the capital to produce and distribute the product or service. This individual may find a financial backer who becomes a partner and supplies the needed capital for a piece of the action (percentage of the profits).

Incentives for key employees. If a partnership wishes to keep a particular employee who contributes a valuable skill, it can make that employee a partner. Many accounting and law firms operate on this principle. When employees realize that it is possible to become part-owner of the company, they have incentive to stay with the company and perform much better on the job.

Legal certainty. Partnerships, though less complicated than corporations, have more legal certainty than proprietorships. The **Uniform Partnership Act** of 1914 established specific guidelines for the function of partnerships. Since then, with more legislation that clearly defines the operation of partnerships, legal arrangements can

be very specific. Specific written agreements at the time of partnership can avoid future problems. A lawyer who deals in partnerships can provide legal advice on most questions quickly at minimal cost.

Wide range of freedom. Like the proprietorship, the partnership is relatively free from government control. Since the partnership is not an entity separate from its owners, it is subject to few reports and taxes. Also, it can conduct business in other states as freely as can an individual.

Disadvantages of Partnerships

The partnership overcomes many disadvantages of proprietorship, but not all.

Unlimited liability. Like the proprietorship, each partner is liable for the obligations of the business. Should the business fail, each partner's personal wealth may be legally taken to fulfill the obligations of the venture. Also, each partner is an agent for the partnership. If one of the partners makes a decision that costs the company a loss, all of the partners are responsible. Such responsibility for the actions of other partners is enough to make a person think twice before entering into a partnership agreement.

Short length of life. There are many situations that can dissolve a partnership. Death, withdrawal, bankruptcy, or insanity of a partner will end the venture. Also, the transfer of one partner's share to someone else or failure of a partner to fulfill contractual agreements can cancel the partnership. Of all the forms of business, partnerships average the shortest life span. When the partnership is terminated, the benefits of long-range planning are often lost.

Owner conflicts. Partners Simon and Blanchard own Kelso Chemical Company. Although the two founders have been in business for ten years, they have not talked with each other for the past three. Blanchard gets to the office before 9:00 A.M.; Simon comes in later to avoid meeting Blanchard. They communicate to each other via memos, which they pass back and forth between their secretaries. The partners have yelled at each other, thrown water on each other, and even got into an old-fashioned fist fight about their differences. Eventually, the business suffered, and a court-appointed receiver now runs the business. Simon and Blanchard are both in their seventies.

Partnership squabbles have become so common — the American Arbitration Association reports a 78% increase in the past two years — that attorneys have developed a new service industry to help partners with their disagreements. Partners must cooperate to run a business effectively. Often, disagreements over decisions, rewards, and business practices create tension between partners. These conflicts can threaten not only the profits but even the existence of the business. Partners may fight over who has the right to enter into a contract, negotiate a loan, hire or fire an employee, or invest in a new product or service. The partnership agreement may have methods for reconciling differences, but it does not prevent them. Unfortunately, partners sometimes dissolve their successful business because of these conflicts.

Difficulties in withdrawing. Unlike a proprietorship, a partnership is not easy to dismantle. As a result, partners may lose control over their investment. For example, a partner may want to sell out, but the other partners may vote against it. If partners want out, they must either find other investors or sell their shares to the remaining partners. Often, this is difficult. Finally, even if the partnership is agreeable to the withdrawal of a partner, it is not legally possible if the partnership is in the middle of a contractual obligation. When a partner insists on withdrawing, the result may be a forced sale at a price less than the value of the business.

Modifications in Partnership Agreements

As partnerships evolved, owners made several adjustments to overcome their limitations. Most changes try to reduce personal liabilities.

Joint venture. In a **joint venture,** a group of people set up a temporary partnership for the purpose of carrying out a single business project. The joint venture lasts for a specified period of time; during the life of the venture, each partner has the same legal obligations as a general partner.

Typically, however, only one person takes responsibility for the management decisions of the project. Historically, joint ventures have been used primarily in real estate developments. For instance, a group may agree to invest money in a project to build and sell six condominiums. If they formed a joint venture, their partnership would last for the time that it took to build and sell the condominiums.

Today, however, joint ventures are becoming increasingly common, especially among high-tech firms. One way that biotechnology firms (those engaging in the new field of genetic engineering) can remain independent and still gain access to marketing and manufacturing expertise that they lack is by forming joint ventures with large drug or chemical companies. Zsolt Harsanyi, an E. F. Hutton vice-president, predicts that at least a dozen joint ventures will be formed this year. Genentech, for example, has set up several joint ventures, the most recent with Baxter Travenol Laboratories, Inc., to develop diagnostic tests.

Limited partnership. In 1822, New York State set the precedent for limited partnerships by passing an act allowing partnerships to limit the liability of one or more of its partners. Many other states soon followed. Sales of limited partnerships were expected to reach a record $18 billion in 1984, up from $14 billion in 1983 and $8 billion in 1982. **Limited partners** have the right to inspect the company's books, receive information from the business, and participate in earnings. If they take an active part in the control of the business, they become liable as general partners. Every partnership must have at least one **general partner** that has unlimited liability and is usually active in management. A business can attract investment dollars by adding limited partners who can invest capital without assuming risks beyond their investment. The law assumes partners to be general partners unless otherwise stated. Oil com-

Major corporations are joining together in limited partnership agreements to cooperate on common research problems and raise money.

panies such as Dyco Petroleum, Sampson Properties, and Saxon Oil have been particularly successful in raising money for investment through limited partnerships. In real estate, another hotbed area for limited partnerships, JMB Realty, Balcor/American Express, and Consolidated Capital have been successful.

Major corporations are also joining together in limited partnership agreements to cooperate on common research problems and raise money. In late 1983, the following firms were talking about limited partnership agreements: National Steel Corp. and Battelle Memorial Institute were looking at a research and development project as a way to finance research on production of steel strips; Semiconductor Research Corp. (SRC) was considering a limited partnership to raise money to develop a 4-million-bit, random-access computer memory; and Boeing, Lockheed, and McDonnell Douglas were looking at the possibility of collaborating in a 10-year program to design and develop the next generation jetliner.

Business trust. The **business trust** is able to limit the liability of its owners by excluding them from control. Typically, a few partners solicit funds from a large number of investors who receive shares in the trust. But the trustee makes all the management decisions, including the distribution of profits. Investors do not even elect the managing group. Investors merely furnish the capital and allow the trustees to speculate with it. A business trust is very similar to a corporation, and it is still rather widely used.

Through these examples of modifications in partnership agreements, we can see the modern corporation emerging. Today's corporations have proven so successful that they have overshadowed proprietorships and replaced nearly all partnerships.

CORPORATIONS

Leonard and Clara Murray have operated a pancake house as partners for 15 years. Recently they decided to incorporate for several reasons: they wanted to get worker's compensation, to be able to deduct the cost of their medical insurance, and to give their son and daughter part ownership of the business. Incorporating made all this possible.

The **corporation** is an actual being in the eyes of the law. It is an intangible person with many of the legal rights, powers, and obligations of an individual. The corporation may make contracts and buy, hold, and sell property; it can sue and be sued in its own name. Chief Justice John Marshall's legal definition of a corporation has become famous. In the case of *Dartmouth College* v. *Woodward* in 1803, Marshall breathed life into the corporate body with a definition that read in part:

> A corporation is an artificial being, invisible, intangible, and existing only in contemplation of law. Being the mere creature of law, it possesses only those properties which the charter of its creation confers upon it, either expressly or an incidental to its very existence. . . . Among the most important are immortality, and, if the expression may be allowed, individuality; properties, by which a perpetual succession of many persons are considered as the same, and may act as a single individual.

Although relatively few in number, corporations dominate today's business world. The two million corporations in the United States account for more than 85% of the total sales of all businesses. Table 4.1 lists the twenty largest corporations, ranked according to sales, in the United States in 1982.

Characteristics of Corporations

Because of their unique legal identity, we create, own, and manage corporations differently from other companies. Since the states define and regulate corporations, the laws may differ slightly from one state to another. Some corporations are owned by individuals; we call these **private corporations.** Most large businesses that you think of — General Motors, the Boeing Company, Sears — are examples. By contrast, **public corporations** are owned by the government, such as the Tennessee Valley Authority (TVA), liquor stores in a few states, park boards, and city governments.

There are several types of private corporations. Some are profit corporations, those organized to make a profit for the owners. Most companies are profit corporations. But some are nonprofit corporations; they may receive and spend money, but their goal is not to make a profit. Nonprofit organizations include charities, churches, public television stations, hospitals, and private schools. An **open corporation** makes its stock available to the public and therefore usually has many owners. Usually a family or only a few people own a **close corporation.** These may also be called privately held companies since they do not offer their stock for public sale, and it is not traded on the stock markets. A company may choose to remain closed for several reasons, including:

■ They do not have to produce a lot of financial reports to the public.

■ They can make decisions with less red tape.

TABLE 4.1 ■ THE TWENTY-FIVE LARGEST U.S. INDUSTRIAL CORPORATIONS IN 1983

Rank		Company	Sales	Assets		Net Income		Stockholders' Equity	
1983	1982		$ Thousands	$ Thousands	Rank	$ Thousands	Rank	$ Thousands	Rank
1	1	Exxon (New York)	88,561,134	62,962,990	1	4,977,957	2	29,443,095	1
2	2	General Motors (Detroit)	74,581,600	45,694,500	2	3,730,200	3	20,766,600	3
3	3	Mobil (New York)	54,607,000	35,072,000	4	1,503,000	11	13,952,000	6
4	5	Ford Motor (Dearborn, Mich.)	44,454,600	23,868,900	9	1,866,900	6	7,545,300	14
5	6	International Business Machines (Armonk, N.Y.)	40,180,000	37,243,000	3	5,485,000	1	23,219,000	2
6	4	Texaco (Harrison, N.Y.)	40,068,000	27,199,000	5	1,233,000	12	14,726,000	4
7	8	E. I. du Pont de Nemours (Wilmington, Del.)	35,378,000	24,432,000	7	1,127,000	13	11,472,000	8
8	10	Standard Oil (Indiana) (Chicago)	27,635,000	25,805,000	6	1,868,000	5	12,440,000	7
9	7	Standard Oil of California (San Francisco)	27,342,000	24,010,000	8	1,590,000	8	14,106,000	5
10	11	General Electric (Fairfield, Conn.)	26,797,000	23,288,000	10	2,024,000	4	11,270,000	10
11	9	Gulf Oil (Pittsburgh)	26,581,000	20,964,000	13	978,000	14	10,128,000	12
12	12	Atlantic Richfield (Los Angeles)	25,147,036	23,282,307	11	1,547,875	9	10,888,138	11
13	13	Shell Oil (Houston)	19,678,000	22,169,000	12	1,633,000	7	11,359,000	9
14	15	Occidental Petroleum (Los Angeles)	19,115,700	11,775,400	21	566,700	25	2,640,900	50
15	14	U.S. Steel (Pittsburgh)	16,869,000	19,314,000	14	(1,161,000)	489	5,355,000	20
16	17	Phillips Petroleum (Bartlesville, Okla.)	15,249,000	13,094,000	18	721,000	18	6,149,000	16
17	18	Sun (Radnor, Pa.)	14,730,000	12,466,000	19	453,000	34	5,236,000	21
18	20	United Technologies (Hartford)	14,669,265	8,720,059	32	509,173	28	3,783,755	31
19	19	Tenneco (Houston)	14,353,000	17,994,000	15	716,000	19	5,822,000	18
20	16	ITT (New York)	14,155,408	13,966,744	17	674,510	21	6,106,084	17
21	29	Chrysler (Highland Park, Mich.)	13,240,399	6,772,300	38	700,900	20	1,143,058	126
22	23	Procter & Gamble (Cincinnati)	12,452,000	8,135,000	34	866,000	17	4,601,000	27
23	25	R. J. Reynolds Industries (Winston-Salem, N.C.)	11,957,000	9,874,000	26	881,000	16	5,223,000	22
24	24	Getty Oil (Los Angeles)	11,600,024	10,385,050	23	494,314	29	5,402,707	19
25	21	Standard Oil (Ohio) (Cleveland)	11,599,000	16,362,000	16	1,512,000	10	8,094,000	13

Source: ''The *Fortune* 500 List of the Largest U.S. Industrial Corporations,'' © 1984 Time Inc. All rights reserved.

BULLETIN

The Most Admired Corporations

Fortune polled over 7000 corporate executives, outside directors, and financial analysts; half responded. Those surveyed were asked to rate only the ten largest companies in their own industry, using a scale of 0 (poor) to 10 (excellent), on eight key attributes of reputation: quality of management; quality of products or services; innovativeness; long-term investment value; financial soundness; ability to attract, develop, and keep talented people; community and environmental responsibility; and use of corporate assets.

RATINGS ON EIGHT KEY ATTRIBUTES OF REPUTATION

Most Admired		Most Admired	
Quality of management	*Score*	*Financial soundness*	*Score*
IBM	9.16	IBM	9.45
Hewlett-Packard	8.75	General Electric	8.88
Dow Jones	8.70	Dow Jones	8.80
		Ability to attract, develop, and keep talented people	
Quality of products or services		Hewlett-Packard	8.42
Dow Jones	9.06	IBM	8.39
Boeing	9.02	Merck	8.29
Anheuser-Busch	8.64		
Innovativeness		*Community and environmental responsibility*	
Citicorp	8.69	Johnson & Johnson	8.44
Merrill Lynch	8.35	Eastman Kodak	8.26
Time Inc.	8.26	IBM	7.95
Long-term investment value		*Use of corporate assets*	
IBM	8.88	IBM	8.47
Dow Jones	8.39	Dow Jones	8.26
Hewlett-Packard	8.08	Hewlett-Packard	8.01

OVERALL RATINGS

Rank	Company	Industry Group	Score
1	IBM	Office equipment, computers	8.53
2	Dow Jones	Publishing, printing	8.35
3	Hewlett-Packard	Office equipment, computers	8.24
4	Merck	Pharmaceuticals	8.17
5	Johnson & Johnson	Pharmaceuticals	8.15
6	Time Inc.	Publishing, printing	7.99
7	General Electric	Electronics, appliances	7.96
8	Anheuser-Busch	Beverages	7.91
9	Coca-Cola	Beverages	7.87
10	Boeing	Aerospace	7.79

TABLE 4.2 ■ EXAMPLES OF SOME LARGE, CLOSE CORPORATIONS

Company	Business
Koch Industries	Crude oil marketing
Hughes Aircraft	Aerospace products
United Parcel Service	Parcel delivery
Reader's Digest	Publishing
Gates Rubber	Rubber, aviation
S. C. Johnson and Sons	Household products
Hallmark cards	Cards, novelties

■ They do not have to hold public stockholder meetings.

Some very large companies remain privately held. Table 4.2 lists several of the largest. We also classify corporations according to where they were organized. A business is a **domestic corporation** in the state in which it is incorporated. To do business in other states, it must register as a **foreign corporation. Alien corporations** have been organized in other countries, but they have received permission to do business in the United States. Figure 4.1 illustrates the various types of corporations.

How to Create a Corporation

The first step in the birth of a corporation is the promotion of the proposed company. Somebody, usually the owner, sees an advantage in creating a new corporation or incorporating a proprietorship or partnership. The promoter must then convince others that they stand to benefit by investing in the venture (by the purchase of stock). The pro-

moter usually prepares a prospectus outlining the potential of the proposed concern, and he or she may enter into certain preincorporation contracts. Professional promoters usually handle the task of selling the new corporation, especially for the larger ventures.

The second step is the filing of the **articles of incorporation** with the appropriate state office, usually the secretary of state. Promoters and lawyers often help in this step. The content of the articles will vary according to state laws, but they generally include:

■ Name and purpose of the corporation.

■ Address of the main office.

■ Number of shares of stock of all classes, and restrictions on transferability of shares, if any.

■ Number of directors and perhaps their names.

■ Names and addresses of the incorporators.

■ Amount of paid-in-stock with which the business will begin.

Once the articles are consistent with the law, the state will grant a charter that gives the company permission to operate as a corporation.

Ownership of Corporations

An owner of a corporation is called a **stockholder. A stock certificate** is evidence of ownership (see the example in Figure 4.2). Stockholders are of two major types: common and preferred. **Common stockholders** are owners who have a right to vote on the corporation's board of directors. **Preferred stockholders** are also owners, but they usually do not have voting

Figure 4.1
Kinds of corporations.

Figure 4.2
A sample stock certificate. *Courtesy of the Coca-Cola Company.*

rights. They do, however, usually have first claim on profits—the reason they are called preferred. The main rights of common stockholders are to:

- Elect the board of directors.
- Receive a share of the profits in the form of dividends.
- Sell and purchase stock on the open market.

Once a year, common stockholders vote on members of the **board of directors,** a group charged with the responsibility of managing the company. Since the owners are usually scattered throughout the country, it would be difficult to get them all together for voting. So owners may sign a **proxy,** a document transferring their voting rights to someone else, and mail it in. Figure 4.3 is an example of a proxy. The board of directors, at the company's expense, mails proxy forms to all owners and asks them to sign and return the forms. By so doing, the owner transfers his or her right to vote to someone else. In large corporations with many stockholders, the owners seldom keep tabs on the board's decisions. So, unless the company has grave problems, the board members usually vote themselves in. Owners often have the right to vote on amendments to the charter, pension and bonus plans for the officers, acceptance of a merger, and other major issues.

The owners receive profits in the form of dividends. **Dividends** are payments to the stock-holders over a given period of time, at a given amount per share. Directors usually decide quarterly how much, if any, of the profits they wish to distribute to the owners. The profits are either distributed to the owners in dividends or they are reinvested back into the company in the form of **retained earnings.** If the company decides to keep the profits, the company may become more valuable and the price of the stock usually goes up. Some investors prefer profit in the way of dividends while others speculate for an increase in the price of stock.

How Corporations Are Managed

In smaller corporations, the major owners may also be the managers. But in larger corporations, the thousands of owners could not possibly manage the daily activities. So the elected board of directors is responsible for running the business. Members of the board are not only principal officers and employees of the company but also some specialists with legal and financial expertise from outside the company. Although stockholders have the right to draw up the bylaws, they usually delegate this task to the board of directors.

The bylaws cover such activities as:

- Time and place of meetings.
- Method of calling meetings.
- Pay for the directors.

Figure 4.3
A proxy statement for General Motors stockholders. *Reprinted by permission.*

BULLETIN

Will There Be More Women on Boards of Directors?

In 1976, there were only 147 women directors in the United States, a remarkably small number. By 1979, the number had more than doubled to 300. In 1979, there were more than 16,000 men on these same boards. While there is no legal penalty for not having women on boards, there are pressures to recruit more women for these positions.

Still, the facts show that most board members, of both sexes, are more than 50 years of age. They grew up in a period where women stayed at home or worked as volunteers to improve the community. For most male directors, this value imprinting has remained strong, and they do not automatically accept women in the boardroom. A major problem is finding women that can make the transition to board membership. To facilitate this, an organization called Catalyst began in 1977. Its purpose is to bring potential women board members and organizations together through the use of files, information, and other data on qualifications and positions.

Source: Felice N. Schwartz, "'Invisible' Resource: Women for Boards," *Harvard Business Review,* March–April, 1980, pp. 6–8, ff.

TABLE 4.3 ■ REVIEW OF THE FEATURES WITHIN THE FORMS OF OWNERSHIP

Features	Sole Proprietorship	Partnership	Corporation
Creation	Easy; no legal requirement	Relatively easy; incorporated by law	Difficult; incorporated by law
Ownership	Single owner	Few or many owners	Few or many owners
Liability	Unlimited	Unlimited	Limited
Freedom	Wide range	Wide range	More limited
Motivation	Strong for owner, weaker for employees	Fairly strong for owners and key employees	Weak for lower level employees, strong for management
Tax	No special income tax	No special income tax	Heavily taxed, and income is double taxed
Size	Limited	Limited	Unlimited
Stability	Unstable	Unstable	Stable
Capital	Hard to attract	Relatively hard to attract	Easier to attract
Ownership transfer	Relatively easy	Difficult	Easy
Government regulations	Fewer by comparison	Fewer by comparison	Many by comparison

■ Identification of management positions.

■ Duties of the major officers.

■ Ways of filling vacancies.

■ Regulations for issuing stock.

■ Methods of altering the bylaws.

The appointment of the principal officers is another responsibility of the board. The charter defines principal officers; they typically include the president, secretary, treasurer, and several vice-presidents. Normally, the board will elect the president, who then chooses the other officers.

A final responsibility of the board is to serve as a watchdog for the owners. Board members should evaluate the performance of the company's officers, and they usually have authority to accept or reject major decisions of the officers. In this role, they often give "rubber-stamp" approval to the plans of the chief officer, resulting in little protection for the owners.

Board members are liable for illegal decisions and fraud. But they are not liable for decisions of poor judgment unless the court decides the actions were blatantly irresponsible. Recently, courts have toughened their stand and, in a few cases, board members have been held personally liable for their "bad judgment." Table 4.3 reviews the features of different ownership forms, and Figure 4.4 summarizes how corporations are managed.

Advantages of Corporations

We have personalized corporations by creating legal advantages that deal with the legal being concept. The major advantages are as follows.

Limited liability. Unlike partners and proprietors, owners in a corporation have **limited liability.** They stand to lose only what they have invested. Suppose you invest $20,000 in the stock of a company and that company goes bankrupt and is left owing a half million dollars. You can lose — because of limited liability — only your investment, even if you have enough wealth to pay the debt. Since the corporation is a legal being, it sues and is sued in its own name.

Ease of transferring ownership. You can withdraw your investment in a corporation simply by selling your stock to someone else. Major stock exchanges list the latest selling price for thousands of stocks by the minute, and they pro-

The relative ease with which corporations attract large amounts of capital is one of the advantages of this form of business ownership.

vide a ready market for buyers and sellers. Many corporations are not listed on the exchanges. And those owners may have more difficulty finding buyers and sellers. But the withdrawal is still easy compared to the other forms of ownership because the sale of an owner's stock does not dissolve the corporation. An owner can usually sell stock to anyone at any time, but the corporation must keep records of who owns its shares.

Continuous life. Unlike proprietorships and partnerships, a corporation can last indefinitely. While some charters specify the length of life of the company, most assume an indefinite life span.

The corporation overcomes the instability caused by change of ownership and also provides management separate from the owners. For these reasons, the corporation has a form of eternal life.

Ease of attracting capital. How can a business get more money for expansion? Proprietorships are limited by the owner's ability to borrow or supply capital. Partnerships have a small advantage; they are limited by their few owners' abilities to raise money or to draw from their personal assets. Corporations have a large advantage. They can raise money by selling shares of stock, and investors know that they cannot lose more than

Figure 4.4
How corporations are managed.

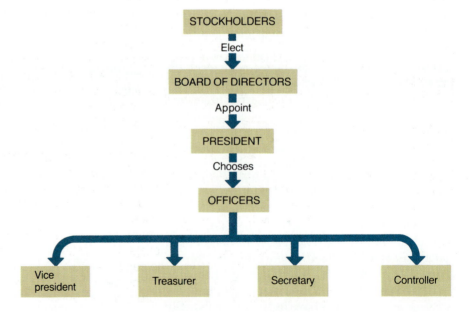

the price of the stock. Thus, it is easier for corporations to become large.

Large size. While all corporations are not large, most large businesses are corporations. Large size offers the advantage of economical production methods: Large companies can buy materials, manufacture products, and ship finished goods in bulk. But even more important is the ability to specialize. In a large company, managers can specialize in financing, production, marketing, legal assistance, and the like. Employees can specialize in their areas of interest and have more opportunity for advancement than in most small compa-

TAKING STOCK

From Proprietorship to Corporation: The National Association for Management

In 1969, Gene Williams began his career as a management consultant. At first, he operated as a sideline on weekends and days off from his regular job. He started because of interests he had in organizational problems and his successes in conducting several projects in his company. Although Gene filed no formal papers, passed no exams, and did not have to be certified by any licensing agency, he was in fact operating a single proprietorship.

By the end of 1975, Gene's earnings in his sideline proprietorship were netting more than $15,000 per year, and he was looking for ways to expand. He did not have time to do promotional work, and he needed more capital then he could raise — two conditions that motivated him to seek a partner. Hugh Burgess, a long-time acquaintance, seemed to be an appropriate candidate for a partner. Hugh, a successful manager in a large firm, had a lot of experience in promotion. After several meetings, Gene and Hugh agreed to become partners in the business. To expand their offerings beyond consulting services, they decided to develop training products: materials, tapes, workbooks, newsletters, and booklets. They each invested $5,000 cash in the project. Hugh agreed to do the promotional work, and Gene agreed to develop the projects and continue the consulting projects.

By 1979, the business was generating gross returns of more than $75,000 per year. Neither partner wanted to take money out of the business for personal use, so they continued to plow their money back into growth and expansion. Because they were getting larger, hiring additional personnel, and entering into contracts with many firms, they thought they should form a corporation.

They met with a lawyer who, for a fee of $750, filed the articles of incorporation with the secretary of state. Total authorized capital for the corporation was $200,000, and the total number of shares that the corporation had authority to issue was 200,000 of common stock. Gene and Hugh took 100,000 shares each, so that between them they owned 100% of the corporation. The state granted the charter, and the business became a corporation in December, 1979. Gene became the president, and Hugh was the vice-president and treasurer. Hugh continued his duties of promoting the firm's products and services while Gene continued to develop consulting services and materials. Thus far, they have declared no dividends; rather, they continue to reinvest the earnings in the company for additional growth. Currently, the owners are considering selling additional shares to another acquaintance to raise capital and to get more management help in the company.

nies. This potential, combined with the ability to pay higher salaries and offer attractive fringe benefits, gives the corporation an advantage in hiring and keeping top-rate employees.

Disadvantages of Corporations

On the one hand, we have supported the corporate form of ownership by legally promoting size and continuous life. At the same time, we are concerned about its control over our lives. Some of the disadvantages of corporation ownership stem from fears associated with its enormous size and vast power.

Government regulations.   The government created the corporation as an artificial being and feeds its offspring with dozens of rules and regulations. State governments begin by reserving the authority to approve each charter before a corporation can exist. The federal government gets into the act with regulations on retirement plans, procedures for hiring and paying employees, safety programs, control of mergers, pricing arrangements, and taxes. Many of these regulations apply to all organizations, but enforcement is focused on the larger corporations. In order to comply with all the regulations, corporations spend a good deal interpreting laws, maintaining records, and reporting to government agencies.

Higher taxes.   Owners pay taxes twice on corporate profits. The corporation pays corporate taxes, and then the owners pay personal income tax on dividends (distributed profits). Corporate taxes vary, but in recent years they have fluctuated between 22 and 30% on the first $25,000 of income and hovered around 50% on profits above $50,000. In addition, corporations pay many fees and special taxes that do not apply to other organizations.

Corporations with fewer than ten shareholders that meet certain legal requirements may elect to be taxed as a **Subchapter S corporation,** meaning that the corporation is taxed like a partnership. If you owned a small business, for example, you might want to incorporate to limit your liabilities to the amount you have invested in the business. In all probability, you could qualify under Subchapter S of the Internal Revenue Code. This would allow you to take advantage of the corporate form of ownership, while avoiding the double taxation on your profits.

Lack of personal interest.   Many employees lose their ability to identify with a giant company. They begin to feel like computer punch cards, cogs in the machine, and six-digit payroll numbers. Many employees do not even know the name of the company president and couldn't care less. This vast gap between managers, owners, and employees leads to many communication problems, indifference, and reduced employee motivation.

Lack of secrecy.   Because corporations have to report so many of their activities and because many government agencies scrutinize their activities, corporations often lose the competitive advantage of secrecy. Corporations must make public reports on profits, total sales, and research expenditures. Competitors can learn much about each other by reading reports and studying the reports from hearings. A competitor can even buy a nominal ownership in the company and receive, by law, information intended especially for the owners. Of course, corporations realize how much of their information is public knowledge. It is common for them to disguise the information reported.

Rigid structure.   A proprietor can have a brainstorm over a ham sandwich at lunch, make a decision, and act on it before the end of the day. But corporations have many departments, committees, and boards that must approve major projects before action can be taken.

Difficulty in creating.   A corporation is more costly and difficult to create than other forms of ownership. Preparing the articles of incorporation, developing a prospectus for potential owners, complying with regulations on stock issues, and registering in other states is costly and time consuming. Filing fees, lawyer expenses, and promotion costs can be expensive.

Modifications of the Corporate Form of Ownership

Cooperatives and mutual companies are two modifications of the corporation that have become popular. Special needs have created both of these forms.

Cooperatives. A **cooperative (co-op)** is a business, owned and operated by the people it serves — mainly for their benefit. They are nonprofit. If, at the end of the year, they have received more money than they have spent, they might distribute these "savings" to their members. The savings are not taxed as business income to the co-op, and this, as you might expect, results in protest from competing corporations. Co-ops organize under state charters and elect a board of directors to manage the business. Each member has one vote.

Co-ops began in the United States with farmers who grouped together to sell their products and make purchases such as feed and seed. Today, co-ops operate retail outlets and provide services such as electricity, telephone service, housing, health care, and credit. Co-ops vary in size from thousands of members to a few families who pool their resources. **Buying co-ops** buy products such as fuel, feed, groceries, and electricity in volume at low cost for the benefit of the members. **Consumer co-ops** are retail outlets owned by the customers. Farmers may organize a gasoline consumer co-op (nonprofit) in order to make purchases at more reasonable costs. **Producer co-ops** market products for its members. Here, crafts people may form a co-op to retail their pottery, clothing, and jewelry. Being nonprofit, they can market the products more efficiently, leaving more profits for the members. A prime example comes from Detroit where a housing co-op for the elderly charges its tenants an average of $40 per month less than other apartments. A member of a California health co-op says, "We have reduced the cost of health care to our members by 50 to 60%."

Still, there have been some problems. Critics say that members are usually surprised by the amount of time and effort required to make the co-op successful. Members become dissatisfied and drop out, and the venture fails. Also, some co-ops, intent on serving more people effectively, invest their profits in new services. The result is loss of savings to members. In these cases, the goal of the co-op saving money for its members is not met.

Farm and electrical co-ops have been the most successful. **Credit unions,** another popular form of co-op, are groups of people who accumulate their savings and loan them to other members at interest. Here, owners buy shares in the credit union as an investment, and they receive interest that is usually higher than bank savings accounts. If you wish to borrow from the credit union, you can make a small investment by purchasing one share, and then get a loan at competitive rates. Most credit unions are quite successful; many are tied into companies as fringe benefits for employees.

Mutual companies. **Mutual companies** are similar to cooperatives in that the users are also the owners. Although mutual companies have a board of directors, they do not normally send out proxies, and most members do not vote. Mutual companies are popular as life insurance companies, savings banks, and savings and loan associations. When consumers purchase policies from a mutual company, they automatically become owners. When people deposit money in mutual savings banks or savings and loan companies, they automatically become owners. Currently, mutual life insurance companies control about two-thirds of the total assets of all life insurance companies; mutual savings banks hold about 12% of all the savings of individuals; and almost nine out of ten savings and loan associations are organized on a mutual basis.

While mutual companies have most of the advantages of corporations, they have a different tax status. Companies return "savings" to their members in the form of dividends. Mutual life insurance policyholders do not have to pay taxes on their dividends. But money returned to owner-members of savings banks and loan associations is regarded as interest and therefore is taxable to its members.

Business Combinations, Breakups, and Buyouts

Many businesses combine with other to form larger businesses. They do this to take advantage of size, add expertise and extra money, spread operating expenses over a larger base, and fill out the product offerings. Mergers and holding companies are the two most popular combination forms.

Mergers. A **merger** is the joining of two or more companies to operate as one. Typically, a larger firm buys enough interest in a smaller one to con-

Should Mergers Be Encouraged or Discouraged?

Traditionally, we have worried when a business such as General Motors or IBM gets too large. We also get a little concerned when the number of firms in a particular industry shrink to four. (Four is no magic number; it just seems to have arisen as subjective benchmark.)

People who wish to discourage mergers argue that large business, or few businesses within an industry, can have unhealthy effects on competition. For instance, it is easier for a few larger firms to get together to fix prices than it is for many smaller firms to do so. Also, one large firm can enter into long-term contracts with suppliers or buyers with the result of driving out smaller competitors. A large producer might also agree to sell only to retailers who do not discount the prices of its product. And we do have examples of such illegal activities. In December 1983, there were seventeen prosecutions in process against thirty-seven construction companies for entering into big-rigging practices.

People who encourage more mergers and cooperative practices between companies say that we need increased size for several reasons. First, we have to compete in the world market, and other governments subsidize and assist large companies. The Japanese government, for example, gives its cement industry special loans and other financial aids to help them compete with the American market. Second, many research and development projects require millions of dollars of investments. This is just too much risk for even our largest firms. Third, companies in ailing industries such as steel need to be able to merge so they can preserve jobs. If a company goes bankrupt, it will disappear from competition. Why not let this firm merge with another rather than go under?

Currently, merger activity has increased. Many firms in basic industries such as steel, railroads, and banks and financial services are consolidating at record rates. Santa Fe and Southern Pacific railroads, two giants in the rail industry, backed off from a proposed merger in 1980 because they feared government disapproval. However, at this writing, they were planning a $6.3 billion merger, leaving just six major railroads in the United States.

Are you concerned about the increasing rate of mergers in the United States?

___ A. Very concerned   ___ C. Somewhat unconcerned

___ B. Somewhat concerned   ___ D. Very unconcerned

Do you think that our Justice Department should encourage or discourage mergers, joint research and development projects, and other consolidated efforts by large businesses in the United States?

___ A. Encourage strongly   ___ C. Discourage

___ B. Encourage   ___ D. Discourage strongly

Give three reasons for your position:

A. _____

B. _____

C. _____

trol it. Stockholders of both companies have to approve this, usually by a two-thirds vote. When two or more firms producing the same type of product or service combine, it is a **horizontal merger.** An example of a horizontal merger was the purchase of Gulf Oil by Standard Oil Co. of California (Socal) for $13.4 billion in 1984, the largest corporate takeover to date. This merger created the third largest oil company in the United States, exceeded in sales only by Exxon Corp. and Mobil Corp.

A **vertical merger** brings under one roof several different firms involved in different stages of the production and distribution process. A manufacturing company might buy a wholesale firm. Or a wholesale company might buy retail outlets. The firms are usually not competing, but the merger links up customer-supplier relationships into one company. If enough firms combine into a vertical merger, they can control the product or service from the point of production to the end user.

Conglomerates, a third type of merger, join two or more companies that offer unrelated products or services, as when Mobil Oil Company bought Montgomery Ward. Most of the world's largest companies grew through conglomerate mergers. In 1982, both Mobil Oil and U.S. Steel tried to buy Marathon Oil Company. Had Mobil bought Marathon, the merger would have been horizontal since both were oil companies. But because U.S. Steel ultimately bought Marathon for more than $5 billion, the merger formed a conglomerate. Had Goodyear Tire Company purchased Marathon, the merger would have been vertical. Figure 4.5 diagrams these three merger types.

Holding companies. Technically, **holding companies** are any firms that own stock in other companies. However, the term is more frequently used to describe companies that own enough voting stock in other companies to have control over them. In this way, one firm combines several different operations under a single policymaking structure. Some holding companies exist only for that purpose.

Traditionally, holding companies have been popular in the utility industry. Before its breakup, American Telephone & Telegraph (AT&T), owned all the stock in at least ten companies and part of

The merger of Marathon Oil with U.S. Steel elicited strong opinions all around. Here, Marathon employees rally in support of U.S. Steel's takeover bid.

the stock of many others. Holding companies may own stock in companies which also own stock in other firms. Figure 4.6 shows the makeup of the Ravelston Corporation, an example of a holding company.

Divestitures. During recent years, at the same time that many firms have been joining ranks through mergers, other large corporations have been selling off many of their holdings, a process called **divestiture**.

Perhaps the most newsworthy divestiture was the federal government's forced breakup of AT&T. In January 1984, AT&T released control of its twenty-two local operating companies, which were formed into seven regional companies. The seven holding companies will retain use of the Bell name, and they will receive about two-thirds of AT&T's $153 billion in switching equipment. This will allow, probably within a 3-year period, competitors such as MCI, Sprint, Longer Distance, Metrofone, and Skyline access to most customers. AT&T will retain Western Electric and Bell Laboratories, and it will be able to enter the data processing and computer markets through a new subsidiary, AT&T Information Systems.

Leveraged buyouts. Another form of breaking up larger companies comes through **leveraged buyout (LBO)**, where investors buy the shares of a company using a lot of debt relative to the equity they have invested. Typically, investors finance leveraged buyouts by big chunks of money that they borrow against the company's assets; then,

(a) Horizontal merger

(b) Vertical merger

Figure 4.5
Different types of mergers.

(c) Conglomerate

Figure 4.6
An example of a holding company.

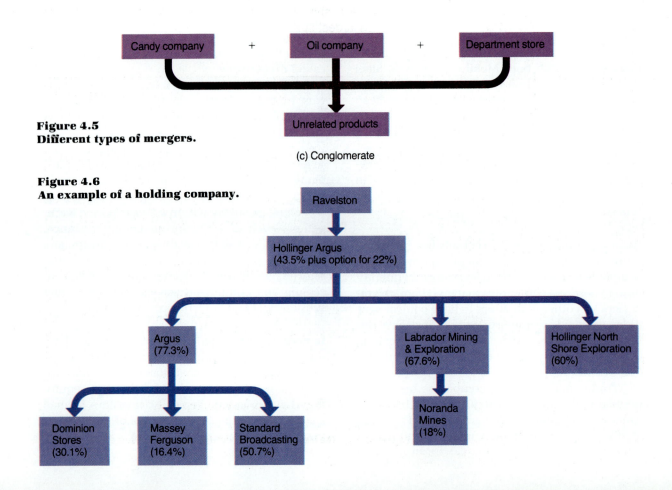

Corporate Sell-Offs

While corporate mergers attract a lot of attention, many companies are actually doing the reverse (that is, they are selling many of their holdings). This process, called divestiture, increased in the early 1980s, while the rate of mergers actually decreased.

There appeared to be several reasons for the wave of demergers, including:

■ Some companies wanted to sell losing operations during the recession before the operations created too much drag.

■ Cash-starved companies sold some of their holdings to get money to invest in better growth prospects.

■ Other companies suffering under high-interest loans and declining sales needed cash.

■ Unions accused some firms of spinning off subsidiaries so they could renegotiate less costly wage contracts.

■ And many experts feel that diversification has just gone too far.

Companies are in so many unrelated ventures producing unrelated products that customers have a hard time identifying with what they stand for.

The accompanying charts show the number of divestitures and mergers from 1978 to 1982 and the ten largest spinoffs in 1982.

Number of divestitures and mergers and acquisitions

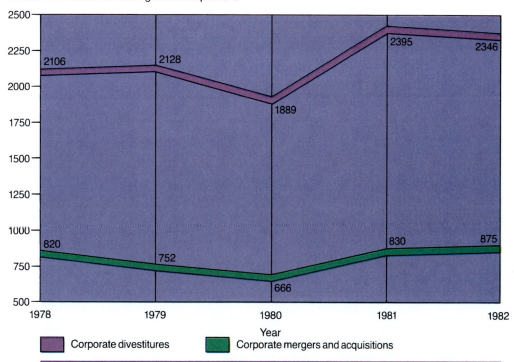

Source: W. T. Grimm and Company, "The Merger Drive Goes Into Reverse," *U. S. News & World Report,* May 2, 1983, pp. 55–56.

they repay the loan out of the company's cash flow. Often, managers of a division of a larger company will use the LBO to buy the division themselves, thus establishing the division as a privately owned company. Some have called this technique "management buybacks" and "deconglomeration."

Partly because of the lower interest rates and liberalized tax rules of today, the trend toward LBOs is increasing. According to W. T. Grimm & Co., a merger brokerage firm, 6% of all divestitures in 1978 used LBOs, and by 1982, the figure had increased to 13%. In 1983, LBOs amounted to more than half of all corporate acquisitions.

SUMMARY

Three basic forms of business ownership have evolved: sole proprietorship, partnership, and corporation.

The proprietorship is ownership by only one person and has the advantages of: (1) being easy to start and to dissolve, (2) a wide range of freedom, (3) strong motivation of the owner, (4) high degree of secrecy, and (5) tax simplicity. Its major disadvantages are: (1) unlimited liability of the owner, (2) limitations on size and capital accumulation, (3) lack of management and employee skills, and (4) instability.

The partnership is an association of two or more owners. It was formed to offset some of the disadvantages of the proprietroship. Advantages of the partnership are: (1) more specialized management, (2) more sources of capital, (3) greater incentives for key employees, (4) more legal certainty, and (5) a wide range of freedom. Because of the following disadvantages, the partnership has very little impact in our current business: (1) unlimited liability, (2) short length of life, (3) potential owner conflicts, and (4) difficulties in withdrawing investment.

The corporation is an artificial being in the eyes of the law. To create a corporation, its promoters must file articles of incorporation indicating what its major purposes will be and identifying owners, addresses, and so on. Owners of a corporation are called stockholders or shareholders; they elect the board of directors, receive a share of the profits in the form of dividends, and buy and sell their stock on the open market. In large corporations, management of the corporation is in the hands of the board of directors who appoint the principal officers of the company. The principal officers manage the day-to-day operations.

The corporation has the advantages of: (1) limited liability, (2) ease of transferring ownership, (3) continuous life, (4) attracting capital, and (5) large size. The disadvantages are: (1) increased government regulations, (2) higher taxes, (3) lack of personal interest, (4) little secrecy, (5) rigidity, and (6) difficulty in starting. Modifications in the corporation include cooperatives and mutual companies. Cooperatives receive a charter from the state and elect a board of directors to run the company. Rather than seeking a profit in the traditional sense, they try to accumulate savings to distribute to their members. Many credit unions make use of this form of ownership today. Mutual companies, like cooperatives, are owned by their users. Life insurance companies, savings banks, and savings and loan associations make extensive use of the mutual form of ownership.

Many businesses combine with other companies through mergers or holding companies. A merger occurs when a larger company buys controlling interest in a smaller company, and they combine their managements. A holding company is one that owns stock in another company, usually enough to control it. Large businesses also break up into smaller ones, primarily through divestitures and leveraged buyouts.

MIND YOUR BUSINESS

Instructions. Check your understanding of the forms of business ownership by matching the items in the right column with those in the left column.

____ 1. Has only one owner.	A. Proprietorship
____ 2. Noncontinuous life is a major disadvantage.	B. Partnership
	C. Corporation
____ 3. Owner conflicts are a disadvantage.	D. Joint venture
	E. Limited partnership
____ 4. An actual being in the eyes of the law.	F. Business trust
____ 5. Common stockholders are owners	G. Cooperative
	H. Mutual company

of this type of business.

___ 6. Proxy is associated with this form of ownership.

___ 7. This form of ownership has the most difficulty attracting capital.

___ 8. Income of this ownership is said to be double taxed.

___ 9. Limited liability is a major advantage.

___ 10. Ease in transferring ownership is an advantage.

___ 11. Government regulations are a disadvantage.

___ 12. A nonprofit organization owned and operated by the people it serves.

___ 13. A popular form of ownership for many financial organizations.

___ 14. There are more organizations of this type than any other.

___ 15. This owner's personal assets may be taken to pay business debts of another owner.

___ 16. A temporary partnership set up for a specified time period.

___ 17. A type of partnership that limits the liabilities of some of its partners.

___ 18. Limits the liability of owners by excluding them from control.

___ 19. Boards of directors are associated with this form of organization.

___ 20. This form of ownership tends to encourage businesses to grow large.

See answers at the back of the book.

KEY TERMS

sole proprietorship, 72
unlimited liability, 73
general partnership, 74
partnership agreement, 74
silent partner, 74
secret partner, 74
dormant partner, 74
nominal partner, 74
Uniform Partnership Act, 75
joint venture, 76
limited partner, 76
general partner, 76
business trust, 77
corporation, 77
private corporation, 77
public corporation, 77
open corporation, 77
close corporation, 78
domestic corporation, 80
foreign corporation, 80
alien corporation, 80
articles of incorporation, 80
stockholder, 80
stock certificate, 80
common stockholder, 80
preferred stockholder, 80
board of directors, 81
proxy, 81
dividend, 81
retained earnings, 81
limited liability, 83

REVIEW QUESTIONS

1. What is a sole proprietorship? Discuss its impact on our economy.

2. List and discuss the advantages of a sole proprietorship.

3. List and discuss the disadvantages of a sole proprietorship.

4. What is a partnership? Discuss the impact of partnerships on the economy.

5. What does the partnership agreement contain?

6. Distinguish between silent, secret, dormant, and nominal partners.

7. List and discuss the advantages of a partnership.

8. List and discuss the disadvantages of a partnership.

9. Distinguish between limited partnerships, business trusts, and partnerships.

10. What is a corporation? Discuss the impact of corporations on our economy.

11. Identify the various kinds of corporations.

12. Trace the process of creating a corporation.

13. How is the management of a corporation set up?

14. List and discuss the advantages of a corporation.

15. List and discuss the disadvantages of a corporation.

16. What are cooperatives? How do they differ from corporations?

17. What are mutual companies? How do they differ from corporations?

18. What is a merger? Describe the different kinds of mergers.

19. What are holding companies? How do they differ from mergers?

20. Explain what a divestiture is. Explain leveraged buyout.

CASES

Case 4.1: A Ban on Mergers?

Some critics argue that the government should place a ban on mergers. They argue that mergers allow companies to become too powerful and that they reduce competition in the following ways: (1) There are a reduced number of competing companies; (2) with the power in fewer hands, there are greater opportunities for cooperation among the company leaders; and (3) some mergers place barriers for firms wanting to enter the market.

Others believe that mergers are healthy for our economy. They argue that mergers: (1) help firms grow so they can compete better in world markets, (2) increase a firm's efficiency and stability, (3) should be judged by the quality of its product or service, not by whether it is large or small.

Questions

1. Which side of the argument do you agree with? Why?

2. Are there other things to consider concerning mergers?

3. Do you think mergers will increase or decrease in the future?

Case 4.2: Ownership Choices

Assume that you and a close friend have the opportunity to buy a locally owned ice cream store. In the past few years, the store has been deteriorating and business has fallen off rapidly to the point that the store is no longer profitable. The owner is ready to retire and has not been doing a very good job of management for the last four years. Yet, the store is in a good location, on a business corner across from the college, and you think that it has good possibilities of becoming a hang out for the college kids. The owner wants to sell both the store and the land. You will need about $20,000 cash to get into the business and carry you the first couple of months while you are rebuilding the ice cream store's image. You have $8000 available from savings and a "friendly loan" from your father. Your friend has the ability to raise another $8000 but this leaves you about $4000 short. There is a possibility of skimping by with only $16,000, but if your first month is bad, you don't know how you will pay your bills.

In discussing the situation with your friend, you consider several alternatives for ownership.

■ You can buy the business, borrow $8000 from your friend, and hire her as one of your key employees.

■ You and your friend can form a partnership with each person putting up $8000 and manage the business jointly.

■ You and your friend can look for a third person who has $4000 to contribute to the business in return for less involvement in management.

■ You and your friend can form a corporation and become the major stockholders. You would then try to sell enough stock to raise the remaining $4000.

Questions

1. What other alternatives can you list?

2. The first two alternatives have the disadvantage of going into ownership with very little cash in case something goes wrong. The second two alternatives have the disadvantage of bringing in other people and having to share the decision making and control.

5

SMALL BUSINESS, ENTREPRENEURSHIP, AND FRANCHISING

Allen E. Paulson, 61, grew up in Iowa during the depression. He sold newspapers and cleaned hotel bathrooms to support himself. After graduating from high school, he went to work for TWA as a mechanic. Eventually, he began advising TWA and other airlines on engine design. He started his own business in 1951, converting surplus passenger planes into cargo aircraft. In 1978, he bought Grummann's corporate aircraft division in Georgia and began making the plush Gulfstream corporate jets. In 1983, Gulfstream went public and Paulson collected cash and stock worth more than half a billion dollars.

"I was an average kid; I was an average student," is the way Neil Hirsch, founder of Telerate Systems, an electronic financial information service, describes himself. Hirsch, whose father ran the buying office of a family-owned department store chain, studied business in college for two years. He dropped out and began hanging around stockbrokerage offices. Hirsch formed Telerate in 1969 to keep track of commercial paper prices. He sent the prices electronically to customers' video terminals. Today, 11,000 subscribers pay an average of $700 per month for the service. When Telerate went public in 1983, Hirsch held shares valued at $67.5 million.

Practically all large businesses start small; usually they begin as these two examples illustrate, with one person's idea. Of course, the vast majority of new businesses stay small; only a fraction grow to be giants. This chapter explores the nature of small business, identifies the characteristics of entrepreneurs, and explains franchising.

WHAT IS A SMALL BUSINESS?

More than 98% of all businesses in the United States have fewer than fifty employees. Because small businesses make up such a vital part of our business system, we are devoting this chapter to small business ownership and management. Before we begin, we need to decide "What is a small business?" The answer to this question has to do with type of industry, number of employees, and annual sales. The Small Business Administration

(SBA) offers us a technical definition of a **small business:**

- Manufacturers who have fewer than 250 employees.
- Retailers with annual sales of less than $1 million.
- Wholesalers with annual sales of less than $5 million.

The Committee for Economic Development (CED) classifies a business as small if it exhibits the following characteristics:

- Independent management.
- Owner-supplied capital.
- Mainly local area of operations.
- Relatively small size within industry.

Owners usually manage their small businesses, and they make all the decisions without boards, committees, stockholders, or partners. They finance the operation out of their personal wealth and their ability to borrow; they often restrict their operations to the local community; and they have little influence in their industry. The SBA and CED definitions combined form our concept of a small business.

The Role of Small Business

Almost 97% (about 10.2 million companies) of all nonfarm businesses are small. Employing almost 60% of all the private, nonfarm workers in the United States, their output makes up 43% of the gross national product. More than 70% of all retail sales are made by small businesses; in the construction industry the figure is 80%.

Despite the recent rise of mammoth businesses, small business remains a mainstay of our economic system. Although writers have, for years, predicted that we would soon see the end of small business, this hearty breed endures. In fact, in percentage of the total assets and income, small businesses have remained fairly steadfast since 1900.

Popular Types of Small Businesses

The SBA suggests that there are five categories of small businesses.

1. *Service businesses,* meaning businesses that provide services to consumers and to other businesses, are a most popular form of small business. Management consultants, printers, graphic shops, janitorial services, CPAs, and computer time sales companies are examples of service companies that deal with other businesses. Personal service businesses include barbers, theaters, restaurants, gas stations, and film developing shops. Agents, people who are commissioned to perform a future service, are also popular small businesses. There are sales, real estate, and travel agents—all usually small businesses.

2. *Retail businesses* sell goods directly to consumers and are another popular form of small business. Small neighborhood shops are everywhere—bakeries, liquor stores, card shops, and record and stereo stores are good examples. Unless part of a larger chain, these types of stores are almost always small businesses.

3. *Wholesalers* are called the middlemen between the producer of goods and the retailer. Here again, local wholesalers tend to be small businesses. They deal in products such as books, records, foods, furniture, clothing, building materials—just about all products.

4. *General construction* firms deal locally and are usually small businesses. They typically agree to build homes, apartments, office buildings, roads, or schools at given prices.

5. *Manufacturing firms* produce actual goods out of raw materials. Because of large costs,

most of these firms are big businesses. But some small manufacturing businesses may deal in crafts, tee shirts, posters, custom clothing and jewelry, and specialized home products.

Contributions of Small Business

Small businesses contribute many valuable qualities to our economic system by providing jobs, stimulating competition, creating new ideas, and supplying goods and services to larger companies.

Provide jobs. During the past 10 years, we have created 20 million jobs in this country. But during the same period, the *Fortune 500* companies have lost 4 to 5 million jobs. Thus, most of the 20 million jobs are in new, small enterprises. The Small Business Administration reports that 60% of the people employed in the United States work for small businesses. This provides livelihood, either directly or indirectly, for approximately 100 million Americans. Small businesses provide jobs and lots of them.

Stimulate competition. Because our leaders have understood the value of small businesses in our competitive system, they have passed many laws to protect them. For instance, laws prevent sellers from charging higher prices to smaller companies than they do to larger companies. And larger companies cannot conspire—say, through pricing or altering supplies—to put smaller competitors out of business. Competition from many thousands of small businesses helps keep larger businesses in check by keeping prices down, encouraging better service, stimulating new product development, and the like.

Consider gasoline sales. Without strict laws, the corporate giants could alter supplies and prices to drive smaller competitors out of business within months. However, the smaller companies, through competition, help keep prices down, provide more specialized and personal service, and cause larger businesses to be more sensitive to competition.

Birth of new ideas. We mistakenly think that all of our important products and services come from large companies. They do not. Small, enterprising businesses have been responsible for the develop-

Several small firms in the early 1980s developed ultralight aircraft for the home consumer market.

ment of insulin, power steering, ballpoint pens, self-winding watches, strained baby foods, frozen peas, and zippers. Henry Ford struggled as a small businessman while developing an automobile. Just two individuals — the Wright brothers — created the airplane. Remember Alexander Graham Bell, Samuel Morse, and Thomas Edison? According to a study by the Office of Management and Budget, firms with fewer than 1000 employees have come up with almost half of the industrial innovations since 1953. *The Wall Street Journal* got attention when it predicted that the infant Elite Corp. would beat both IBM and Hewlett-Packard into the market of high-performance desktop computers for engineers and scientists. Because of smaller staff, less overhead, and heightened innovation, Elite's lead system, the Consultant, is between one-sixth and one-half the cost of its competitors. Sales for 1985 were predicted to top $10 million, up from $3 million in 1983.

Smaller businesses often serve as a proving ground for new ideas because they have greater freedom to experiment.

Smaller businesses often serve as a proving ground for new ideas because they have greater freedom to experiment. The bureaucratic approval machinery of big business — committees, boards, staff experts, research departments, and complex decision methods — usually causes them to be less innovative and flexible.

Suppliers to large companies. Large companies rely heavily upon smaller businesses to furnish parts, subassemblies, and specialized services. Costly overhead and lack of flexibility make it difficult for large businesses to produce these parts or services. For example, General Motors may include a motorized sunroof in less than 5% of their cars. Rather than go to the expense of manufacturing the electric motor themselves, they will contract with a specialized smaller firm to provide the motors they require. The result is lower costs and lower prices. In fact, General Motors relies on thousands of smaller firms to provide specialized parts. During the 1982 recession, when American car manufacturers were forced to cut back drastically, many of these smaller firms went out of business.

In a similar vein, many of the large chain stores find it too costly to build in small communities. Thus, the corner department store steps in to fill these needs. Small businesses remain important in filling the gaps by providing goods and services that the large corporations cannot.

Small Business Trends

How are small businesses adapting to changing needs? One trend is an increase in support of big business. Huge corporations are relying more and more on small businesses in supplying parts, goods of all kinds, and services. Ford Motor Corporation, for example, may rely on as many as 30,000 smaller companies to provide goods and services for their operation.

A second trend shows small retailers and wholesalers holding their own against competition from giant chain stores and mail-order houses. Still, 95% of retail firms hire fewer than twenty employees. Opportunities in wholesaling for small business have diminished. Large manufacturers and retailers have taken over many of those functions. However, the small business wholesaler still provides many valuable services.

Finally, the most noticeable trend is the increase in small businesses in the service industry. Smallness is a distinct advantage in service firms because, through small size, they can offer a high degree of personal contact. Examples of thriving small service businesses include hair styling salons, repair shops of all types, storage companies, and food outlets.

STARTING A SMALL BUSINESS

What happens when skilled white-collar workers lose their jobs? Many of them decide to start their own businesses. In all, people started more than 581,000 new businesses in 1983. Not including farmers, almost 8 million people own their own businesses, and practically all these businesses are small.

Most small businesses that fail are either poorly planned or inadequately financed. The first step in starting a business is a specific, realistic plan. Other arrangements include financing, legal requirements, taxes, and insurance.

The Business Plan

A **business plan** is a method of projecting income, expenses, and expected profit of a venture. It is a road map or blueprint for the small business-person. It not only reveals the success possibilities of the venture, but sets goals. After the business has begun, the plan provides a yardstick to measure how well the venture is doing. A well-conceived business plan may also help the owner obtain financing. A business plan offers at least four benefits:

1. The most important benefit is that a plan gives you a path to follow. A plan helps make the future what you want it to be.

2. A plan makes it easy to let your banker in on the action. By seeing the details of your plan, your banker will have valuable insight into your situation.

3. A plan can be a communications tool to orient sales personnel, suppliers, and others about your operations and goals.

4. A plan can help you develop as a manager. It can give you practice in thinking about competitive conditions, promotional opportunities, and situations that seem to be advantageous to your business.

Although there are abbreviated forms of business plans, many plans are more than 100 pages long. A detailed example of a proper business plan can be obtained from the SBA, or seen at the Center for Entrepreneurial Management in New York, where a library has been started of original plans for some of the country's well-known and not so well-known companies. The library already includes the original plans of Federal Express and Pizza Time Theatre, both of which weigh nearly half a pound.

Financing

According to the Small Business Administration, inadequate financing is the major reason for small business failure. Successful owners secure adequate financial arrangements before they begin their business. As one owner who had started several successful businesses said, "It is best to have capital resources well beyond your needs. Something always happens that you did not anticipate. If you are on a shoestring, the slightest mishap can put you under."

In any new venture, the cost of capital to the owner is directly related to the risk of the business. That is, if the business is one where the failure rates are high, the owner will have to pay more interest for money borrowed. Conversely, if the chances of failure are low, the owner can get

Whether money is borrowed from an institution or an individual, the prospective small business owner must convince the lender of the soundness of the investment.

money more easily and more cheaply. The following are eight possible sources of capital for a new business venture.

Owner investment. "I scraped and saved and finally decided to put up my money in a new business" is a typical statement of an owner. The majority of all new businesses start with the owner's personal savings. Eager proprietors have been known to sell their cars, stocks, interests in family estates, and even their homes to finance a venture. It is usually better for the owner to put up as much of the original investment as possible. This allows a return of maximum profits, while avoiding high interest payments and dividing profits (and decision making powers) with other investors.

Investment from family and friends. Wealthy relatives or friends are a popular capital source for new ventures. However, a prospective owner should be careful to keep money and personal matters separate. Failed investments have destroyed valuable personal relationships many times in the past.

Commercial banks. Although it may be hard to get venture money from banks, they do have the advantage of charging the lowest interest rates (among capital suppliers). Banks usually want to see a sound investment plan and a substantial owner investment, and they also like to use your tangible assets as security for loans. Before a bank approves a loan, bank personel will need to be convinced that there is little risk of losing the bank's money. In fact, the bank might even insist that the owner repay bank loans before dividing profits among investors.

Mortgage loans. A mortgage loan is when the lender loans money and the borrower pledges property as security. The lender likes this arrangement, because he or she can take the property if the business fails and the owner cannot repay the loan. Examples of mortgage loans are second mortgage on a house, a lien on equipment or other company assets, or even using a car as collateral. Again, interest rates are usually reasonable because the lender faces little risk.

Government agencies. Many government agencies will help small business owners secure money. (See page 110 for further discussion of these sources.)

Credit from suppliers. Suppliers may agree to sell supplies or perhaps even inventory to you on credit for as much as 30, 60, or in a few cases, 90 days. They do this to get your business. It helps if you can sell the inventory within the credit period and repay the supplier from the proceeds of the sale. In the case of equipment or supplies, the seller may allow you several months to pay off the debt. For instance, a new restaurant may be able to purchase an expensive walk-in cooler and pay for it over several years, or a clothing boutique may be able to pay for its inventory 30 to 60 days after purchase.

Finance companies. Finance companies make loans in somewhat the same way that banks do. However, because they take riskier projects than banks, they may charge interest rates 5 to 6% higher than banks.

Venture capital companies. Venture capital companies organize investors who are willing to take higher risks for a much higher return on their investment. Venture capitalists usually are not interested in a project unless it promises a sparkling tenfold return within a five-year period. Venture companies need this type of heady potential to return to their investors the 35 to 60% annual returns they require. Venture capital companies usually specialize in investments such as real estate, banking, manufacturing, and retailing. In the early 1980s, high-technology companies were the darlings of venture capitalists. In 1982, the 100 most active venture capital companies launched a blur of new businesses by investing $1.38 billion in entrepreneurial companies. Table 5.1 shows the top ten venture capital companies of 1982.

Legal Arrangements

Obtaining financing is the hardest part, but a new owner must clear other hurdles. For instance, most cities and states require a license to do business. The owner must secure the license before opening a business. Licensing allows local governments to keep track of business activity. It also clears the use of business names so that they will not conflict with other local businesses.

Some businesses also need permits. A restaurant or food manufacturer may need food handler permits for its employees. Businesses dealing out of state may require a special permit. A business that serves or sells alcohol typically needs a permit; retailers may require a vendor's permit; and a manufacturing firm may need a permit so agencies can check on employee safety.

Since requirements for licenses and permits vary, it is helpful to visit a local attorney who specializes in small businesses. City governmental offices and Chambers of Commerce may also help.

Taxes

There are always taxes. Each new business must collect and pay several kinds of taxes. A retail firm must collect sales taxes; an employer may have to collect and pay various taxes on employees' wages; and the owner may have to pay a self-employment tax. The Internal Revenue Service has two publications that help: *Mr. Businessmen's Kit* and *Tax Guide for Small Business.* An owner might also want to call state and local tax revenue departments for information.

TABLE 5.1 ■ THE TEN TOP VENTURE CAPITAL COMPANIES OF 1982

Rank (Last Year)	Firm Name	Total ($) Invested	No. of Deals	Startups ($)	Startups Deals	Buyouts, Others (Buyouts Alone) ($)	Buyouts, Others (Buyouts Alone) Deals	Follow-On Investments ($)	Follow-On Investments Deals	General Partners
1 (1)	The Hillman Co. Pittsburgh, Pa.	101.5	39	NA	14	NA (17.5)	11 (5)	NA	14	Henry L. Hillman, president Carl G. Grefenstette, Senior VP
2 (9)	Allstate Insurance Co. Venture Capital Div. Northbrook, Ill.	64.2	30	8.8	7	36 (25)	9 (2)	19.4	14	Charles Rees, director
3 (2)	First Chicago Investment Corp. Chicago, Ill. (First Nat'l Bank of Chicago)	48.5	45	5.4	5	27.7 (13.5)	14 (5)	15.4	26	John A. Canning Jr., president
4 (27)	General Electric Venture Capital Corp. Fairfield, Conn. (GE Corp.)	41.6	20	NA	4	11.4*	4	30.2	12	Terence E. McClary, president
5 (10)	Brentwood Associates Los Angeles, Calif.	35	20	10	8	20	7	5	5	Frederick J. Warren, B. Kipling Hagopian, Timothy Pennington, George M. Crandell, Roger C. Divisson
6 (12)	E. M. Warburg Pincus & Co. New York, N.Y.	33.9	30	3.5	6	22.9 (10.7)	10 (2)	7.5	14	Lionel I. Pincus, chairman; John L. Vogelstein, president
7 (4)	TA Associates Boston, Mass. (Tucker Anthony & R. L. Day)	32.3	21	8.3	7	20.5	9	3.5	5	Peter A. Brooks, David B. Croll, C. Kevin Landry, managing partners
8 (8)	Security Pacific Capital Corp. Newport Beach, Calif.	32.25	11	.94	1	30.7 28.7	6 (4)	.6	4	Timothy Hay, president
9 (3)	Citicorp. Venture Capital Ltd. New York, N.Y.	30.5	54	8.0	12	12.0 (6)	13 (4)	10.5	29	William T. Comfort, president
10 (45)	BT Capital Corp. New York, N.Y. (Bankers Trust N.Y.)	26	16	—	—	26 (20)	16 (9)	—	—	James G. Hellmuth, president

1982 Investments (in millions)

NA = Not available.
* = estimate.
Source: Reprinted from the June, 1983, issue of *Venture, The Magazine for Entrepreneurs,* by special permission. © 1983 Venture Magazine, Inc., 35 West 45th St., New York, N.Y. 10036.

TABLE 5.2 ■ KINDS OF INSURANCE COVERAGE

Fire insurance

Liability insurance

Automobile insurance

Worker's compensation

Business interruption insurance

Crime insurance

Glass insurance

Rent insurance

Group life insurance

Group health insurance

Disability insurance

Retirement income

Key-man insurance

Insurance

A business needs several kinds of insurance. If customers come into a place of business, the owner will need liability insurance. If you serve food, you will need additional insurance. Should the business hire employees, you will need insurance—both mandatory and optional—to protect both yourself and the employees. Employees may also require accident or disability insurance as well. Again, a small business lawyer and local government agencies can be very helpful. See Table 5.2 for a listing of the kinds of insurance coverage (and see Chapter 19 for more discussion of insurance).

THE SUCCESS OF SMALL BUSINESS

Although they have been called an endangered species, the traditional, small, mom-and-pop businesses are still around. Businesses with fewer than ten people, according to government statis-

---

After one year of operation, about one-third of all new small businesses discontinue; about half close after two years; and only one-third make it as long as five years.

---

tics, make up 70% of all businesses. Not that they have an easy time. By percentages, the success rate is not very high. After one year of operation, about one-third of all new small businesses discontinue; about half close after two years, and only one-third make it as long as five years. Even against these odds, about 5 million small businesses start up each year. These businesses can increase their chances for survival if they maximize their advantages and guard against the causes of failure.

Why Small Businesses Succeed

Flexibility, personal touch, lower overhead, and owner motivation are natural strengths of small business. And these are the reasons that the successful ones make it.

Greater flexibility. Surveys show flexibility to be an important benefit of being small. Small firms have more informal organization and, likewise, more efficient communication. Within minutes, they can create, alter, implement, and terminate a plan. This allows the small company to take advantage of fleeting opportunities and to avoid bad situations. Systems, approval procedures, and communication channels of larger companies cause them to adapt with dinosauric clumsiness, while small firms deftly outmaneuver them.

More personal service. Small business owners usually have a rather close personal relationship with their customers and employees. Personal friendships encourage trust and understanding between owner and customer. Owners who know their patrons take more pride in customer satisfaction, which in turn enhances old-time client loyalty. Small business owners may also be more intimately involved with the community, and they get an understanding about consumer needs and wishes that sophisticated market research could never uncover. Friendly relationships with employees improve communication, commitment to owners' objectives, and responsibility. Employees of small businesses are much less prone to organize unions or develop adversary relationships with the owner. These first-hand relationships reveal the owner as more human and understanding than distantly removed owners and managers of larger companies.

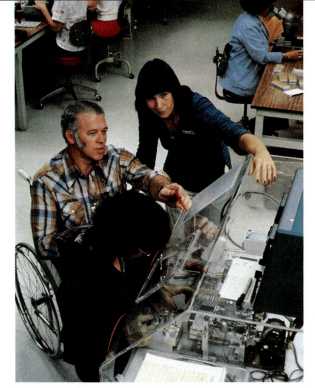

Small business operations often can generate close relationships between owner and employees, resulting in a deeply committed work force.

Low overhead. Small companies have less capital tied up in costly investments such as building, machinery and equipment, executive salaries, fringe benefit programs, and research departments. Therefore, small companies can take on ventures of only a moderate return. Smallness is less expensive. A look at the minicomputer industry provides an example. Most of the early innovations in minicomputers were made by small business owners. They had much more to gain personally, and their risk of failure was much less. The development of the Apple computer may have cost as little as 5% of IBM's similar product. Because the IBM venture was on a much larger scale and because IBM had much more to lose by any mistakes, their investment was massive by comparison.

High motivation of owners. Horace and Joan Gimbell work in their small grocery store from 8:00 A.M. until 7:00 P.M., six days a week. Many nights after they close the doors, they stay around to clean up, keep records, and stock shelves. For this, they earn about $20,000 per year. Yet, in order to be independent and free, they are willing to work harder for less income. The most outstanding quality of a small business owner is an untiring dedication to work. This allows smaller businesses to overcome many of the disadvantages of small size.

Why Small Businesses Fail

Although different sources will show slightly different figures, small businesses have high failure rates, and they do not make their owners worshipful of wealth. Of the 5 million sole proprietorships that form every year, nearly 50% of them fail within two years. What's more, 40% of small business owners earn less than $15,000 per year.

According to _Dun & Bradstreet_, 90% of all

business failures are due to poor manage-

ment.

According to **Dun & Bradstreet,** a financial credit rating organization for businesses, 90% of all business failures are due to poor management. And James D. McKevitt, director and chief lobbyist of the National Federation of Independent Business (NFIB), says that small business owners often have only themselves to blame for their failures. More specifically, lack of experience and aptitude, improper record keeping, and unwise handling of money usually account for small businesses not lasting.

Limited experience and aptitude. Research shows that the combination of formal education and experience offers the highest probability of success. Also, experience with ownership itself seems to be more important than expertise in a particular line of business. Similarly, much of the owner's formal education does not necessarily have to relate to his or her line of business in order to be helpful.

In failure, many small business owners state that they had little control over their problems. Economic recessions, rising interest costs, street relocations, labor situations, changes in laws, and sudden style changes can cause failure of a small business. Yet, successful owners find ways to soften these blows and even turn them into oppor-

tunities. Large corporations, with special research departments, tend to be more aware of these problems. The successful small businessperson makes every effort to keep informed of potential problems.

Inadequate record keeping and planning. Failing small business owners are not aware of how they jeopardize their venture by not keeping proper records. These records may well detect poor business practices. Poor records are either outdated or deficient in such key areas as sales volume, accounts receivable, assets, inventory, expenses, and employment records. Too many owners are content to drop their income into a cigar box and take the money out as needed or as bills become due. In fact, they may not even know if they are making a profit until the end of the year when their accountant files their income tax.

Too many owners let wholesalers, brokers, and suppliers suggest what they ought to buy. As a result, they find their money is tied up in some merchandise while they are out of stock in other items. Some owners may keep a record of gross sales, but few know how many of each item they are selling, and they cannot distinguish between high-profit and low-profit goods. Records on costs associated with accounts receivable are valuable, but seldom available.

Planning beyond a day or two seldom occurs. Intuition and hazy judgment serve in lieu of reasonable forecasts of cash, supply, and capital needs. Many small companies let tremendous opportunities for growth slip away because they do not adjust their capacity to manufacture more goods, sell more products, or furnish more services. Often, small business owners fail to plan for employment needs. Finally, they only lightly consider economic situations. Failure to consider an economic boom or recession can be costly.

Unwise handling of money matters. Ultimately, most businesses fail because they cannot pay their bills. Most businesses feel the pinch of money problems now and then. At no time is awareness of money needs more important than during start-up. It is important to consider and properly forecast all expenses and cash requirements. Even after a successful start, money problems are more acute for smaller businesses. Generally, they face a limited source of funds. It is

Small Business Failures

The early 1980s, with high interest rates, slow-paying customers, and sluggish orders, took the zest out of many small businesses. Nineteen eighty-two saw more than 25,000 business failures, most of which were small businesses.

However, it now appears that the economic turnaround has arrived just in time for many small businesses. The chief economist for the National Federation of Independent Business (NFIB) says that demand is increasing, employment is improving, and companies are adding to their inventories. Experts say that small businesses are being helped primarily by interest rate declines. Not only do lower interests reduce borrowing costs to customers, they allow the small business owner to borrow for expansion. The accompanying chart shows business failures from 1973 through 1982.

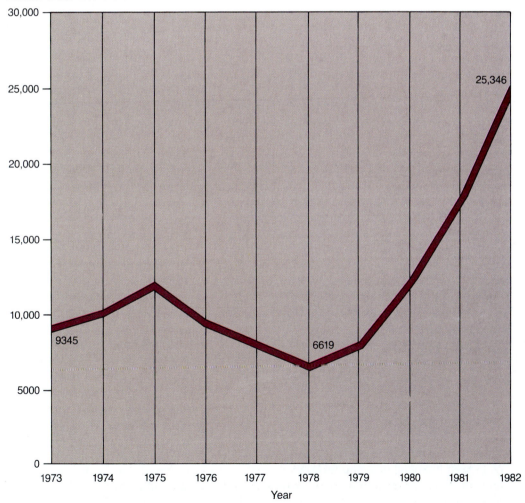

Number of business failures

Year

Source: ''The Famine is Over for Small Businesses,'' *U.S. News & World Report,* July 4, 1983, p. 55.

hard to get additional money for working capital or long-term expansion, especially when interest rates are high. Insufficient cash flow, uncollected accounts, and high debt are usually serious blows for the small business owner.

THE ENTREPRENEUR

"Give me enough Swedes and snuff and I'll build a railroad to hell," the entrepreneur James J. Hill is supposed to have said before he built the Great Northern Railway across the plains in the 1880s. An entrepreneur is one who takes the risks of starting and managing a business. Many an everyday citizen envies this hard-driving, risk-taking independent of the business world. Entrepreneurs have the nerve to put their money and skill on the line. If they succeed, life is glamorous and independent. Fear of failure, however, is a constant companion. Millions of Americans take the risk and start their own businesses; most of the rest of us flirt with the idea at some time during our careers.

Some entrepreneurs are visionary dreamers. Carter Canada, a successful real estate developer, has spent eight years trying to raise money to develop huge pyramids to house a resort hotel complex in Nevada. William Kumm wants to start a company to transport oil via a fuel-driven cell underneath Alaska's North Slope to the East Coast. While these two visions may have long odds against them, Alan Boyd and Lawrence Gilson, two former Amtrak executives, might see their dream realized. In 1987, their dream project, the first "bullet" train in America, is scheduled to begin whisking passengers between Los Angeles and San Diego. Most entrepreneurs, however, are much more practical.

Purdue University professors Arnold C. Cooper and William C. Dunkelberg, after studying 890 business founders, identified three basic types of people that start their own businesses:

1. Crafts people who exploit a personal skill (mechanics, hair stylists, and plumbers).
2. Growth-oriented people who start a business to seek financial or personal goals.
3. People who start their own businesses to avoid working for others.*

---

* "Small Business," *The Wall Street Journal*, July 15, 1983.

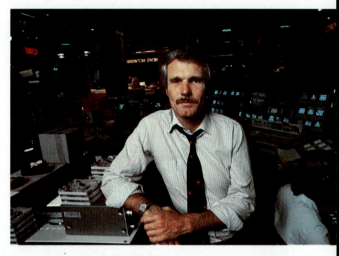

Ted Turner, a well-known example of the successful entrepreneurial personality, has become a major force in the telecommunications industry.

Businesses started by crafts people, according to the study, tended to have a slower growth rate than other types of businesses. Even though each entrepreneur is unique, there are some common traits found in successful entrepreneurs.

Personal background. The entrepreneur is likely to be the first or oldest child in the family. His or her parents are usually not involved in any kind of corporate bureaucracy. In a study of eighty people who started their own businesses, only 3% had parents who were managers in large or medium-sized organizations. Sixteen percent of the entrepreneurs' parents were professionals, clerks, or salespeople. Nineteen percent had parents who were farmers, and 25% of the parents were independent business owners. The largest group, 30%, had fathers who worked as skilled or unskilled laborers. Almost 79% of the owners described their family as poor, while less than 30% came from affluent backgrounds. This study suggests that dire childhood circumstances serve as the primary catalyst for the entrepreneur in starting a business. Although few independents go from rags to riches, their alternatives are often less promising.

Studies have shown that self-employeds have more education than average students but less than corporate executives. Learning from "the school of hard knocks" is common. More current research shows that, for self-employeds, a master's degree in business management or some technical field is quite common.

Independence

The cherished values of independence and self-sufficiency radiate from small business owners. They toss aside the selection and promotion practices of large organizations for the right to be their own bosses. The enterpriser resists being pigeonholed or following routine habits. In fact, entrepreneurs become frustrated when they have to follow someone else's direction. They have to be the boss. They like to be in control. They find it difficult to work under the direction of others.

High Achievement

People who operate their own businesses have a great need to achieve. They strive to take personal responsibility for finding their own solutions to problems. And they crave tangible, measurable feedback on their accomplishments. They like specific answers to the question, "How am I doing?" Contrary to popular opinion, achievers are not long-shot gamblers who stake their life savings on hundred-to-one odds. They are moderate risk takers. Typically, their choice is a calculated risk that can be achieved by their labor and devotion. While their careers are much less secure than a nine-to-five job, their risks are still somewhat moderate.

Hard Work

Willingness to work — and work hard — is an outstanding trait of entrepreneurs. They seem able to work endless, 12-hour days. You can bet that the successful business owner has paid with tedious, sweat-filled hours, emotional stress, and perseverance. Most likely, the business verged on failure many times in the beginning, but the owner simply would not let it die. A successful entrepreneur described his early experiences: "When I started, may workday began at 6:00 A.M. and often lasted until 8:00 or 9:00 P.M., sometimes later. I worked this pace at least 6 and sometimes 7 days a week. You might say it was my whole life."

BUSINESS BULLETIN

Characteristics of Entrepreneurs

In 1983, *Inc.* magazine published findings of their study of the chief executive officers of America's 100 fastest growing companies. Some of the characteristics of these people are:

Parents who were entrepreneurs	43%
Would like to see children become entrepreneurs	75%
Between the age of 25 and 35 when they started the company	41%
Initial source of capital — personal savings	69%
Initial source of capital — outside investors	39%
Initial source of capital — banks	28%
Share equity with key employees	96%
Undergraduate degrees in engineering	30%
Graduate degrees	46%
Worked in a Fortune 500 company	49%
Started the business with one or more partners	67%

Source: Curtis Hartman, "Who's Running America's Fastest Growing Companies," *Inc.*, August, 1983, pp. 41–47.

WHERE SMALL BUSINESS OWNERS CAN GET HELP

To stimulate the important role that small businesses play in our business system, we have devised several sources of aid. Some banks have advisors who specialize in small business. And suppliers can be a prime source of information.

The Small Business Administration remains the major source of organized assistance for small business owners.

Many books and articles are written on the subject, and colleges and universities offer courses, workshops and seminars on small business ownership. But the Small Business Administration remains the major source of organized assistance. Other resources include the Department of Commerce and professional organizations.

The Small Business Administration

The federal government established the **Small Business Administration (SBA)** with the *Small Business Act of 1953*. The SBA helps small businesses to secure funds, find management assistance, and bid for government contracts. Since its origin, the Small Business Administration has:

- Made or guaranteed loans for 461,000 businesses.
- Attracted more than 300,000 people per year to seminars and workshops.
- Provided 905,000 disaster loans totaling $12.2 billion.
- Created 33.4 million person-hours of work.
- Created $468 billion of additional gross national products.
- Provided $67.3 billion of income tax revenue.

Source of funds. The SBA helps small businesses secure funds by helping to provide three kinds of loans:

1. **SBA direct loans** are made by funds directly from the SBA. These are made only in special circumstances, where the SBA feels that the enterprise has merit and where the owner is not able to get financing from other sources.

2. **SBA participating loans** are situations where the SBA supplements the required funds from loans from banks or other investors.

3. In an **SBA guaranteed loan,** the funds come totally from a bank, while the SBA guarantees that 90% of the loan will be paid. Should the venture fail, the SBA will pay the bill. Because this loan is much more secure, the owner may not only get the loan, but usually, because of the guarantee, it is at a lower rate of interest.

However, the SBA is limited to a commitment of $350,000 in guaranteeing and sharing loans. Also, the SBA can commit for capital funds up to 15 years and working capital loans for up to 6 years.

Disaster loans. To businesses that suffer losses from floods, storms, or earthquakes, the SBA can make **disaster loans** of up to a half million dollars for 30 years. To qualify, the business must be in a presidentially declared disaster area.

Low-income loans. Since 1964, the SBA has been able to make loans to low-income individuals who exhibit potential for running a business but do not qualify under the standard program. It may loan up to $50,000 for 15 years and usually relaxes credit standards, looking instead at managerial ability and financial responsibility.

Small business investment companies. Finally, the SBA regulates some 500 privately owned **small business investment companies (SBIC).** These SBICs are organized specifically for the purpose of helping small businesses with their long-term capital needs. An SBIC helps finance firms by direct loans and equity investments. In the direct loans, the SBIC will provide funds and accept collateral when banks will not. As this is a private transaction, the interest rate is usually negotiable. However, the transaction must be regulated by the SBA. With equity loans, the SBICs usually share in the growth and profit of the venture. Sometimes, the SBIC will purchase common stock in the firm. Because these ventures are usually high-risk, they demand a high rate of interest. The owner usually must pay a high percentage of the profits and increased value of the company back to the private investors. The SBICs are similar to venture capital companies, except that they operate within the framework of the SBA.

In 1983, the nation's SBICs were seeking to sever their ties to Congress and the Small Business Administration, which polices and doles out funds to them. Walter Stults, president of the National Association of Small Business Investment Companies, says that by taking the program out of government hands and putting it in the private sector much more money could be provided for SBICs, which would mean more money for small business loans and investments.

Management assistance. A variety of management help, from direct counseling to advising and training programs, is available to proprietors. First, the SBA assists owners in locating sources of funds through regular lending agencies. It assists them in preparing their financial statements, shows them how to approach lenders, and helps them evaluate the proposal. Also, it gives specific guidance to entrepreneurs in competing for government contracts.

Small Business Institute (SBI) programs sponsor student-faculty teams from universities to provide consulting help with decisions such as seeking loans, collecting debts, hiring and supervising employees, improving records, managing cash, selecting location sites, controlling inventory, and increasing sales. Student-faculty teams serve only as staff advisors; the decisions remain with the owners.

Finally, the SBA provides management assistance through Small Business Development Centers (SBDC). Although not available in all states, the program organizes the resources of the community, university, and state government to offer management help to small businesses.

Service Corps of Retired Executives. The SBA also sponsors a group of about 5000 retired executives who volunteer their time to serve as part-time consultants for small business owners **(the Service Corps of Retired Executives (SCORE)).** A small business owner can usually get assistance from SCORE by calling the nearest SBA office. These consultants are usually free for the first 90 days, although they do ask the owner to cover out-of-pocket expenses. After 90 days, some compensation is established between the owner and the consultant.

Small business owners can call on the experience of retired executives who serve as consultants for SCORE.

Active Corps of Executives. ACE is organized and sponsored in much the same way as SCORE, yet it involves executives that are still active in business management **(Active Corps of Executives (ACE)).** They can provide valuable counseling for the small business owner.

Small business innovation research program. Under an act of Congress, the SBA in 1982 established a research program that makes eleven federal agencies set aside 1% of their research funds for small businesses. In 1983, more than 1700 proposals were submitted by small businesses hoping for further research funding. This source was expected to provide $50 million in 1984 for new companies developing products for government use.

Information. A wealth of information is provided for the new business entrepreneur. The Small Business Administration publishes many booklets, pamphlets, and research reports on starting and managing a small business. Some of these are specifically focused on particular types of business, such as restaurants, services, and manufacturing firms. Commercial publications, such as *Entrepreneur Magazine, Inc., Venture,* and *Money* magazines can provide valuable information. Standard business publications such as *The Wall Street Journal, Forbes, Business Week,* and *Fortune* can also provide crucial information to keep the small business owner aware of current events.

Too Much Help for Small Businesses?

Some argue that small businesses actually receive too much help from the government and other sources. These critics say that small businesses should succeed or fail on their own merits, and aiding them actually encourages inefficiencies in our system. They point to the money and time invested in the Small Business Administration and suggest that this should not really be a government effort. They further argue that many of the most successful small businesses made it without government help.

However, others say that small businesses are vital to our economy for both practical and psychological reasons. Practically, they provide most of the new jobs in our economy; they provide products and services that would not be available otherwise; and they are more creative than larger businesses. Psychologically, they make it possible for people to have the freedom to "chase the American dream" by starting a business, be their own boss, and perhaps become wealthy. Finally, this side says that the actual amount of government aid is really not all that great in the first place.

Do you believe that the government offers too much assistance to small businesses?

___ A. Offers way too much   ___ C. Offers too little

___ B. Offers too much   ___ D. Offers way too little

List three reasons for your position:

A. _____

B. _____

C. _____

Minority Business Development Agency. Since 1969, the federal government has made some special attempts to help small minority enterprises. These programs try to provide financial, technical, and management assistance to blacks, Puerto Ricans, Mexican Americans, native Americans, and other minorities. In 1969, the Department of Commerce established the **Minority Business Development Agency (MBDA)** (formerly the Office of Minority Business Enterprise or OMBE). Also, there are two agencies within the MBDA that assist minority enterprises.

Minority Business Opportunity Committee. The Minority Business Development Agency cre-

ated the **Minority Business Opportunity Committee (MBOC)** to help coordinate programs from over sixteen different federal agencies that serve minority businesses. MBOC promotes opportunities for minority enterprises, helps them find risk capital, and serves as a watchdog to ensure that funds and assistance get to the people who need it.

Minority Enterprise Small Business Investment Company. This agency works much the same way as the SBICs yet they specialize in raising money for minority ventures. The **Minority Enterprise Small Business Investment Company (MESBIC)** aids in securing starting and long-term capital requirements.

Professional Organizations

Small business owners have been especially difficult to organize in lobbying for laws and in resisting regulations unfavorable to them. This type of group activity goes against their independence. Proprietors tend to want to take care of themselves. However, two groups have emerged and have gained some impact. The **Junior Chamber of Commerce** organized the **National Small Business Association** in 1937, and the **National Federation of Independent Businesses** in 1943. These groups represent small business owners' interests in Washington. They strive to improve the competitive position of small businesses by opposing monopolistic practices, reducing government burdens on small businesses, and helping small companies get their share of government business. **Better Business Bureaus** are local nonprofit organizations that help police the activities of businesses. They protect consumers and businesses against unfair and unethical business practices.

FRANCHISING

In 1984, the third largest pizza franchise, Godfather's, opened war on the two leaders, Pizza Hut and Domino's, by entering its deep-dish pizza into the market. Deep-dish pie now accounts for about two-thirds of all pizza sales. Godfather's has taken the offensive in their promotion with a slogan that says, "We'll get very specific about our pan pizza versus their pan pizza." Even though both Pizza Hut and Domino's continued to rock along quite successfully, Godfather's aimed to open 200 to 300

TAKING STOCK

Aggressive Management Plus Speed Equals Success

Domino's Pizza, with estimated sales of $400 million in 1983, is one of the fastest-growing companies in a rapidly expanding fast-food industry. Key executive and founder Thomas Monaghan says that his success is due to speedy delivery and aggressive management.

Domino's Pizza, Inc., is a home delivery chain, and he promises to get a pizza to customers within 30 minutes. Monaghan says he can make a pizza in 11 seconds flat.

Although there are a few large pizza chains, local chains and mom-and-pop stores tend to dominate. However, Monaghan felt that there was a market for a chain that delivers, and he aggressively set out to capture it. His strategy paid off; in 1982, pizza sales hit $250 million ($76 million from owned units, and the rest from franchises), and his total number of outlets ranked second only to Pizza Hut's. By 1988, according to current projections, Domino's and Pizza Hut will be neck and neck with about 5000 stores each.

Showing a strong preference for growth over profits, Domino's earned only $3 million last year. Investment bankers say Domino's could easily raise $150 million with a public stock sell, but Monaghan prefers to keep control of the firm himself. He has a $52 million revolving loan which he can use for expansion, and the company has little debt. Monaghan says, "My competitors want a return on investment. I don't care about that, I just want to be No. 1 in every market we're in."

Source: "Domino's Pizza: How It Became the No. 2 Chain," *Business Week,* August 15, 1983, p. 114.

TABLE 5.3 ■ PROFILE OF A FRANCHISE

Name of franchise	Kentucky Fried Chicken
Address	P.O. Box 32070, M-680, Louisville, Kentucky
Product or service	Fried chicken
Year business began	1930
Franchising since	1952
1980 — Number of franchises	4928
Company owned	1198
1981 — Number of franchises	5146
Company owned	1203
1982 — Number of franchises	5200
Company owned	1286
Range of capital needed	$385,000 – 486,000
Franchise fee	$10,000
Royalty	4%
Advertising royalty	5%
Financing provided	No
Industrial rank	12

stores a year until they reached about 4000 stores. At the end of 1983, Pizza Hut had a little over 4000 stores.

A few examples of franchise arrangements are McDonald's, Walgreen's, Kentucky Fried Chicken, and H & R Block.

Franchising has been around for some time, but it has undergone a whirlwind growth since the middle 1950s. A **franchise** is an exclusive arrangement between a manufacturer or operating company and a private owner. Franchise arrangements can be divided into two broad classes: (1) product distribution arrangements in which the dealer is to some degree, but not entirely, identified with the manufacturer/supplier, and (2) entire business franchising, in which there is complete identification of the dealer with the buyer. A few examples of franchise arrangement are McDonald's, Western Auto, Walgreen's, Kentucky Fried Chicken (see Table 5.3), Coca-Cola distributorships, and H & R Block. The parent company gives an individual or group the right or privilege to do business. These rights, provided in a written contract, usually establish the method of business, the period of time, and the location. The parent company is called a **franchisor**, the privilege is a franchise, and the private owner is called the **franchisee**. The franchisee is an independent owner tied to the parent company by the contractual agreements.

The franchise method provides several advantages to the small business owner. There are also some disadvantages.

Advantages to the Owner

Why would an individual owner prefer a franchise to the more independent form of ownership? Franchising allows small business owners to enjoy the advantages of smallness while offsetting many of the disadvantages. The major advantages include instant recognition, management assistance, financing assistance, and reduced failure rates.

Instant recognition. The franchisor develops a highly visible trade name, usually through flashy national advertising that is easily recognized by the public. The positive image created through national promotion is transferred to franchisees. When they first open the new business, the company name and product is already familiar to most customers. This helps franchisees compete with the nationwide advertising of larger businesses. While traveling, for example, most consumers would prefer stopping at McDonald's over the local hamburger stand. This is because they are familiar with the quality, prices, and types of food available.

Management assistance. Many franchisors have gathered specific information on the location, design, and management of their outlets. They have important data on store layout, methods of hiring and training employees, pricing policies, preparation of the product or delivery of the service. They provide continuing advice on markets, prices, and changes in the economy. Through mass purchasing and production, they can provide better supplies at less cost. The franchisor's prior experience with the products and services is a great advantage. Their expertise helps prevent failures; the small business owner does not have to learn about them the hard way. Finally, the franchisor will often counsel the owner on unusual problems.

One young, fast-growing series of franchising operations actually specializes in management assistance for dentists. The franchise company offers to oversee all the details of managing the dentist's office — choosing and leasing the site, hiring the staff, and marketing the dentist's services. The dentist merely buys the franchise and shows up for work. The franchisor does all the rest. United Dental Network, one of the largest such franchisors, has sixty-two franchisee offices.

Service stations have long been franchised operations, the owners benefiting from the financial, marketing, and management assistance provided by the franchisor.

Financial assistance. Franchisors may aid the franchisee with direct loans or leasing agreements. Or franchisors can help the owners prepare their loan applications and even use their influence with lending agencies. While financing is still the responsibility of the owners, they receive expert help and get to trade on the reputation of the franchisor.

Reduced failure rates. Some estimates on the odds for success favor a franchise over a privately owned small business by 20 to 1. While this figure may be exaggerated, there is no doubt that the help provided by the franchisor greatly reduces the risk of business failure by the owner.

Disadvantages to the Owner

While the advantages are the reason for the rapid growth rate of franchising, there are some disadvantages: franchises are becoming rather expensive; their reputation has been tainted by a few fly-by-night outfits; some owners resent the control of the franchisor; sometimes the quality and personalized services are lacking; and legal confusion may become a problem.

Increasing expense of franchising. In addition to the initial fee, most franchisors have ongoing charges for their services. The fee may range from $3000 to over $1 million, but most fall between $20,000 and $50,000. And their continuing services can be expensive. More than 90% of all franchisors charge a royalty fee ranging from 3 to 20% of sales. Also, about 70% assess owners for advertising services. New franchises tend to be less expensive. Here, there may also be an advantage to the franchisor. If the owner buys in early and the franchise becomes unusually successful, the franchise may be sold for considerable profit.

Fraudulent practices. The aura of success in franchising has been somewhat dimmed by fly-by-night operators. An owner who put a hard-earned $20,000 into a new franchise explained his feeling, ''When they came in, it looked like they were going to start a massive advertising campaign within the week. I gave them my money, they sent me some materials, and kept promising a lot of results. As my patience wore thin, I found it harder and harder to get them to respond to my questions. Finally, they seemed to disappear into thin air." New franchises, like new businesses, have a greater threat of failure.

Silk-tongued opportunists capitalize on success stories by promoting nonexistent trade names, peddling undeliverable services, and selling illegal pyramid schemes. They make numerous blue-sky promises, most of which they never intend to fulfill, take their franchise fee, and go out of business, leaving the owner on his own. Others have been known to raise their fees or change their practices, resulting in great pressures on the profits of the business. Sometimes, they charge exorbitant prices for goods and equipment, and the franchisor has no choice other than to pay those prices.

Franchisor control. The benefits of standardized practices are diminished when the owner loses control over the management of the business. A major benefit of small business—independence and autonomy—is often lost in the regimen of a franchise. Franchisors usually insist on a particular layout, set procedures for processing customers, and may even dicatate store hours, methods of hiring, employee salaries, and prices.

BUSINESS BULLETIN

A Checklist for Evaluating Franchise Opportunities

In checking out franchises, you will want to get "yes" answers to most of the questions in this list.

check if yes

I.   Is the franchisor successful?
  1. Has the franchisor been in business for more than five years? _____
  2. Does the franchisor have a good reputation and credit rating? _____
  3. Have you found out how many franchises are operating? _____
  4. Is the failure rate small? _____
  5. What assistance will the franchisor offer you? _____

II. What about the product or service?
  6. Has it been on the market long enough to gain acceptance? _____
  7. Is it priced competitively? _____
  8. Is it a staple product, not a fad? _____
  9. Would you buy it on its merits? _____
  10. If product and supplies must be purchased exclusively from the franchisor, are prices competitive? _____

III. What do you know about the franchise contract?
  11. Does the fee seem reasonable? _____
  12. Do continuing royalties appear reasonable? _____
  13. Does the cash investment include payment for fixtures and equipment? _____
  14. Can you, as the franchisee, return merchandise for credit? _____
  15. If there is an annual sales quota, can you retain your franchise if it is not met? _____

The potential conflict becomes clear: the highly valued independence of the enterpriser versus the rigid rule of the franchisor. For example, a successful owner of a national fast-food restaurant that was located in a Mexican American neighborhood wanted to add four Mexican dishes to the menu. The request was strictly forbidden by the franchisor.

Legal confusion. The growth of franchising raced ahead of legislation governing its practices. In order to control illegal and unethical practices, some states passed laws regarding franchising. The more respectable franchises encouraged these laws. Still, there were variations between state laws, and some states had no laws whatsoever. In 1971, the Federal Trade Commission, recognizing this problem, proposed a trade regulation requiring full disclosure of all facts to prospective investors. The law requires a **uniform offering circular**, with a disclosure of all financial information and details regarding the specific arrangements between the franchisor and the franchisee. It is now more difficult for the franchisor to make promises that are left unfulfilled.

16. Do you have an exclusive, protected territory? _____
17. Can you terminate your agreement if you are not happy? _____
18. May you sell your business to whomever you please? _____
19. Did you have a lawyer study each paragraph of the contract and approve it? _____
20. Does the contract cover all aspects of your agreement with the franchisor? _____

IV. What about your market?
21. Are your boundaries completely and understandably defined? _____
22. Does your product or service have a market in your territory? _____
23. Does your territory provide an adequate sales potential? _____
24. Is the existing competition not too well entrenched? _____

V. What about you, the franchisee?
25. Do you know where you are going to get the money to invest? _____
26. Have you compared the costs to starting other similar businesses? _____
27. Are you prepared to give up some of your independence? _____
28. Are you prepared to accept rules and regulations you may disagree with? _____
29. Are you capable of accepting some supervision from the franchisor? _____
30. Are you ready to spend much or all of your remaining life with this franchisor? _____

Source: Adapted from Wendell O. Metcalf, *Starting and Managing a Small Business of Your Own,* Washington, D.C.: Small Business Administration, 1973.

**Figure 5.1
Franchise ads that
appeared in *The Wall
Street Journal*.**

State laws governing pricing and territorial arrangements may conflict with those of the franchisor. There exists a legal question as to whether territorial agreements are anticompetitive. These unsettled laws may create problems for franchising. They may also mean numerous reports for both franchisor and franchisee.

Future of Franchising

While the rapid-paced growth of franchising may not continue indefinitely, the immediate future of franchising looks rosy. Fast-foods have been booming for the last few years and seem likely to continue thriving. Restaurants now capture 37% of the family food dollar, and projections aim at

50% by 1990. Fast-food franchises, buoyed by past successes, are continuing rapid expansion. Table 5.4 lists the top ten franchises of 1982.

Convenience food stores are surviving their hot competition with supermarkets by locating close to residential areas and staying open at odd hours. Thanks to shorter work weeks, longer vacations, rising incomes, and early retirements, leisure and travel businesses continue to thrive. But while new franchising fields offer greater growth opportunities, the traditional franchises—fast-food restaurants, automobile dealers, gasoline stations, soft drink companies, and retailing outlets — continue to dominate (see Figure 5.1).

TABLE 5.4 ■ THE TOP TEN FRANCHISES OF 1982

1. McDonald's
2. One Hour Martinizing
3. Hanna Car Wash
4. Parts Plus
5. Domino's Pizza
6. Diet Center
7. Wendy's Old-Fashioned Hamburgers
8. Burger King
9. American International Rent A Car
10. Nutri/System Weight Loss Medical Center

SUMMARY

Small businesses make up the vast majority of our enterprises. The Small Business Administration (SBA) defines a small business as:

1. Manufacturers who have less than 250 employees.
2. Retailers with annual sales of less than $1 million.
3. Wholesalers with annual sales of less than $5 million.

The SBA also defines the five general types of small businesses: service, retail, wholesale, general construction, and manufacturing.

Even though we are increasingly dominated by large corporations, small businesses still thrive because of their unique contributions. They are adaptable and flexible. Smallness allows the firm to make decisions much more quickly than the bureaucratic giants. Because of less overhead costs, small firms can take risks that larger companies cannot. Smaller businesses are better able to serve local needs, and they can offer more specialized goods and services. Also, small business owners are usually more motivated and have more control than do corporate employees. However, small companies have problems in raising capital and attracting key employees. Because of their small size, their costs are often greater due to economies of operation. Finally, small firms do not usually have the recognition enjoyed by larger companies.

Small businesses contribute to our business system by stimulating competition, providing new ideas, and serving larger companies. In starting a small business, the first step is a specific business plan. Other early considerations are financing, legal arrangements, taxes, and insurance. Sources of small business financing are owner investment, investment from family and friends, commercial banks, mortgage loans, government agencies, credit from suppliers, finance companies, and venture capital companies.

Small companies succeed when they capitalize on their flexibility, personal contacts, low overhead, and strong owner motivation. However, small businesses have a high failure rate, which can be attributed to the owner's lack of education and experience, inadequate record keeping and planning, and improper handling of finances. According to Dun & Bradstreet, 90% of all business failures are due to poor management.

Entrepreneurs—owners and managers of small businesses—have unique characteristics. Thirty percent have parents who work in skilled or unskilled labor; another 25% have parents who also owned businesses. Enterprisers retain strong values of independence. They demonstrate high achievement needs and prefer to take moderate, calculated risks that they can influence. Finally, independents are motivated to work harder than most people.

The primary source of help for small businesses is the Small Business Administration (SBA), which was created by the federal government with the Small Business Act of 1953. Its main contribution is helping the small business obtain financing, both for start-up and working capital. It also provides management assistance and valuable information for the entrepreneur. Minority businesses get special help from the Office of Minority Business Enterprise (OMBE), created by the Department of Commerce in 1969. Also, professional organizations, such as the Junior Chamber of Commerce, offer crucial assistance.

A franchise is an exclusive agreement between a manufacturing or operating company and independent owners; the franchisor gives the owner (or franchisee) specified privileges to operate in a particular territory, and the owner handles only the franchisor's products. The advantages to the owner are recognition, management assistance, financial assistance, and reduced failure rates. The major disadvantages of franchising are the increasing expense, potential fraudulent practices, reduced independence, and legal confusion. The recent growth rate of franchising has been phenomenal and the future looks bright.

MIND YOUR BUSINESS

Instructions. Indicate whether each statement is true (T) or false (F).

_____ 1. An entrepreneur is most commonly the oldest child of the family.

_____ 2. Most entrepreneurs are men.

_____ 3. Most entrepreneurs are not married.

_____ 4. Most entrepreneurs start their first company in their twenties.

_____ 5. The entrepreneurial tendency first appears when an individual is between 30 and 40 years of age.

_____ 6. When beginning a first business, an entrepreneur typically has a master's degree.

_____ 7. The major reason entrepreneurs start their own business is to make money.

_____ 8. An entrepreneur typically starts only one business in his or her life.

_____ 9. The entrepreneur's high need for achievement is based on his or her relationship with his or her father. .

____ 10. To be successful in a new venture, the entrepreneur needs an abundance of luck.

____ 11. Entrepreneurs are frequently in conflict with financers.

____ 12. A successful entrepreneur relies on no one but himself or herself for critical advice on how to run the company.

____ 13. Entrepreneurs are excellent planners.

____ 14. Entrepreneurs are high risk takers (big gamblers).

____ 15. The only really necessary ingredient for a successful business is money.

See answers at the back of the book.

Source: Adapted from Joseph R. Mancuso, *How To Start, Finance, and Manage Your Own Business,* Englewood Cliffs, New Jersey: Prentice-Hall Publishing Co., 1978.

KEY TERMS

small business, 98

business plan, 101

Dun & Bradstreet, 106

Small Business Administration (SBA), 110

SBA direct loan, 110

SBA participating loan, 110

SBA guaranteed loan, 110

disaster loan, 110

small business investment company (SBIC), 110

Service Corps of Retired Executives (SCORE), 111

Active Corps of Executives (ACE), 111

Minority Business Development Agency (MBDA), 112

Minority Business Opportunity Committee (MBOC), 112

Minority Enterprise Small Business Investment Company (MESBIC), 112

Junior Chamber of Commerce, 113

National Small Business Association, 113

National Federation of Independent Businesses, 113

Better Business Bureau, 113

franchise, 114

franchisor, 114

franchisee, 114

uniform offering circular, 117

REVIEW QUESTIONS

1. What is a small business? How are the SBA and the CED definitions of small business similar? Different?

2. What are the most popular types of small businesses? Give some local examples of each.

3. Discuss the advantages and disadvantages of small business. What businesses do you know of that provide examples of these?

4. Nationally, what role do small businesses play in terms of: (a) number or percentage of all businesses, (b) percentage of all sales, and (c) percentage of all employees?

5. What specific contributions do small businesses make to our economic system?

6. List the steps that should be taken in starting a small business. What should the business plan include and why is it important? List the sources of business financing with the advantages of each.

7. What factors most contribute to the success of a small business? Discuss the major reasons for small business failure.

8. Define entrepreneur. List and discuss the ways that entrepreneurs differ from most people.

9. What is the SBA and how can it help small business owners?

10. What are the three major types of SBA loans and how do they differ?

11. What are the three major organizations that operate within the SBA? Name each, along with the specific services they provide.

12. What are the three major organizations that assist minority business owners and how, specifically, can they help?

13. What are the four professional organizations, as discussed in the text, that work in the interest of small business?

14. What is a franchise? How does it work? Name at least ten examples of franchises. What franchises have you recently patronized?

15. List and discuss the specific advantages and disadvantages that a franchise offers an owner.

16. What is the future of franchising?

17. What specific questions would you ask before buying a franchise?

CASES

Case 5.1: When Do You Quit?

Jack Hand has owned his own small appliance repair shop for over 23 years. With help from his wife, he has managed to raise three children and get them through college. While he has always worked long hours, he does enjoy being his own boss.

But problems are mounting, and his wife has asked him the very reasonable question, "What is going to happen in the future?" Jack is 49 years old, but his business income has been dropping during the past 5 years until it now averages less than $20,000 per year. They have some savings and they own a couple of small apartments which they rent. The area where the business is located has changed so that the income level of those that live in the area is less than half of what it was a few years ago. Many of his regular customers have moved away, and he has not received enough additional customers to replace a lot of tools and buy some additional equipment. He talked with his banker, who discouraged additional investment at his current location. Jack and his wife have talked seriously about their future, and they have considered several options:

1. They could move. They have found a possible location, and they could also arrange the financing.

2. They could stay where they are and try to hold on until retirement.

3. They could retire now, sell their properties, and invest in blue chip securities. This, along with social security and his retirement fund which he has been carefully building for years, would allow them to maintain their standard of living at close to their current level.

Questions

1. Which alternative do you think they should take? Why?

2. What other alternatives can you think of? Are these better or worse than what they were considering?

Case 5.2: A Fabulous Franchise

Fabulous Franchise Company has approached you about buying a franchise to sell their product in your city. They promote high-cost candies and cakes that appeal primarily to the "gift for the person who has everything" market. Assume that you have funds for the purchase. You are considering the merits of purchasing the franchise and hiring someone else to manage it for you. The owners of Fabulous Franchise say that they expect to lay out several hundred thousand dollars during the next couple of years to build product identity and create a demand for their confections. Since they are just beginning, their products are not yet known in your city.

Questions

1. Make a detailed list of the information that you would require from the company to help you make your decision. Do you think you would be able to obtain all of this information? Explain.

2. Other than the company, where else would you go to look for information? What type of information would you look for?

3. Set the criteria that you think would be necessary for you to reach a decision to buy the franchise.

This is the first of six sections in this book that we have prepared hoping to involve you in a process of career planning. You will be examining yourself and your interest in four different business specializations: management, marketing, finance, and data processing. You will be trying to find out if the business world is appropriate for you and how you can fit into it in the most satisfying way possible.

Career decision making is a long process. You may change your mind often. Our purpose in writing these Careerscopes is to help you to organize your thinking about topics that are important in choosing a career. We will not tell you which specific career you should choose. Instead, we will suggest careers for you to explore, and some guidelines will be provided to help you narrow your choices. **Thomas F. Harrington, Ph.D.** *(Professor of Counselor Education, Northeastern University)* **Arthur J. O'Shea, Ph.D.** *(Professor of Psychology, Boston State College)*

PERSONALITY AND CAREER SATISFACTION

Many psychologists believe there are six basic kinds of people — scientific, artistic, crafts, social, clerical, and business. They also tell us that there are six basic kinds of work environments — the same six — and that you are more likely to find satisfaction if you go into a job that matches your personality.

What kind of person are you? Finding out may help you to develop a career plan that will lead to job satisfaction.

Which one of the following personality types is most like you? Put a check mark in front of those adjectives and statements that most closely describe you. (Obviously, we don't mean to suggest that these descriptions are absolutely accurate, but they should give you a good sense of each personality type.)

Under each personality type, you will find two lists. The one on the left has jobs that provide a work environment that is usually distinctively reflective of the type. To the right, jobs are listed that reflect the type in question and also include a strong business component. Psychological research shows that most of us possess personalities that are a combination of types.

The Scientific Person

___ Analytical

___ Curious

___ Likes science

___ Creative

___ Likes math

___ Intellectual

___ Independent

___ Studious

___ Theoretical

___ Precise

___ Enjoys working alone

___ Organized

___ Philosophical

___ Persevering

___ Enjoys solving problems

The Scientific Worker

Chemist
Physicist
Biologist
Engineer
Mathematician
Physician

The Scientific-Business Worker

Programmer
Sales engineer
Electrical engineer
Systems analyst
Actuary
Technical sales worker

The Artistic Person

___ Imaginative
___ Nonconforming
___ Enjoys music
___ Introspective
___ Sensitive
___ Independent
___ Creative
___ Enjoys writing

___ Impractical
___ Uninhibited
___ Enjoys painting
___ Expressive
___ Unsystematic
___ Critical
___ Complex

The Artistic Worker

Singer
Dancer
Actor/actress
Novelist
Artist
Musician

The Artistic-Business Worker

Industrial designer
Advertising worker
Public relations representative
Advertising copywriter
Radio-TV announcer
Movie-TV producer

The Crafts Person

___ Uncomplicated
___ Conforming
___ Likes to work with hands
___ Practical
___ Prefers the outdoors
___ Mechanical
___ Predictable
___ Shy

___ Unassuming
___ Unphilosophical
___ Detached
___ Blunt
___ Persistent
___ Materialistic
___ Conservative

The Crafts Worker

Carpenter
Auto mechanic
Plumber (pipefitter)
Farmer
Sewing machine operator
Long-distance truck driver

The Crafts-Business Worker

Buyer
Blue-collar worker supervisor
Computer service technician
Warehouse manager
Optician
Agribusiness manager

The Social Person

____ Friendly
____ Trustworthy
____ Helpful
____ Genuine
____ Understanding
____ Open
____ Tolerant
____ Idealistic

____ Kindly
____ Skilled in teaching
____ Sharing
____ Sympathetic
____ Verbal
____ Compassionate
____ Cooperative

The Social Worker

Counselor
Nurse
Secondary school teacher
Social worker
Clinical psychologist
Clergy

The Social-Business Worker

Human resources manager
Labor relations specialist
Employment interviewer
Social service director
Training and development worker
Community recreation director

The Clerical Person

____ Conscientious
____ Organized
____ Likes well-structured tasks
____ Persistent
____ Conventional
____ Efficient
____ Precise
____ Conservative

____ Systematic
____ Orderly
____ Stable
____ Enjoys office work
____ Practical
____ Submissive
____ Conforming

The Clerical Worker

Secretary
Bookkeeper
Bank teller
File clerk
Typist
Receptionist

The Clerical-Business Worker

Credit manager
Accountant
Market researcher
Insurance underwriter
Bank officer
Real estate appraiser

The Business Person

___ Aggressive
___ Energetic
___ Willing to take risks
___ Social
___ Eager to lead
___ Persuasive
___ Ambitious
___ Confident

___ Outgoing
___ Status-seeking
___ Exhibitionistic
___ Daring
___ Personable
___ Materialistic
___ Verbal

The Business Worker

Insurance agent
Investment fund manager
Government administrator

Stockbroker
Real estate agent
Business executive

The lists above show how the business personality combines with the other five types.

You have had a brief introduction to the broad range of occupations within the world of work, with particular emphasis on the business world. A more careful examination of yourself and your vocational future is essential.

In the remaining Careerscopes of this book you will find exercises designed for you to explore your interest in major business areas: the Careerscope in Part II focuses on management; the Careerscope in Part III on marketing; the Careerscope in Part IV on finance; and the Careerscope in Part V on data processing. The Careerscope in Part VI discusses work values commonly associated with the business field.

II

1234567890

11112222333344445556666677778889

THE MANAGING OF BUSINESS

After completing this chapter, you will be able to:

■ Identify the four basic functions of management.

■ Describe the planning function and give examples of common types of plans.

■ Describe the organizing function.

■ Describe the directing function.

■ Discuss leadership and leadership styles.

■ Distinguish between Theories X, Y, and Z.

■ Describe how the controlling function works and identify four typical problems with controlling.

THE PROCESS
OF MANAGEMENT

Peter Drucker, a $1500-a-day consultant, says that management ability is the most important ingredient in the success of a business or a nation. Regardless of how wealthy a company is, how smart its people are, and how good their intentions, it will soon be turning out bleak status reports unless staffed by capable managers.

Management is the process of accomplishing group objectives through the functions of planning, organizing, directing, and controlling human activities.* **Managers** help accomplish these group objectives by performing the functions of management to get the work done through others. Managers do not actually perform the work themselves; the president of General Motors surely could not single-handedly assemble a Corvette. Like chemical catalysts, managers cause things to happen. When the catalyst is too strong, it becomes a monster to the other elements; when it is too weak, desired actions never happen.

The manager's job is to plan what employees are supposed to do, organize them to do it, direct the employees, and check to see that the work is properly done. Some management positions, especially at lower levels, may include actual work assignments as well as management responsibilities. Figure 6.1 is a diagram of the four management functions.

THE PLANNING FUNCTION

Planning involves establishing objectives and deciding on the strategies and tasks necessary to accomplish the objectives. Planning is primary to the other management functions; it is impossible to organize, direct, and control effectively without proper plans. And planning is demanding. As an experienced manager commented, "Planning re-

---

* Traditionally, writers of business books also considered staffing as a management function. However, we include staffing in *Human Resources Management* (Chapter 9), as do most current business writers.

quires the accumulation of intricate details, the discipline of highly structured thinking, and the persistence of Sherlock Holmes." After discussing planning time periods and offering examples of plans, we will examine the planning process.

The Planning Time Period

Plans may be either short-range or long-range.

Short-range planning. Normally, **short-range plans** cover a period of a year or less. Some people refer to short-range planning as **tactical planning**; that is, they represent tactics for

**Figure 6.1
Functions of management.**

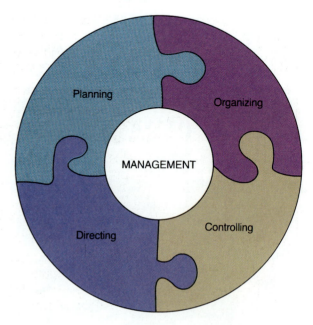

reaching longer-range goals. It should be obvious that short-range plans need to be integrated with long-range plans. But experience shows that too often managers do not attain this coordination. As a result, some short-range plans contribute little or nothing to long-range purposes. A middle manager discusses this hitch: "Our long-range plans called for an ability to increase sales by 40% over a 5-year period. However, we found that budgets had been cut in recruiting and training to meet some temporary, short-term financial projections. This really unraveled our long-range hopes, and we had to alter them."

Long-range planning. Since planning concerns the future, this spurs the question, "How far into the future should managers plan?" In actual practice, planning periods vary widely. But to be long-range, by most definitions, plans must cover more than 1 year into the future. Some companies have **long-range plans** of only 2 years, while others devise 20- or 30-year plans. But the most

The most common form of long-range planning is strategic planning.

common long-range planning period seems to be from 3 to 5 years, and almost all organizations plan for at least 1 year.

The most common form of long-range planning is strategic planning. Typically, **strategic planning** includes (1) determining the major mission of the organization, (2) analyzing the organization's environment, (3) analyzing the organization's internal strengths and weaknesses, (4) setting 5-year targets of accomplishment, and (5) developing strategies for implementing the plans.

Common Types of Plans

In the broadest sense, any provision for the future is a plan. Most plans include objectives, policies, procedures, rules, and budgets.

BUSINESS BULLETIN

Managerial Skills

Managers are responsible for seeing that others (their subordinates) perform the work. To do this effectively, managers must become skilled in the four functions of management discussed in this chapter. And to be successful in a particular position, managers need to develop competencies along three dimensions:

1. *Technical skills.* While it is not necessary for managers to know all the technical aspects of the work they are managing, they must have enough technical knowledge to communicate effectively with their subordinates and superiors. And they must have enough technical knowledge to gain some credibility with their subordinates.

2. *Human skills.* As one writer put it, "Good managers must have a way with people." Managers need to practice good, sincere human relations with their people. A manager can be a technical expert, but if he or she does not generate confidence and commitment from his or her subordinates, the group will be ineffective.

3. *Conceptual skills.* Finally, managers need to be able to think of problems and solutions in a logical and systematic way. Rather than concentrating solely on a short-term solution to an immediate crisis, good managers put all of their smaller decisions in a broader, long-term perspective that benefits the total organization.

Objectives. **Objectives,** sometimes called goals, are the end result of our efforts. An objective is where we want to be or what we want to have accomplished when finished. While profit is the most frequently mentioned objective, businesses also have objectives of growth, efficiency, increased market share, resource attraction, employee development, public responsibility, and customer service. Well-defined organizational objectives serve managers by (1) establishing priorities, (2) serving as standards against which results are measured, and (3) unifying management-employee efforts.

Many organizations do not get the maximum impact from their objectives because they are improperly conceived and stated. To be effective, objectives should be:

■ Challenging yet realistic.

■ Stated in specific, measurable terms.

■ Strongly supported by superiors.

■ Able to generate enthusiasm and commitment from subordinates.

■ Communicated to all subordinates involved in attaining the objectives.

■ Put in writing.

■ Regularly discussed at departmental meetings.

Policies. **Policies** are plans that guide thinking. They create boundaries that encourage consistent decisions throughout the many facets of the company. Firms create policies in nearly all areas, including employee relations, financial commitments, profit, growth, community relations, and sales. Policies may be broad as "satisfaction guaranteed," for example. They may be more specific, such as "satisfaction guaranteed or money refunded in full if returned within 10 days." Either way, managers use some discretion in interpreting the policy. They do not decide, in this example, whether the company sells on credit, but they may have to determine what "satisfaction guaranteed" means.

Procedures. More limiting than policies, **procedures** are specific guides to action. They outline steps for such activities as hiring, requesting capital equipment, accounting for inventory, re-

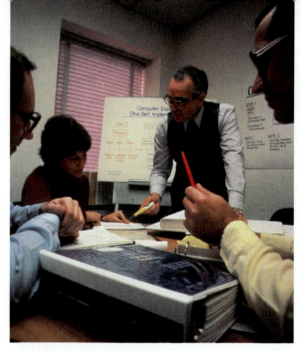

Companywide procedures provide guidelines for action at all levels of large firms.

questing transfers, returning merchandise, utilizing scrap, and the like. An example of a purchasing procedure reads, "To purchase supplies, you must complete four copies of Purchase Requisition Form PR-3A. The yellow copy goes to your manager, the green copy to purchasing, and the pink copy to the business office. Keep the white copy for your files."

Critics complain that procedures are bureaucratic and time-wasting red tape. Employees may become impatient with procedures they do not understand and usually feel that they create unnecessary paperwork. The purpose of procedures, however, is to help managers and employees complete their work efficiently.

Rules. Narrowing still further, **rules** are specific guides to action. Rules tell people what they can and cannot do in well-defined situations. Rules need no interpretation and allow no exceptions. "Hard hats must be worn in this area" and "An employee will be given a three-day layoff for his/her third absence in a six-month period" are examples of rules.

Budgets. **Budgets** express future expectations in numbers. Cash budgets predict the need for

TABLE 6.1 ■ EXAMPLES OF COMMON PLANS FOR AN ACTUAL ORGANIZATION

Objectives	1. To gain a reputation as the most reputable and innovative firm in the industry within 10 years.
	2. To earn an annual rate of 10% on investment.
	3. To improve sales by 15% each year for the next 3 years.
Policies	1. We promote employees on the basis of skill value, performance, and tenure.
	2. We extend credit to customers with good ratings.
	3. Our product standards exceed those of our major competitors.
Procedures	1. To purchase capital equipment, three copies of Form 304-B must be prepared, showing justifications for the purchase. The original and one copy go to purchasing; retain one copy for your files. Requests above $2000 must be approved by the finance manager.
	2. On customer complaints, salespeople must make a record of the complaint on Form 601, including the specific reason for the complaint. Unless the item shows obvious customer abuse, the customer must be allowed to exchange the item or receive a cash refund. If there is customer abuse, refer the customer to the sales manager.
Rules	1. Lunch breaks will be from 12:00 P.M. to 1:00 P.M. for all employees.
	2. All employees in the assembly area must wear steel shoes, protective clothing, and goggles.
	3. Employee theft will result in automatic termination.

cash; operating and expense budgets show profit expectations; and sales forecasts estimate future sales. But budgets need not be financial. Labor budgets, for instance, are expressed in hours. Tables 6.1 and 6.2 show common examples of plans.

The Planning Process

Effective managers follow a logical, well-developed approach to planning, similar to the steps in scientific decision making.

Recognize opportunities. Certainly, good planning requires awareness of opportunities. Can we offer a desirable service? Is there any historical evidence of a contrary need? What does our market research tell us? Are our competitors doing anything of concern? Can we obtain additional resources? Can we produce or market additional but similar lines? Great successes occur when a manager has the insight to recognize an opportunity.

Select planning objectives. Each plan must have a purpose. Where is it leading us? What is the target? Without a clear, measurable objective, a plan will fail. Conversely, a precise goal gives direction and meaning to the planning steps.

Identify and create alternatives. Effective planners try to identify several alternatives for reaching and planning objectives. At this stage, creative thinking is important because some of the best alternatives may not be immediately obvious.

Evaluate alternatives. Precise evaluation of alternatives is crucial. Each alternative must be judged in light of the objectives. Success requires a careful study of the advantages and disadvantages of each plausible alternative. What are the costs? What are the probable outcomes? Do we

TABLE 6.2 ■ EXAMPLE OF BUDGET PLANNING

Projected Labor Budget for Project 29

Work Station	Hours	Rate	Estimated Cost
Cutting	500	$7.00	$3500
Lathes	100	8.50	850
Assembly	230	8.20	1886
Finishing	80	8.40	672
Shipping	100	7.00	700
TOTALS	1010		$7608

have the necessary resources? How much time will it take?

Select an alternative. If we have performed the previous steps carefully, we can be more confident of our selection. However, the pros and cons of each alternative may be unclear. Managers never have all information they would like and they cannot be sure they have chosen the correct alternative; still, they have to make a selection.

Follow-up. Because of uncertainties and imperfect decision makers, even the best plans need to be checked. Follow-up continually checks the plan and helps a manager decide whether it is best to switch to other alternatives.

THE ORGANIZING FUNCTION

While the planning function provides purpose and direction to the company, the **organizing** function makes it possible to pursue these plans collectively. Because organization structure is so important and rather complex, we devote Chapter 7 to this topic. In this section, we will discuss the purposes of organization, how managers relate to the organization's structure, and the benefits of an effective organization.

The Purpose of Business Organization

The theory of business organization presents five major purposes:

1. To provide the structure for defining job functions, descriptions, and relationships.
2. To establish lines of authority and responsibility. Organization makes clear who is in charge and who is responsible for what tasks.
3. To create communication channels. The organizational structure establishes channels for upward, downward, and interdepartmental communication.
4. To establish methods for reaching organizational objectives.
5. To provide for hiring and placement of human resources. As a company hires employees, the employees join a department, branch, or division with specific duties.

How Levels of Management Differ

Within complex organizations, there exist various levels of management. We can divide managers into three levels: top management, middle management, and operating management (see Fig. 6.2).

Figure 6.2
Pyramid of management levels with examples of responsibilities.

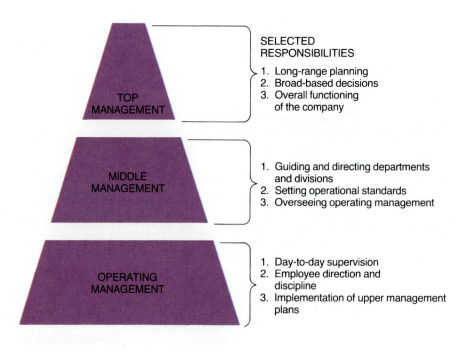

SELECTED
RESPONSIBILITIES

TOP MANAGEMENT
1. Long-range planning
2. Broad-based decisions
3. Overall functioning of the company

MIDDLE MANAGEMENT
1. Guiding and directing departments and divisions
2. Setting operational standards
3. Overseeing operating management

OPERATING MANAGEMENT
1. Day-to-day supervision
2. Employee direction and discipline
3. Implementation of upper management plans

TABLE 6.3 ■ TOP PAY FOR TOP MANAGEMENT

	Salary	Bonus	Total
John H. Gutfreund, *cochairman,* Phibro-Salomon	$344,495	$2,200,000	$2,544,495
Robert Anderson, *chairman,* Rockwell International	$977,083	$1,340,560	$2,317,643
Steven J. Ross, *chairman,* Warner Communications	$350,000	$1,951,497	$2,301,497
Henry Kaufman, *vice president,* Phibro-Salomon	$264,495	$1,880,000	$2,144,495
Gedale Horowitz, *vice president,* Phibro-Salomon	$264,495	$1,880,000	$2,144,495
Donald R. Beall, *president,* Rockwell International	$668,333	$ 804,336	$1,472,669
Fred Hartley, *chairman,* Union Oil Co. of California	$561,667	$ 838,675	$1,400,342
Rawleigh Warner, Jr., *chairman,* Mobil	—	—	$1,388,072
Clifton C. Garvin, Jr., *chairman,* Exxon	$800,000	$ 536,350	$1,336,250
Harry J. Gray, *chairman,* United Technologies	$760,350	$ 520,000	$1,280,350

Source: Company proxy statements.

Top management. Top management develops the broad plans for the company and makes decisions that shape the direction 2 to 10 years or more into the future. Through careful analysis, top managers establish major objectives of the firm, based upon the resources and capabilities of the company. While they spend a lot of time planning, they must also guide their team through effective organizing, directing, and controlling. Top managers usually go by such titles as chairman, president, vice-president, treasurer, and secretary (see Table 6.3).

Middle management. Middle management, including levels below top management and above operating management, does the tasks of top management but on a more specialized level. Middle managers are usually responsible for certain areas, departments, divisions, or subdepartments of the team. They make decisions and carry out plans within the broad guidelines set by top management. Titles may include department head, divisional manager, head buyer, chief engineer, plant manager, regional manager, and so on.

FUNNY BUSINESS

Drawing by Saxon; © 1982 The New Yorker Magazine, Inc.

"I suggest you take your proposition to Mr. Hodkiss at the office. He may send you to Sam Watson or Bob Exum. Eventually, of course, you will have to talk to me."

Operating management. At the lowest management level, **operating management** is responsible for putting into operation the plans of higher and middle management. On the firing line, operating managers direct their people to get the work out. Most authorities believe that this is the hardest of all management positions because operating managers have to get employees to do what upper-level management has planned. Supervisor and foreman are the most common titles of operating managers. While all these managers perform the functions of management, they do not spend the same amount of time and energy in each function. Figure 6.3 shows how management effort at differing levels relate to function.

Most authorities believe that operating management is the hardest of all management positions because they have to get employees to do what upper-level management has planned.

Educational Backgrounds of Successful Managers

Psychologists Douglas Bray and Ann Howard have for more than 25 years been studying college graduates in entry-level management ranks for AT&T. Here are some of their findings:

1. Master's degrees can be helpful. Howard says of master's degree holders, "They bring us greater administrative and interpersonal skills and more motivation for status and money, but they're not any smarter." This applied equally to holders of an M.A., M.S., and M.B.A.

2. There are key differences between technical and nontechnical majors. Business majors led the pack in organizing, planning, and decision-making skills. Humanities and social science graduates also scored high. Math, science, and engineering majors scored much lower in these skills. Technical majors did have higher general mental ability, but they were not as creative or as good at interpersonal skills. As you might expect, social science majors were quite low on quantitative skills. Business majors were the ones most eager to get ahead.

For future managers, AT&T is still looking for about a third each of business, technical, and liberal arts majors. While they are still looking for master's degrees, some firms say the era of the M.B.A. has passed. Many companies offer the same management training programs for their new people, whether or not they have a master's degree.

Regardless of the success/failure studies of managers, educational background is probably less important than the actual skills that people develop. Leo J. Corbett, vice-president of sales management for Salomon Brothers, says, "We're really looking for a particular kind of person, rather than a particular degree."

Source: Peter Hall, "Surprise! Liberal Arts Students Make the Best Managers," *Business Week's Guide to Careers,* Fall/Winter, 1983, pp. 16–19.

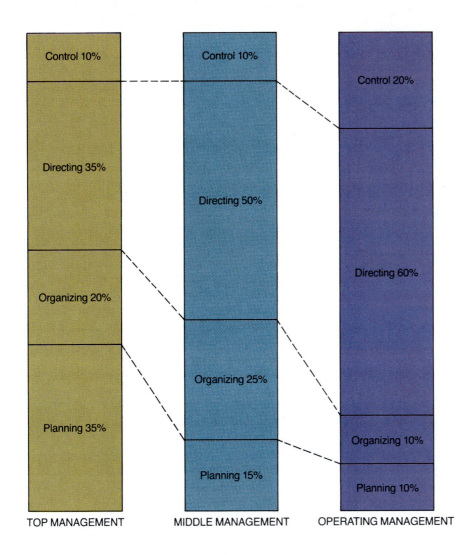

Control 10%
Directing 35%
Organizing 20%
Planning 35%
TOP MANAGEMENT

Control 10%
Directing 50%
Organizing 25%
Planning 15%
MIDDLE MANAGEMENT

Control 20%
Directing 60%
Organizing 10%
Planning 10%
OPERATING MANAGEMENT

Figure 6.3 Distribution of a manager's time. *Source: Adapted from H. Mintzberg,* The Nature of Managerial Work, *New York: Harper & Row, 1975.*

THE DIRECTING FUNCTION

After we have planned where the company is going and organized people to accomplish goals, we push the starter button. **Directing** leads employees to carry out company objectives by performing their duties. **Leadership,** the exercise of influence and power, is necessary to perform the directing function. Without leadership, the department or company drifts aimlessly, but effective leaders give form and purpose to the group. They seek out, identify, and articulate group objectives and influence subordinates to work toward these objectives. Communicating and motivating are also important to the directing function; we cover these topics in detail in Chapter 10.

Theories of Leadership

The study of leadership has travelled many paths. One of the earliest ideas of leadership was the **traitist theory,** a belief that capable leaders have personality traits that differentiate them from ineffectual leaders. This theory specifies personality criteria such as intelligence, initiative, tenacity, fairness, and creativity. A few traitists still exist, but this approach lost much of its thrust because researchers could not agree on a list of traits.

Later, the **situationalist theory** developed, which states that traits necessary for leadership vary according to the situation. A construction crew foreman might require different leadership traits than a manager of a shoe department. Situationalists do not believe in absolute leaders who emerge in any situation; rather, they say the situation dictates the leader. The same group might prefer one individual for its work supervisor, another to captain its softball team, and still another to plan the office party. The situational approach switched the emphasis from leaders to situations.

More recently, theorists have been considering both traits and situations, and they add a relational dimension. These comprehensive theories consider such variables as leadership personality, nature of the job, characteristics of the employees, and the relationship between leaders and followers.

Leadership Styles

To the practicing manager, leadership styles are more important than theory. There are three predominate leadership styles: autocratic, democratic, and free-rein (laissez faire). **Autocratic leaders** make decisions without consulting their subordinates. Autocrats tend to be dogmatic and task-oriented, and they fully expect subordinates to heed their commands. **Democratic leaders,** by contrast, involve their subordinates in decision making. Before making a major decision, a democratic leader will get opinions and ideas from staff. Democratic leaders, though they may hold high expectations, tend to be more open, cooperative, and supportive than autocrats. **Free-rein leaders** provide very little, if any, direction to their subordinates. Rather, they leave their subordinates to figure things out for themselves. Figure 6.4 shows this range of leadership styles.

Some assume that one style of leadership is best for all situations, that there is an "ideal" style. However, the **contingency approach** to leadership assumes that different situations require different leadership styles. For instance, if a leader were in charge of a group of immature employees performing routine tasks, an autocratic style might be more effective. By contrast, a very mature and responsible work group would probably respond better to a more democratic or even free-rein style. **Style flexibility** is the ability of leaders to adapt their style to the situation.

Figure 6.4
Range of leadership styles. *Source: Adapted from Robert Tannenbaum and Warren H. Schmidt, "How to Choose a Leadership Pattern,"* Harvard Business Review, *March–April, 1958, p. 96.*

AUTOCRATIC — DEMOCRATIC — FREE-REIN

Use of authority by leader

Area of subordinate freedom

1	2	3	4	5	6	7
Leader makes decision and announces it	Leader sells decision	Leader presents ideas and invites questions	Leader presents tentative decision subject to change	Leader presents problem, gets suggestions, makes decision	Leader defines limits, asks group to make decision	Leader permits subordinates to function within limits defined by superior

RANGE OF BEHAVIOR

THEORY X ASSUMPTIONS	THEORY Y ASSUMPTIONS
1. Most people work as little as possible.	1. It is as natural to work as it is to play.
2. Most people lack ambition.	2. Most people exercise self-direction toward the objectives to which they are committed.
3. Most people avoid responsibility.	3. Most people seek responsibility under the proper conditions.
4. Most people prefer to be led.	4. Imagination and creativity are widespread throughout the population.
5. By nature, most people resist change.	5. Motivation and desire for improving are widespread throughout the population.
6. Most people are rather gullible and uninformed.	6. People will be committed to objectives if they receive rewards for attaining them.
7. Without management direction, most subordinates would do very little to serve the organization.	

Figure 6.5
Theory X and Theory Y leadership assumptions.

Theory X and Theory Y

Noted researcher Douglas McGregor, recognizing that leaders could choose from wide ranges of behavior, said that much leader behavior is the result of how the leader views people. To make this point, McGregor identified two opposing sets of assumptions that leaders make about people. He labelled these assumptions **Theory X** and **Theory Y** (see Fig. 6.5).

CROSS FIRE

Do We Have a Shortage of Executive Leaders?

"Wanted: corporate leaders. Mere managers need not apply," is the title of an article in the May 30, 1983 issue of *Fortune* magazine. Warren Bennis, Professor of Management at the University of Southern California School of Business Administration, says, "Business schools are training people who are good staff members but not good leaders." Do we have, as Bennis and others suggest, a shortage of effective leadership in our corporations?

Whereas managers focus on doing things right, leaders focus on doing the right things. Critics suggest that we have lost some of the fabric for creating leaders. Parents, because their children are involved in so many activities outside the home, no longer pass along strong values needed for success in leadership. Companies, because they want to maintain good images, do not allow subordinates and others to diagnose their failures, a necessary ingredient for building leaders. Bureaucratic organizations encourage teamwork and harmony at the expense of experimentation and failure. Business schools, with their emphasis on logical, rational, financial analysis, reduce risk taking, also a necessity of leadership.

Others suggest that the critics are being too harsh. At any time in history, we can make a case for producing more and better leadership in our corporations and in society. However, this does not mean that our current approach is ineffective in producing good leaders.

Do you think that we have a severe shortage of leaders running our business corporations today? Why?

____ A. Definitely, yes   ____ C. Probably, no

____ B. Probably, yes   ____ D. Definitely, yes

Noted researcher Douglas McGregor argued that the assumptions leaders had about their employees actually had a lot to do with how subordinates behaved; the assumptions became self-fulfilling.

McGregor argued that the assumptions of the leader had a lot to do with how subordinates actually behaved. In other words, the assumptions became a self-fulfilling prophecy. That is, if you believe something to be true, you act as if it were true, and your actions make your belief come true.

To illustrate, suppose a leader believes that most of her subordinates are hard-bitten Theory Xs. Because the leader assumes that employees are lazy and gullible, the leader will employ a directive, autocratic leadership style. After a period of time, most employees will rebel against this smothering direction by doing only what they have to, resisting management, avoiding responsibility, and calling in sick at the first sniffle. Then the leader will say, "See there, I was right. They will not do anything unless you make them." But suppose the leader assumes that most employees are Theory Ys. This leader, believing that subordinates are mature and responsible, will tend to use a more democratic, supportive leadership style. Employees, after a period, will respond by taking responsibility, acting maturely, and not calling in sick even when feeling badly. This leader is likely to brag that "I have a good group of employees. They're cooperative, motivated, and work themselves to a frazzle on tough projects."

Are most subordinates like Theory Y, or is this just wishful thinking? In reality, few of us are pure

4. *Productivity through people.* Managers of effective organizations really do believe that people will respond well if you treat them as adults. A researcher in one study asked twenty Hewlett-Packard executives why their company was successful. Eighteen of the twenty spontaneously said, "It is our people-oriented philosophy." Founder Bill Hewlett puts it this way, "It is the tradition of treating every individual with consideration and respect and recognizing personal achievements." They call it "The HP way."

5. *Hands-on, value-driven.* To the authors, this means good companies pay a lot of attention to values. Founders and executives spend a lot of time encouraging and reinforcing their key values. The shared values create teamwork. For instance, an executive at Delta Airlines explains, "There is a special relationship between Delta and its personnel that is rarely found in any firm, generating a team spirit that is evident in the individual's cooperative attitude . . . , cheerful outlook on life, and pride in a job well done."

6. *Stick to the knitting.* This simply means keep doing what you do best, what has made you successful. Former University of Texas football coach Darrel Royal put it this way, "We are going to dance with the people that brung us." Many firms make a mistake by diversifying into too many areas. Sooner or later, they get into trouble.

7. *Simple form, lean staff.* Bigness tends to create complexity. Not so with effective organizations. They want to keep their structure simple, clear, and autonomous. They also want a lean staff, that is, too few rather than too many assistants. One official said, "I believe management is more effective when they cannot control everything."

8. *Simultaneous loose-tight properties.* The excellent companies believe in freedom to fail, experimentation, risk taking, room to perform, and the like; but every one of them was also a stern disciplinarian. Employees could do many things on their own, but if they violated a key value like customer service, they were out of a job.

Source: Thomas J. Peters and Robert H. Waterman, Jr., *In Search of Excellence,* New York: Harper & Row Publishers, 1982.

Theory X or Theory Y. But we tend to lean in one direction or the other. Because some people had Theory X parents, teachers, or previous employers, they may have become a Theory X before they ever went to work. And if a leader tries to treat a Theory X employee with a Theory Y management style, the results are often plainly disastrous. If an employee insists on being a Theory X, leaders would probably be more effective in getting their attention by presenting the work in a tougher style. Then after the leader has the confidence of the employee, he can try to bring him along toward a Theory Y by using a more democratic, supportive approach.

Theory Z

Theory Z management emerged in the 1970s, primarily as a result of the Japanese influence on our markets. Professor William Ouchi, in his best-selling book, *Theory Z,* described the principles of **Theory Z.** In essence, Theory Z includes the following:

1. *Commitment to lifetime employment.* For all practical purposes, when a company hires an employee, the company commits to employing the person until retirement.

2. *Slow evaluation and promotion.* Evaluations occur over a relatively long period of time, and promotions come very slowly.

3. *Consensus decision making.* Managers encourage input into decisions by all who will be affected by the decision. Also, they try to reach a consensus; that is, everyone agrees, at least to some extent, with the decision.

4. *Collective responsibility.* Responsibility for success or failure of the organization is shared by the group as a whole. One individual is not necessarily responsible for more productivity than another.

5. *Informal, implicit control.* Within the formal organization, younger employees are not expected to disagree with or rebel against their superior managers. However, managers are expected to take their employees out for frequent social gatherings. In these settings, employees can make their disagreements known in a subtle, kidding way.

6. *Wholistic concern for employees.* The company's influence extends into almost all aspects of their employees' lives. The company sponsors many group vacations and social outings, and it may subsidize their employees' housing and transportation.

While most of these ideas may have emerged from the Japanese culture, Ouchi's description of Theory Z management was largely derived from the practices of American companies.

THE CONTROLLING FUNCTION

After charting the course, organizing the members, and directing employees, managers complete their duties by making periodic readings and corrections. The word "control" evokes a host of meanings, many of which are negative. But the essence of **controlling** is adjustment—checking actual events against plans and reconciling the differences. More specifically, controlling involves the following: (1) management sets standards of performance covering some future time period, (2) they measure the actual performance during the period, (3) they compare actual to expected performance, and (4) they reconcile the difference between the actual and the expected performance. Sometimes this means finding out why things did not go right and figuring out what to change in the future. Other times, it might mean reexamining plans to see if they were off base. A manager described his controlling function in this way, "I keep a constant check on how well we are doing by looking at weekly and monthly reports. Since we plan our work well in advance, I know where we are supposed to be each week. When we are behind or ahead of our plans, I have to find out why. If something unusual happened, I probably will not make any changes. But if we fall behind consistently, I have to find out why and make some changes."

How Controlling Works

Controlling begins with plans. As you recall from the earlier part of the chapter, objectives tell us where we are going. Policies, procedures, rules, and budgets offer guidelines as to how to get there. We begin controlling by communicating these plans to all the people involved in the effort.

Communicating expectations. Managers begin the controlling process by communicating plans to all the people involved. People should know exactly what is expected of them. And they should know what is expected of the group effort. Good communication helps prevent problems

and provides a benchmark by which to judge performance.

Getting feedback. After we develop and communicate plans, we need information on the progress of actual events. This is the role of feedback. Feedback may vary from simple observations such as taking a look now and then to very complex, computer-based monitoring techniques.

Exchanging information and ideas is vital to fulfilling management's controlling function.

Some examples of feedback include such historical information as financial records, turnover reports, sales figures, and quality control records. Other data are more immediate, for example, supervisors watching and checking employees' work methods. Whatever its form, to be useful, feedback must allow us to compare the actual with the expected.

Evaluating results. When activities compare favorably to plans, we assume things are going well. But suppose events do not match exactly (and they hardly ever do) with what we expected. To evaluate the difference, we raise the questions: How much deviation is allowed? What caused the deviation? Are events out of line, or were the plans off? The analysis of these questions may come in rule-of-thumb judgments or through complex cause-and-effect formulas.

Reconciling the differences. When deviations fall outside an allowed limit, we want to correct them. If some unusual event caused the deviation — the salesperson was ill and did not work 3 days — we probably would let it go without making any changes. But if the difference becomes consistent, we need to fix it. Correcting actual events may require training, improved procedures, reassigning or adding personnel, using different types of people, managing more effectively, getting more information, using different equipment, and so on. But improperly set

plans can also cause deviations. If the objective is far too high, we are not likely to achieve it consistently, regardless of how determined our efforts are at plucking the prize. In this case, management needs to restudy its information and set more realistic goals.

Major Problems in Controlling

Control methods are an attempt to prevent and correct problems, but they sometimes create problems of their own.

High cost of control. Control costs money. Quality control departments in some companies have budgets running into hundreds of thousands of dollars. If we compute the hours managers spend in everyday control functions — budgeting, performance appraisal, correcting mistakes, and constructive criticism — the total cost mounts.

Repressive control. Sometimes managers place so many demands on their employees, trying to control their behavior, the controls become repressive. This overcontrol may gain observable compliance, but employees become frustrated, tense, and anxiety-ridden. They express their resistance in creating alibis, slanting the truth, passing the buck, and undercutting the boss's wishes. At the same time, job satisfaction and morale go down, while absenteeism and turnover go up.

Objective displacement. Displacement occurs when policies, procedures, and rules become more important than objectives. Guidelines are necessary, but their only purpose is to help people achieve the organization's objectives more effectively. Too often, policies, procedures, and rules outlive their usefulness, yet someone in the organization may insist on following them.

Feedback problems. Control relies on feedback as a measure of success, but some managers get so involved with the numbers that they forget other important issues. And sometimes employees and managers try to manipulate measurement data just to make the numbers look good. In fact, overemphasis on numbers may lead employees to inaccurate reporting, distrust, and hostility.

THE MANAGEMENT PROCESS AND THE ENTREPRENEUR

This chapter has presented management in the context of large organizations. While these concepts do apply to small business entrepreneurs, applications may differ. Entrepreneurs still plan, organize, direct, and control their organizations, but they do it on a smaller scale and with fewer people. Typically, this means that the manager is unable to specialize. For instance, large organizations will likely have different managers for sales, finance, production, and so on. Each of these managers is specialized. However, in smaller organizations, one manager may be responsible for sales, finance, hiring, discipline, customer service, inventory control, and sweeping up after closing the doors.

Lack of specialization may be a drawback, but small business managers also have some advantages over larger companies. For instance, employees today insist on participation in decision making. Larger companies are trying to do this, but smaller companies can probably do it more effectively. Because smaller companies are more informal and spontaneous, it is easier for the manager to seek input from employees in decision making. Further, participation requires a lot of

A computer game under development receives an impromptu staff appraisal. Such informality is often the rule in the small startup companies of this growth industry.

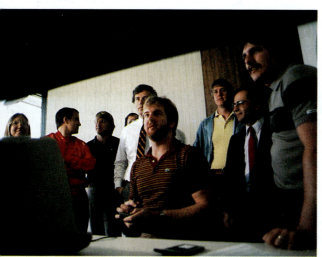

information. Again, smaller companies, with their informal associations between manager and employee, can more easily communicate information to the employees. Small companies also are better able to get their people to think about themselves as a total group, as a team. Smaller companies are less likely to have separate dining and parking privileges for management and employees, and this makes it more comfortable for them to work together as a team. Finally, smaller organizations can be more flexible in dealing with their employees. If, for example, a single parent needs to schedule unique working hours, the small business manager is more likely to be aware of this and more likely to be able to accommodate the worker.

SUMMARY

Management functions include planning, organizing, directing, and controlling. Planning is deciding in advance the objectives to be accomplished and developing guidelines for reaching them. Nearly all companies have monthly and yearly plans; many plan for 5 years and some plan for 20 or 30 years.

Examples of common plans are objectives, policies, procedures, rules, and budgets. Effective planners follow a sequential, rational approach to the planning process, including the following steps: recognize opportunities, select planning objectives, identify and create alternatives, and follow up.

Organizing is the management process of arranging employees of a business so that they can best accomplish the organization's objectives. Lines of authority and channels of communication are established. Organizing is most often accomplished by means of an organization chart. Such a chart also provides structure for the organization and methods for hiring and training employees.

There are three basic levels of management: top management, middle management, and operations management. At each of these levels, the manager's time is divided into a different combination of management processes. Effective organization provides many worthwhile benefits to a company.

Directing involves leading, motivating, and aiding employees toward the accomplishment of the firm's objectives. It ensures that tasks are performed properly. The process of control includes communicating plans, checking actual events against plans, and correcting the differences. While there are some negative effects of control, it is necessary to be certain that efforts are successful and effective.

MIND YOUR BUSINESS

Instructions. Check your knowledge of the management process by answering true (T) or false (F) to the following questions.

____ 1. When you get into management, success depends only upon human, interpersonal skills; technical skills are not needed.

____ 2. To be effective, objectives need to meet all of the following requirements: challenging but realistic, specific and measurable, supported by superiors, and communicated to all people in the organization.

____ 3. Procedures are guides to thinking, while policies are specific guides to action.

____ 4. One purpose of organizing is to define job functions, descriptions, and relationships.

____ 5. "Most people work as little as possible," is a Theory Y assumption.

____ 6. "Commitment to lifetime employment," is an aspect of Theory Y.

____ 7. Excellently managed organizations tend to have a strong bias for action, that is, doing something.

____ 8. High cost is a problem with most control systems.

____ 9. It is easier to get employee participation in smaller organizations than it is in larger ones.

____ 10. Research clearly shows that a business or M.B.A. degree will more likely lead to managerial success than a liberal arts degree.

See answers at the back of the book.

KEY TERMS

management, 130
manager, 130
planning, 130
short-range planning, 130
tactical planning, 130
long-range planning, 131
strategic planning, 131
objective, 132
policy, 132
procedure, 132
rule, 132
budget, 132
organizing, 134
top management, 135
middle management, 135
operating management, 136
directing, 137
leadership, 137
traitist theory, 137
situationalist theory, 137
autocratic leadership, 138
democratic leadership, 138
free-rein leadership, 138
contingency leadership, 138
style flexibility, 138
Theory X, 139
Theory Y, 139
Theory Z, 142
controlling, 142

REVIEW QUESTIONS

1. What is a manager? What do managers do?

2. Define planning. How far into the future do managers plan? Explain. Distinguish between strategic planning and tactical planning.

3. Identify and describe the most common types of plans.

4. Explain the planning process and identify the six major steps to planning.

5. Define organizing. What is involved in the organizing process?

6. Identify the levels of management with examples of job titles for each.

7. How do the levels of management differ?

8. Explain the differences of duties for each of the three levels of managers.

9. What are the benefits of good organization?

10. Define directing. What does it involve?

11. Discuss the theories of leadership.

12. What is the difference between a Theory X and a Theory Y manager? How does Theory Z differ?

13. Define controlling. How does an organizational control system work?

14. Explain the four major steps in the controlling process.

15. Describe the four major problems of the controlling process.

CASES

Case 6.1: A Tough Leader?

Phil Drew is the supervisor of a construction crew. He often argues with his people, berates them, and curses when they make mistakes. Turnover is high, but Phil can always hire additional people because the pay is good and unemployment is high in the local area. The workers despise Phil, but they work pretty hard because they do not want him on their backs all day. They are actually afraid of Phil, who has been known to become violent from time to time. The crew seldom talks back and they stay out of his way as much as possible. Phil can never leave, even for a few minutes, because the crew will loaf around or ruin a job.

Phil is known by contractors as a very responsible supervisor who gets the job done on time and in the manner planned. They know that once Phil agrees to do a job they can depend upon him.

Questions

1. How would you analyze Phil's leadership style?

2. Would you like to work for Phil? Why?

3. Would you like Phil to work for you? Why?

4. Would you regard Phil as a good leader? Explain.

Case 6.2: A Business Failure

As director of marketing for the Sony Corporation, manufacturers of stereo equipment, Roberta had her hands full. Because she felt the need for more control over her forty-five sales representatives, she quickly designed a complex form that they were to complete after each work day. Because the form took about one hour to complete—mostly on their own time after the day's work—the sales force was up in arms. Roberta insisted upon receiving the forms and has four months' worth on her desk. Roberta has had three secretaries in the past six months. They say they leave because there is not enough flexibility and freedom on the job. They had to deliver coffee to her at precisely the same time, four times a day. If their work was not completed at the end of the day, they stayed late regardless.

Roberta has three regional sales managers, yet she works and communicates directly with each representative whenever possible. She spends most of her time directing her forty-eight salespeople and staff of five. Because of morale problems, turnover, and lack of results, Roberta was put on probation three months ago. Last week she was fired.

Questions

1. Of the six steps of the planning process, which did Roberta fail?

2. Why was Roberta unsuccessful as a leader? What style of leader was she? How could she have changed her tactics and become a more successful leader?

3. What was the one glaring mistake she made with regard to the organizing process? How could better organizing practices have benefited her?

4. Which steps of the control process were ignored by Roberta? What should she have done in order to have been successful?

After completing this chapter, you will be able to:

■ Define the term "corporate culture."

■ Identify and describe the four elements of corporate culture.

■ Describe how heroes, storytellers, and priests help create and promote corporate culture.

■ Relate the importance of rites and rituals to corporate culture.

■ Compare and contrast the four generic corporate cultures.

■ Explain why corporate culture must sometimes be changed.

■ Relate some of the most successful ways of managing corporate culture change.

A

CORPORATE

CULTURE

Every company has a culture. Sometimes we are given insights into this culture by the organizational motto or the things we hear others say about it. For example, General Electric's motto is "Progress is our most important product." From this, we are led to believe that this firm strives to recruit and keep personnel who are highly educated, innovative, creative, and hardworking. Would someone who enjoys working in a stuffy bureaucracy consider applying for a job at GE? Probably not. The corporate culture would be viewed as too threatening to such an individual. Or consider IBM. This company's image is one of quality products and timely service. It is a no-nonsense firm in which people work hard and are well rewarded, but there is no place for laggards or goldbricks.

Corporate culture is the norms, beliefs, attitudes, and philosophies of the organization. Organizational culture is shaped by the values of the people who start the organization and those who carry on its leadership. In successful firms, these managers actually shape and encourage the "right" types of personnel values. In fact, most of these companies share three common organizational culture characteristics: (1) they stand for something, that is, they have a clear and explicit philosophy about how they should conduct their business; (2) management pays a lot of attention to shaping and encouraging values so that they conform to the environment in which the company operates; and (3) these values are both known and shared by the personnel. These characteristics create a sense of identity for the people who work there. The personnel feel special. And this sense of togetherness helps build and maintain high esprit de corps.

Organizations with a strong culture also have an informal system of rules. The personnel know how they are supposed to behave most of the time. A strong culture also helps the personnel feel better about what they are doing. For example, an IBM salesperson can proudly say, "I'm with IBM. It's a great firm!" And the individual means it. He or she feels a commitment to the organization, and this translates into greater efficiency and higher sales.

ELEMENTS OF CULTURE

How does a company create an organizational culture that encourages high productivity, efficiency, and esprit de corps? Often it does so by consciously fashioning a specific value system. For example, during his early years at IBM, Thomas Watson, Jr., taught the salespeople his own personal philosophy of work and life. By putting strong emphasis on selling, urging them not to waste time, and encouraging them always to think, he built the company into the premier office equipment corporation in the world. Today he is gone, but his values live on because the three

The major elements of culture are heroes, rites and rituals, and a communication network.

major elements of culture are still present at IBM: heroes, rites and rituals, and a communication network that conveys Watson's values to every part of the corporation.

Heroes

Heroes are an integral element of corporate culture. They serve as role models for the personnel. People identify with them and attempt to emulate them. Every company has its heroes. Watson was a hero at IBM. Edwin Land, founder of the Polaroid Corporation, has been a hero there for years; young employees are continually encouraged to follow his examples of innovativeness and hard work. Yet it is not necessary to be a giant in the field to serve as a hero or role model in the organization. Consider the following two cases:

> Richard A. Drew, a banjo-playing college dropout working in 3M's research lab in the 1920s, promised to help some colleagues solve a problem they had with masking tape. Soon thereafter, DuPont came out with cellophane. Drew decided he could go DuPont one better and coated the cellophane with a colorless adhesive to bind things together — and Scotch tape was born. In the 3M tradition, Drew carried the ball himself by managing the development up through the ranks; he went on to become technical director of the company and showed other employees just how they could succeed in a similar fashion at 3M.
>
> Mary Kay Ash, founder of Mary Kay Cosmetics, believes in offering herself as a visible role model to her employees. She trains saleswomen not simply to represent her but to believe that they *are* Mary Kay. To inspire them with her own confidence, she awards diamond bumblebee pins and explains that, according to aerodynamic engineers, the wings of the bumblebee are too weak and the body is too heavy for the insect to fly. But bumblebees don't know this, and so they fly anyway. The message is clear: anyone can be a hero who has the confidence and persistence to try *

Heroes play a very important role in promoting corporate culture. First, they symbolize the organization to the outside world. Consider some of the popular top managers who do their own commercials, like Lee Iacocca of Chrysler Corporation. These people, heroes in their organization,

convey an image to the TV viewer of the type of company they represent. A second important role played by heroes is preserving what makes the corporation special. The values that have helped bring the company to its current position are maintained, thanks to the hero's ability to inspire emulation by the personnel. Third, the hero helps set a standard of performance in the organization. The hero represents the very best, and, as other employees attempt to emulate this person, they achieve higher standards of performance than would be the case otherwise. Heroes serve to motivate employees.

Rites and Rituals

Rites and rituals are important to corporate culture because they help reinforce desired behavior. For example, when someone does something well, like sell $1 million of insurance, the company will often award the individual a plaque. This is just a token; however, it serves as a way of saying thank you. In many instances, these plaques or awards are given at a dinner or special ceremony. For example, at Mary Kay there is an awards night in which the spotlight is placed on those who have done well. There is an extravaganza in which the leading saleswoman of the year is crowned. Diamonds, minks, and cars are given to those who have done well. At the end of the ceremony, it is

The annual awards presentation of Mary Kay Cosmetics is a distinctive ritual in this company's culture.

* Terrence E. Deal and Allan A. Kennedy, *Corporate Cultures* © 1982 Addison-Wesley Publishing Company, Inc., Reading, Mass., pp. 39–40. Reprinted by permission.

obvious to all that the number 1 rule in the firm is to sell.

Yet these rituals need not be so elaborate. In hospitals, it is common for surgeons to scrub down for about 7 minutes before an operation. In fact, most germs are destroyed within 30 seconds. However, the 7-minute scrub-down time is a ritual and to stop before this time is to break the ritual — a signal that the surgeon is ill-prepared. Other rituals are geared more for recognition. Consider the following.

> At Intel, when someone does something well, the founder calls him or her in, reaches in his desk, and produces a handful of M&Ms as a sign of recognition. The ceremony began years ago, and now everyone keeps a supply of these candies ready.

The giving and receiving makes everyone feel good.

> At Addison-Wesley Publishing Company, a bronze star is passed from one achiever to the next. At the same time, a "Martyr of the Week" award consoles the person having the roughest time. The point here is the recognition that even a good worker can have a bad time.*

Rites and rituals are important because they reinforce the actions of those who are doing well. Others in the organization who want to be rewarded need to emulate the behavior of these individuals. Additionally, rites and rituals legitimatize the reward process. They say, "Here is

---

* *Ibid.*, p. 72.

Example of a Hero

"He has been compared to an evangelist, a football coach, and all sorts of things. He gives chances to people who would never have had it," is the way Judge William Enfield describes Sam Walton, the founder and "hero" of the very successful Wal-Mart Discount City Stores.

Sam Walton has made Wal-Mart successful by locating stores in smaller communities, hiring rural strivers with a strong work ethic, and living the simple, small-town philosophy. He also makes a strong effort to infuse enthusiasm and pride in their work. On most Saturday mornings, Sam Walton will be in Bentonville, Arkansas, leading cheers for his buyers, truckers, clerks, warehouse workers, and other executives.

Many storytellers relate incidents that perpetuate the Walton value system. John Jeffers, president of the Bentonville Chamber of Commerce, says, "The Waltons are givers, not takers. They don't live in a mansion in the center of town and try to run everything." The community banker said, "I am totally convinced that if a petition was passed around, you could legally change the name of the town to Waltonville. They're super great people."

Sam Walton appreciates small-town values, and small-town consumers appreciate him. He still starts each day with a predawn breakfast at the Bentonville Holiday Inn. And he holds the annual stockholder's meeting in the high school gym. People say he likes to hunt quail and he likes to work. He named his line of dog food after his favorite bird dog, "Old Roy, 1970 – 1981. Gone but not forgotten."

According to former Wal-Mart president, Ferold Arend, Sam's philosophy is simple: "You treat your people right, pay 'em right and listen to them, and you can't go wrong." These values lived out by this corporate hero have made consumers and employees happy, stockholders wealthy (if you had bought a thousand shares in 1970 for $2000, you would be worth $2.5 million today), the community prosperous, and Sam Walton the second-richest man in the United States.

someone who did an outstanding job. This is the reward we gave that person. Do the same and you will be rewarded."

Communication Network

While rites and rituals help communicate desired behaviors, effective organizations try to influence the behavior of personnel from the moment they begin working for the company. These firms tell their people what they expect of them and try to guide them along the desired paths. In this regard, it is common to find heavy reliance being made on "storytellers" and "priests."

The storyteller's basic theme always remains the same: Work hard and you will succeed.

A **storyteller** is an individual who has been around the organization a long time and has done an outstanding job. The individual is someone whom the organization would like its personnel to emulate. One way of achieving this is by having the old-timer share some stories with the new people. The exact story will differ from storyteller to storyteller, however, the basic theme always remains the same: Work hard and you will succeed.

The following is a typical example of what a storyteller might relate.

When I was just starting out with this firm back in 1946 I was given three western states and told "get out there and sell our new calculators." Well, I had never been to Utah before so when I got there in mid-December I couldn't believe how cold it was. Coming from Alabama, I was unaccustomed to this weather. Nevertheless, I checked into the biggest hotel in Salt Lake City and turned in early so that I'd be up on time for my 9 A.M. meeting with the president of the largest bank in the city. When I awoke, it was snowing hard. I couldn't believe my eyes. I got dressed and ran out in front of the hotel. The flakes were coming down so fast, I couldn't see 10 feet ahead of me. Nevertheless, I knew where the bank was and figured I could walk over there in a few minutes. First, however, I ran back inside and asked the desk clerk where the nearest hardware

store was. He told me and I walked over there. When the store opened at 8:30 A.M. I went in and bought a snow shovel. I then went over to the bank and positioned myself outside the main door. I knew the president would be showing up early because he wanted to talk to me before starting business for the day. As soon as I saw a car drive up at 8:45 I knew it was him. I shoveled a path from the bank door to his car. When he got out, I said, "Hi. I'm Bob Petersen. I think we have a 9 A.M. meeting. I thought I'd get here early and help you get through all of this snow." He was impressed by my initiative and assistance. And later in the bank when I made my sales presentation to him, I continually stressed that our business sells products and stands behind them. I told him, "You can rely on us." He smiled and told me, "If you take as good care of me as you did this morning, I know I'll be in good hands." He then gave me a large order for calculators. We won't leave you out in the snow. We shovel a path for you and make sure that you stay on it. If you have a problem, we're there to pick you up.

This type of story is typical of those told by storytellers. It is particularly effective when employed by old-timers around the corporation who can recall the early days when things were difficult. Young people joining the firm identify with these stories and those who tell them. It is not uncommon to hear these stories repeated over and over again. It becomes part of the folklore of the firm.

Quite often the storyteller will enhance the tale by showing some type of physical evidence related to the episode. For example, the individual in the preceding story might have a snow shovel mounted on the wall of his office. Everyone dropping by sees the shovel and is reminded of the story. New employees who see the shovel but have not heard the story will undoubtedly ask questions. So they too will learn what happened. The shovel story serves to reinforce certain values that the organizaton wants its people to accept; work hard, be prepared for any eventuality, and show the customers that they can count on us.

Priests in the corporation are very much like clerical priests. They try to guard the congregation's values and keep the flock together. They also, in their own way, listen to confessions and offer recommendations for action.

In organizatonal culture terms, priests are those who have been around the firm for a long time and have seen a lot of things happen. They are very familiar with the past history of the organization, and, while a priest in a religious order might respond to a question by citing the Bible, an organizational culture priest will cite a past event in the firm's history. For example, a young manager might ask an older one about a recommended plan of action she is considering, involving special price discounts to large-quantity buyers. The older one might reply, "We suggested that same plan to the board of directors back in 1963. They rejected it because they felt this firm sells quality. They don't want us to get a reputation as a discounter. No one has ever again suggested discounting." Result? The young manager

CROSS FIRE

Are the Skills of Managing Different from the Skills of Leading?

With the new emphasis on heroes, storytellers, and corporate culture, an old debate is emerging, "What skills or abilities are necessary for effective leadership?"

For some time now, we have been teaching that a good manager needs to be skilled at planning, organizing, directing, and controlling an organization. This typically requires skills in financial analysis, long-range planning, structural design, and control systems. Managers, to be effective, must be rational, logical, controlled, and able to take the initiative in problem solving. The image of a good manager, oversimplified of course, is one who can use intelligence to analyze a problem, discover the most reasonable alternative, and execute the decision.

However, Dr. Abraham Zaleznik, endowed chairholder at the Harvard Business School, says that the psychology of leaders differs dramatically from that of managers. He says that managers, without much emotion, get things done through contractual relationships within an organization. But leaders, often with much emotion and perhaps even irrational thinking, change the course of events.

A typical manager might try to get people to do things for money or other rewards, or out of fear. For instance, a manager might communicate, "We need to work hard to reach our quarterly projections of 5% increase in return on investment." But a leader, relying upon more intuitive "gut feeling," might passionately exhort his group to, "Apply yourselves to the highest task of all, providing our customers with satisfaction and joy."

Typical Freudian managers have strong consciences that keep them feeling guilty with low self-confidence. Their aggressive tendencies will then result in attacks on themselves and others. The result will likely be distrust of subordinates and peers, overuse of corporate policies, battles over turf, win–lose confrontations, and demoralizing of others.

Leaders, because they do not have such strong consciences, are more secure and look for help from others. They are more willing to turn people loose, but at the same time, more forthright. Leaders might bluntly tell people when they are not performing up to the mark and they may even fire people and worry about it less than managers. The manager tends to be a worrier, the leader a doer. The manager says, "How well am I doing?" The leader says, "Are we getting the job done?"

Do you believe that managers and leaders are psychologically different? Why?

___ A. Yes   ___ B. No

Given the preceding descriptions of managers and leaders, which do you think would be most effective guiding an organization over the long term? Why?

___ A. A manager   ___ B. A leader

scraps her plan. She knows from past history that it won't work. It flies in the face of the company's values. Thanks to the priest, she has saved herself from making a proposal that will be turned down. Deal and Kennedy offer additional insights of priests in action.

> Priests also aid people in event of defeat, frustration, and disappointment. The person who handles worldwide assignments of managers is one company's favorite priest. A young manager will walk into his office and say, "My God, I've been assigned 18 months with our South American divisions. I'll be away from the heart of the action, and I came here to get a lot of experience. What's the use?" By the time he leaves the priest's office, he will have been told indirectly about how the company's chief executive officer spent 10 years working in Brazil. The manager won't know what's happened to him because of the meandering, eccentric way storytellers work, yet he'll trudge off feeling, "Maybe I can spend 10 years with this division and wind up as CEO." Stories are parables that motivate others and extend the power of the effective storyteller.*

IDENTIFYING CULTURES

The easiest way to examine a particular organization's culture is in terms of risk and feedback. What kinds of risk does the firm take? How much time elapses before the organization finds out if it made the right or wrong decision? Risks can be classified into two categories: high or low. Feedback can be classified into two categories: fast or slow. The result is four generic cultures. These cultures are briefly sketched out in Table A.1.

Tough-Guy, Macho

The **tough-guy, macho culture** is typical in organizations where people make high-risk decisions. For example, a person producing a Broadway play may invest $10 million (along with other backers, of course) and spend three months in rehearsal and on the road before bringing the play to New York City. There, after opening night, the individual learns whether the play will be a success or not. The risk is great, and within 24 hours of the Broadway opening there is feedback.

---

* *Ibid.*, p. 89.

Tough-guy, macho types are opportunistic, individualistic, and enjoy winning.

People who function well in this environment are often young and stress speed over endurance. The entrepreneur who makes $1 million before the age of 21 is an example. Tough-guy, macho types like the fast-paced environment. They are opportunistic, individualistic, and enjoy winning. They are also creative both in terms of their work (they look for unique solutions) and their life-style (they wear designer clothing, drive expensive sports cars, and live in one-of-a-kind houses).

Work Hard/Play Hard

The **work hard/play hard culture** is typified by individuals who are successful in a low-risk, fast feedback environment. Sales organizations typically fall into this category. If the salesperson does not make a sale, it usually is not the end of the world. However, the individual often finds out very quickly if the sale is made. Some of the firms that fall into this category include Mary Kay Cosmetics, IBM, Bloomingdale's, Xerox, and Digital Equipment.

Survivors in this environment tend to be supersalespeople. They are also team players, knowing that the success of the enterprise depends on their ability to work in unison with one another. For example, the people in sales know the importance of coordinating their efforts with production so that delivery promises can be kept.

Survivors in the work hard/play hard environment tend to be very high achievers, but they do not go to extremes.

Research and development knows the value of its input to new product lines and the importance of having these products ready for manufacturing at the agreed-upon time. Survivors in this environment also like feedback on how well they are doing and tend to be very high achievers. They dress well and often live in nice houses. However, in contrast to the tough-guy, macho types, they do not go to extremes.

TABLE A.1 ■ ORGANIZATIONAL CULTURE PROFILES

	Tough-Guy, Macho	Work Hard/Play Hard
Type of risks that are assumed	High	Low
Type of feedback from decisions	Fast	Fast
Typical kinds of organizations that use this culture	Construction, cosmetics, TV, radio, venture capitalism, management consulting.	Real estate, computer firms, auto distributors, door-to-door sales operations, retail stores, mass consumer sales.
Ways survivors and/or heroes in this culture behave	Have a tough attitude. Are individualistic. Can tolerate all-or-nothing risks. Are superstitious.	Are supersalespeople. Often are friendly, hail-fellow-well-met types. Use a team approach to problem solving. Are nonsuperstitious.
Strengths of the personnel/culture	They can get things done in short order.	They are able to produce a high volume of work quickly.
Weaknesses of the personnel/culture	They do not learn from past mistakes. Everything tends to be short-term in orientation. The virtues of cooperation are ignored.	They look for quick-fix solutions. They have a short-term time perspective. They are more committed to action than to problem-solving.
Habits of the survivors and/or heroes	They dress in fashion. They live in "in" places. They like one-on-one sports such as tennis. They enjoy scoring points off one another in verbal interaction.	They avoid extremes in dress. They live in tract houses. They prefer team sports such as touch football. They like to drink together.

Source: Adapted from Terrence E. Deal and Allan A. Kennedy, *Corporate Cultures: The Rites and Rituals of Corporate Life*, Reading, Mass.: Addison-Wesley Publishing, 1982, Chapter 6.

Bet Your Company

The **bet-your-company culture** is characterized by high risk and slow feedback. There are many examples of organizations that fit into this

Oil exploration firms typify the high-risk, slow-feedback nature of the bet-your-company culture.

category. Banks, aerospace firms, oil exploration firms, capital goods manufacturers, and the military are examples. People in these organizations often put their careers on the line by risking the future of their entire enterprise. Michael Murphy, an investment analyst for Venture Capital Management, says that Apple Computer is "betting the whole company on the Macintosh," their new personal computer that is competing head to head with IBM's PC. "If Mac is a flop," says Murphy, "Apple doesn't stand a chance. It will just disappear."

Consider oil explorers. It may cost $5 million and a year's time from when a firm decides where to look for oil until it finds out whether there is oil in that location. If the company is right, it stands to make a lot of money. If it is wrong, the entire investment is lost. Or consider the military. If the navy builds a superaircraft carrier but sea power over the next 10 years is decided by submarines, the organization has made a serious mistake. Any time a decision is made regarding defense spending, whether it be for a new fighter aircraft or an MX missile system, a mistake can be detrimental to

TABLE A.1 ■ (Continued)

Bet Your Company	Process
High	Low
Slow	Slow
Oil, aerospace, capital goods manufacturers, architectural firms, investment banks, mining and smelting firms, military.	Banks, insurance companies, utilities, pharmaceuticals, financial service organizations, many agencies of the government.
Can endure long-term ambiguity. Always double-check their decisions. Are technically competent. Have a strong respect for authority.	Are very cautious and protective of their own flank. Are orderly and punctual. Are good at attending to detail. Always follow established procedures.
They can generate high-quality inventions and major scientific breakthroughs.	They bring order and system to the work place.
They are extremely slow in getting things done. Their organizations are vulnerable to short-term economic fluctuations. Their organizations often face cash-flow problems.	There is lots of red tape. Initiative is downplayed. They face long hours and boring work.
They dress according to their organizational rank. Their housing matches their hierarchical position. They like sports where the outcome is unclear until the end such as golf. The older members serve as mentors for the younger ones.	They dress according to hierarchical rank. They live in apartments, or no-frills homes. They enjoy process sports like jogging and swimming. They like discussing memos.

the interests of the country. There is a lot at risk in bet-your-company cultures, but the participants only find out if they were right or wrong after a number of months or years have elapsed.

Survivors in this environment need to have the stamina to endure the long-run ambiguity and lack of feedback. For this reason, it is common to find them checking and double-checking their decisions. They don't want to make a mistake. These individuals also respect authority and technical competence since they are so important to success in this environment. Their life-style is much more sedate than the tough-guy, macho people. For example, their housing tends to fit with their rank in the organizational hierarchy.

Process

The **process culture** environment is characterized by low risk and low feedback. Typical examples operating in this culture include banks, insurance companies, utilities, and governmental agencies. Consider banks. Customers are judged

on the basis of their credit worthiness. Does the person have collateral to back up the loan? Can the individual repay the principal and the interest? If so, the person usually is judged a good risk and given the money. The risk is (or at least is supposed to be) low. How does the bank know it will get back its money? Only time will tell. However, given the fact that the applicant has been checked out, the loan should be safe. Of course, it does not always turn out that way. For example, in the last couple of years, many banks that have loaned money to South American governments have found the latter unable to repay. Mexico and Poland are other examples. Unfortunately, the banks were unable to forecast economic problems in these countries. So only after a nation announced that it was unable to meet debt obligations did it become evident that the loan was much higher risk than was initially believed.

Survivors in the process culture tend to be very cautious and protective. They follow the rules, write memos on everything, and observe all procedures. Titles and formalities are very important. Bureaucratic behavior is commonplace. It even affects life-style. For example, when it comes to athletics, personnel like process sports like jogging and swimming.

RESHAPING CULTURES

Corporate culture is an important area in business today because it helps dictate how people in the structure will behave. However, this behavior is not fixed; it can be changed through a reshaping process should this be necessary.

When Change Is Necessary

Change in corporate culture can become necessary in certain instances. One instance is when the environment in which the firm is operating undergoes fundamental change. The culture may have to be altered. For example, in the case of AT&T, there have been significant changes over the last 5 years. Local operating companies have been taken away, and the firm now consists of but three major parts: Bell Laboratories (research and development), Western Electric (manufacturing equipment) and long lines (long distance). AT&T used to have no competition. Now it must vie with a host of competitors. In the case of manufactured equipment, there are many companies currently offering telephones to the general public. It is no longer necessary to get a phone from Ma Bell. In the case of long distance calls, MCI, Sprint, and a host of others offer reduced long-distance rates. How is all this affecting AT&T? While it is still too early to tell, there must be a tremendous internal change taking place.

Second, when an industry is highly competitive and the environment changes quickly, the

TAKING STOCK

Creating a Corporate Culture

Harry V. Quadracci, president of Quad/Graphics, has been very successful in creating a strong work-oriented culture among his employees. His firm, employing about 700 people, is a printing company with customers like *Newsweek, Harper's,* and *U.S. News & World Report.*

Like most companies that have a strong culture, the president, Quadracci in this case, takes a significant role in establishing shared values. He personally instructs the beginning printing course that all new employees must take. And he says that he does not automatically trust new employees to be responsible. New hires cannot even wear the company uniform until they have served a rigorous 2-month probation period. He believes that most of his new people are "kids," and "they don't all have their heads screwed on right." Half are under 24, and most have never had a full-time job.

Quadracci admits, "They get indoctrinated, brainwashed. . . . They're raw recruits, and as far as we're concerned, they're in boot camp for about 2 years," he adds. The values most cherished by Quadracci, and therefore spread to the work force, appear to be:

- Performance is everything.
- Nobody gets points for seniority.
- Absenteeism and sloth will not be tolerated.
- Most important is pride and exacting standards in the work they turn out.

However, the company also encourages participation and freedom among its people, after they have served their proving period, of course. Each year, the entire

Organizational changes in AT&T after the 1983 divestiture ruling no doubt have altered its culture as well.

culture may have to change as well. For example, the Digital Equipment Corporation (DEC) has always been very competitive in the computer field. Every time there has been a change in customer needs, the firm has adapted to that end of the market and succeeded. However, in recent years, DEC has not moved into the microcomputer field quickly enough. For whatever reason, the firm allowed Apple and IBM to get a big jump on them. The DEC personal computer (PC) does not appear to be a serious challenge to IBM's PC. DEC's culture has not changed fast enough to keep it strong in this part of the computer market.

Third, when a firm is mediocre or worse, a change in culture is needed. Eastern Airlines is a good example. Before Frank Borman took over, the firm was in terrible shape. Although Borman has not managed to turn the airline into one of the big money makers, he has prevented collapse.

top management team leaves the workers in charge of everything while they retreat to do their planning. The early cultural indoctrination process apparently develops employees management can trust. Quadracci says, "Our people shouldn't need me or anybody else to tell them what to do." When the firm was growing and adding new operations, he tapped people with expertise—both internal and external—and told them they were entrepreneurs and turned them loose. They were very successful; some of the groups won awards for innovations and many sell some of the products to others—including competitors.

On the one hand, Quad/Graphics is very demanding; and on the other hand, people have a lot of freedom and participate significantly in major company decisions. The company also appreciates its employees by providing:

- An employee stock ownership plan.
- A profit-sharing program.
- An extensive list of benefits.
- Numerous employee education and training programs.
- Luxurious working facilities.
- A $3 million sports center.
- Original art, even in the locker room.

All this is apparently working; 1983 sales volume for the 11-year-old company was $75 million.

Source: Ellen Wojahn, "Management by Walking Away," *Inc.,* Oct. 1983, pp. 68–76.

This was done by changing the culture to an overriding orientation toward customer service, coupled with a sense of shared commitment to the firm's welfare by both management and employees.

Fourth, when a firm is on the threshold of becoming a large company, a change in culture is often required. Things cannot go along as before. There has to be greater attention to building teamwork, as opposed to encouraging everyone to go their own way as they did when the firm was small and growing.

Managing Cultural Change Successfully

Cultural change has to be managed skillfully. While there are a number of ways of doing this, most are complementary. Some of the most useful

BUSINESS BULLETIN

Changing the Corporate Culture

The vast majority of companies believe that shared company values are very important to the success of a firm. This was the finding of a survey of 305 chief executives by William M. Mercer, Inc., a New York consulting firm.

The need to be able to change seems to be greater than ever, because of deregulation, technological upheavals, competition from abroad, and rapidly changing markets. Yet, according to top management consultants, only about one company in ten can successfully effect a significant change. They believe the reason that change is so hard to execute is an inability to deal with the organization's culture.

The Management Analysis Center (MAC) of Cambridge, Massachusetts, has developed a plan called the CEO's Change Agenda which they use to help organizations change their culture. Their plan involves the following steps:

1. Top managers of the firm examine the company's history, culture, skills, and traits.
2. The chief executive should then forge a new vision, a new strategy, and new values for the firm.
3. The chief executive officer (CEO), in speeches, memos, and informal contacts, sells the new way at every opportunity.
4. CEOs are told to reflect their new values in everything they do: who they spend their time with, what they choose to emphasize with their subordinates, and the like.
5. CEOs should reshuffle their power figures and hire outsiders specifically for the new values the firm is preaching.
6. Managers must use the budgeting process, internal public relations, and all other levers at their command to encourage the change.

While the MAC group treats corporate culture as a global process linked to strategic planning, other consulting groups rely upon more traditional methods. For instance, many rely upon surveys to determine how people perceive the organization. Then they provide feedback to the managers, based on their surveys. Finally, they design a plan for changing the values and attitudes they feel need changing.

Source: Bro Uttal, "The Corporate Culture Vultures," *Fortune*, Oct. 17, 1983, pp. 66–70.

successful steps have been the following:

1. Put a hero in charge of the process. Many people in the organization already identify with this person. When he or she encourages them to change, do things a different way, accept a new approach to their jobs, etc., they are likely to listen and respond accordingly.

2. Use transition rituals to bring about change. By setting up meetings in which people can talk about their concerns and learn how the company is changing and why, there is the opportunity to win personnel support for the new cultural values.

3. Bring in outside assistance. Where useful, consultants should be brought in from outside to discuss necessary changes and make useful recommendations regarding how these changes should be implemented.

4. Ensure security during the transition. A company must ensure that no one is arbitrarily fired along the way. Otherwise these people become martyrs, and the change process breaks down. Keeping people around is an important ingredient of successful change.

Steps such as these are vital in helping reshape corporate culture. They also assist in seeing that the new values result in the desired behaviors.

SUMMARY

Corporate culture is the beliefs, attitudes, values, and philosophies of an organization. This culture helps dictate what personnel will do and how they will do it. There are three elements of corporate culture: heroes, rites and rituals, and communication of the culture. Heroes are individuals who symbolize the company to the outside world and set standards of performance. They also serve as a role model for other personnel. Rites and rituals are behaviors and ceremonies that are carried out in support of the desired culture. Typical examples include monetary rewards, plaques, vacation trips, etc., which are given out at recognition dinners. The culture itself is communicated through these formal recognition procedures. However, there are additional ways of communicating culture including the use of storytellers and

priests. Both use past company history and experience to guide and shape the thinking of personnel, reinforcing the culture in the process.

There are four basic types of corporate culture: tough-guy, macho; work hard/play hard; bet your company; and process. There are certain types of industries or environments in which one culture is much more prevalent than the others. Those who survive in their respective culture tend to adopt the values and behaviors that allow them to adjust most effectively to their environment.

Sometimes it is necessary to reshape a corporate culture. This can occur when the environment undergoes a fundamental change, when the industry is highly competitive and the environment changes quickly, when the firm is mediocre, or when the firm is on the threshold of becoming a large company. In successfully managing cultural change, there are a number of things managers should consider doing. Four of the most helpful include: (1) put a hero in charge of the process; (2) use transition rituals to bring about the change; (3) bring in outside assistance; and (4) ensure personnel security during the transition.

MIND YOUR BUSINESS

Instructions. Answer each of the following questions with a Y (yes) or N (no).

____ 1. Is organization culture something that can be defined?

____ 2. Are heroes important to the organization's culture?

____ 3. Are storytellers harmful to the organization's culture?

____ 4. Are priests in the organization culture much like clerical priests?

____ 5. Is the tough-guy, macho culture one that is likely to take a long-term view of things?

____ 6. Would supersalespeople likely be associated with the work hard/play hard culture?

____ 7. Are order and slow response to change characteristic of the bet-your-company culture?

____ 8. Would executives of the process culture be likely to enjoy jogging and swimming?

___ 9. If you wanted to change the organization culture, would you be likely to put a hero in charge of the process?

___ 10. Are outside consultants considered helpful when trying to change an organizaton culture?

_____

See answers at the back of the book.

REVIEW QUESTIONS

1. In your own words, what is meant by the term "corporate culture"?

2. How can a hero help a company develop a corporate culture? Give an example.

3. How do rites and rituals help develop corporate culture?

4. What role is played by storytellers to help develop a corporate culture? Explain.

5. What role is played by priests in developing a corporate culture? Explain.

6. How does a survivor in a tough-guy, macho culture behave?

7. In what kinds of businesses are we likely to find a work hard/play hard corporate culture? Cite at least two examples and explain each.

8. How do survivors in a bet-your-company culture behave?

9. What types of people would do best in a process culture? Why?

10. When it comes to reshaping corporate culture, what are some of the most useful guidelines for the manager to keep in mind? Identify and discuss three.

CASES

Case A.1: The Bardell Way

The Bardell Corporation is a very successful construction firm. During the last 12 months, the company has won a series of state and local contracts for major building projects. It has also bid successfully on seven new office buildings located from New York to Los Angeles.

Many of the people who work on these construction projects are union laborers who are hired from the local area. However, the company maintains a solid core of management staff. Some of the staff work out of the home office in Chicago. The rest are in management positions in the field.

Because of the large increase in business over the past year, Bardell has found it necessary to recruit more managerial personnel. Some of these people have been hired right out of engineering programs. Others are M.B.A. graduates. Still others have been hired away from competitive firms. In all cases, they know very little about Bardell and its operating philosophy.

The head of the personnel department has suggested that each of these new people be put through a 3-day in-house seminar in which they are taught the history, values, and operating philosophy of the firm. In particular, the personnel manager would like to see some of the top staff and up-and-coming middle managers take 15 to 30 minutes to talk to these new people about the company. "We've got to get these new personnel thinking the Bardell way," the manager told the company president. "If we start them out right, they'll be more effective as members of our management team." The president agreed, and the first 3-day seminar is scheduled to begin next week.

Questions

1. In scheduling people to talk at her seminar, how likely is it that the personnel manager will use some heroes? Why? Explain.

2. What type of corporate culture best describes Bardell? (Use Table A.1 to help you.) Defend your answer.

3. How valuable will this 3-day seminar be? Why? Defend your answer.

Case A.2: Bob's Choice

When Robert Flaherty decided to retire from the military, he was already under consideration for promotion to general. Nevertheless, he decided to get out and enter industry. "I want to start a new career, and, if I am promoted to general, I know I'll stay in at least another five years," he told his wife. "I've enjoyed my military career, but I'm now ready to move on."

Bob already had his eye on a job with a large computer firm. The company has been very prominent in the industry for over 30 years and the individual who recruited him told him, "Bob, you're used to taking charge. You know the importance of assuming responsibility and getting things done. You'll fit in well with us. We think it's a natural step from a military career to one in the world of business, especially computers." Bob agreed with the recruiter and is scheduled to start his new job in five weeks.

He will be vice-president of sales for western operation. In this capacity, Bob will be responsible for directing the sales force in a ten-state area. He will have five people reporting directly to him and a total of 375 people in the entire region. In addition to handling the management side of the job, Bob will be expected to pitch in and help out with sales to large business and military customers. "I'm really looking forward to getting started," he told the president of the firm yesterday. "Well, we're glad to have you with us, Bob," the CEO told him.

Questions

1. In your own words, describe the organization culture of the military.

2. What does the organizational culture of a successful computer sales organization look like? Compare it with your answer to the preceding question.

3. Are there any particular problems Bob is likely to have in adjusting to this new job? What are they? Be complete in your answer.

LEARNING OBJECTIVES

After completing this chapter, you will be able to:

- Define the function of organization.

- Describe five means for subdividing work in organizations.

- Draw three kinds of organizational charts.

- Define authority, responsibility, chain of command, delegation, accountability, and span of control.

- Distinguish between line and staff authority.

- Distinguish between centralized and decentralized authority.

- Define and describe the key aspects of the informal organization.

- Draw and explain five alternate forms of organization structure.

7

BUSINESS

ORGANIZATION

AND STRUCTURE

Suppose you recruited twenty people to accomplish a task; for example, you might want to produce a new piece of furniture that you designed. What would happen if you hired the people, explained that you wanted to manufacture your uniquely designed furniture, and told them to go to work? No doubt, the result would be confusion. Your employees would not know what you expected them to do and they would not know where to start. In fact, there is a strong likelihood that several employees would soon become frustrated and begin arguing about who should be doing what. Chances are slim that any useful product would result, even though the effort of the people might be quite serious.

To reduce such chaos, a manager could organize the work groups by:

- Determining what tasks are necessary.
- Dividing tasks into work groups.
- Assigning managers to be responsible for each group's tasks.
- Giving each manager the authority to complete the tasks.

For instance, the manager might organize as follows:

- Determine the tasks to be cutting, sanding, polishing, sewing, assembling, and painting.
- Group the tasks according to ordering the materials, producing the product, and selling the furniture.
- Select a manager for each grouping of tasks, that is, a manager for purchasing, production, and sales.
- Give each manager the authority to complete the tasks, for example, buying materials, supervising employees, and making the sales.

In complex organizations, it is impossible for one person to do everything. To produce airplanes, automobiles, or windows requires thousands of varied jobs.

As discussed in Chapter 6, the four basic functions of management are (1) planning, (2) organizing, (3) directing, and (4) controlling. Organizing, because of its complexity, is covered in greater detail in this chapter. Topics include formal organization, authority and responsibility, informal organization, and alternative forms of organization.

FORMAL ORGANIZATION

The underlying purpose of organization is to divide, and subdivide if necessary, the work into groupings. We call this process departmentation. Organization charts show us the relationships between departments.

Departmentation

To organize, we divide the work into large groups (divisions, regions, plants, etc.); then we divide into smaller groups (departments, shifts); and finally, we have a job description for each employee. By dividing work into small units, we benefit from specialization. The process of creating these divisions of work is called **departmentation,** and we call the divisions **departments.**

Departmentation by function. A functional division of work separates tasks into the company's major activities such as manufacturing, sales, finance, and personnel. Everything related to manufacturing goes into the manufacturing department, everything related to sales comes under the sales department, and so on. For instance, the function chart in Fig. 7.1 shows marketing, human resources, finance, and production to be the four major company divisions. The work of each major division is further divided into sub-departments. Advertising and promotion departments are under marketing, personnel is under human resources, and the like. Division by function is popular at top organizatonal levels.

Departmentation by territory. Division by geographic location (territory) is popular in marketing departments. When a company promotes its products or services over large territories, it is effective to divide the work according to these territories. Then each manager can make decisions that take into account the unique characteristics of that particular territory.

A company with only twenty salespeople may have only four sales managers, with each responsible for five salespeople. However, if a firm has one hundred salespeople, each of the four regional managers may supervise three or four district managers. District managers would then be in charge of salespeople for their own districts.

Departmentation by product. Companies that produce varied products often organize their work by product or class of product. General Motors, for example, has Cadillac, Chevrolet, and Buick divisions. A clothing manufacturer may have divisions such as boys' wear, junior miss, men's wear, and women's wear.

Departmentation by process. Creating departments by process is popular, especially in manufacturing companies. Division of labor by process creates departments for each step of what is usually a continuous process. Consider a shoe manufacturer which may organize into departments of design, cutting, sewing, gluing, and finishing. Employees in each department could specialize in the activities of the department.

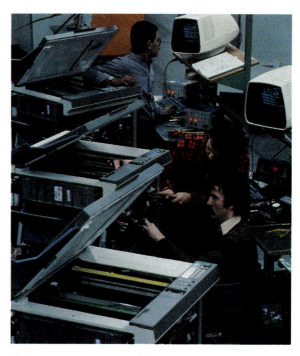

Final testing, the responsibility of this department, marks the end of the manufacturing process for these copying machines.

Departmentation by client. When a company departmentalizes by client, it groups its activities by customer. For instance, a major producer such as Crown-Zellerbach might produce nonbrand-labeled products for several different types of customers. The company may have special departments for major clients, such as Safeway, Luckies, Sears, and the like. Or a publishing company might divide its activities according to its reading markets — trade, textbooks, reference books, children's books.

In reality, companies usually employ a combination of these departmentation schemes. At one level, they may organize by function; they may choose territorial departmentation for another level; and they might departmentalize by product at another level. See Fig. 7.1 for examples of the various methods of departmentation.

Organization Charts

An **organization chart** is a diagram of the departments and their relationships to each other. There are three major types of organization charts: (1) vertical, (2) pyramid, and (3) horizontal.

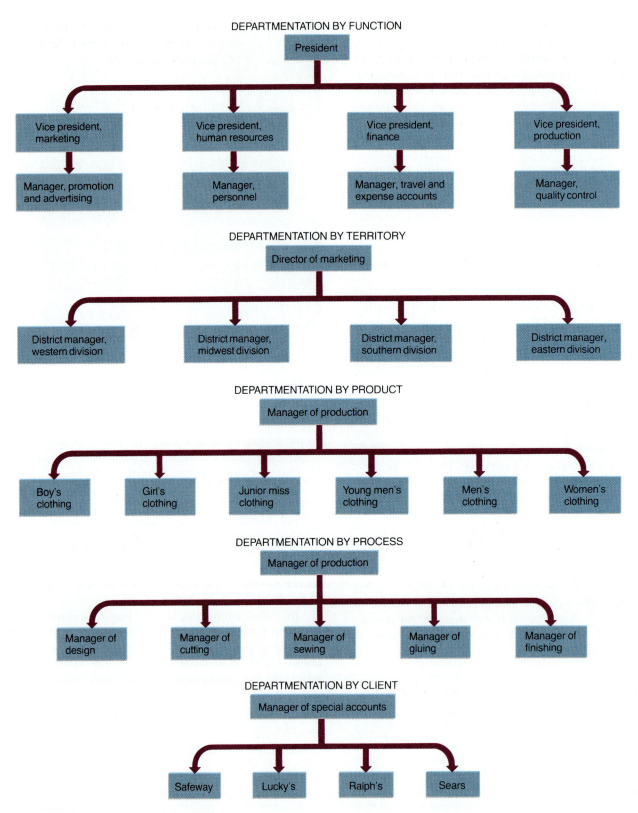

DEPARTMENTATION BY FUNCTION

President

Vice president, marketing

Vice president, human resources

Vice president, finance

Vice president, production

Manager, promotion and advertising

Manager, personnel

Manager, travel and expense accounts

Manager, quality control

DEPARTMENTATION BY TERRITORY

Director of marketing

District manager, western division

District manager, midwest division

District manager, southern division

District manager, eastern division

DEPARTMENTATION BY PRODUCT

Manager of production

Boy's clothing

Girl's clothing

Junior miss clothing

Young men's clothing

Men's clothing

Women's clothing

DEPARTMENTATION BY PROCESS

Manager of production

Manager of design

Manager of cutting

Manager of sewing

Manager of gluing

Manager of finishing

DEPARTMENTATION BY CLIENT

Manager of special accounts

Safeway

Lucky's

Ralph's

Sears

Figure 7.1
Various methods of departmentation.

The vertical chart. An example of a vertical organization chart appears in Fig. 7.2. As you can see, the power positions appear at the top levels of the chart, and the subordinate positions would be at the lower levels. The lines show the relationships of the departments to each other. For example, in the **vertical chart** in Fig. 7.2, the manager of advertising reports to the director of marketing who, in turn, reports to the president.

The pyramid chart. The **pyramid chart,** although much like the vertical chart, is usually ex-

Figure 7.2
Various types of organization charts.

THE VERTICAL CHART

President

Director of marketing

Manager of advertising | Manager of direct mail sales | Manager of the sales force | Manager of internal marketing efforts

THE PYRAMID CHART

President

Director of marketing

Director of promotion

Midwestern manager | Western manager | Eastern manager | Manager of advertising | Manager of direct mail advertising | Manager of internal marketing efforts

THE HORIZONTAL CHART

President

Director of marketing

Midwestern manager
Western manager
Eastern manager

Director of promotion

Manager of advertising
Manager of direct mail advertising
Manager of internal marketing efforts

panded to show more detail. Like the concept of a pyramid, it reflects power at the top and lower management levels at the bottom (or the base) (see Fig. 7.2).

The horizontal chart. Although not so frequently used as the vertical and pyramid charts, the **horizontal chart** shows the higher levels of management at the left with the lower management levels extending to the right. Some companies developed the horizontal chart because they did not want to emphasize the fact that the higher positions were on top and the lower positions were on the bottom. Figure 7.2 shows an example.

AUTHORITY AND RESPONSIBILITY

The organization chart is useful because it shows relationships between departments, but it does not show precisely just how much power one department has over another. This aspect of the relationship involves the concepts of authority and responsibility. **Authority** is the organization's right to do something, to make decisions regarding the tasks of the department. **Responsibility,** on the other hand, is an individual's personal obligation to carry out the activities assigned.

Let us consider the example of a community hospital located in a small midwestern community. The hospital administrator has the right to make decisions necessary to manage the hospital. Her job description states that she has the authority to purchase supplies and equipment; hire, assign, and terminate personnel; engage in fundraising; appoint and delegate appropriate authority to departmental executives; make decisions regarding financial control; and develop and maintain a sound organization. And, although it is not specifically stated, she also has the responsibility to carry out these duties to the best of her ability. Even if she delegates some of her authority to her department heads, she still remains responsible for the overall operation of the hospital.

A serious problem occurs when authority and responsibility are not equal. Suppose the board of trustees of the hospital told the administrator that they would hold her responsible for running the hospital. But if the trustees did not give the admin-

istrator the authority to make decisions regarding subordinates, finances, purchasing, and the like, the administrator would be unable to fulfill her responsibilities.

To fully understand authority and responsibility, we need to know something about the chain of command, authority delegation, accountability, span of control, line and staff authority, centralization, and decentralization.

Chain of Command

The **chain of command** is the established set of authority relationships between the departments. It shows who reports to whom. The hospital administrator mentioned previously reports to the board of trustees; and her assistant director, a director of nursing, and other staff department directors report to her. Figure 7.3 traces this chain of command.

To illustrate how the chain of command works, let us suppose one of the nurses complains, "I don't like my work assignment. I always get scheduled at the most undesirable hours." To complain through the chain of command, the nurse should talk to the director of nursing. If

Figure 7.3
Chain of command at a community hospital.

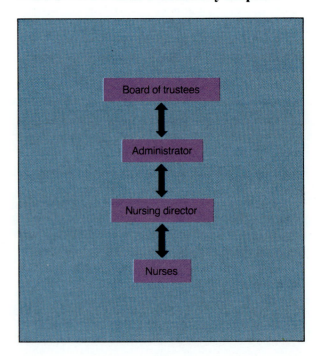

things are beyond the director's immediate control, both the nurse and his director might visit with the administrator. Likewise, the administrator should not make work assignments directly to the nurse. Rather the administrator, through authority delegation, asks the nursing director to run the nursing department. The nursing director then makes work assignments to the nurses.

Authority Delegation

Authority delegation means (1) assigning a task to a subordinate, (2) granting the rights and freedom to accomplish the task, and (3) checking to see that the subordinate performs the task properly.

Effective managers learn to delegate, but many managers insist on making all decisions themselves.

Effective managers learn to delegate, but many managers insist on making all decisions themselves. By adopting the idea "If you want something done right, you have to do it yourself," they spread themselves too thin. This creates stress for the manager and frustrates subordinates. Typically, managers who refuse to delegate use excuses such as that subordinates will not do a task correctly, there is not enough time to delegate, this is too important to delegate, the employees have not been trained well enough, or they just do not feel comfortable letting someone else do this. These excuses often signify that the manager is not secure enough or does not have enough self-confidence to delegate properly to subordinates.

Accountability

Once subordinates accept the authority to do a job, they should be held accountable for its accomplishment. **Accountability** is the liability of subordinates to accomplish tasks and objectives as agreed upon. Accountability is more narrow in scope than responsibility. Responsibility is an assumed obligation to do the best that one can in performing one's duties. Accountability is that part of the job that higher authorities will evaluate

to determine whether they should reward or punish the subordinate. For example, the nursing director is in a general way responsible for doing the best that she can. But she can be held accountable only for the specific aspects of the job that can be evaluated.

Span of Control

Span of control refers to the number of employees reporting to a manager. Authorities debate the proper span of control, but most agree that it varies with different situations. Lower-level supervisors who manage employees completing routine, stable tasks may manage as many as forty employees. However, at upper levels where jobs are complex and constantly changing, the span of control may be as few as three or four subordinates.

C. Northcote Parkinson, in _Parkinson's Law_, reasoned that (1) officials want to multiply subordinates, not rivals; (2) therefore, top officials have a tendency to add staff; (3) the added staff make work for one another; and (4) this results in the need for more staff.

C. Northcote Parkinson in _Parkinson's Law_ says that the number of subordinates that a manager can control reduces as you move up the organizational hierarchy. He believed, for example, that presidents could effectively control fewer subordinates than first-line supervisors. Drawing upon his experiences, Parkinson, somewhat tongue-in-cheek, offered an explanation for why organizations add more staff at the management level. His reasoning, known as **Parkinson's law,** goes like this: (1) officials want to multiply subordinates, not rivals, (2) therefore top officials have a tendency to add staff, (3) the added staff make work for one another, and (4) this results in the need for more staff. When a department gets too large, the top official divides the department and

The M-Form Structure

In his latest book, *The M-Form Society,* professor and writer William Ouchi prescribes a way for American companies to increase their teamwork and recapture their competitive edge.

Ouchi identifies three structural forms of large companies: the U-form structure, the H-form structure, and the M-form structure.

The U-form structure, the most common, is simply a functional organizational structure. As the drawing below suggests, a chief executive officer (CEO) oversees functional divisions. In the U-form, all departments must exist alongside one another. Sales would have nothing to sell unless production produced a product or service. No subunit can exist by itself and no subunit can measure its performance independently of the other units. Because the subunits are dependent on each other and because there is no simple measure of performance for each unit, the decisions tend to be highly centralized. Such organizations typically do not develop a long-term view.

The H-form structure identifies a holding company, typically with a small central staff that keeps financial controls over separate operating units. Each unit stands alone, independent from all other aspects of the business. The top management of the holding company knows very little about the separate units but can evaluate each one independently by using profits as a guideline. Since top management has a simple measure (profits) of each unit, decisions are usually very decentralized. The corporate management team does get to know quite a bit about the top managers of each unit, and the home office financial people are usually well-versed in the financial affairs of each unit. The drawing below shows a hypothetical example of an H-form structure.

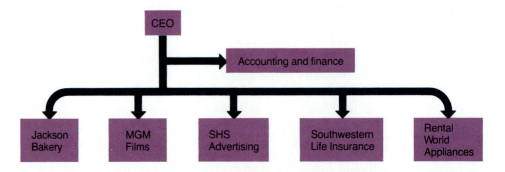

Existing between the U-form and the H-form, the M-form structure (or multidivisional organizaton) is the high-performing type, with partially independent operating units. Each operating unit makes a product or creates a service that is independent from the other units, but they all draw from some common pool such as technology, skill, or other features. Hewlett-Packard is an example of an M-form structure. H-P has nearly fifty semiautonomous divisions. One division manufactures oscilloscopes; another produces computers; another makes hand-held calculators; and so on. Each sells to a slightly different market, and each may use different methods of production. But they all draw from a common base of electrical engineering expertise, and they depend to some extent on the inventions from their central laboratories to supplement their own research. In short, subunits of the M-form structure are both partially independent and partially dependent upon the overall organization.

Top management may ask each division to maximize its profits, and it can measure this easily enough. However, managers of each division usually have to draw on central office skill, technology, marketing ability, and the like. And each divisional manager is concerned about the performance of the division as well as the performance of the overall operation. The success comes from providing a proper balance of independence and teamwork. The drawing below shows an M-form structure.

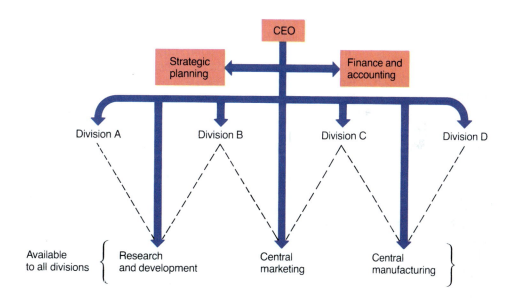

Summarized from William Ouchi, *The M-Form Society,* Reading, Massachusetts: Addison-Wesley Publishing Co., 1984.

creates two department heads. These two department heads, both of whom are subordinate to the top official, also create work for each other. In fact, Parkinson said that the number of people in any working group tends to increase regardless of the amount of work to be done. In reality, until very recently, organizations in both England and the United States have shown a tendency to increase their management positions at a much faster rate than their employee positions.

Wide spans of control tend to produce a **flat organization**; that is, a manager has large departments, and there are fewer managerial levels. By contrast, narrow spans produce a **tall organization,** the result of small departments and many management levels. Figure 7.4 diagrams examples of spans of control.

Research suggests some advantages to both wide and narrow spans of control. Some advantages of wide spans are:

- Communication is better because of fewer levels.
- Subordinate initiative is encouraged.
- Employees feel closer to top management.
- Lower-level employees have more responsibility.

Some advantages of narrow spans are:

CROSS FIRE

The Authority Dilemma

The vice-president of an information processing firm, concerned about cutting costs, issued an unconditional order forbidding managers and supervisors to authorize overtime under any circumstances. On a Thursday morning, the data processing manager called the vice-president's assistant and explained that water damage from the recent storm had damaged some of their records and equipment. They called the repair service, but they do not expect to get the equipment running until late Friday night.

A systems supervisor, a subordinate of the data processing manager, has requested overtime for ten people so that they can get the monthly dividend statements mailed on time. When the dividend checks are late, owners become angry and complain. The data processing manager forwarded the overtime request to the vice-president's assistant, but he said he could not authorize the overtime. He tried to get in touch with the vice-president, but he was out of town and could not be reached. Finally, the vice-president's assistant told the data processing manager to use his own discretion in the matter. The data processing manager explained to the systems supervisor, "I could not get in touch with the vice-president. The vice-president's assistant told to us to use our own judgment. So I guess you will just have to use your own discretion about whether you ask your people to come in this weekend."

What decision do you think the systems supervisor made?

___ A. Told his people to come in and turn in the overtime.

___ B. Did nothing over the weekend; reported to work Monday as usual.

Explain the reasoning behind your choice.

A. _____

B. _____

C. _____

D. _____

Wide span

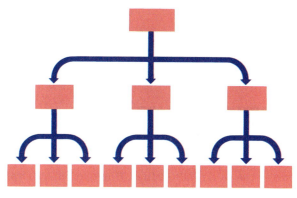

Narrow span

Figure 7.4
Examples of wide and narrow spans.

- More levels of management are created, providing more promotion opportunities to quality employees.
- Each manager is allowed to specialize more narrowly.
- More control over employee behavior is provided.

Line and Staff Authority

Thus far, we have been discussing **line authority,** the formal right to tell others what to do. However, because of increasing complexities in organizations, a more elaborate system has developed. **Staff authority** supplements line authority by providing specialized advice. Staff managers can only make recommendations to other departments. As one manager put it, "The line tells, the staff sells."

In many organizations, the human resources department has staff authority with other departments. Human resources people might, for example, interview people and make recommendations for hiring; nevertheless, the line manager of the department probably has the final say on hiring. Or, computer specialists might develop a new system for recording costs in a department, and they may recommend this new system to the manager of the department. The department manager then can accept or reject the plan.

In practice, line and staff relationships are often major sources of conflict. In looking for better methods, improved procedures, or greater efficiency, staff people usually initiate changes. And staff people may even specify certain procedures and actually control the line manager's resources to some extent. It is easy for a line manager to think that a staff person is infringing upon his territory. For instance, staff engineers may specify what materials will be used in making a product and how the product is to be manufactured. But line managers are responsible for the output of their production subordinates. Understandably, a line manager might feel a little resistant when staff people begin suggesting to — often telling — the line manager's subordinates how they ought to perform part of their production jobs. In such situations, a line manager frequently thinks, "I do not have complete authority to tell my subordinates what to do, but I am still responsible for the output."

To compound this dilemma, line and staff managers usually have different personal backgrounds. Staff people tend to have more formal education, they come from different social backgrounds, and they tend to be younger than line managers. Staff managers, because of their specialized knowledge and frequent association with upper-level management, are also closer to the power structure. All these things cause line managers to worry about staff people usurping some of their influence. Figure 7.5 diagrams line and staff relationships.

Centralization and Decentralization

Managers must decide how much authority to vest in each managerial position. **Centralization** occurs when a few managers at the top reserve most of the important decisions for themselves. By contrast, **decentralization** of authority means that employees at lower organizational levels

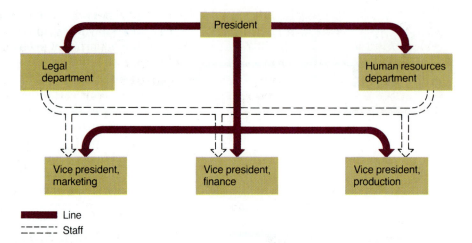

**Figure 7.5
Line and staff
organization chart.**

Line
Staff

Routine, recurring decisions are generally decentralized; less routine, critical decisions are usually centralized.

---

have more power to make decisions. Generally, routine, recurring decisions are decentralized, whereas decisions that are less routine and more critical are centralized.

Which is better: centralization or decentralization? Many feel it is better to decentralize whenever possible. By giving lower-level managers and employees more authority, you create initiative and develop better-trained managers for the future. Centralization tends to frustrate many employees. Suppose the mailroom manager had to get permission to buy stamps. Perhaps she is even required to submit a daily report on postage costs. This could become tedious and frustrating. In a decentralized firm, upper-level management would likely give departments a postage budget. Department managers could spend their postage as they wished so long as they stayed within the budget. Upper-level managers would want to look only at special problems. However, if decisions have a great impact on the firm, they are likely to be centralized. Or if lower-level managers and employees are not responsible enough to make proper decisions, upper-level management may need to centralize more of the decisions. IBM, General Motors, and Kodak are a few examples of decentralized companies.

INFORMAL ORGANIZATION

The planned, formal organization structure, which we have been discussing, has divisions, departments, and relationships. However, members of a working group develop their own informal relationships as they work together. This **informal organization** involves group norms, roles, status, personality traits, and the grapevine. The impact of the informal organization upon the goals and policies of the formal organization depends upon management's approval of the informal groups.

Group Norms

Group norms are standards that the group informally sets for themselves. Norms may involve performance standards, ways of relating to managers, and ways of interacting within the group. An observer reported, "I found three major norms to exist within my group: (1) you should not produce more than to 70% of your capabilities, (2) you should avoid brownnosing the manager, and (3) you should share gossip with the other employees."

Often the social pressures of the group may overpower the authority of the manager. Suppose an individual in the preceding example decided to break with the group and begin producing to 100% of her ability. This rate buster may become such an outcast with the department that the manager may have to let her go even though her performance is superior.

Characters in the Informal Organization

According to writers Deal and Kennedy, 90% of what goes on in an organization has nothing to do with formal events. Rather, the informal network, the "hidden hierarchy," is in reality how an organization operates. They describe several characters in the informal culture. In addition to the storytellers and priests discussed in Enrichment Chapter A, several other roles emerge in the informal culture.

Whisperers

Whisperers are the powers behind the throne. They are the movers and shakers, but they do not hold formal authority. They get their power because people know that they are doing the boss's dealings. No one wants to cross whisperers because of the influence they have with Mr. Big.

Gossips

Gossips pass the latest "Have you heard . . . ?" like lightning throughout the organization. They are not always taken seriously, and they do not have to always be right; but they entertain and the organization tolerates them. They also reinforce the informal culture.

Secretarial sources

A knowledgeable person who wants to tap into the power network goes to the clerical people. They know what the organization is really like. Acting in a noninvolved role, they can tell you about the argument in the boardroom, a memo the vice-president's secretary is about to send, and who is about to do what to whom.

Spies

Every good manager has spies. Good spies are well-liked; people trust them enough to confide in them. They know all of the stories and the names that go with them. Cultural spies do not work with cloak and dagger; they seldom say a bad word about anyone, and most people like them. They know what is going on because they keep their fingers on the pulse of the organization.

Cabals

Two or more people who secretly join together for a common purpose form a cabal. The common purpose is usually to advance themselves. Two junior officers in the Dutch navy made a pact. They decided that, at cocktail parties and other social gatherings, each would go out of his way to tell people what a great guy the other was. One might say, "Charlie is the best man in the navy. I can't believe how good he is with people." Or, "Did you hear about the brilliant idea that Dave had?" These two revealed their deal the day they were promoted to admiral — the two youngest ever appointed in the Dutch navy.

Source: Terrence E. Deal and Allan A. Kennedy, *Corporate Cultures,* Reading, Mass.: Addison-Wesley Publishing Co., 1982, pp. 85–97.

Effective managers are sensitive to informal norms and can even make them work in their favor.

Effective managers are sensitive to informal norms and can even make them work in their favor. The manager may create a norm of "employees liking their boss," and this can create better communication and cooperation.

Role

A **role** is a set of expected behaviors. Job descriptions outline formal work expectations, but the group may develop other views. Few job descriptions, for example, dictate that bank officers get involved with community projects. Yet, as one officer said, "I soon learned that the top managers expected you to help the bank's image by doing visible things to help the community." This was an informal role or expected behavior that came with the position.

Status

Status is the way that other people perceive an individual's prestige. The formal chain of command defines the authority ranking, but informal, social opinions may alter the manager's actual prestige and power.

Sometimes a manager or employee with low formal authority may attain high status with other employees. This might frustrate higher-level managers, causing conflict and disruption. For example, suppose the office manager has formal authority over the receptionist. Because the latter is outgoing, sociable, and well-liked by everyone in the office, she may have a higher status than the manager. Feeling the loss of power, the manager might decide to reassign the receptionist to a lesser position, claiming that the receptionist wasted too much time talking. However, the receptionist, with the strong support of the remainder of the office staff, might balk at the move and perhaps actually cause the manager to change her mind.

High-status managers sometimes use their power to build an empire and gain even more status, often at the expense of the organization's objectives. Many such managers become very ineffective while chasing fancy titles, hiring excessive subordinates, requesting oversized desks, and wearing $700 suits.

Personality Traits

Ways of acting socially — **personality traits** — also affect the informal organization. Employees may be outgoing or shy, active or docile, wild or straight, naive or informed. Employees make social connections with other employees according to their tastes, and some of these relationships can cause problems. Information meant to be confidential may be passed along among friends. And interoffice dating might create awkward and uncomfortable situations. Effective departments achieve a balance of personality traits where peo-

FUNNY BUSINESS

Stockworth by permission of Sterling & Selesnick, Inc., and The New York Times Syndication Sales Corp.

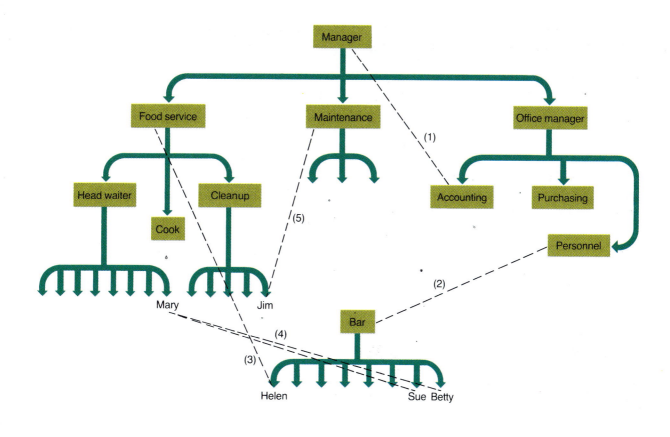

Figure 7.6
An organization chart showing informal relationships.

Formal relationships
---- Informal relationships

The Grapevine

Much information passes around the formal chain of command. In fact, rather stable networks develop and spread information informally. This informal communication network is a **grapevine.** While the grapevine often carries accurate information, it also carries rumors, exaggerations, and gossip. Some employees, wanting to be "in the know" spend a lot of their time gossiping about company business and employees. Sometimes rumors and exaggerations carried along the grapevine can seriously damage an organization. As a manager explained, "We had a rumor that the plant was closing down. Before we could get it stopped, we lost some of our best people and created so much confusion that it was 3 months be-

ple can accept, although not necessarily like and respect, each other's personality.

fore things got back to normal." Figure 7.6 diagrams part of an informal organization in a restaurant.

Management and the Informal Organization

Whether or not the informal organization works for or against management depends upon management's approach. Managers who effectively deal with the informal organization both recognize and accept its existence. They do not send informal networks underground with their policies or actions. Effective managers also identify informal leaders and try to get them to support the department's goals. As a manager who took over a group commented, "The previous supervisor tried to control all the informal discussions among the people. He even posted rules against rumors, discussing salary schedules, and the like. He

Sex in the Office: Changing Norms and Roles

In a 1976 survey by *Redbook* magazine, 90% of those questioned said that they had experienced some form of sexual harassment on the job. Phyllis Schlafy, an antifeminist crusader, says, "Sexual harassment on the job is not a problem for virtuous women." More and more women are entering the work force, and the norms governing relationships between the sexes appear to be unclear. In a recent, *Redbook-Harvard Business Review* study, nearly two-thirds of the respondents felt that their company should issue formal statements decrying sexual harassments. But only one-third said their companies had done so.

Historically, the role of women in business has been to work in low-power, serving jobs — secretaries, clerks, receptionists, and the like. And the norms regarding sexual behavior were more clearly defined. Certainly, there always have been and always will be office romances, but the traditional norm was to avoid them. The male adage expressed it as, "Don't fish off the company pier," or "Don't play where you work and don't work where you play."

However, the woman in business today is clearly creating new roles. Better educated and more ambitious, she is vying with males, often on equal terms, for power positions. It should be no surprise that this is straining traditional sexual norms at work. Working in close contact for long periods makes it possible to develop trust and affection for each other. And working on a risky venture with an attractive partner can create romantic, exciting feelings: adrenalin pumps, you feel nervous, elements of success create confidence. For many, this high-wire balancing act quite easily translates into sexual attraction.

In fact, the *Redbook* survey showed that more than half of the working women in their late thirties admitted to having affairs, compared to only 24% of housewives. Twenty-six percent of the readers of *Self* magazine admitted to having an "office affair."

Both men and women agree that working in offices with the opposite sex is both more exciting and enjoyable than working with a group of the same sex. A woman editor said, "Men make me feel good. I'm funnier, sharper, and feel more competent with them around." A male engineer agreed, ". . . we tend to show off a little more, to be at the top of our form when there are women around. It just makes work more fun, less rigid and demanding."

During this evolution of roles and norms, people differ about what the most effective relationships should be. Some say that office romance should be avoided by both sexes, that it is too risky on both a personal and professional level. Yet some say that the office is the best place to meet people and learn to trust them. This state of flux creates problems. Some women are bright, intelligent, and sexually emancipated, looking for action. Others are bright, intelligent, and equally appealing, but will not tolerate sexist remarks. And it is sometimes hard for men to tell the difference until they embarrass themselves and create an uncomfortable relationship. And women have to face the dilemma of wondering whether a potential relationship is sincere or a male power trip by an aggressive executive. While these informal relationships may be confusing, they can have just as much impact upon the organization as the formal relationships.

Source: Patrice D. and Jack C. Horn, *Sex in the Office,* Reading, Mass.: Addison-Wesley Publishing Company, 1982.

treated the informal association like a weed, and all he succeeded in doing was driving it underground.''

In any formal organization, there are numerous informal relationships. The dotted lines in Fig. 7.6 show a few of the informal relationships between people in a large restaurant.

1. The manager is having an affair with the accounting manager.

2. The bar manager and the personnel manager are good friends. Both attended the same college for a short period, and their wives are good friends.

3. The food service manager is recently divorced, and he has been spending some time talking with Helen, a cocktail waitress.

4. Mary, a waitress, and Sue and Betty, both cocktail waitresses, are very good friends. They carpool to work and take most of their breaks together. This group is also one of the first to hear company gossip.

5. The maintenance manager has three part-time employees, but he is something of a loner. About the only person that he gets along well with is Jim in food service. Both worked together at another restaurant, and they developed a trust in each other.

ALTERNATIVE FORMS OF ORGANIZATION

Organizational critics suggest that the traditional structure is too inflexible to meet the fast-paced changes of today's modern business world. They criticize the formal structure for thwarting individual autonomy and development. Modern theorists suggest some new forms of structure that are more fluid.

The Matrix Organization

While the formal structure builds on power centers, the **matrix organization** identifies a project and puts together a team based on what members can contribute. Both the aerospace industry and the high-tech industry, recognizing the inflexibility and inappropriateness of a traditional structure, have adopted matrix forms of organization. Rather than being strictly divided by

Complex aerospace projects (such as the engines of the Space Shuttle) often require the flexibility of a matrix organization.

functions, project members may come from marketing, finance, production, and personnel departments. A **project manager** with line authority takes charge for the duration of the project. After completing the project, members return to their respective departments.

Figure 7.7(a) shows a matrix structure. It has the flexibility of temporarily drawing resources to various projects. But uncertainties and vague relationships sometimes result in confusion over authority. Suppose an employee leaves the marketing department and works for a project manager for 8 weeks. The project requires him to do things that his regular boss would not OK. He gets confused and a little insecure. Also, permanent managers may disagree with project managers over merit ratings, raises, promotions, and the amount of employee time that goes into the special project.

The Xerox Corporation's market share in copy machines fell to 45% in the early 1980s, down from a high of 96% in 1970. Although foreign competition accounted for a lot of the market share loss, Xerox executives freely admit that they strangled themselves with a matrix organization. While the heads of such groups as product planning, design, service, and manufacturing were based in Rochester, New York, they reported to separate executives at their Stamford, Connecticut, headquarters. Insiders admit that the groups had endless debates over features and design trade-offs. Many of the debates ran all the way to the president's office. It seemed that no one had the responsibility for getting the products out the door. Xerox redesigned its structure to set up four

THE MATRIX ORGANIZATION

(a)

THE BEEHIVE ORGANIZATION

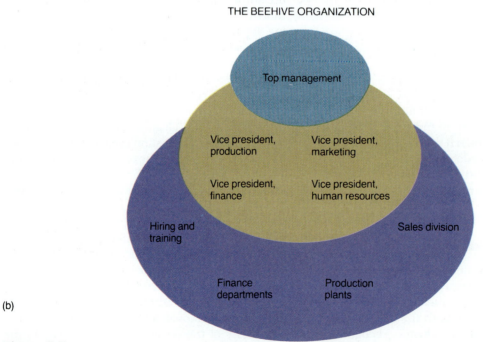

(b)

Figure 7.7
Organization charts for alternative forms of organization.

THE DOUGHNUT ORGANIZATION

(c)

THE LADDER ORGANIZATION

(d)

THE PYRAMID ORGANIZATION

(e)

divisions that were relatively independent of each other. Productivity immediately improved 10%.

Obviously, as with any form of organization, some problems with the matrix structure can be expected, but there are also many advantages: it allows for more interaction between functional groups; it reduces boredom by getting employees involved in new areas; participating employees feel important because their opinions seem to matter; and managers are surprised at the creativity and success generated by the matrix form.

The Beehive Organization

The **beehive organization** is an example of another modern, less structured organizational form. As Fig. 7.7(b) shows, the beehive consists of two to five circles on top of each other. Each circle represents a different level of management, and each level can deal directly with any of the managers at the next lowest level. While this structure encourages more communication between departments at different levels, it also creates some confusion in authority and responsibility relationships. Further, evaluation and promotion channels are less clear. Still, people who value less structure and more freedom benefit from the beehive organization.

In Fig. 7.7(b), the top circle might be the president and the board of directors; the second circle might consist of the vice-presidents; and the third level could be middle managers.

The Doughnut Organization

Somewhat similar to the beehive is the **doughnut organization** (see Fig. 7.7c). The doughnut shows two to five circles, with the inner circles being top-level managers and the outer circles representing lower-level managers. One of the circles may consist of staff managers or outside consulting relationships. The doughnut, like the beehive, encourages more interaction between levels, while providing both the benefits and hazards of less structure.

The Ladder Organization

The **ladder organization** is similar to the typical line organization except for the way it deals with staff managers. The ladder shows all staff functions at the side of the chart, resembling a ladder in appearance. Staff functions appear as a function of each level. This form allows the clarity of line organizations, while specifying staff functions more clearly. See Fig. 7.7(d).

TAKING STOCK

How Structural Changes Led to Improvement at Brunswick Corp.

Brunswick Corp. originally became successful making bowling and billiard balls. However, the company acquired a medical products division, Mercury Marine outboard motors, a fishing tackle company, and many defense and energy-related divisions. And profits began to decline.

CEO Jack F. Reichert began, in 1977, to change things. He said as the company expanded they got more and more managers, and "the pyramid was too tall." During the past year, Reichert has consolidated eleven divisions into eight, increasing the span of control and shortening the chain of command. Further, all the division managers report directly to Reichert and they vie equally for his attention.

In restructuring the organization, Reichert also reduced overhead by reducing 400 white-collar workers and middle managers from the payroll at a savings of $18 million. And along with the management cuts went two corporate jets and the executive dining room. Partly as a result of this restructuring, Brunswick Corp. netted $31 million in profits during the first half of 1983, up 148% over the previous year.

Source: Jill Bettner, "Bowling for Dollars," *Forbes,* Sept. 12, 1983, p. 138.

TABLE 7.1 ■ ADVANTAGES AND DISADVANTAGES OF ALTERNATIVE ORGANIZATIONAL FORMS

	Advantages	Disadvantages
Matrix	Flexibility Pooling talents More interaction Reduces boredom Employee participation	Confusion over authority Disagreement over merit ratings, promotions, pay raises
Beehive	Encourages communication More freedom Less structure	Confusion in authority and responsibility relationships Less clear evaluation and promotion channels
Doughnut	More interaction More freedom	Uncertainty Some confusion over formal relationships
Ladder	Specifies staff function Clarity More certainty	Less flexible More rigid Slower to change
Pyramid	Clarifies relationships and incentives in sales departments	Not adaptable to most functions

The Pyramid Organization

Direct sales firms sometimes use a unique organizational form called the **pyramid organization.** Some people are sensitive to the term "pyramid" because there are pyramid structures that are illegal. Under this organizational form, each salesperson usually gets a percentage or bonus, based on the sales of the employees that work under him or her. Employees' positions on the chart are determined by the date they were hired and by the number of people they hire to work for them. Companies selling health foods, household products, and lingerie are most likely to use a pyramid organization. The pyramid provides clear relationships for sales groupings, but it is not readily adaptable to all functional areas. For example, see Fig. 7.7(e). (And see Table 7.1 for a listing of the advantages and disadvantages of these five alternative organizational forms.)

SUMMARY

Organizations are given structure through departmentation. These departments are created by function, territory, product, process, or client. Organization charts are used to illustrate graphically each department and its relationship to other segments of the company. The three major types of charts are vertical, pyramid, and horizontal.

The major purpose of business organization is to establish channels of authority and responsibility. It also helps define job functions. Channels of authority are referred to as the chain of command. Delegation is when authority is passed on from one level of management to another. When a manager or employee accepts authority, there is a corresponding responsibility to be certain that tasks are accomplished as agreed. The acceptance of authority implies accountability.

The span of control refers to the number of employees responsible to any one manager. When a manager has authority over many employees, it is called a flat organization. A tall organization is where the manager has authority over only a few employees. Depending upon the situation, there are advantages to both a wide and a narrow span of control. Line authority is the right to direct the work of others, while staff authority is usually advisory and outside direct authority relationships. While conflicts often occur between line and staff employees, most firms have found this form of organization useful.

Centralization is a term that refers to authority and decision making being at the top or upper levels of the organization. When much of the authority is delegated to lower levels, it is called decentralization.

The informal organization refers to relationships and events that occur as people interact within the firm. This less structured behavior creates group norms, roles, status, friendships, and informal means of communication. These all have an impact upon workers and managers.

Alternatives to the line and staff forms of organization are the matrix, the beehive, the doughnut, the ladder, and the pyramid types of organization.

MIND YOUR BUSINESS

Instructions. The following are statements of managers describing their relationships with their subordinates. Check the statements that you believe describe ineffective relationships.

____ 1. I watch over my subordinates very closely at all times.

____ 2. I am aware that my subordinates will make some mistakes.

____ 3. I believe that a subordinate should be held responsible for everything that has been assigned to him or her.

____ 4. I perform many jobs that my subordinates could do because I enjoy the job very much myself.

____ 5. I ignore many mistakes that my subordinates make.

____ 6. I insist that subordinates check with me before they try anything that I have not previously approved.

____ 7. I like to have only a very few subordinates reporting to me at any one time.

____ 8. I have a firm policy against employees discussing rumors and grapevine information among themselves.

____ 9. I ask my subordinates to make an appointment when they wish to visit with me; this allows me to plan my day better.

____ 10. I do not allow my subordinates to go around me to a higher level of management.

See answers at the back of the book.

KEY TERMS

departmentation, 166
department, 166
organization chart, 167
vertical chart, 169
pyramid chart, 169
horizontal chart, 172
authority, 172
responsibility, 172
chain of command, 172
authority delegation, 173
accountability, 173
span of control, 173
Parkinson's law, 173
flat organization, 174
tall organization, 174
line authority, 175
staff authority, 175
centralization, 175
decentralization, 175
informal organization, 176
group norms, 176
role, 178
status, 178
personality traits, 178
grapevine, 179
matrix organization, 181
project manager, 181
beehive organization, 184
doughnut organization, 184
ladder organization, 184
pyramid organization, 185

REVIEW QUESTIONS

1. Discuss the benefits of effective organization within a business. Why should a manager be concerned with organization?

2. What is departmentation? List the five major methods, with examples of each.

3. Why do managers create organization charts? What benefits do they provide? Describe the three major types of organization charts.

4. Define authority and responsibility. Explain the relationship between the two and give examples. What is the most common mistake that managers make with regard to these two concepts?

5. Explain chain of command; give an example.

6. What is delegation? What are the advantages and disadvantages of delegation within an organization?

7. Explain the concept of accountability. While it is similar to that of responsibility, what is the difference between the two terms?

8. What is meant by the span of control? How are the two extremes termed? What are the advantages of each?

9. Define both line and staff authority. How do they differ? Discuss the problems that tend to occur between the two.

10. Explain the difference between centralization and decentralization. How do these concepts affect the span of control? What is the major misconception regarding centralization?

11. What is meant by informal organization? In what specific ways does it affect the formal organization discussed earlier? Discuss the formal organization with regard to: (1) group standards, (2) expected behavior, (3) prestige, (4) friendships, and (5) communication.

12. The text covers five alternative forms of organization. Explain each of them and discuss their similarities and differences. What are some of the advantages of each?

CASES

Case 7.1: The Whole Earth Bakery, Part I

Esther Chavez owns and manages a bakery called the Whole Earth Bakery. The bakery makes health foods and sells them in local grocery and health food stores in Syracuse, New York. The enterprise employs sixty people: twenty-five in production, fifteen in marketing, two in finance, three in management, seven in maintenance, three in promotion and advertising, one general manager (Esther), two in purchasing and inventory control, and two in personnel. Esther also has a lawyer and a CPA on retainer.

Questions

1. Create an organization chart for the Whole Earth Bakery. Be sure to consider departmentation, authority and responsibility, chain of command, span of management, line and staff authority, and centralization. Explain the rationale behind your organization chart.

2. Consider modifying your chart to include some of the optional organizational forms (matrix, beehive, doughnut, ladder, and pyramid) presented in the latter part of the chapter.

Case 7.2: The Whole Earth Bakery, Part II

Several interesting conditions exist within the Whole Earth Bakery, which Esther Chavez owns and manages. For example: (1) Only five employees smoke. Many of the other employees are applying considerable pressure to prevent smoking on the work premises. The smokers feel repressed, and they think their rights are being violated. They only smoke in the areas designated for smoking. (2) Although Maria, one of the cooks who works in the kitchen, has no official management position, she exerts a lot of influence. She has been with the company a long time, and most employees hold her opinions in high regard. (3) Three employees, known as the "wild ones," are always throwing parties. They invite most of the firm's employees, but few attend. The parties sometimes get out of hand, and there is a feeling that the group attending the parties is immature and a bit irresponsible. (4) The kitchen employees work, by their own admission, at about 70% of their capacity. Individuals who try to be more productive are sure to feel the scorn of the group. (5) Roberta, a secretary, is the company gossip. She is always talking about personal and professional information that, as the secretary, she is privy to.

Questions

1. Analyze the case in terms of group norms, roles, status, personality traits, and the grapevine.

2. Explain how each of the five conditions in the case could be either beneficial or harmful to the company.

3. If you were the general manager, what would you do to ensure that each of the situations was as beneficial as possible?

After completing this chapter, you will be able to:

■ Describe the purpose of production management.

■ Discuss seven criteria that firms evaluate when deciding where to locate a plant.

■ Explain four different kinds of plant layout designs.

■ Identify the following production scheduling techniques: program evaluation and review technique (PERT), critical path method (CPM), and materials requirements planning (MRP).

■ Describe standard purchasing policies and procedures.

■ Explain the benefits and drawbacks of just-in-time inventories.

■ Explain the production process and production control.

■ Explain computer-aided design/computer-aided manufacturing (CAD/CAM) and flexible manufacturing systems (FMS) production.

8

PRODUCTION AND OPERATIONS MANAGEMENT

During the 1981–1982 recession, many companies became very much concerned about productivity, a measure of goods produced in consideration of resources used. For many years, the United States had led the world in increased productivity rates and innovative productivity methods. However, in the past few years, the United States has lagged behind while other nations, especially Japan, have continued to increase their productivity rates. In 1981, Japan replaced the United States as the number 1 automobile producer in the world. Why has the United States fallen behind? Many reasons are given. While productivity methods is only one ingredient in the overall productivity rates, this chapter aids our understanding of production and operations management by exploring (1) the purpose of production management, (2) product planning, (3) materials management, and (4) the plant in operation.

THE PURPOSE OF PRODUCTION MANAGEMENT

A bicycle is produced by molding metal, rubber, plastic, and paint into a frame with wheels, spokes, handlebars, and a seat. We buy bicycles for fun, exercise, and transportation; but the scattered raw materials would not do us much good. **Production,** the process of creating goods and services, creates value by converting raw materials into finished forms. Conceptually, production includes: (1) input, (2) processing, and (3) outputs.

Production is crucial to the overall economy; the more effectively we produce goods and services, the higher the standard of living we can attain. Economists use the term **utility** to refer to the extent to which a good or service satisfies consumers. Thus, the major purpose of **production management** is to increase utility by better satisfying consumers' wants and needs.

Traditionally, production concepts have been applied strictly to the production process. More recently, however, managers are applying production techniques to other business functions, including finance, marketing, and general management. The application of production techniques to the broader scope of business operations is called **operations research** (OR). Using scientific, computer, and mathematical systems, OR implies that accounting firms, police departments, banks, and repair shops face many of the same problems in delivering their services as do manufacturing companies in making a product. While most of the examples in this chapter refer to manufacturing methods, we endorse the broad perspective of production and operations management.

PRODUCTION PLANNING

Like all areas of management, production management requires good planning. For our purposes, important aspects of production planning include plant location, plant layout, production scheduling, and capital requirements.

Plant Location

One of the first crucial decisions in establishing a production facility is location. Plant location decisions include where to place new facilities, as well as continuing evaluations of current facilities. Location decisions move through three phases. First, management selects the region of the country (the South, West, East, Midwest) it wants to build in. Second, choices narrow to cities and communities within the region. And third, they must select a specific site, a spot where they will build. These decisions usually hinge on a set of rather standard factors.

Labor supply. Any plant requires labor. Highly automated factories need few employees, but some plants employ thousands of people. Such companies try to determine if the community has a large enough labor force; then they check for skills. If the local labor force does not have the skills, the company considers the feasibility of training programs. A successful firm built a branch plant in another city. The executive explained, "We like the city we are in, but the labor market is so tight, we can't hire the right people.

Other things being equal, a company would prefer to locate where labor unions are weak or nonexistent.

We had to build our branch where workers are available." Labor costs were once a significant concern, but geographic wage differentials have become smaller than in the past. Like wages, labor

BUSINESS BULLETIN

Modern Production Characteristics

Several terms characterize modern production methods.

1. **Mechanization** is the replacement of human labor with machines. While this process was popular during the Industrial Revolution (Chapter 1), it is becoming even more popular today. We are using machines and robots to perform many routine, diverse, and complex functions. Companies like machines because they do not join unions, demand higher wages, go on strike, need rest breaks, argue with each other, or call in sick. As one manager commented, "Machines can often work 24 hours a day while performing tasks consistently and accurately."

2. **Standardization** is the production of uniform and interchangeable parts. Via standardization, we can produce parts that can be used in many different kinds of products. For example, because of standardization, we can interchange many of the parts in cassette tapes, tape decks, and recorders.

3. **Automation** occurs when managers divide the production process into routine, standard (automatic) functions. This clear definition of tasks makes it easier for machines to perform the work.

4. An **assembly line** is a production process whereby an item moves along a designated route, sometimes on a conveyor belt, and people or machines perform specific operations at various stages along the line.

5. Because of mechanization, standardization, automation, and the assembly line, we are able to manufacture products in great quantities, that is, by **mass production.** Mass production, in turn, results in lower per unit costs, which makes the product affordable to more people, thereby raising the standard of living.

Although bidding for high-technology companies, these ads cite several of the location factors that any business must consider in production planning.

union strength is less of an issue than it was in the past. Other things being equal, a company would prefer to locate where labor unions are weak or nonexistent. Traditionally, unions have been stronger in the East, North, and West, than in the South and Midwest.

Raw materials. A skilled and plentiful labor force may be useless without raw materials. Many production companies require a plentiful supply of raw materials — unprocessed resources such as oil, coal, minerals, and agricultural products. A component part or semifinished product might also be a raw material: tires are finished goods for a tire manufacturer, but they are raw materials for automobile producers. To avoid prohibitive transportation costs, plants are located near weighty and bulky raw materials. For example, chemical companies select the Mississippi riverbanks of Louisiana to be near sulfur, salt, limestone, and oil deposits. Likewise, brick manufacturers locate near clay deposits, and lumber mills operate near forests. Firms that depend on highly perishable resources, such as the fishing industry, try to locate close to the source. Canning operations choose to locate in agricultural areas so they can reduce spoilage losses. Some products use raw materials that are geographically dispersed and their manufacturers locate nearby in order to reduce transportation costs; for example, a brewery may choose to locate in Oregon rather than Arizona.

Markets. If firms can transport raw materials economically, then they like to locate near their markets. As an analyst commented, "Market proximity is particularly important where customers require quick delivery, flexibility, and fast service." For example, many subcontractors for airframe manufacturers locate in Wichita, Kansas, where Beech, Cessna, and Gates Lear jet, the largest producers of small aircraft, are situated. For national markets, branch plants and warehouses enhance customer contact and service. However, when raw materials are costly to transport and finished products can be moved cheaply, it is better to be located near the input source rather than the prime consumers.

Power and water. Power and water are costly to store or transport. And both may be crucial to a manufacturer. Companies that need reasonable power sources or large quantities of water may be forced to locate near these resources. Chemical companies require a lot of power, whereas textile and furniture manufacturers are more concerned with labor resources. Major sources of power are electricity produced from dams, natural gas, coal, and more recently, nuclear energy. These power sources are limited, and prices vary widely within different locations.

A few companies choose to generate their own power, but for most this is an expensive venture. Similarly, steel mills and pulpwood plants are thirsty operations: They seek out rivers and lakes. The Coors brewery has been considering a plant in California, the state drinks 40% of its product. But Rocky Mountain spring water, an essential ingredient, anchors the company in Golden, Colorado.

Transportation. Except in very localized operations, either the raw materials or the finished products must be moved. Speed, flexibility, and cost considerations underlie most transportation decisions. Airplanes transport products rapidly, but the high cost may be prohibitive. Truck deliveries are flexible enough to alter days, hours, and routes to fit almost any schedule. The slower means of water and rail transporting are less expensive, but they are inflexible, both in terms of source and destination. And because of building and maintenance expenses, pipelines usually have to be in service for several years to justify their costs.

Rails still carry most of the freight in this country — several billion tons per year. Trucks are becoming more popular because of flexibility and the vast network of highways. Waterways are prime movers of grain, gravel, coal, lumber, and other massive materials. Air transportation is used for small, expensive items such as computer parts. Because the cost of transportation varies within locations, these cost factors are considered in the plant location decision.

Community inducements. Communities, cities, and states have been recruiting industry for years. Recently, most states have greatly increased their efforts to attract new industry. They offer lavish, well-organized proposals. The wide variety of lures includes tax-free bonds, low-cost financing, easing of local zoning laws and even pollution standards, and free or nominal land cost. City and state officials say they need new industry to widen their tax bases and reduce unemployment. Texas officials persuaded Diawa Spinning Company of Osaka, Japan, to build a $20 million

COST FACTORS	SITE FACTORS	COMMUNITY FACTORS
Energy	Accessibility (roads, rails, airports)	Educational systems
Labor	Availability of goods and materials	Fire and police protection
Construction	Location of markets	Medical services
Taxes		Zoning laws
Real estate	LOCAL BUSINESS FACTORS	Legal restrictions
Rent		Cultural opportunities
	Related business activities	Political environment
RESOURCE FACTORS	Service businesses	Crime rate
	Available transportation	Tax rates and regulations
Manual labor	Subcontracting firms	Public services (business)
Skilled personnel	Vendor resources	
Natural resources		EMPLOYEE CONSIDERATIONS
Energy		
Land		Shopping facilities
		Housing costs
		Religious facilities
		Cost of living
		Public facilities and services

Figure 8.1
Considerations of plant locations.

cotton spinning mill in Leveland, Texas. Japanese textile companies are the biggest importers of Texas cotton. The state agency spent 3 years convincing Diawa to locate in Texas. Japanese officials inspected 32 possible sites, and each community submitted a bid for the plant. Leveland won by offering land and water rights for a mere $10. In explaining their decision, the city officials said, "The cotton plant will mean 120 new jobs, and as many as 1000 in the near future. It was worth the cost of the land and water to have the plant in our community."

While the factors described here are the major considerations for plant location, there are many others. Some of these appear in Fig. 8.1. Of course, not all these factors are equally important to all types of companies. For example, an oil refinery must be near a source of oil, regardless of other issues.

Evaluating location factors. Where a company locates is usually a compromise between several factors. One site has a more desirable labor supply, but another has better transportation facilities. One community offers an outstanding incentive package, but it would place the company in an inaccessible location. In almost all decisions,

key managers visit several sites, study the variables, and make individual evaluations. They may prepare elaborate estimates of total costs and expected returns at various volume levels for each

TABLE 8.1 ■ COMPANY LOCATION FACTORS

	Value 1–10	Relative Importance to Company 1–10	Total Points
Labor supply	6	10	60
Raw materials	8	9	72
Power and water	7	7	49
Transportation	8	9	72
Markets	4	4	16
Community inducements	9	3	27
Site factors	3	7	21
Cost factors	7	8	56
Community factors	9	5	45
Employee considerations	4	4	16
TOTAL POINTS (This Location)			454

location. Some use a point-rating system by which they list and assign points to the important factors. The list of factors and point values might appear as shown in Table 8.1.

This point system helps managers clearly evaluate the alternatives as they apply to their company. The site with the highest rating may not automatically be the final choice, but this system certainly helps in making an informed decision.

Plant Layout

Once plant location has been settled, the next planning task is plant layout. If all the plant location factors did not give you a headache, consider-ing all the criteria for plant layout may. **Plant layout** refers to the physical positioning of machines, work space, storage, shelving, and equipment within the building. First, we have to decide how big a plant we are going to build.

Plant capacity. The sales forecast is the major determinant of **plant capacity.** But sales in most industries fluctuate. So managers have to consider the cost of both unused space during slack times and lost orders due to shortages in peak periods. Size and number of machines also influence plant capacity. Larger and faster machines may produce lower per-unit costs, but higher sales volume is needed to justify them. Shift work also has an

TAKING STOCK

Auto Producers Come Back

After a deep recession in the auto industry, manufacturers of automobiles in the United States staged a strong comeback in 1983. In the second quarter of 1983, quarterly earnings rose 86% for General Motors, 165% for Ford, and 190% for Chrysler.

The auto comeback also means good news for suppliers, many of which have been operating below 50% capacity since 1979. The Eaton Corporation, which sells engine components to auto producers, says that both sales and profits are up. National Steel, which lost $52 million in the second quarter of 1982, made a $9.3 million profit in the second quarter of 1983. They credited the turnaround to increases in auto-related orders.

Machine tools, which are also very dependent upon the auto industry, are also beginning to fare better. "When the auto industry reaches 80% capacity, machine tools take off," a spokesperson said.

As a nation, we are very much concerned about what happens to the auto industry because it has such a tremendous impact upon our economy. For example, the auto industry:

- Provides, directly and indirectly, about 12 million jobs.
- Generates about $25.8 billion taxes annually.
- Uses about 15% of U.S. steel.
- Uses 60% of U.S. rubber.
- Uses 62% of U.S. lead.
- Totals about one-fourth of all retail sales.

Therefore, success among auto producers usually means success in many other aspects of our economy.

Source: "Spreading Impact of Auto Comeback," *U.S. News & World Report,* Aug. 8, 1983, p. 44.

Figure 8.2
Example of a process layout.

impact on plant size. If an around-the-clock, three-shift operation is practical, a smaller plant is adequate. A one-shift plant would require a much larger plant for the same output.

Manufacturing processes. As plant capacity affects layout, so does the type of manufacturing process. An **intermittent process** has periodic starting and stopping points. Product #612 may appear on the production schedule for 25 days, be off the schedule for 13 days, and back on again for 22 days. The schedule may change often, according to the demand of that product. Intermittent processes turn out products in small volumes and use easily adaptable, general-purpose equipment. A **continuous process** operates for long, uninterrupted periods—months or even years. But "continuous" does not mean "indefinite." New developments and style changes may cause changes in the process. Continuous operations employ specialized, highly efficient equipment to create large volumes of standardized output. **Custom manufacturing,** or producing to special customer specifications, has declined in popularity because it is so expensive. Standardized, mass-produced products are much less expensive. Some clothes, a few automobiles, and some homes are still custom-made, primarily for status-seeking and wealthy customers.

Examples of plant layouts. Used primarily for intermittent manufacturing, the **process layout** clusters all functions of a particular type. Processes such as welding, painting, assembly, drilling, and finishing are all done in specific, prees-

tablished sections of the plant. Processes such as inspecting, planning, and receiving also have their designated areas. The more dangerous operations are often grouped and separated. Each product may flow through the plant in a different path; flexibility is necessary because one piece of equipment is used for several different products. However, having a different flow pattern for each product reduces operating efficiency. And it requires careful planning. See Fig. 8.2 for an example of a process layout. Note how the products follow different routes. Product A comes into receiving and moves to the planning department, is routed through punching, drilling, and welding, then shipped. Product B is received and goes from planning to grinding, punching, painting, and shipping.

In a **product layout,** operators and equipment are stationed in one spot; assembly line conveyer belts move materials and semifinished products through each station. Unlike a process layout, the same types of processing equipment

Figure 8.3
Example of a product layout.

are frequently located in different parts of the plant. Product layouts that are more adaptable to continuous operations are desirable where a company produces a few highly standardized products in large volume. Straight-line flows that require minimum movement in transporting parts between operations are most common. Raw materials enter one end, flow straight through, and come out the other end as finished products (see Fig. 8.3). Other product layouts may utilize U-shaped, circular, or S-shaped flow patterns as shown in Fig. 8.4. The U-flow is convenient when construction requires shipping and receiving at the same end of the building. A circular flow also permits shipping and receiving at the same end of the building. When operations are physically crowded, the serpentine or S-flow lends efficiency. With each method, the type of production process also affects the type of flow pattern.

Fixed-position layouts move employees, equipment and even machinery around the stationary product. It is impractical to circulate large products such as some airplanes, ships, and bridges. Fixed layouts are flexible, but because they are slow, tend to be more expensive. Many plants use **combination layouts** — utilizing elements of all three layout types. Here, combinations of the process and product layouts and flow patterns are essential. Wrong choices can result in the failure of the venture.

Production Scheduling

After the plant location and layout have been settled, the next production planning step is scheduling. **Scheduling** identifies the sequence and timing of each step in the production process. By scheduling, a planner can forecast the time of each production process and project costs, sales, and profits. Each of the several methods of scheduling usually includes:

- A listing of all things that have to be done.
- An estimate of the time each operation will take.
- Which operations have to come before others.
- An estimate of the total time required for each project.

Control charts are used to illustrate the production processes and chart the time required for

U-flow   S-shaped   Circular

Figure 8.4
Basic flow patterns for product layouts.

each step. Many scheduling techniques use control charts. We describe three popular scheduling techniques here.

Program evaluation and review technique. One of the most popular scheduling techniques is **program evaluation and review technique (PERT).** Originally developed by the U.S. Navy, PERT identifies each job that makes up the project and details the time required for each step. It also recognizes that some jobs are dependent upon other jobs and that some jobs must be completed before others. Planners estimate the time for each task and identify a sequence of operations that requires the longest time period. This becomes

Fixed-position layouts are employed in jet aircraft production, bringing workers, machinery, and pre-assembled parts to the stationary product.

the critical path, that is, the sequence of processes that takes the longest to complete.

The longest path through the diagram is the critical path; it is the quickest the job can be completed.

To illustrate how PERT works, consider the process of manufacturing shoes. In a much-simplified example (see Table 8.2), we can divide the process into ten different tasks, each requiring a given number of time units. Now, look at the PERT diagram in Fig. 8.5. Notice that Tasks #4, #5, and #8 must be completed before Task #9, as must Tasks #2, #6, and #7. The longest path through the diagram, represented by the heavy line, is the critical path; it is the quickest the job can be completed. The circles indicate the completion of a task. Often, the length of the lines indicates the time required for each task.

Critical path method. When planners use the longest process within a task to estimate production completion times, it is called **CPM (critical path method).** In the shoe manufacturing example, the critical path is sixty-two time units (which

could be hours, days, weeks, or months). The total for all processes is eighty-eight time units. Once the critical path is determined, other processes are planned around it. For example, the work on heels and soles takes less time; fewer employees will be required to complete those tasks. Scheduling will allow for the proper number of soles, heels, and tops to be completed and received for the next process of sewing them together.

Materials requirements planning. In planning, managers need to get the proper number of products or the right amount of materials to a specific place at a certain time. The method of accomplishing this task is called **materials requirements planning (MRP).** Looking again at the shoe example, notice how heels (eighteen time units), soles (twelve time units), and tops (thirty-three time units) must arrive at the same point for assembly. If too few parts arrive, it will stop the rest of the operation. If too many are completed, storage and stockpiling problems occur. MRP allows for the exact number to arrive at the proper place and time.

Of course, these methods can be used in other functions of production management. PERT charts, for example, are used in plant operation as well as production control. These methods are critical in production scheduling, however. Like the other aspects of production planning, scheduling can make the difference between success and failure.

TABLE 8.2 ■ THE TASKS AND TIME UNITS REQUIRED TO MANUFACTURE SHOES

Task No.	Task	Number of Time Units
1	Receiving	1
2	Cutting heels	8
3	Cutting soles	8
4	Cutting pattern	12
5	Dyeing leather	8
6	Glueing heels	4
7	Glueing heels to soles	6
8	Sewing tops	13
9	Sewing tops to heels and soles	14
10	Finishing	10
11	Packaging	2
12	Shipping	2

Capital Requirements

While capital or finance topics are covered in several other places within the text, some discussion is fitting here because of the tremendous investment required for modern production plants. As costs of equipment may change rapidly, accurate forecasts are difficult. Too often, investment is much greater than anticipated. The U.S. government's planning of the B-1 bomber is a prime example, as are many atomic energy plants. Large businesses, especially production companies, have the same problems. Consider the costs of land, buildings, technical equipment and machinery, design and engineering costs, storage facilities, and transportation. Many of these are difficult to forecast 5 years into the future, not to mention the cost of capital itself. The cost of spe-

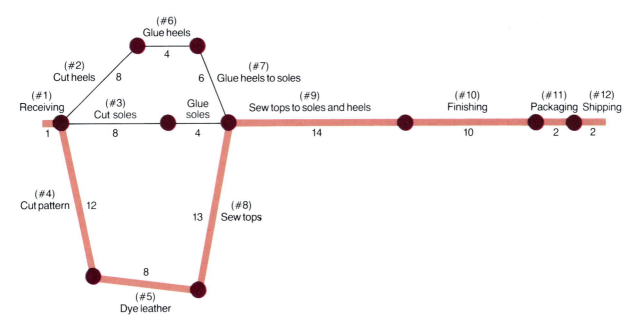

Figure 8.5
PERT chart for the manufacture of shoes.

cialized manufacturing equipment and machines is staggering. For these reasons, planners need not only adequate financing but large funds for unexpected costs.

MATERIALS MANAGEMENT

Once the specifics of product planning have been established, the next function is materials management. Effective plant management requires proper handling of materials used in the production process, including purchasing and inventory control.

Purchasing

Have you ever purchased a car, a suit, a pair of shoes, or an electric blender? Think of all the decisions you had to make. "What model, brand, or size should I get? How much should I pay? Does the seller have a good reputation? When will the product be available? What is a reasonable price?"

Since few businesses exist entirely on their own, thousands of purchasing decisions must be made. To make a large product, a company might purchase from as many as 14,000 different suppliers located throughout the United States and other parts of the world. Purchases include raw materials for products, supplies, services from other companies, land, buildings, and even automobiles and insurance. The aim of purchasing is to get the right amount, quality, and price from the right place at the right time.

Purchasing policies. Large and medium-size firms devote a department to the purchasing function. The department head is called an agent or general purchasing agent. This manager may supervise a staff of buying specialists. A company establishes policies on exactly how the purchasing will be done. These policies assign the buying authority and responsibility to certain departments and individuals. Policies also set limits on what can be purchased. For example, the personnel department may be in charge of the purchasing office, but only up to certain quantities and amounts. The mailroom manager may purchase postage and mailing supplies. Different people in production may be responsible for purchasing raw materials, semifinished products, production supplies, and various services. The purchasing authority may vary, according to budget, need, and company projections. This authority may be centralized, with the decision making in the higher levels of the organization. Other firms decentralize this authority, giving it to various departments or local branches.

In establishing purchasing policies, managers have to resolve several issues, including the following:

1. *Make-or-buy decisions.* **Make-or-buy decisions** involve a firm deciding whether they should make a part or buy it from another firm. Sometimes a larger company may produce many of its own needs; other times, the company may choose to buy many things. Should a car manufacturer purchase tires or create its own department to produce them? Should a winery grow or purchase its grapes? A cheese producer may have a large farm operation or purchase milk from a local farmers co-op.

2. *Hand-to-mouth buying vs. forward buying.* In **hand-to-mouth buying,** a company places orders frequently and usually in small amounts. This style of buying is popular when products are perishable, needs vary, or storage is a problem. In **forward buying,** a company usually purchases large quantities less frequently. For example, a winery may purchase vast amounts of grapes only once a year, whereas a cheese producer may purchase varying amounts of milk daily.

3. *Contract buying.* Producers may enter into contracts with suppliers, or **vendors,** to purchase goods of certain quantities over several years. A contract may be necessary because both the buyer and seller must be certain of the deal. The producer needs the materials to ensure smooth running of the plant, and the vendor needs to know that the products will be purchased. **Contract buying** is popular in heavy industries, such as automobiles, electronics, construction, and transportation.

4. *Bidding.* Often a producer will resort to **bidding** from vendors. Vendors are told the quantities and specifications of a certain good and then submit bids on what they will charge for a good or service. In large purchases, it benefits the buyer by creating competition between the vendors. Usually, the lowest bid will result in business for the supplier.

5. *Reciprocal buying.* Sometimes companies will agree to buy from each other. This form of **reciprocal buying** is popular in some types of business. However, both illegal and unethical practices may result unless this type of agreement is carefully guarded. For example, a computer company and a television manufacturer may become vendors for each other. But if the arrangement is too restrictive, each may lose business to other companies.

Purchasing goods. To help understand the kinds of goods that companies purchase, we have divided them into four general catagories.

1. *Raw materials.* Raw materials are the resources from which a product is produced. These include lumber, iron, oil, dairy products, rubber, plastics, chemicals, and minerals. These raw materials are combined in the production process to create the finished products that we buy in the stores.

2. *Semifinished goods.* Sometimes production companies purchase goods that are already partially manufactured. These are called semifinished or semimanufactured products.

3. *Supplies.* Supplies do not go into the actual product, but they assist in its production. Examples include cleaning materials, sandpaper, saw blades, and office supplies.

4. *Capital items.* Machinery and major equipment used to produce the product are called capital items. Examples are robots, finishing machines, drill presses, saws, lifts, trucks, and conveyors.

Purchasing services. In addition to goods, production companies also purchase a wide range of services, such as the following:

1. *Industrial services.* Firms may hire other companies to clean their shops, building, and machines, remove their waste products, protect against theft, or provide food for employees. Outside companies can often provide these industrial services more efficiently than the company itself.

2. *Professional services.* Companies may also hire outside professionals to perform a variety of services including advertising, printing,

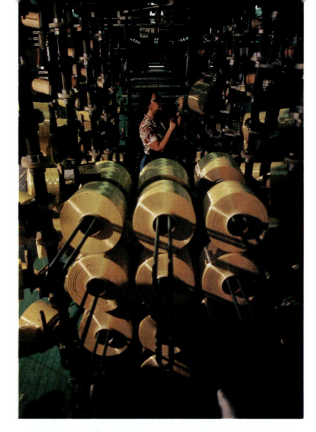

These fibers being readied for shipment are semifinished goods, the material basis for a variety of finished products.

data processing, accounting, legal assistance, and management consulting.

3. *Subcontracting work.* Sometimes a firm will hire other companies to complete all parts of a particular job. The original company is called the prime contractor, and the firms doing the work are called subcontractors. This arrangement is most common in the construction business. A contractor may hire or subcontract other companies to complete the electrical, plumbing, paint, glass, or insulation aspects of a job. Manufacturing companies often subcontract parts of their work on a permanent or part-time basis to other companies.

Purchasing procedures. The actual purchase usually follows a plan with well-established steps. While these procedures vary from firm to firm, they usually include describing specifications, completing a purchase requisition, selecting a

supplier, placing the order, and receiving the goods.

1. *Specifications.* Various departments within the company usually cooperate in creating the specifications (specs) of the goods to be puchased. Engineering, production, quality control, and sales departments may all contribute to the desired specifications. For example, an office might require a calculator to compute square roots, have a certain storage capacity, and perform so many calculations per minute. For repetitive purchases such as nuts, bolts, and screws, there are industry-wide standards that are usually graded; establishing specs in this case simply means identifying the grade.

2. *Purchase requisition.* The need for materials, supplies, or services is recognized either by the people who use them or by someone in a materials management department. When inventories run below the desired level, they indicate the need to reorder with a **purchase requisition** — a form listing the quantities, specifications, and date needed. Usually, this form is routed to the proper department for approval and then to the purchasing department to initiate the buying process.

3. *Supplier selection.* Where does a company buy? From the vendor with the lowest price? Not always. While price is important, there are other considerations: Speed of delivery, dependability, quality of product, the salesperson, reputation of the firm, and previous experiences with the vendor all affect the final decision.

4. *Order placement.* When agents select a supplier, they complete a **purchase order.** This, in effect, is a contract to buy. If the purchase is large, agents will probably make frequent follow-ups to see how the order is progressing and make sure that the delivery is on time.

5. *Receiving.* Upon delivery, a receiving clerk checks the quantity, price, and other qualities against the purchase order to be certain that they fit the specs. If the shipment is correct, the clerk makes a note on the supplier's invoice and sends it to the purchasing department where it is approved for payment. If the

Production Techniques in Service Organizations

Unlike a product, a service is intangible and perishable. Services are usually used at the time they are created; and, for the most part, they cannot be stored.

How services differ from products

Services differ from products in at least four ways. One, services are intangible. When producing a product, employees can see, touch, and perhaps taste and smell the item. But since services are intangible, neither employees nor customers can touch or taste them. Further, producers cannot get a patent on services. When Hertz, the car rental company, created the Hertz #1 Club to make it possible for customers to get a car without filling out all the forms, Avis and other competitors were quick to copy this service.

Two, services are perishable. Nothing is more perishable than an airline seat, a hotel room, or an hour of a consultant's time. If these are not used at the time they are available, you cannot inventory them. Three, services are heterogeneous. Holiday Inn may train all of their reservation clerks in the same way, but there is no way they can ensure that service in Los Angeles will be the same as service in New York. The same services will differ among locations and from hour to hour, depending upon the mood and motivation of the clerk. Four, we typically produce and use services at the same time. While we design manufacturing facilities with employees and products in mind, we design service facilities with the customer in mind.

Applying production techniques to service operations

Even with these differences, we can apply many production techniques to service operations. Here are three examples of plant layout applied to the creation of services.

- *Straight-line flow.* In straight-line flow layouts, products move from one station to another through the production process in a straight line (for example, an assembly line). A cafeteria is an example of a straight-line flow for service operations. Customers move in a straight line through the process as they are "served" with food of their choice.

- *Job shop.* In a job shop, employees may produce many different types of products by using different sequences and combinations of activities. A job shop usually produces custom-made products for customers. An example of a service job shop is the more traditional restaurant, which provides meals to order. Medical doctors who are general practitioners are another example of a service job shop.

- *Intermittent processes.* While both line and job shop processes provide a continuous flow of products, some require intermittent processes. For instance, service firms have to manage the periodic task of introducing new services to their customers. Further, architects and movie studios often find themselves managing the services of projects. They have to concern themselves with the starting and stopping of operations as well as with their integration.

Thus even though the creation of services differs from production of a product, production techniques are still useful to service companies.

order is deficient, the purchasing agent usually works out the difference with the supplier.

Inventory Control

Purchasing policies and procedures are influenced by how much inventory a company maintains and the size of the order. When the plant runs out of materials, production stops, resulting in costly waste. Too much inventory can result in storage costs, bottlenecks, obsolescence, insurance, theft, deterioration, and waste. While inventory control is important to all companies, it is crucial to a production company.

Small inventories require frequent, small orders. They result in increased ordering costs and paperwork. But small inventories reduce storage and handling costs. Larger inventories allow for volume discounts, ensure necessary levels, and incur less ordering costs. But they require the necessary inventory and handling costs. Many techniques are used to balance these storage and ordering costs. One popular method is called **economic order quantity (EOQ).** Assume that a plant annually uses 10,000 units of Part 40B. Placing an order costs $20, and the annual inventory costs average $.10 per unit. Economic order quantity is obtained by determining the point at which the combined costs are the least. EOQ is illustrated in Fig. 8.6.

This is the most economic order size because it balances the inventory and ordering costs. While other technical methods provide guidelines for ordering quantities, additional practical reasons also affect the decision. **Anticipation inventories** exist because of some planned future need. Model changeovers, anticipated strikes, vacation shutdowns, recessions, or intensive sales

Annual cost (in thousands of dollars)

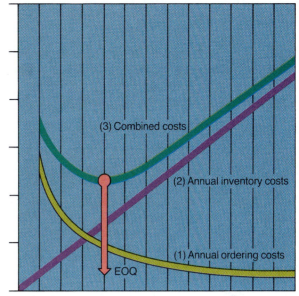

Order quantity (in number of units ordered at one time)

Figure 8.6
A chart for determining economic order quantity (EOQ).
(1) The annual costs of ordering; this cost decreases as the size of the order increases. (2) Annual inventory costs; this cost increases as larger quantities are ordered. (3) This is the combination of ordering costs and inventory costs.

campaigns are factors that affect future needs. **Buffer inventories** are additional orders that serve as safety measures against unforeseen events; demands may exceed forecasts, or output may deviate from plans. Figure 8.7 lists factors favoring large and small inventories.

Finally, to keep an accurate record of inventory on hand, people actually count the materials and supplies at scheduled times. **Materials in-**

Figure 8.7
Factors that favor large or small inventories.

MAINTAIN LARGER INVENTORIES WHEN:	MAINTAIN SMALLER INVENTORIES WHEN:
1. Cost of placing an order is great	1. Inventory costs are high
2. Storage is inexpensive	2. Goods deteriorate rapidly
3. Quantity discounts are substantial	3. Storage costs are expensive
4. Prices are expected to rise	4. Goods are easy to get
5. Shortages are anticipated	5. Cash is hard to get or in short supply
	6. Prices are expected to drop

ventories record the materials that go into the finished product; **supplies inventories** register the supplies on hand; and **merchandise inventories** count the finished products.

To cut inventory costs, many firms are switching to the just-in-time method popularized by Japan.

To cut inventory costs as much as possible, many firms are switching to the just-in-time method popularized by Japan. **Just-in-time inventory** means ordering smaller quantities more frequently and receiving them as close to their use as possible. This drastically reduces the need for large shipments that have to be stored and controlled on the premises. At Apple Computer's new Macintosh plant in Fremont, California, no more than 5 days' worth of supplies for any one component are kept at the site, reducing inventory costs and the possibility of damage in storage. When large purchasers convert to such a system, suppliers often have to move closer to their customer. When General Motors modernized its plant in Bal-

Inventory control functions for Apple Computer's production of the Macintosh personal computer are handled by a single Macintosh.

timore, many suppliers called to ask about sites nearby.

Apart from cost reduction, other benefits develop when suppliers cluster near the producer. Because deliveries and contacts occur more frequently, engineers from both supplier and purchaser get together more often and help solve common problems. However, there is a disadvantage to the supplier because they have to depend rather heavily upon one outlet for their products.

THE PLANT IN OPERATION

Now that the plant has been located, the layout established, and all materials arranged for, the stage is set for plant operation: production processes and production control.

Production Processes

Routing specifies the particular path through which a production process will take place. While it is planned for in, say, a PERT chart, those plans have to be put into effect within the plant. Back to the shoe example. At #9 on the assembly line, sewn tops arrive at the same place as the glued soles and heels. Routing allows not only for the separate process, but also for the right number to arrive at the proper place for the next step of the production process.

Dispatching provides work orders to managers and supervisors, allows for the resources of labor and materials, and outlines the schedule of completion for the specific task. It activates all the resources necessary for the actual performance of production, the next step of the process. **Performance** is, simply, the action of machines and labor in the actual production process. It requires supervisors to be certain that each step is completed properly and to solve any problems or interruptions. The finished product now comes off the production line.

There are two major types of production processes: the analytic and the synthetic processes. The **analytic process** is the breaking down of raw materials into one or more products. The final product may or may not resemble the raw materials. A good example would be the making of records out of plastic products. The **synthetic**

process is the combining of two or more materials in the production of one final product. Cleaning fluid, for example, may contain several raw materials that are combined in special quantities in order to produce the final product.

Production Control

Even with the most careful plans and execution, results often fall short of the goal. Production control compares production progress to plans and checks for proper product quality. Quality control reflects deviations in schedule, quantity, and quality of the finished product.

Progress control. With **progress control,** managers compare actual production time to the

schedule. An individual or a department may have responsibility for production control, and there are a number of ways to check actual progress. For an intermittent process, each department's foreman may prepare daily reports listing work ordered, work completed, and work still in progress. Another method is to issue job tickets that go to production control, signifying that the job is completed. Also, standard forms may be filled out as each job is completed. Production control receives these reports to get an accurate progress status.

The **Gantt chart,** developed by Henry Gantt, uses a bar graph to compare what was planned to what remains to be done. Figure 8.8 is an example. Order numbers are listed in the left column. Solid bars show planned starting and stopping times,

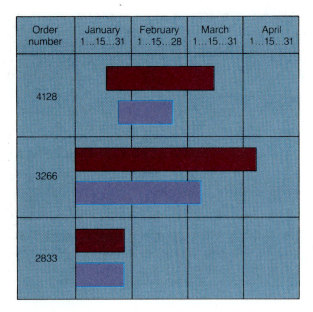

Order number	January 1...15...31	February 1...15...28	March 1...15...31	April 1...15...31
4128				
3266				
2833				

Figure 8.8
A Gantt chart.

and light bars represent actual progress. The Gantt chart is simple and revealing, but it is used less frequently today because of the time required to keep its data current. Much of this same information is recorded and displayed by modern computers.

The basics of progress control are similar for continuous manufacturing. They begin with the authorization to produce. Planning issues a production schedule with quantities and dates. A tally, comparing the actual number produced with that planned, is kept at regular intervals. Production control then uses a variety of charts such as the one in Fig. 8.9 to compare actual and scheduled output.

Production that is behind schedule usually adds to the costs and may delay delivery dates, so production control tries to detect problems early. Lags result from breakdowns, improper planning, poor material handling, supervisory errors, employee disturbances, or strikes. The plant tries to catch up by working overtime, adding shifts, pressuring suppliers, and hiring additional or part-time people. Ahead-of-schedule problems are less serious, but production control must find out why there is a variance. They may put other items into production sooner than expected, build

up inventories, or cut back production as a result.

Computer-aided design and computer-aided manufacturing. Of course, more recently, companies have been using computers quite extensively in all aspects of their manufacturing processes. In **computer-aided design (CAD)** systems, designs can be sketched on an electronic drafting board or directly on a computer screen, thereby allowing the operator to view from any angle or modify in any way a stored design. CAD systems are typically used by aerospace, automotive, and manufacturing companies for mechanical design and drafting; by electronics firms for printed circuit and integrated circuit design; by architectural and construction organizations for structural design; by energy companies and utilities for plant design and layout; and by government agencies and private companies for various mapping applications. General Motors, for instance, uses a CAD system to help with complicated engine and chassis design problems.

Computervision Corporation, the industry leader in CAD/CAM products, says that the 1970s was the decade of CAD and that the 1980s will be the decade of **computer-aided manufacturing**

Figure 8.9
A control chart.

Cumulative output

Days

Using a CAD/CAM system, a small firm like Compo Industries can quickly and cost-efficiently design and manufacture a variety of their product-molds for shoe soles.

(CAM). It is not unusual, during batch manufacturing, for a part to stand idle for weeks, waiting at each step of the manufacturing process for a machine tool to become available. About 95% of the time required to manufacture a typical part is spent waiting for machines; 3.5% is devoted to setup; and only 1.5% of the time is actual machining. By intelligently collecting, integrating, and using information, CAM systems can increase productivity and cut manufacturing costs. Compo Industries, a firm that designs and fabricates injection molds for shoe manufacturers, uses a CAD system to design shoe molds and a CAM system to machine the finished mold designs.

The next step in industry automation, in realizing the fully automated factory of the future, is **computer-integrated manufacturing (CIM),** the integration of design and manufacturing activities and of all ancillary elements of manufacturing operations. Electronic manufacturing is an important and growing segment of CIM. Automated numerical control drilling for printed circuit boards, automatic component insertion, and automatic testing are a few examples of CIM technologies.

Flexible manufacturing systems. Flexible manufacturing systems (FMS), the newest thing in production, integrate all the elements in the production process. Computer-driven systems control practically everything, including machine shop operations, transporting parts and products within the plant, and even replacing worn-out or broken drill bits.

A flexible manufacturing system can cost $25 million or more, but it is infinitely more flexible than conventional, numerically controlled operations. For instance, designers can instantly reprogram an FMS to make new parts or products. Thus, one machine can replace several conventional lines and save in capital investment. General Electric uses an FMS to produce 2000 different versions of an electric meter, and IBM was able to shorten the time needed to introduce new products by adopting an FMS that made it possible to build several successive models on the same production line.

To date, one of the largest FMSs exists near Mount Fuji in Japan's Fanuc Ltd.'s plant, which produces machine tools and parts for robots. The part of the plant that produces machine tools covers 54,000 square feet, and a single controller supervises the whole area via closed-circuit television. If something goes wrong, the controller can shut down the part of the operation with the problem and reroute the work to other stations.

CROSS FIRE

Robots versus Jobs

Every time a nation steps up its automation efforts, people debate whether the overall impact will be positive or negative. Today, the concern centers around the increasing use of robots. About 15,000 robots were in use in the United States in 1983. By 1993, the figure is expected to balloon to 268,000.

Industry sees these "smart" machines as a blessing because they expect them to cut labor costs while, at the same time, increasing both quality and productivity. However, labor fears that the machines will take away jobs. An Arthur D. Little, Inc., expert says that three jobs will be taken over by every two robots installed by 1993. Other experts place the displacement figure even higher; maybe as many as 3.8 million jobs will be affected. However, some of the displaced workers will be transferred or retained within the company, maybe as many as 85% in some cases.

Donald Smith, director of the University of Michigan's industrial development division, says that if firms do not use robots, "silent firings"—loss of jobs because industries cannot compete—may reduce the jobs available. General Motors contends that, with almost 2000 robots in place, workers have not lost jobs. Another company says that robots will result in net additions to the work force because they will create jobs in the "care and feeding" of robots.

Still, Harley Shaiken, labor analyst at MIT, asks, "What of the welder in Flint, Michigan? He's being asked to commit economic suicide so GM can return to profitability."

Briggs & Stratton Corporation, however, resists robots. As the world's leading producer of low-cost engines, used mostly in lawn mowers and garden tractors, they have been profitable for years. What's more, they maintain that human skill and agility, not automation, are responsible for their high-quality, successful products. Briggs & Stratton, which may put as many as 500 parts into one of its machines, emphasizes effective management, good communication, worker participation, and a piecework incentive payment system. Some workers earn as much as $30,000 per year; one visitor said, "They even run to and from the bathrooms." The company says they will consider automation whenever practical, but they do not believe they will ever go to a completely automated, unmanned plant.

What overall impact do you think the increasing use of robots will have upon our economy? Do you believe we will be:

___ A. Much better off   ___ D. Somewhat worse off

___ B. Somewhat better off   ___ E. Much worse off

___ C. No significant change

Give reasons for your response.

A. _____

B. _____

C. _____

Sources: "Will Robots Bring More Jobs—or Less?" *U.S. News & World Report,* September 5, 1983, p. 25; "Where Robots Can't Compete," *Fortune,* February 21, 1983, p. 64.

Abusing Products before Using Them

United Laboratories (UL), a nonprofit organization that tests products strictly for safety, burned and bashed, torched and trashed, sank and smashed nearly 60,000 products in 1982 in their testing procedures. Firms are willing to pay $2000 and more to UL to test their products. Consumers look to the UL label as proof of a product's safety, and the imprimatur may even help a manufacturer defend itself against product liability suits since it proves the manufacturer sought independent evaluation. Here are a few examples of their testing methods:

- UL, with a machine, opened and closed a waffle iron 6000 times. They opened refrigerator doors 30,000 times and microwave ovens 100,000 times. Technicians then examined the wiring and other parts for possible danger.

- A 150-pound technician (the likely maximum weight of a child) rode and bucked for 25 minutes on a coin-operated toy elephant while observers checked volts, watts, ampheres, and motor temperature.

- To test an electric sander, technicians dropped it three times from a 6-foot height onto a concrete floor. Then they looked for cracks and exposed wires that might be dangerous to an operator.

- UL staff drilled holes in the bottom of a fiberglass skiff, slashed the seats, and held it submerged for 18 hours. If the boat got back to the surface horizontally, they declared it seaworthy.

A safe is tested for resilience to a cutting torch in the burglary-proofing section of Underwriters Laboratories.

Source: ''The Lively Art of Product Abuse,'' *Fortune,* May, 1983, pp. 93–98.

Although there were about thirty FMS in the United States in early 1983, Japan had as many as thirty in one large company.

Once again, Japan seems to be leading the world in a manufacturing advancement. Although there were only about thirty flexible manufacturing systems in place in the United States in early 1983, Japan had as many as thirty in one large company.

Quality control. As it is necessary for products to be completed on time, so it is necessary for products to be of a certain quality. Perfection is not essential for all products, but some must be exactly according to the specs. So what if we produce 5000 calendars a day, if 2000 have October missing? Poor quality might reduce sales, waste materials and labor, and even cause a repeat of the same process. A given product may have many different attributes. Some must be precise in the production process, others may not be so crucial. As in progress control, records are kept to compare the actual quality with that planned. Most products have acceptable ranges of deviance. Figure 8.10 shows a control chart for measuring the deviations in the weight of manufactured hot dogs. If periodic checks show that some of the weights are beyond the upper or lower control limits, production is usually stopped and adjustments are made.

In **quality control,** there are periodic checks of products to test their standards. A natural question regarding this process is "How many of the items do we actually check?" For large volumes of standard-sized products, quality control may decide that a 10% sample is enough to make predictions about the remaining products. Larger sample sizes ensure less chance of error, but they are more costly. For grander, more expensive products, a 100% sampling may be used, which means a quality check of each item. Manned space rockets might require 400 or 500% inspection — meaning each item is checked four or five times. The actual test might require simple operations such as weighing, measuring, or testing function, for example, screwing a light bulb into a socket.

Weight (in grams)

Figure 8.10
Control chart for acceptable weight ranges in the manufacture of hot dogs.

More complex tests employ highly sensitive measuring instruments such as x-rays or electron microscopes. And some testing requires destroying the product, as with shotgun shells.

SUMMARY

The purpose of production management is to manufacture the best possible products at the lowest possible cost. Production provides utility for businesses and countries alike. Operations management is like production management, but is a broader term that applies some of the same concepts to the running of the entire company. Production management utilizes many of the concepts of mass production in order to accomplish its goals.

In planning the production plant of the future, location and layout are two of the main considerations. Production scheduling, also part of planning, plans the exact process whereby the product will be produced. Arranging for the capital requirements is another function of production planning.

Materials management includes purchasing and inventory control. Purchasing procedures and policies help implement the acquisition of goods and services. Inventory level and order size are the primary concern of inventory control. Just-in-time inventory, a relatively new policy in the United States, means ordering smaller quantities more frequently.

The six major steps within the production process are planning, scheduling, routing, dispatching, performance, and control. The two most common types of production processes are called the analytic and the synthetic processes. A Gantt chart is used for progress control, and various charts and methods are used in quality control. CAD/CAM and FMS are both recent developments that use computers to increase manufacturing efficiency. Increased productivity is the goal of every plant, and it will become an even more important issue in the future.

MIND YOUR BUSINESS

Instructions. Answer each of the following statements with true (T) or false (F).

_____ 1. For the past 10 years, the United States has led the world in productivity rates.

_____ 2. Communities, cities, and states may offer tax-free bonds, low-cost financing, and free or nominal land costs to attract plants.

_____ 3. An intermittent manufacturing process operates continuously for long, uninterrupted periods of time.

_____ 4. PERT is a scheduling technique.

_____ 5. A firm that practices buying materials and supplies from one of its customers is practicing reciprocal buying.

_____ 6. Just-in-time inventory refers to the practice of buying inventories in large quantities so they will be available when they are needed.

_____ 7. An analytic production process involves breaking down raw materials into one or more products.

_____ 8. By 1990, robots will be operating 90% of the manufacturing functions of our plants.

_____ 9. The United States leads the world in the design and use of flexible manufacturing systems (FMS).

_____ 10. Authorities agree that, during the next 10 years, robots will increase unemployment by more than 30%.

See answers at the back of the book.

KEY TERMS

productivity, 190
production, 190
utility, 190
production management, 190
operations management, 190
mechanization, 191
standardization, 191
automation, 191
assembly line, 191
mass production, 191
plant layout, 195
plant capacity, 195
intermittent process, 196
continuous process, 196
custom manufacturing, 196
process layout, 196
product layout, 196
fixed-position layout, 197
combination layout, 197
scheduling, 197
control chart, 197
program evaluation and review technique (PERT), 197
critical path, 198
critical path method (CPM), 198
materials requirements planning (MRP), 198

layout, what two types of manufacturing process have impact on the choice of a particular plant layout?

5. Describe the three major methods of production scheduling as discussed in the text.

6. How are PERT and CPM used together?

7. What is MRP? Why is it important in running a production plant?

8. What are five issues that managers have to resolve in establishing purchasing policies?

9. Discuss the four types of goods and three services that a production may require.

10. What is the purpose of inventory control? What happens when inventory control is not done properly?

11. Define and describe just-in-time inventory.

12. What are the six major steps within the production process? Describe and differentiate between each of them.

13. Scheduling and routing are quite similar. Exactly how do they differ?

14. What is the difference between progress and quality control?

15. Exactly what is productivity? How is it measured? How is productivity important to a business? To a country?

16. Discuss the three recent developments in production management as they are mentioned in the text.

17. Briefly describe CAD/CAM. Describe FMS. How are these systems similar? Different?

REVIEW QUESTIONS

1. What is the purpose of production management? Describe the five methods used to accomplish this purpose.

2. What are the four major steps in production planning? How is each important to the production process?

3. Describe the factors in choosing a plant location. When are more or fewer of these factors considered? Give an example.

4. What factors affect plant layout? Discuss the five major types of plant layout. In terms of

CASES

Case 8.1: How Far Should the Community Go?

A large manufacturing company was considering locating a branch plant in a small community of about 25,000 people. Supposedly, the plant would create about 250 jobs initially and add another 500 jobs over the first 5 years of operation. The community had a relatively low unemployment rate, about 5%, but the wage level for the community was lower than the national average. Many people thought that the plant would help in getting wage rates up. There was a bit of a problem with pollution from the new plant, and there was some concern about taxes. The company was looking at several locations, and some communities had offered tax exemptions and even agreed to help raise money for building the plant.

Many people were a little concerned about bringing in the new facility. Since it is mostly a farming community, some thought that the factory, the first in the area, would change their lifestyles. The local chamber of commerce was in favor of attracting the new plant to their community, but its leaders were aware of community concerns.

Questions

1. What are the major advantages of a new plant to such a community? Disadvantages?

2. How could such a community attract the new plant? What are the disadvantages to the company of locating in such a community?

3. If you lived in the community, what would you recommend? Why?

Case 8.2: Cost versus Safety in Product Manufacturing

Each year, 50,000 people die in auto accidents. And people continue to argue about how to make this vital product more safe. Most deaths occur upon impact when the driver is thrown against some part of the auto's interior. Thus, most testing and design changes attempt to protect the driver and passengers from these impacts.

Auto engineers say that the cheapest way to reduce injuries and deaths is to pass a federal law requiring seat belt usage. Critics say that the federal government has no business requiring people to do such things against their will, and there is no way to prevent the determined driver from removing his or her seat belt. Some people say that the law should require air bags that inflate upon impact. Still others add that manufacturers should put more padding around the dashboard instruments.

Manufacturers are using computer-aided design systems to come up with more effective means of preventing auto injury. However, practically every possible protection design has one or more drawbacks: it adds to the cost of the auto, people will not use it, or people do not like the design changes necessary to accommodate the protection.

Questions

1. Who has the major responsibility for reducing auto-related injuries and deaths? Why?

   ___ A. The manufacturer

   ___ B. The government

   ___ C. Drivers

2. How would you like to see manufacturers design cars differently to reduce injuries and deaths?

3. How much more would you be willing to pay for a car that is substantially safer? Why?

   ___ A. Much more

   ___ B. A little more

   ___ C. No more

After completing this chapter, you will be able to:

■ Identify the functions of a human resources department.

■ Discuss major laws affecting human resources and personnel matters.

■ Distinguish between a job analysis, a job description, and a job specification.

■ Identify ten external sources for recruiting employees.

■ Explain the seven steps in the employee selection process.

■ Discuss the training and development function.

■ Explain the nature and purpose of performance evaluations.

■ Describe the major types of wage payment plans.

INCENTIVE COMP
PURPOSES

9

HUMAN
RESOURCES
MANAGEMENT

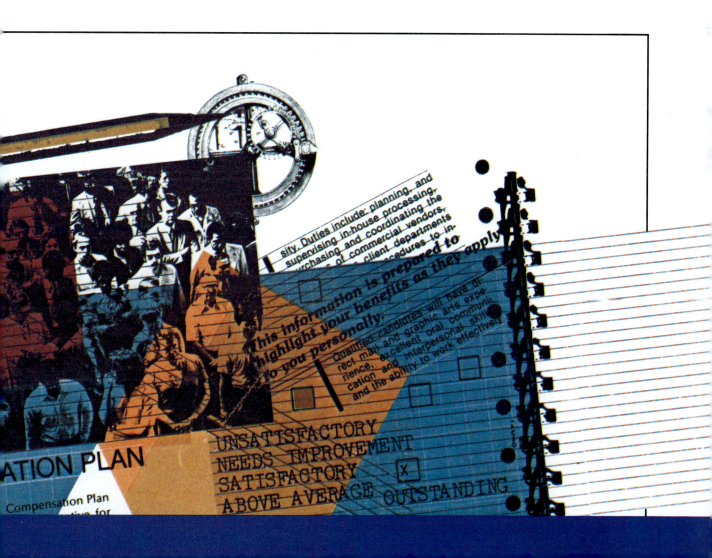

People are our most important assets," is the watchword of many organizations today. More and more, we are realizing that we cannot have a long-term successful firm without selecting, training, and treating our people properly. Of course, it is the responsibility of all managers to treat their people with dignity and respect, but people in the human resources area devote all, or most, of their time to people.

Have you ever wondered how organizations select people to work for them? What they do to train and develop their people? How they evaluate employees' performances? How they decide what to pay their people? These are the concerns of human resources management. After a brief description of human resources administration, this chapter deals with these topics.

WHAT IS HUMAN RESOURCES ADMINISTRATION?

Human resources tries to develop a zestful, highly motivated work force. They want employees to be happy and to experience high levels of job satisfaction. Although this is the responsibility of all managers, human resources specializes in matching people with jobs and providing a good reward system. **Human resources management,** a modern term that replaces "personnel management," is usually a staff position responsible for staffing, training, compensating, and providing services for the entire company.

The Functions of Human Resources

From its humble clerical beginnings in the early 1900s, the human resources profession has grown to include more than 170,000 specialists working in government and industry. Though human resources departments still keep numerous employee records, they now participate with top management in diagnostic and policy-making functions. Like any other department in the orga-

nization, human resources now administers programs that directly affect profitability. In small companies, human resources shares more of these responsibilities with line managers. Human resources departments expend considerable effort in advertising job openings, recruiting, and selecting the right people. Selecting also implies training, and human resources is usually responsible for training. In addition to in-house programs, training specialists investigate and sponsor general education and employee development programs with universities, professional associations, and workshop consultants. Human resources specialists also analyze jobs according to skill level and contribution to objectives before recommending wage and salary systems. Table 9.1 lists twenty-four critical issues (or pressure points) ranked by priority that human resource managers identified in a recent survey.

As companies grow, the human resources department tends to receive those duties that really don't fit anyplace else. Human resources carries out a wide range of employee services from company parties to managing benefits, from providing information about the company to producing the company newsletter. Other human resources functions often include labor relations, conducting research, maintaining records, providing supplies, and implementing safety programs. Figure 9.1 profiles some of the typical responsibilities of human resources administrators.

Human Resources Department Structure

Structural relationships of the human resources department depend somewhat upon the size of the company, but management philosophy and practical concerns have the greatest influence on structure. As the need for human resources services has grown, human resources departments have become more visible and influential.

In smaller companies, the human resources department may consist of an assistant to the president or may report directly to the operations manager. In about 15% of the departments, the head administrator has the title of vice-president of human resources. Other common titles are personnel administrator, industrial relations manager, head of employee relations, manager of labor relations, director of personnel administration, and human resources manager. Although more than 80% of human resources administra-

tors have college degrees, many have not been formally trained in human resources. More recently, larger departments have begun to hire trained specialists. Entry-level jobs include interviewers, training specialists, analysts, counselors, and labor negotiators.

The human resources department does not exist in isolation; its major purpose is to help other departments handle employees through service, control, and advisory relationships.

Service relationships. Specialists provide many services to other departments. Record keeping is paramount, but other services include issuing the company newspaper, managing the

TABLE 9.1 ■ HOW 309 HUMAN RESOURCE EXECUTIVES RANKED THE IMPORTANCE OF 24 HUMAN RESOURCE ISSUES

Ranking	Pressure Point	Average Critical Value (on a scale of 10)	Ranking	Pressure Point	Average Critical Value (on a scale of 10)
1	Productivity improvement programs	7.74	13	Promotional opportunities for female and minority employees	5.76
2	Controlling costs of employee benefits	7.72	14	Employee relocation costs	5.61
3	Compensation planning and administration	7.57	15	Recruitment of mid-level and senior technical and/or engineering personnel	5.42
4	Employee communications	7.38	16	Labor relations and contract negotiations	5.23
5	Upgrading management training development programs	7.16	17	Improvements to employee benefits program	5.07
6	Organizational development programs	7.13	18	Compliance with OSHA/ EEOC and other governmental regulations	5.01
7	Management succession planning	7.12	19	Administering health and accident prevention programs	4.88
8	Improving employee morale	6.80	20	Reducing employee turnover	4.82
9	Human resource information systems	6.47	21	Employee willingness to relocate	4.81
10	Quality improvement programs	6.22	22	Recruitment of entry-level management talent	4.76
11	Recruitment of mid-level and senior management talent	6.12	23	Outplacement counseling	4.37
12	Union avoidance programs	5.85	24	Union decertification programs	2.59

Source: Jack Herring, "Human Resource Managers Rank Their Pressure Points," *Personnel Administrator*, June, 1983, pp. 113–116, 137.

SELECTION	TRAINING	WAGES AND SALARIES	SERVICES
Recruiting	Technical training	Job analysis	Pensions
Interviewing	Supervisory training	Job descriptions	Life insurance
Testing	Management development	Job specifications	Retirement
Evaluating	General education	Job grades	Profit sharing
Placing	Correspondence programs	Wage standards	Recreation
Orienting	Off-campus programs	Wage surveys	Health facilities
Promoting	Company library	Employee classifications	Credit union
Transferring			Cafeteria
			Newspaper
LABOR RELATIONS	**SAFETY**	**RESEARCH AND RECORDS**	Parking
			Medical insurance
Grievances	Standards	Personnel records	Legal aid
Labor contracts	Inspection	Personnel audits	
Collective bargaining	Contests	Labor market surveys	
Hours overtime	Safety engineering	Organizational analysis	
Work conditions	Rules	Design of reports	
Suggestion plans	Accident investigation	Manuals	
Affirmative action	Prevention	Policies	
		Statistical analysis	
		Turnover studies	

Figure 9.1
Examples of human resources functions.

cafeteria, planning the company picnic, scheduling vacations, and keeping the inventory on such items as table tennis balls. Specialists also write job descriptions, place recruiting ads, perform preliminary interviewing, and handle employee testing for the departments. Line departments are usually quite willing for human resources to take over these headache-producing activities, but there are a few friction points. For example:

■ Line and human resources managers sometimes disagree over how well a service fulfills a need.

■ Line departments may resist directions from human resources services.

■ The line may make requests that human resources thinks are the responsibility of line managers.

■ Conflicts sometimes exist over who has the right to do what.

Control relationships. Although service activities were the first concerns of human resources work, now human resources departments are becoming responsible for controlling company policies and procedures. Increased government regulation stimulates the need to control hiring, firing, wage administration, and safety practices. In a typical control relationship, line management has to clear certain decisions with the human resources director. For example, suppose a middle manager in the line wants to promote a subordinate into a supervisory position. Before he or she can implement the decisions, the line has to check with human resources to see if all the affirmative action guidelines are being followed.

Advisory relationships. Perhaps the most significant role for modern human resources departments is developing recommendations and providing advice for line managers. Human resources members work on policies for promoting managers, improving hiring, building better union relationships, designing modifications in organizational structure, and incorporating the newest ideas of employee motivation. This advisory relationship is usually tricky because the human resources manager has to persuade line managers to accept advice. Line managers resist the inconveniences of change and often perceive the recommendations as a threat to their authority. Human resources advisors must spend time developing the trust and confidence of line managers before identifying problems and offering assistance.

Legal Considerations

Human resources managers are concerned about some legal aspects of their work. Even when there is a separate legal department, human resources oversees some company activities to ensure legality in several areas, especially in the areas of safety, hiring, and firing. Safety has long been a human resources concern, and the passage of **Occupational Safety and Health Act (OSHA),** which sets safety standards for industry, has drastically increased the need for safety administration. Human resources is still charged with the all-important but tedious task of record keeping on almost all facets of the employee's work life. And human resources departments conduct internal surveys on attitudes, morale, employee feelings, and audits of skills and talent.

The **Civil Rights Act of 1964** prohibits discrimination in all phases of the job. And the government appointed an Equal Employment Opportunity Commission (EEOC), a federal agency to enforce the civil rights act. By law, companies cannot make selection decisions on the basis of race, color, national origin, religion, or sex. The only exceptions are very small companies (employing fewer than 15 employees for less than 20 weeks per year), religious organizations, and private clubs exempt from paying income taxes.

In 1973, the EEOC got the attention of the nation and most large companies when it won a pay discrimination suit against AT&T. The suit forced AT&T to pay $15 million in back pay and $23 million a year in raises for discriminatory practices in job assignments, pay, and promotion. This judgment was based on the premise that people doing the same jobs should be paid equally.

More recently, some groups have tried to replace the concept of equal pay for equal work, with comparable worth. Under **comparable worth,** dissimilar jobs would be paid at the same rate if the content of the work — the skills, responsibility, hazards, and mental and physical effort — is similar. According to job evaluators in Illinois, for example, the predominantly female job of secretary is roughly comparable in value to the predominantly male job of electrician. However, the average monthly salary for electricians in Illinois is $2826 while the average monthly salary of a secretary is only $1486. The Equal Pay Act of 1963 requires equal pay for equal work, but unions and women's groups say that equal pay for comparable work is needed to fully eliminate sex discrimination in employment compensation. Worried about the wide disparity in pay between male- and female-dominated jobs, the city of Spokane, Washington, recently granted $200 pay equity increases for lower-paid women office workers. In past negotiations, the city had given the same percentage increase to all of its workers. However, the city agreed to recognize the comparable worth concept and grant raises on the content of the work rather than trying to ensure that all people doing similar jobs get equal pay.

In mid-1984, the U.S. Equal Employment Opportunity Commission had 250 wage discrimination complaints pending. If the comparable worth notion is applied to these cases, it could dramatically restructure wages and salaries for women and men in organizations. Employers and conservatives are fighting the issue, saying that the marketplace should determine the value of jobs.

Executive Order 11246 created the Office of Federal Contract Compliance Program (OFCCP).

These power company engineers are testimony to the success of affirmative action programs.

Every company that has forty or more employees and government contracts of $50,000 or more is subject to affirmative action policies.

Among other things, this order requires an **affirmative action** program which states in part:

Every company that has forty or more employees and government contracts of $50,000 or more must develop a detailed plan that identifies weaknesses in hiring and promoting minorities and women, and a specific plan, along with dates, for correcting them. In short, affirmative action requires an effort by employers to:

- Identify barriers of race, sex, religion, national origin, and other factors that keep employees from reaching their full potential.

- Eliminate barriers quickly.

- Set up special programs to speed corrections.

Affirmative action also guides recruiting and selection policies. Recruiters, for instance, cannot legally ask questions that allow management to make prejudiced decisions. Questions such as, "How do you plan to combine marriage and a career?" "Where were you born?" and "Do you have an honorable discharge?" are examples of discriminatory questions. Figure 9.2 shows a list of

**Figure 9.2
Examples of interview questions that would be likely to be judged discriminatory.**

1. Are you married?
2. How do you plan to take care of your children?
3. Have you changed your name recently?
4. Do you have any handicaps?
5. What is your religious affiliation?
6. How many times have you been arrested?
7. What is your draft classification?
8. What is the date of your military discharge?
9. What were the conditions of your military discharge?
10. Where were you born?
11. What is your nationality?
12. What is your mother tongue?

interview queries that are discriminatory and therefore illegal.

As an example of affirmative action, the courts recently ordered General Motors to contribute $42 million to programs to correct for past pay discriminations. The cases had been in the courts for 10 years, but there was evidence that the company had paid different wages to people doing similar jobs. In another case, Lockheed California Co., a division of Lockheed Corp., agreed to hire and promote several hundred women over the next few years to settle a sex discrimination suit. Since the company just received a $2 billion contract from NASA, it appears that they will create between 1500 and 2000 new jobs in the next few years. Women will probably get half of them.

The **Age Discrimination in Employment Act of 1967** outlaws discrimination against candidates between the ages of 40 and 65. The law does not prevent a company from asking a candidate's age on an application blank, but the company cannot legally use age as a reason for not hiring. In 1979, Congress amended this act to prohibit mandatory retirement before the age of 70.

Are quotas necessary for affirmative action programs? Most people automatically associate hiring and promoting quotas with affirmative action. However, there has been a continuing debate about whether companies need to develop hiring quotas for women and minorities in order to fulfill affirmative action requirements.

Some experts contend that affirmative action was never intended to require quotas. They say it was to prevent discrimination against certain groups of employees. Further, advocates of this view add that Labor Department regulations say that hiring goals should not be used to discriminate against any applicant because of race, color, religion, sex, or national origin. Goals, they say, are just that: goals. They are not intended to be strict quotas. Finally, the use of goals is just one aspect of a company's total effort to reduce discrimination.

The other view says this may sound good in theory; in actual practice, however, hiring quotas are often necessary to meet affirmative action guidelines. For example, suppose an employer has ten jobs to fill and a goal of hiring two minorities. If the first eight people the company hires are white, in reality, the next two hires will have to be minorities. Thus, the goal turns into a quota. This side also quotes court decisions and practices to support their conviction, for instance: (1) a court ordered the Boston Police Department to hire a fixed number of minorities until the work force reached roughly the community percentage of minorities, and (2) Kaiser Aluminum reserved 50% of all openings in its craft apprenticeship program for minorities until their percentages were equal to the percentage of minorities in the local work force.

What is reverse discrimination? Reverse discrimination occurs when companies give hiring and promotional preferences to women and minorities who are less qualified than whites. Congress says they never intended to promote reverse discrimination with the law; rather, they were just trying to make sure women and minorities got an equal chance. However, critics say that some companies have overreacted and actually hired and promoted some women and minorities who were less qualified than white, male applicants.

In the *Bakke* decision of 1978, a highly publicized reverse discrimination case, the U.S. Supreme Court ruled that Allan Bakke, a white male, had been the victim of reverse discrimination. Bakke applied to the University of California School of Medicine at Davis but was not admitted.

It will probably be some time before there is

a clear understanding of just what consti-

tutes reverse discrimination.

He sued, saying the university had admitted less-qualified minority applicants. The university agreed that they had admitted some minorities under "special admissions programs" to get a more equal minority representation. The Supreme Court said the school's special admissions program was unconstitutional because its quota system amounted to discrimination against whites. In a confusing statement, though, the court said that schools wanting a more diverse student body could use race as a factor in determining admission standards. Many other reverse discrimination cases are still in the courts, and it will probably be some time before there is a clear

understanding of just what constitutes reverse discrimination.

STAFFING

As a human resources specialist described part of her job, "I spend a lot of time recruiting and selecting employees. I also have to determine how many employees are needed and what kinds of skills the company requires." The staffing function includes planning employment needs, recruiting prospective employees, selecting the best candidate, and finally, hiring the employee.

Planning Employment Needs

Employment planning forecasts the future needs of the company's human resources. These employment forecasts are determined, in part, by sales forecasts, budgets, and growth estimates. Of course, planners must also consider employee turnover in the planning. Employment planners try to meet the challenge of hiring top-flight employees, ideally qualified for the tasks, at exactly the right time.

Forecasting needs. Planners consider the company's growth plans and anticipated turnover when projecting employment needs. **Turnover** is the number of employees that leave a company over a period of time—typically a year. Turnover occurs when employees quit, retire, die, or are terminated. By considering the company's turnover history and allowing for situations such as retirements, possible layoffs, transfers, and probations, managers can project the future turnover rate.

After projecting turnover, specialists consider growth projections of the firm. Is a new department planned? What will production requirements be? Are sales expected to increase? While these methods of projecting employment needs may, in some cases, be quite accurate, most human resources managers get some real surprises. And quick action is often required to fill positions that suddenly become vacant.

Accurate employee forecasting is very important to the company's profitability. Should a forecast provide too few employees, the company will likely lose sales because it will not be able to deliver the needed goods or services on time. And if the firm hires too many employees, the result will be higher-than-necessary labor costs.

Defining the job. The staffing task would be easier if all jobs in a firm were similar. However, the best salesperson could probably not replace the controller, and the ace producer probably could not substitute for the sales manager. Planners use job analysis and job descriptions to help them identify the particular skills that the firm will need.

Job analysis determines the exact tasks that make up a job. By detailing the precise requirements of the job, recruiters can find potential employees with necessary skills and aptitudes. Figure 9.3 shows a sample checklist for job analysis.

Information gathered from the job analysis is used to write a **job description,** a summary of the employee's job duties and responsibilities. A good manager will be certain that these job descriptions are kept up to date. Incomplete or inaccurate job descriptions result in criticism by employees and make it difficult to match the employee to the task. Highly technical or rapidly growing departments require job descriptions to be revised at regular intervals — say, every six months. Figure 9.4 shows an example of a job description.

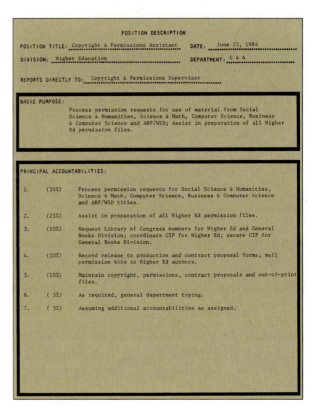

Figure 9.4
An example of a job description.

Figure 9.3
A sample checklist for job analysis.

TASKS PERFORMED

1. What is actually done?
2. How is it done?
3. Why is it done?
4. How much time is required to do it?
5. What tools are used?
6. Where is the work accomplished?
7. What is the employee's responsibility?

REQUIRED PHYSICAL AND MENTAL SKILLS

1. What technical skills are required?
2. What kinds of job knowledge are needed?
3. Does it require special training?
4. Will employees have to cooperate with other employees?
5. What personality characteristics are desirable?
6. What are the intelligence requirements?

Job specifications list the physical, mental, and emotional requirements of a job. Physical specifications are usually the easiest to identify. In minute detail, they list the job demands for walking, lifting, crouching, climbing, grasping, sitting, and the like. Mental specifications set minimum requirements for mental capabilities, and they may be defined by indirect means such as a high school degree, two years of college, a certificate of accomplishment, or a college degree. Other, more direct examples of mental specifications spell out standards for general intelligence, memory, planning ability, reading proficiency, abstract reasoning capability, and judgment. Although not as precise as physical or mental specifications, there is a trend among analysts to look more closely at emotional and social requirements.

For jobs that require working with the public or with other groups, social skills may be more important to success than technical or mental aptitudes. Difficulty of measurement causes the same conflict over emotional specifications. How can you predict when an employee will behave immaturely? Some companies rely upon testing to judge emotional stability and social skills; other submit their people to examinations by psychologists. Still another input is recommendations from prior employers on the prospective employee's ability to work cooperatively with others, react objectively under stress, and handle personal problems. Figure 9.5 is an example of job specifications for a particular job.

Recruiting

It is one thing to know labor needs. It is quite another to recruit people with the necessary skills. Companies begin recruiting by projecting a public reputation that attracts qualified employees. Everything that the company does reflects upon this image and thereby influences the success of recruiting. Recruiters select from internal and external sources, making their decisions after following a systematic screening process.

Internal sources. Internal sources are the present work force, and there are two good reasons to fill vacancies with current employees. Present employees are easier to find and evaluate, and human resources already has records on their backgrounds, education, experience, skills, mental abilities, attitudes, and work habits. The second advantage of replacing from within is the effect on morale and motivation. Internal transfers and promotions are concrete evidence that the company is concerned about employee development and loyalty.

Of course, internal sources pose potential problems. A major barrier is inbreeding. Employees, being aware of current policies and pro-

Figure 9.5
An example of a set of job specifications.

QUALIFICATIONS:

Minimum of 45–50 wpm accurate typing.
Knowledge and use of CRT.
Knowledge and understanding of manufacturing process and terminology.
Good organizational skills and an aptitude for figures.
Effective communication and interpersonal skills.
Minimum of two years of college.

cedures, understand the company much better than outsiders, but insiders have more trouble seeing and judging improved methods. If companies *only* promote from within, they may become stagnant. Industry analysts say a large part of the operational problems that Digital Equipment Corporation was wrestling with recently was due to President Kenneth Olsen's tradition of promoting from within, which, these critics feel, has created an insular management team. "Top management is not open to new ideas, and the atmosphere is stifling," complained one observer.

Availability of supply is another limitation of internal sources. It is unlikely that expanding companies can find all the skills they need within their present work force. Current employees can often be retrained to meet changing labor needs, but not all workers are both willing and able to make adjustments.

External sources. To fulfill all a firm's employment needs from internal sources is virtually impossible. But where can the company go for people? It is not practical to kidnap drunks as shipping companies used to do. Nor can human resources lay back and wait for the employees to scamper enthusiastically to their world of opportunity. Effective recruiters go outside to several standard sources.

1. *Walk-ins.* Most companies regularly receive unsolicited applications, especially when the unemployment rate increases. Walk-ins usually find their way to the human resources office where someone records preliminary information in recruiting files. Periodically, a staff member scans the information to determine whether any of the walk-ins' skills match company needs. Although the source is unpredictable — companies never know the number of applicants or variety of skills that may come in — it is inexpensive and good for public relations.

2. *Public employment agencies.* The U.S. Employment Service was created as a subunit of the Labor Department during World War I to recruit civilian workers into war industries. To combat the depression ills of the 1930s, states added their own public employment offices, and they became more important with the passage of the Social Security Act,

which requires unemployed workers to register at state agencies before they can receive benefits. Today, public agencies are funded by employer contributions to unemployment compensation funds, and they are clearinghouses for jobs and information. Additionally, many agencies have expanded their services to include counseling, psychological testing, aiding handicapped workers, and giving special attention to war veterans. Many public agencies have recently become heavily involved in helping disadvantaged and minority employees overcome their unique problems in finding work.

3. *Private employment agencies.* Private employment agencies have grown along with public services. But private agencies specialize more in registering technical or professional personnel such as typists, programmers, engineers, and salespeople. Some private placement groups specialize in low-skilled labor, but they are generally inadequate sources for most blue-collar workers. To improve their services, private agencies have joined forces to exchange computerized lists of talent. Many have added sophisticated testing procedures, counseling services, and vocational guidance programs. Employers say the major advantages of private agencies are their more specialized human resources services. A disadvantage of private agencies is

High-technology professionals are often recruited through specialized private employment agencies.

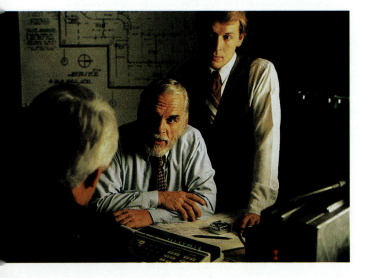

the cost; they charge a percentage of the newly hired employee's salary. Most often, this fee is paid by the hiring company, but for some types of jobs, the employee must pay the agency for securing employment.

4. *Employee referrals.* An RCA Corporation facility pays $1000 to its current employees for recommendations that result in hiring new people. In three years, they have hired at least 100 employees through the program. Several divisions of Wang Laboratories, Inc., pay from $300 to $500 each for employee referrals that result in the right person for the right job. During a recent six-month period, one Wang division hired 43 employees, all of whom passed the 90-day probationary period. Company officials say the program boosts the self-esteem of their current employees and saves a lot of money in recruiting expenses. Recruiting expenses for a new engineer or scientist, including advertisement, employment agency fees, relocation expenses, and visits, may go as high as $9000 for a single hiree. Some human resources officers fear that extensive use of employee referrals could possibly throw the workforce out of balance in the eyes of the EEOC. For instance, a predominantly white group might tend to refer other whites, thereby causing this composition of the work group to be unrepresentative of the community. While new, employee referral has gained a lot of popularity, and more companies are likely to use this method.

5. *Labor unions.* Labor unions, with their hiring halls and job listings, are a source of unskilled and skilled labor for certain industries. Through apprenticeship programs and labor agreements, some unions have maintained firm control over labor supplies. It is illegal for unions to insist that employers hire only union members, but this law has not been vigorously enforced in some industries. Union referrals are particularly important in industries with small companies where demand for unskilled labor fluctuates erratically. Examples include construction, trucking, printing, maritime, and Saturday-night dance bands.

6. *Professional associations.* Many professional societies and trade associations operate placement services for their members. At regional and national meetings, special recruiting

1. Listing of career jobs available from companies.
2. Publishing of newsletters that update job listings.
3. Career counseling.
4. Career testing.
5. Career planning.
6. Computer matching service.
7. Arranging on-campus interviews between hiring companies and student prospects.
8. Listing of temporary and part-time jobs.
9. Holding seminars on interviewing techniques.
10. Holding seminars on resume preparation.
11. Holding seminars on making a job search.
12. Making salary surveys available.
13. Maintaining a career resource library of information on companies and positions.

Figure 9.6
Examples of services offered by college placement centers.

rooms are set up where recruiters meet with prospective employees. In conjunction with the formal procedures, recruiters flush out hot prospects through informal meetings at dinner, cocktail gatherings, and hallway conversations. A few associations regularly publicize lists of openings and applicants in their newsletters and journals.

7. *Educational institutions.* Almost all colleges and universities operate placement or career development centers that assist graduates in their job search. A few centers screen applicants, but most concentrate on coordinating information and securing physical arrangements for bringing recruiters and prospective employees together. Typically, placement directors attract recruiters to the campus, publicize the visits to graduating students, and make appointments between interested students and company recruiters. Placement offices may also compile folders on student qualifications and distribute brochures, pamphlets, and other recruiting literature. After a preliminary on-campus interview, the recruiter normally invites the best candidates to additional interviews on the company's premises. Most companies visit university campuses to seek professional, managerial, and technical talent. Figure 9.6 lists examples of services offered by college placement centers.

8. *Advertising.* Companies have long used advertisements in newspapers, trade journals, posters, billboards, radio, television, and roving sound trucks to attract employees. Advertisements have the advantage of attracting a lot of attention about job openings, but their disadvantage is they produce an uncertain range of candidates. Even with properly written and well-timed ads, employers attract many unqualified applicants. Companies increase their advertising efforts when labor supplies are scarce and reduce them during periods of plenty.

9. *Computer matching.* Although not widely used as yet, computers are very adept at gathering and distributing information in quantity. IBM, Western Union, the U.S. Employment Service, and the College Placement Council operate computer-oriented job banks, which they hope will eventually match skilled applicants and openings nationwide. The computer is best suited for handling jobs with tangible specifications; it is less effective for filling professional and managerial needs.

10. *Job fairs.* Some organizations promote job fairs where several potential employers gather for a day, rent booths, and offer literature on available jobs. They invite people to attend the fairs and talk with representatives of the firms who might ask applicants to fill in applications. And they might conduct some preliminary interviewing with prospects.

11. *Pirating.* Many companies are not beyond pirating employees from other employers. For instance, at professional meetings, representatives from Company A might informally talk with a top-notch professional from Company B about the prospect of changing jobs. Pursuing specific employees from another company may be a quick way to get high-level executives at a modest recruiting cost, but pirated employees may be as disloyal to their new firm as they were to their old.

The Selection Process

True, many organizations, especially smaller ones, observe a candidate's hairstyle, mannerisms, and personality and hire on the basis of some mysterious chemistry. As one president put it, "I look for a prospect that turns me on." No selection procedures entirely eliminate subjective judgments, but good procedures assist the "gut feelings" in two ways. One, they reinforce the positive or negative feelings of company officials. Two, they may ascertain information contradictory to the subjective feelings and cause an executive to reconsider. The selection decision usually moves through several steps, with each step narrowing the field of applicants until only one person is left. Some organizations find the total process to be too expensive and time-consuming, and they skip some of the steps.

1. *Preliminary screening interview.* The preliminary screening interview determines whether the candidate is in the ballpark. Receptionists usually accomplish the preliminary interview with a few questions such as: "How many years of college do you have?" "Can you type and take shorthand?" "Do you have welding experience?" The interviewer also observes the candidate for dress style and general appearance if these are important to the job. If the employee is clearly unqualified, the process ends here. If there is a reasonable chance of qualifying, the interviewer asks the prospect to complete an application blank.

2. *Application blanks.* Practically all companies require candidates to complete an application blank because it is an efficient instrument for gathering data on education, experience, location, achievements, and personal references. See Fig. 9.7 for an example of an application blank.

3. *Testing.* Companies have been using employment tests for more than 50 years, but they are still controversial. Tests may attempt to determine an employee's skill, aptitude, knowledge, personality, and the like. Objectivity is the primary purpose of testing, but some administrators use the scores as a peg to hang the entire selection decision on. Interviewers' subjective judgments are good selection inputs, but there is a tendency to suppress judgments in favor of test scores. Sometimes, when testing for middle- or upper-level management positions, a company may test both the applicant and the manager for whom the applicant would work. This, ideally, would reduce potential personality conflicts. To improve testing validity, companies can compare test scores to employee performance to

Figure 9.7
An employment application form. *Courtesy Digital Equipment Corporation.*

see if good performers actually outscore low achievers. This is called validity, a determination of whether the test truly measures what it is supposed to measure. Obviously, tests should be reliable; that is, they should unfailingly measure the same thing every time. Although test publishers supply national norms, it is misleading for companies to apply the norms indiscriminately.

Tests may not be used as often today as they were a few years ago. Now, you have to be sure that the test does not discriminate between sexes and races and that it does not invade a person's privacy. All applicants must have an equal opportunity for the job. A human resources manager of a smaller firm who had quit testing said, "It just got to be so much trouble that it was not worth it. The cost in time and effort was too great to justify the results. And we had to worry that we did not violate some of the newer legal requirements."

However, **bona fide occupational qualification (bfoq)** testing — determining if someone can meet specific, tangible requirements of the job — may not cause the concern of other types of testing. For instance, if you need an employee to lift 50-pound boxes as part of the job, you could, through strength tests, determine with precision whether the person could lift the weight.

4. *Reference checks.* For those candidates who make it through testing, firms contact references either before or after the interview stage to check on background. Although some firms check personal and school references, previous employers are the most preferred references. Recruiters want to know the applicant's title, nature of work, quality of work, length of experience, and reason for leaving. Recommendation letters are usually required, but they rarely turn up negative information because candidates select references who are likely to write favorable evaluations. Previous employers are reluctant to criticize because of concerns over the individual's right to privacy and lawsuits arising from derogatory evaluations. Personal interviews or telephone calls to former employers are more likely to elicit candid comments, and the interviewer can probe questionable areas.

5. *Employment interviews.* According to surveys, more than 98% of companies use interviews to judge candidates. Opinions vary about whether interviews should be structured or unstructured. Structured interviews follow a predeveloped format. Interviewers ask questions from a checklist and record responses on the space allotted. Unstructured or nondirective interviews are more spontaneous. The interviewer probes with a few general questions such as: "What do you think about your future employment?" "Will you tell me more about that?" The purpose is to get the candidates to do most of the talking on the assumption that they will reveal many things about themselves.

6. *Physical examination.* Responding to increasing emphasis on employee health and safety, almost all firms require applicants to pass a physical examination. Since physical exams are expensive, they are used toward the end of the selection procedure when the field has narrowed. The physical exam tries to accomplish three purposes. First, the company wants to protect itself against paying workmen's compensation claims for health problems the employee had at the time of hiring. Second, managers wish to determine that the employee is physically capable of performing the job. Third, the organization is obligated to avoid hiring someone with a serious communicable disease. While effective for detecting current health problems, physical exams have been poor at predicting future ailments.

7. *The employment decision.* All the preliminary steps lead to the crucial question: to hire or not to hire? Employment decisions have far-reaching implications for training, discipline, and turnover. Even the best training programs do not overcome all hiring mistakes. Assigning an unsuitable person to a job is sure to cause troubles. Replacement costs range from $1000 for unskilled positions to $7000 for semiskilled positions; for specialists and management, human resources hiring expenses might zoom to $25,000 or more.

Hiring Employees

After making the employment decision through the selecting process, the actual hiring takes place. But it cannot be assumed that the employee will accept the job when offered. Prime applicants usually interview with several companies. Also, the candidate may have become less enthusiastic about the job during the screening process. Good human resources management requires a talent for "closing the deal." Often, salary and benefits are negotiated. Enticements, such as a research budget, additional equipment, or tempting bonus plans, are offered to hire the ideal prospect. The hiring process begins with a formal offer from the company. It includes the salary, benefits, and conditions. Usually, the candidate has a short period to consider the offer. Hiring the best candidate may be as important to the company as closing a large sales contract.

Terminating Employees

Because of many potential legal liabilities, human resources managers usually get involved when employees are **terminated,** that is, leave the company. In most cases, the human resources department conducts an **exit interview** with the person to try to determine the specific reasons for leaving. Frequently, an interviewer will ask, in an exit interview, such questions as: "Do you have any suggestions that could help us improve?" "What was your relationship with your supervisor?" "What frustrations did you experience while you worked here?" Employees typically leave a company in one of four ways: (1) retirement, (2) resignation, (3) layoff, and (4) firing (terminating).

CROSS FIRE

Should Employers Be Allowed to Use Lie Detector Tests?

The use of polygraph (lie detector) tests is increasing rapidly. About 1 million Americans take polygraph exams each year. There are approximately 5000 polygraph examiners in the United States today, about twice the number 10 years ago. Firms such as Montgomery Ward, Coors brewery, Zale's jewelers, and 7-Eleven stores use them regularly. However, there is a hot debate over polygraph use, centering around validity.

Points in favor of the use of polygraph testing include:

1. It reduces theft. The Jack Eckerd Corporation tests each of its 30,000 employees annually. An official says, "It's a good tool in maintaining an honest corps of employees. We have one of the lowest levels of internal theft in the chain drug industry."

2. It helps eliminate "bad apple" job applicants. "If an applicant knows that he or she is going to have to undergo a polygraph," says an examiner, "unethical applicants will be less likely to apply."

3. It is more accurate than most people think. The technology has been available for 60 years.

Points against the use of polygraph exams include:

1. The exams are not always accurate. People frequently "fail" not because they have lied but because they get nervous during the exam.

2. The questions many examiners ask are an invasion of a person's privacy—questions on sex habits, drug abuse, and personal relationships.

3. Courts agree that many who failed exams have been wronged. For example, a Florida man won a $250,000 suit against a company who dismissed him on the basis of a polygraph test concerning missing cash. A Connecticut jury awarded $219,000 to 22 persons who were wrongly dismissed for failing a lie detector test.

To what extent do you agree or disagree with the following statement: "Employers should not be allowed to require employees to take polygraph exams for any reasons." Why?

    ____ A. Strongly agree   ____ C. Disagree somewhat

    ____ B. Agree somewhat   ____ D. Strongly disagree

How accurate do you think polygraph exams are? Answer by circling the appropriate number on the following scale:

    Very accurate   7 6 5 4 3 2 1   Very inaccurate

The Age Discrimination in Employment Act makes it illegal for companies to force people out of work strictly because of their age.

Retirement. Employees retire at different ages and for different reasons. Ill health, boredom with the work, or attractive retirement benefits may cause an employee to retire early. In some cases, a manager may want an employee to retire early to replace him or her with a more specialized or up-to-date person. The Age Discrimination in Employment Act makes it illegal for companies to force people out of work strictly because of their age. Sometimes retirement is negotiated, just like hiring is negotiated. Many companies now make both early and late retirement available to their employees. It is human resources' responsibility to make sure that retirement situations go as smoothly as possible for both the retiree and the firm.

Resignation. Employees often decide to leave a company voluntarily. Sometimes they leave because they obtain a more attractive position with another firm. Other times they leave because they are dissatisfied with their current jobs. Here again, human resources personnel, through exit interviews and other means, try to find the real reason for a person's resignation.

Layoffs. Sometimes downturns in economic conditions require a company to reduce its work force through layoffs. Human resources personnel may be responsible for seeing that the layoffs occur in an orderly and rational fashion. They may also try to reduce the ill feelings of layoffs by providing severance pay or by helping employees find positions with other companies. Some human resources departments have developed extensive programs, called **outplacement,** for finding work for employees that they have to lay off.

Less serious economic conditions may result in temporary layoffs where employees lose their jobs for a temporary time period, say 6 weeks, or 3 months. If conditions improve during the temporary layoff, many or all of the employees may be called back to work. But if economic conditions worsen, the company may have to extend the layoff period. Layoffs challenge the human resources department to be as fair as possible because they create a lot of stress and potential ill will for employees and the firms.

Firing. The most delicate human relations task of a firm is firing an employee. Usually, the company will put an employee on probation and give him or her several chances to improve before they actually terminate the employee through firing. During the probation period, progressive managers ask such questions as: "Has the employee been properly trained?" "Is there a way to improve the employee's attitude?" "Would a transfer solve the problem?" "Are there legal implications involved?" Termination usually occurs for one of two reasons: The employee does not perform up to a minimum level of expectations, or the employee continues to violate some of the company's policies such as attendance, safety regulations, tardiness, and the like.

Recently, there has been an erosion of the "employment at will" idea. **Employment at will** is a legal doctrine, accepted by the courts, which says an employer or an employee can terminate a relationship at will. That is, an employee can quit at any time and an employer can terminate at any time. However, some union contracts now guarantee employment for some workers. Further, consider the salesperson in one large company who made a large sale to a customer. The company, rather than pay the commission to the salesperson, terminated the employee. The courts, though, said the company could not legally do this because the termination was based on malice. In another case, a company fired an employee because he refused to testify for the company in a price-fixing case. Again, the courts said that the company could not legally do this. These, and similar cases, have demonstrated that there are limits to the employer's ability to terminate a relationship with an employee.

Before terminating an employee, it is very important to document, in writing, the evidence against him or her.

Before terminating an employee, it is very important to document, in writing, the evidence against him or her. For instance, a company had to

Late Retirement

Many U.S. companies are altering the usual pattern of employee retirement. They are keeping some older workers on the job by offering inducements such as reduced hours, job changes, and job sharing.

Changing demographics are responsible for many of these new corporate responses to retirement. Largely because of the "baby bust" that started during the 1960s, businesses see a relative shortage of young people entering the work force. The problem, says Lawrence Olson of Sage Associates, a Washington management consulting firm, is that the work force will increase by only 1.2% a year from 1985 to 1990 and grow by no more than a mere 0.8% a year in the 1990s. Therefore, says Olson, there must be a reversal of the early retirement option for the elderly and increased incentives for voluntary delays in retirement.

A number of companies have varied retirement options available for their employees. For example, Polaroid Corporation, in Cambridge, Massachusetts, uses "retirement rehearsal" and "phased retirement" to ease the anxieties of their workers who want to test the water before retiring. Rehearsal retirement allows older employees a 3-month, unpaid leave of absence with all benefits. Phased retirement allows them to cut back to 4 days a week or less at reduced pay. Polaroid's hope is that some workers will feel so good after a leave or a shortened week that they will want to extend their working life beyond the traditional retirement age of 65 or the legal retirement age of 70.

Source: "Why Late Retirement Is Getting a Corporate Blessing," *Business Week*, January 16, 1984, p. 69.

---

terminate a minority employee. He refused to follow company rules and policies, caused major disruptions, and called in sick about 20% of the time. After termination, the employee filed suit against the company for discrimination. A series of carefully worded memos and documentation from managers and other employees allowed the company to uphold the termination.

TRAINING AND DEVELOPMENT

Training and development occurs after an employee has been hired. Training includes teaching an employee to perform specific skills, whereas development includes more general education about such things as leadership, communication, economic understanding, and the like. Some companies offer extensive training and development; others offer little or none.

New Employee Orientation

Most companies offer some type of orientation for new employees. The **orientation program** introduces new employees to the company and explains corporate policies to them. A larger company may have a formal, classroom-type training session for new employees. Smaller organizations may use the first line supervisor to orient the new employee to the company. Studies show that orientation is important to both the company and the employee. A good orientation program increases the likelihood of training the employee effectively and helps the employee become productive more quickly. Figure 9.8 offers a checklist of topics to consider including an orientation program.

Training and Development Programs

Regardless of the experience level of an employee, some training is almost always necessary. Some

ORIENTATION CHECKLIST

Informal relations
- _____ name
- _____ introduction
- _____ sponsor
- _____ prepare other employees
- _____ your leadership style
- _____ group norms

Organizational objectives
- _____ departmental objectives
- _____ employee contribution
- _____ major product/service
- _____ growth
- _____ major competitors
- _____ position in industry
- _____ deadlines

- _____ greatest hopes
- _____ biggest problems

The job
- _____ training
- _____ help
- _____ learning period
- _____ standards
- _____ common mistakes
- _____ quality
- _____ quantity

Policies and procedures
- _____ check-in, check-out
- _____ discipline
- _____ safety

- _____ parking
- _____ rest breaks
- _____ smoking areas
- _____ coffee
- _____ lunch facilities
- _____ chain of command
- _____ forms, paperwork
- _____ grievance procedure
- _____ suggestions
- _____ transfers
- _____ performance appraisals
- _____ first aid

Rewards
- _____ pay
- _____ benefits

- _____ insurance
- _____ vacation
- _____ payday
- _____ incentive plans
- _____ promotions
- _____ sick pay
- _____ payroll deductions
- _____ pay increases
- _____ work stability
- _____ athletic activities
- _____ social activities
- _____ hobbies
- _____ clubs
- _____ security
- _____ pride
- _____ prestige

Figure 9.8
Items typically covered by employee orientation programs.

companies conduct their training in-house; that is, their own staff, usually from human resources, conducts the training. Other companies encourage their employees to attend programs at universities or other training centers at company expense. Of course, many companies use a combination of these two approaches.

Some examples of typical types of training and development programs are:

1. *On-the-job training (OJT).* The supervisor or an experienced co-worker has the responsibility of teaching the employee skills on the job.

2. *Job instruction training (JIT).* This instruction method breaks a job into logical steps and lists them in a sequence. The trainer, perhaps a supervisor or someone from human resources, teaches the employee how to perform the steps.

3. *Apprenticeship training.* A new employee is given a temporary, lower-status position to

In-house classroom training is one way to upgrade employees' value to a company.

learn basic skills of a job. Once he or she attains the necessary expertise, the **apprenticeship** title is dropped, and the employee moves up in status and pay.

4. *Vestibule training.* **Vestibule training** creates a simulation of a working situation so an employee can sharpen his or her skills in a mock experience. An early part of flight training, for example, may include learning in a flight simulator that simulates actual flying.

5. *Job rotation.* Job rotation provides a series of assignments, moving trainees from one job to another on a planned basis. Normally, the trainee receives coaching from individuals in each assignment, as well as from the training specialist in charge of the program.

6. *In-basket training.* Usually reserved for management development, in-basket training begins with a series of written materials describing the background of a firm and the job the trainee is assumed to perform. An instructor presents memos, letters, notes, phone calls, and typical problems. The trainee has to react to the situation as he or she might in an actual situation.

7. *Films.* Some firms put certain skills on films or slide-tape presentations. An employee watches the film or tape to attain a set of skills.

TAKING STOCK

Emerging Roles of the Human Resources Manager

Patricia McLagan, chairperson of the 1981 Competency Task Force of the American Society for Training and Development, has identified several new activities that are emerging as having a major role within the profession of human resources management:

- Strategist: the role of projecting what human resources management will be in the future.

- Policymaker: the role of determining broad values or principles that will guide human resources managers.

- Researcher: the role of developing theories that verify, advance, or change human resources views of the alternatives available in human resources work.

- Evaluator: the role of identifying to what extent a curriculum, program, product, or service is achieving or has achieved its stated goals within the mission, strategy, and policy framework of the human resources department and the overall organization.

- Transfer agent: the role of ensuring that competencies learned in education, training, and self-development are remembered, reinforced, and used in the appropriate contexts.

These new roles imply a shift in two directions. There will be a need for human resources specialists to have a more significant influence on top management concerning the use and development of human resources. What's more, human resources specialists will have to become more adept at utilizing the sophisticated techniques of research, evaluation, and maintenance and reinforcement of learning.

Source: Neal Chalofsky and Carnie Ives Lincoln, *Up the HRD Ladder: A Guide for Professional Growth,* Reading, Mass.: Addison-Wesley, 1983, pp. 74–75.

8. *Classroom training.* Many firms also conduct traditional classroom training for their employees. Such training may consist of information about company policies, plans, and history, as well as management and supervisory development programs. Sometimes company trainers instruct the sessions; other times, the firm hires an outside trainer to teach the classes.

9. *Off-site seminars.* Many firms take management retreats periodically where they may conduct management development training for their middle- and upper-level managers. Typically, a selected group of managers meets at a resort area for 2 to 3 days to attend a program conducted by an outside expert. Additionally, many consulting firms conduct seminars throughout the country on management topics. Firms may select one or a few of their management people to attend these programs. Most programs are 1-day events, but some continue for 2 or 3 days.

PERFORMANCE EVALUATION

Performance evaluation is the activity that the firm uses to judge whether employees are performing their jobs effectively. Most companies require managers to appraise their subordinates formally and periodically, typically once a year. While evaluation programs vary, some objectives and techniques tend to be common.

Evaluation Objectives

The most obvious and most common reason for formal evaluations is to determine rewards for productivity. So they can "water where the flowers grow," managers wish to distinguish between employees who do a lot and those who do a little. Merit ratings justify granting one employee a 12% increase in wages or salary, while another employee gets only 4%. Superiors use rating results to back up their decision when subordinates dispute their raises. Managers also rely upon performance evaluations to select employees for promotions.

Employee improvement is the second objective of evaluations. In the review, supervisors can

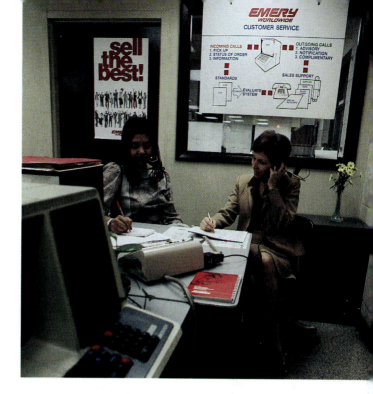

On-the-job evaluations help assess an employee's job skills. Here, a manager listens in on a customer service situation.

point out weaknesses that could be overcome with training. Honest progress reviews, although potentially painful, help employees and managers isolate behaviors that need correcting or work habits that need improving. In this way, the evaluation develops data for counseling, coaching, and attitude change to help employees overcome barriers to their development. Properly done, the review also motivates employees because they receive continuous feedback on how well they are doing. Reviews also assist with transfers. If an otherwise good worker experiences problems because of a personality conflict with a superior or unique circumstances surrounding peer relationships, the review folder can help determine if a transfer would solve the problem.

Third, evaluation can help justify disciplinary action. If, after training and counseling, employees do not perform to a minimum standard, dismissal or discipline for poor performance may be necessary. The review can be solid documentation for the company that is called upon to defend its decision before union committees or in court.

Employee Evaluation Form

Employee's Name _____ Classification _____

Division/Branch _____

Period Covered by Report: From _____ To _____

Circle the appropriate score for each factor and write a short statement explaining why the employee was rated at the particular level.

I. **Output:** Ability of the unit supervised to meet required standards as to quality and quantity.

1	2	3	4	5
Unsatisfactory	Needs improvement	Satisfactory	Above average	Outstanding

Why _____

II. **Job knowledge:** Clear understanding of the facts or factors pertinent to the job.

1	2	3	4	5
Unsatisfactory	Needs improvement	Satisfactory	Above average	Outstanding

Why _____

III. **Organization and planning:** Ability to devise work methods and anticipate needs; Systematic, etc.

1	2	3	4	5
Unsatisfactory	Needs improvement	Satisfactory	Above average	Outstanding

Why _____

IV. **Judgment:** Ability to make effective decisions without undue delay, etc.

1	2	3	4	5
Unsatisfactory	Needs improvement	Satisfactory	Above average	Outstanding

Why _____

V. **Work relations:** Builds morale; public relations; personal relations; leadership qualities, etc.

1	2	3	4	5
Unsatisfactory	Needs improvement	Satisfactory	Above average	Outstanding

Why _____

VI. **Delegation of authority and responsibility:** Frees self of details; Unit continues to function in absence, etc.

1	2	3	4	5
Unsatisfactory	Needs improvement	Satisfactory	Above average	Outstanding

Why _____

VII. **Initiative:** Earnestness in seeking increased responsibilities; Self starting; Unafraid to proceed alone.

1	2	3	4	5
Unsatisfactory	Needs improvement	Satisfactory	Above average	Outstanding

Why _____

VIII. **Capacity for advancement:** Can assume additional responsibility; Understands related functions, etc.

1	2	3	4	5
Unsatisfactory	Needs improvement	Satisfactory	Above average	Outstanding

Why _____

IX. **Personal qualities:** Personality; appearance; sociability; integrity.

1	2	3	4	5
Unsatisfactory	Needs improvement	Satisfactory	Above average	Outstanding

Why _____

X. **Overall performance:** Consider all factors.

1	2	3	4	5
Unsatisfactory	Needs improvement	Satisfactory	Above average	Outstanding

Why _____

Figure 9.9
A sample employee evaluation form. *Reprinted from the June 1983 issue of* Personnel Administrator, *copyright, 1983, The American Society for Personnel Administration, 606 North Washington Street, Alexandria, VA 22314, $30 per year.*

Merit reviews also help to prevent indiscriminate, personalized discipline.

Evaluation Techniques

What should be evaluated? To this question, most managers will answer, "We look first for results. How well did the employee accomplish the tasks as assigned?" Firms use a variety of indicators to focus on results. Surveys of actual practices show that quality of work, quantity of work, job knowledge, and obedience are the most popular.

A second quality to evaluate is personality. A worker's personality may detract from the overall group performance if he or she does not fit in. Or some personality factors may keep the employee from performing up to potential. A supervisor describes this dilemma, "Henry was one of the most promising employees we had in the department. He had all the skills and was most capable. But he just could not get along with the other workers. He was always arguing and would not cooperate." Surveys of actual practices show that initiative, cooperation, and dependability are the personality factors most popular for evaluation.

There are many techniques for rating job performance. Sometimes called a checklist, the graphic rating scale is the oldest and most widely used technique. The evaluator rates each employee on several qualities that relate to the job. The rating scale is simple to construct, easy to understand, and convenient to use (see Fig. 9.9). But, like grades in school, the evaluation is often judged to be unfair by the employee. With the ranking method, a supervisor lists employees from the highest to the lowest on performance. This overcomes the problem of rating everyone high. But managers do not like to rank anyone toward the bottom of the scale. It does, however, give the evaluator some idea of the relative performance of the workers.

Another increasingly popular method of evaluation is setting objectives. At the beginning of the period — usually six months or a year — the manager and employee jointly set performance goals. These may be for measurable performance or subjective evaluations by the manager. At the end of the period, the evaluation is based on how well the objectives were met. Whatever method of evaluation is used, the goal is generally the same: to give the company an accurate idea of job performance and to help the employee improve.

WAGE AND SALARY ADMINISTRATION

Employee evaluation dovetails with wage and salary administration. The reward system should pay employees according to their contribution to departmental and company objectives. This requires not only evaluating employee performances, but also determining how important each job is relative to all other positions. Why do secretaries earn less than engineers? Why do some engineers earn more than others? Why do medical doctors earn more than doctors of philosophy?

While there is little argument that clerks, salespeople, research chemists, maintenance mechanics, and computer programmers should receive different salaries, there is little agreement on what the differences should be. Specialists debate job evaluation methods and the best procedure for paying wages to employees.

Evaluating Jobs

Before compensation can be determined, the relative worth of each job needs to be considered. While many methods are used to determine the value of each position, the following factors are a prime consideration:

- Degree of expertise required. This includes education, experience, aptitude, physical ability, and social skills.
- Availability of qualified applicants. Is there a shortage of people with the necessary skills?
- Relative contribution to the company's success.
- Available resources in terms of budgets for compensation.
- Current success in the operation of the business.
- Economic conditions.
- Growth plans for the company.

Once these factors are considered, a compensation level can be set.

Wage Payment Plans

After determining the appropriate pay range for each job, managers turn to the riddle of pay method. How should the company pay? By the hour? By the day? By the week?

By far the most widely used pay plan is **day work,** where the company simply pays according to the hours worked. To compute wages, payroll accountants multiply the number of hours each employee works by the hourly rate. Employees know exactly how their salaries are determined, but this method has received criticism for not providing an incentive to produce. **Straight salary,** a variation of day work, also pays according to time worked. But the method is figured by week, month, or year, rather than hours. Straight salary is quoted in such terms as $250 per week, $900 a month, or $13,500 annually.

A second grouping of pay plans bases payment on worker performance in an effort to use money as an incentive. Although relatively popular 30 to 40 years ago, the use of incentive plans is declining. **Piecework,** the most widely used incentive plan, pays according to units produced. If the piece rate for a certain part is $0.03 and a worker produces 1800 parts in a day, his wage for the day would be $54 ($0.03 × 1800). **Group incentive plans** operate on a similar premise to piecework, but they pay according to a group rather than an individual effort. Supervisors keep records of group performance when the group achieves above the standard. Many firms pay a percentage, called a commission, of the value of the sale. Although commissions are not referred to as piecework plans, they are quite similar to them. **Profit sharing,** a modified group incentive plan, pays employees a percentage of the profits each year. Percentages vary, but 25% is typical. Companies frequently pay upper-level managers a bonus — extra pay related to the performance of their companies or divisions. For large companies, the total annual salary of a key executive may contain more than 50% bonus pay.

Which is the best method of wage payment? At this point, there is no clearly superior plan. Companies have experienced success and failure with all the approaches. Piecework and other incentive plans are more conducive to job stability and the ability to measure output. Where change and improvement are important to the company, day work and straight-salary methods are more appropriate.

Some firms, usually because of a union-negotiated agreement, provide **guaranteed annual wages (GAW)** or guaranteed annual employment. These plans typically guarantee an identified group of employees a certain amount of wages or a certain amount of work during the year. Employees like it because it gives them some degree of economic security; however, companies usually resist because these plans create a built-in cost that is hard to reduce should sales tailspin. Procter & Gamble, Hormel, Nunn-Bush, and some automotive plants are examples of firms that have GAW plans.

Regardless of the plan in effect, a number of uncontrollable factors also affect the company's compensation system. For example, local wage rates, supply and demand for labor, a firm's financial condition, laws, and union agreements are a few phenomena that influence pay.

Promotions

A promotion is a type of compensation that results in greater status and responsibility and higher salary. Human resources works with managers in making promotion decisions. While most companies like to reward their employees with promotions, care must also be taken. Mistakes can be serious. Employees placed improperly may cause turnover, inefficiency, and poor morale.

Some executives may also feel hurt or rejected when they have been passed over for promotions. Graber Industries of Wisconsin tries to provide counseling for those who are passed over because they want to keep them in the organization. Garber's president, James Sheridan, says, "It [the counseling] has been highly successful in every case." Most workers feel thankful for the counseling, and they especially like to know what they can do to improve their chances for future promotions.

Fringe Benefits

According to Hewitt Associates, a nationwide consulting firm, fringe benefits account for 41% of salary costs. Fringe benefits are company-sponsored programs that take care of employee needs. While employees have received nonpay benefits for years, complex benefit packages have been evolving in the last few years.

According to a survey of 1507 companies in 1982 by the Chamber of Commerce of the U.S., fringe benefits averaged $7187 per worker. The fringes were divided as shown in Table 9.2. Richard L. Adams, director of employee benefits for Reynolds Metals Company, says, "Our benefits have grown like mad. It's amazing to look at old

TABLE 9.2 ■ FRINGE BENEFITS PER WORKER

Social Security (employer's share)	$1274	Paid rest periods	$523
		Unemployment compensation	269
Life, health insurance	1274	Workers' compensation	258
Pensions	1040	Sick leave	244
Paid vacations	902	Profit sharing	218
Paid holidays	553	Other fringe benefits	632

Source: Chamber of Commerce of the U.S.

BUSINESS BULLETIN

How to Communicate Employees' True Earnings

Research shows that many employees are not fully aware of their total earnings, that is, they do not know what they are being paid. Some firms try to communicate to employees what they are making by sending out information at least once a year on their total pay package. Here is an example of a letter that communicates this information:

Dear _____ :

We thought you might be interested in knowing the total you earned this year, including salary, fringe benefits, and bonuses. Your annual salary was _____, plus benefits totaling _____ and bonuses of _____, for a total of _____.

The breakdown of your fringe benefit package includes:

1. Life insurance _____
2. FICA (Social Security) _____
3. Worker's compensation _____
4. Entertainment _____
5. Counseling services _____
6. Medical/dental insurance _____
7. Value of vacation time _____
8. Sick leave value _____
9. Contribution to pension plan _____
10. Company's sponsorship of clubs _____
    Total Benefits Paid _____

We are pleased that we could provide you with these rewards, and we appreciate the contribution that you made to our organization.

Sincerely yours,

Companies report that they have had good experiences in communicating the total pay package to their employees.

documents from the early days of our program in the 1940s to see how far we have come." Much of the expansion has come in health and welfare coverage. U.S. Steel, as an example, now covers workers' hospital stays of up to 2 years per illness; the limit was 120 days 10 years ago. Fringe benefit programs have been expanding in other areas also. However, the economic recession of the early 1980s considerably slowed the expansion of fringe benefit programs.

Many companies today are offering their employees "cafeteria-style" benefits. Instead of providing fixed programs to everyone on the payroll, a number of major firms are offering flexible programs that allow employees to pick and choose their benefits. For example, employees whose spouses already have family medical coverage might prefer added vacation time or child-care coverage to a second medical coverage program.

Proponents of fringe benefits argue that these indirect incentives build employee loyalty, commitment, and satisfaction, while reducing absenteeism and turnover. Others counter that since most of the benefits automatically apply to all employees, few workers actually understand what they are and how much they cost. Thus, benefits have little of the hoped-for impact. According to a spokesperson, "We are in a delicate trap; we spend billions of dollars on fringes with few positive results, yet we must continue to add to these packages or face the wrath of disgruntled employees and upset labor unions."

To help identify the skills the company will need, experts study jobs in the company. Job analysis determines the tasks that make up a job, the job description summarizes the employees' duties and responsibilities, and job specifications list physical, mental, and emotional qualifications required by the job. Companies recruit internally and externally. Major external sources include walk-ins, public and private employment agencies, employee referrals, labor unions, professional associations, educational institutions, advertising, and computer matching. In selecting employees for jobs, effective recruiters follow a systematic process involving (1) a preliminary screening interview, (2) an application blank, (3) testing, (4) reference checks, (5) employment interviews, (6) physical examination, and (7) the employment decision.

Companies formally evaluate their employees in order to reward employees according to their contributions to company objectives. Other reasons for evaluations are to obtain data for counseling and training employees and to justify disciplinary action. Five evaluation techniques are graphic rating scales, ranking, paired comparisons, forced choice, and field reviews.

Wage and salary administration begins with job evaluations. Job evaluation is the process of determining the relative worth of different jobs. After jobs are evaluated, managers must choose to pay employees according to a day work or the incentive-based method. Rewards, in addition to money, include a host of fringe benefits.

SUMMARY

Human resources departments concentrate on developing a motivated and fulfilled work force. In its beginnings, human resources was mostly a clerical function, but recently it has broadened to include employee selection, training, wages and salaries, services, labor relations, safety, and research and records. For other departments, human resources provides services, control, and advice.

A major function of the human resources department is to assist with recruiting and selecting employees. This begins with planning the work force. Planners try to project how many employees the company will need by analyzing turnover records and sales and production forecasts.

MIND YOUR BUSINESS

Instructions. Select the correct answer for each of the following by placing the appropriate letter in the blank at the left.

____ 1. All the following would likely be considered functions, or responsibilities, of human resources personnel except:
  a. Productivity improvement programs
  b. Market segment analysis
  c. Compensation planning and administration
  d. Training and development programs

____ 2. Which of the following best illustrates the concept of comparable worth?
  a. Equal pay for equal work

b. Equal pay for equal experience
c. Equal pay for equal skills, responsibility, and effort
d. Across-the-board pay increases

_____ 3. All the following are part of defining the job except:
a. Job history
b. Job analysis
c. Job description
d. Job specifications

_____ 4. Which of the following selection techniques is the most controversial?
a. Application blanks
b. Testing
c. Reference checks
d. Physical examinations

_____ 5. Which of the following training methods depends upon creating a simulated work environment?
a. On-the-job training
b. Job instruction training
c. Apprenticeship training
d. Vestibule training

_____ 6. Which of the following pay plans pays according to the number of hours worked?
a. Day work
b. Straight salary
c. Piecework
d. Group incentive plans

See answers at the back of the book.

KEY TERMS

human resources management, 216
Occupational Safety and Health Act (OSHA), 219
Civil Rights Act of 1964, 219
comparable worth, 219
affirmative action, 220
Age Discrimination in Employment Act of 1967, 220
reverse discrimination, 221
turnover, 221
job analysis, 222
job description, 222
job specifications, 222

bona fide occupational qualification (bfoq), 227
termination, 227
exit interview, 228
outplacement, 229
employment at will, 229
orientation program, 230
apprenticeship training, 232
vestibule training, 232
performance evaluation, 233
day work, 236
straight salary, 236
piecework, 236
group incentive plan, 236
profit sharing, 236
guaranteed annual wage (GAW), 236
cafeteria-style benefits, 238

REVIEW QUESTIONS

1. Describe the characteristics of today's workers.

2. What are the major functions of human resources departments? Who performs these functions in small companies without human resources departments?

3. How are human resources departments in larger companies organized?

4. Explain the service, control, and advisory relationships between human resources departments and other departments.

5. Explain the laws discussed in the chapter that influence the legal aspects of human resources.

6. Discuss affirmative action and comparable worth.

7. What is reverse discrimination?

8. What does employment planning involve? How do companies forecast their needs for employees?

9. Distinguish between a job description, job analysis, and job specification. How are they used in employment planning?

10. What are the advantages of recruiting internally? Externally? What are the disadvantages of recruiting internally? Externally?

11. Identify the standard external sources of recruiting. Briefly describe each.

12. Explain the selection process for making an employment decision. Which steps in the process are most critical? Which steps could a company eliminate?

13. Explain employment at will.

14. What is employee evaluation? What purposes does evaluation serve?

15. Why is documentation so important in the evaluation process?

16. Identify and briefly describe the more popular techniques for evaluating employees.

17. What is job evaluation?

18. How are day work and incentive pay systems alike? Different? Identify and describe examples of each method. Which is the most common? Why?

19. Analyze the role of fringe benefits in the reward system.

CASES

Case 9.1: A Contrast in Attitudes

The following are comments from two employees relating their differing attitudes toward their organizations.

A younger employee describes his first few years of experience:

"I was really excited when I first took the job. I thought I would advance fast. But after a few months, I began to feel like I was just going to be doing the same routine things for a long time. I had finished high school, but an eighth grader could do what I was doing. The pay was good, better than I expected, but I just wasn't able to do very much. I could see that they were doing a lot of things that could be improved. I tried to make a few suggestions for improvement. They didn't really listen. There was always some reason why they could not take my ideas. I suspect they just did not want to go to the trouble to make the changes. Finally, I just seemed to lose interest. Now, it's just a job. I do my work, at least most of the time. I'm not too happy; I'll probably start looking around for a new job in a few months."

An older employee describes her many years of experience:

"I've been around for a long time. I see the new people coming in, and they want to change things overnight. If things do not go right, they get upset. Most don't seem to worry if they lose their job, and they are sure not as loyal as people were 30 years ago. At one time, I was unhappy with my job also, but after awhile, you realize that the world is not perfect. I take my job seriously; I know some things could be changed. And we *have* changed a lot of things. But many of the things younger people want to change have served us well. They are into so many things, a job is sometimes just another hobby for them. It seems that their job is not central to their lives."

Questions

1. Discuss some possible reasons why these two employees see things differently.

2. Which set of attitudes is more helpful to the organization? To the employee?

Case 9.2: The Employment Decision

You are considering two applicants for a management trainee position in your sales department. For the first two years, the trainee will work in several different jobs in the department to learn how your company does things. Then the employee will be assigned a position as assistant to one of your department managers. The trainee's progress thereafter will depend upon how well he or she performs. You have interviewed several applicants and have narrowed your choice to two people. Both are young college graduates with little or no experience.

Wally Hendrich is a bright young graduate with a B+ average and a major in business. He scored very well on your tests and has excellent references from his professors and from an employer for whom he worked part-time while attending school. Other people in your company have been somewhat impressed by Wally, but not as much as you have been. They feel that he has done all the "right" things, but they worry that he does not have the ambition to be a successful sales manager. Wally places high priorities on getting married, raising a family, being at home, and living a "normal" life. You are aware of this, but since

Wally has been successful at everything he has done, you feel that he will be successful in his work.

Sally DeWolf is also a college graduate with above-average grades in business. She has an outgoing personality, dresses attractively, and communicates a feeling of confidence. She has worked part-time at several different jobs, never staying in one job for very long. When asked why she changed jobs so often, she said she got bored. Her test scores are a little below Wally's but still above average. Others in the organization really like her and think that she has the personality and drive to be a success. You also think she is a good prospect, but you feel that she is too self-centered. You get the impression that she will put her personal growth and advancement ahead of her desire to make the department look good. Also you have a slight fear that she will try shortcuts and might leave if the company does not "take care of her."

Questions

1. Analyze the strengths and weaknesses of Wally; of Sally.

2. How will you consider the opinions of others in relation to yours? Which will you give the most attention to? Why?

3. On the basis of this information, which candidate would you select? Why? What are the potential problems with your selection? What would you do to prevent or reduce these problems?

**After completing this chapter, you should be
able to:**

■   **Discuss Maslow's hierarchy of needs theory
    of motivation.**

■   **Diagram and explain Herzberg's motivation-
    hygiene theory.**

■   **Explain the role of money in employee motivation.**

■   **Describe job enrichment.**

■   **Explain management by objectives (MBO).**

■   **Discuss the history and process of quality circles.**

■   **Describe quality of work life (QWL) programs.**

■   **Identify eight practical ways managers can
    motivate today's employees.**

UNDERSTANDING
AND
MOTIVATING
EMPLOYEES

In a recent survey by the Public Agenda Foundation of New York, only 23% of the respondents told interviewers they were working as hard as they could in their jobs. Management expert Peter Drucker says, "The quickest way to quench motivation is not to allow people to do what they've been trained to do. In other words, take the nurse in the hospital and make her spend 80% of her time on paperwork that has nothing to do with patient care."

The management at Owens-Illinois, in an effort to restore employee confidence and build employee commitment, holds periodic meetings with employees to report on company performance and to answer questions. Management says they are trying to motivate employees through terms and concepts they can understand; they do not want to rely strictly upon financial objectives. Their program also wants to show a close link between individual prosperity and company success.

At a time when technology and robotics seem to be dominating management decisions, Owens-Illinois and many other companies are making special efforts to understand and motivate their people. A researcher asked twenty Hewlett-Packard executives why their company was success-

ful. Eighteen of the twenty spontaneously said, "It is our people-oriented philosophy." Explaining the reasons behind their long-term success, an executive at Delta Airlines said, "There is a special relationship between Delta and its personnel that is rarely found in any firm, generating a team spirit that is evident in the individual's cooperative attitude . . . , cheerful outlook on life, and pride in a job well done." Hideo Sugiura, chairman of Honda Motor Company, explains their people-oriented philosophy: "Our workers are not tools of production. We never say we want to hire welders, or lathe operators, or whatever." Sugiura further explained that if you hired a welder and found a robot to replace him, there is nothing you can do with the welder. But if you hire someone and train him in all the skills of assembling a motorcycle, to him a robot is just another machine to make his work easier.

This chapter examines major motivational theories, practical applications of the theories, and methods of motivating employees.

On their own initiative, active and retired employees of Delta Airlines purchased this 767 airliner and presented it to the company.

MAJOR MOTIVATIONAL THEORIES

Two theories of motivation, Maslow's hierarchy of needs and Herzberg's motivation-hygiene theory, have stood the test of time.

Maslow's Hierarchy of Needs

Maslow, a well-known psychologist, believed that needs were the underlying causes of all behavior. The only reason a person does anything is to satisfy **needs.** Thus, we can understand human **motivation** if we understand needs.

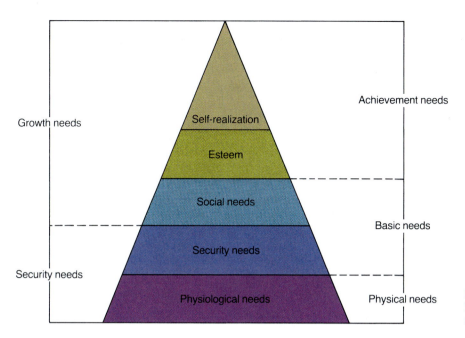

Growth needs

Security needs

Achievement needs

Basic needs

Physical needs

Self-realization

Esteem

Social needs

Security needs

Physiological needs

**Figure 10.1
Maslow's hierarchy of
needs.**

Based on his research and experience, Maslow divided human needs into five levels: physiological, safety, social, esteem, and self-realization. These needs are arranged in **Maslow's hierarchy** as shown in Fig. 10.1 and Table 10.1.

Physiological needs include the basic needs necessary for survival. Examples are oxygen, food, rest, sex, and water. We have to satisfy these needs regularly to keep ourselves alive. The next higher level is security needs, originally called

safety needs by Maslow. **Security needs** reflect the desire for certainty, predictability, safety, and stability in our lives. We like to believe that some things will remain the same tomorrow as they are today. We try to satisfy these needs through such activities as fringe benefit programs, hospitalization insurance, retirement programs, life insurance, savings, and the like. The need to love and be loved, to have friends and be a friend, to enjoy the companionship of other humans is a **social need.**

TABLE 10.1 ■ MASLOW'S NEEDS: PERSONAL, SOCIAL, AND PHYSICAL ASPECTS

Maslow's Needs	Personal Aspects	Social Aspects	Physical Aspects
Physiological needs	Personal, physical comfort		Food, water, oxygen, sex, rest, temperature
Security needs	Personal safety, continuity, comfort, no future threats		Security of a continuance of physiological needs without threat of loss in future
Social needs	Acceptance, friends, a feeling of belonging	Acceptance by others, prestige and value acknowledged by peers	Feeling comfortable, accepted, and secure in social situations
Esteem needs	Respect for self, pride, achievement	Evident respect from others, professional accomplishment acknowledged by peers	More basic needs fulfilled; threats to safety, comfort, and social acceptance overcome
Self-realization needs	Total self-development, fulfillment, maximum personal growth	Unusual accomplishment acknowledged by peers	Concern about basic needs seems petty; of course, basic needs will be met

And these social needs form the third level in Maslow's hierarchy. We try to satisfy these through marriage, parties, office groups, coffee breaks, fraternities, and clubs. At the fourth level is esteem needs. **Esteem needs** mean respect from others and respect for one's self. We want to feel that we are doing something that is worthwhile, and we want others to respect us for it. The need for esteem is the need for our peers to say, "You are a person of value, of worth." "You are doing something we respect." "You are good at what you are doing." We try to satisfy this need through reputation and expertise gained through knowledge, preparation, experience, and accomplishments.

Maslow said a housewife could achieve

---

self-realization by creatively preparing a

---

bowl of soup.

Finally, at the apex, is the need for **self-realization,** the need to do the very best that we are capable of doing. We do not have to be corporation presidents or world-renowned artists to satisfy these needs. Maslow said that a housewife showed him that she could achieve self-realization by creatively preparing a bowl of soup, a football player by executing a block to perfection, and a high school janitor by expertly performing his duties. We achieve some degree of self-realization when we do a task or create an idea that utilizes all, or practically all, of our abilities. See Fig. 10.2 for characteristics of people who operate at the self-realization level.

Maslow also agreed that some people were out of sync with his theory. Some artists, religious leaders, and creative people seek to satisfy higher-level needs without first fulfilling lower-level needs. Without sufficient shelter, security, or social life, they toil away, driven by their quest for self-realization. Maslow explained this by saying they were exceptions to his general theory. Numerous research studies have shown that this theory helps to explain the behavior of most people in our culture.

Herzberg's Motivation-Hygiene Theory

Like Maslow, Frederick Herzberg, a psychology professor and world-famous management consultant, used needs as the basis of his theory of motivation. As seen in Fig. 10.3, **Herzberg's motivation-hygiene theory** divides our needs into two categories: (1) hygiene and (2) motivational.

Hygiene needs. The group of needs outside the circle, Herzberg called hygiene needs. Generally, **hygiene needs** represent factors that are peripheral to the job itself (that is, they are job-context

Figure 10.2
Characteristics of people who operate at the self-realization level. *Source: Adapted from Abraham H. Maslow,* Toward a Psychology of Being, *Litton Educational Publishing, Inc., 1968.*

Evaluate yourself on the following scales by selecting the number that describes how you see yourself.

Clear perception of reality	1 2 3 4 5 6 7 8 9 10	Unclear perception of reality
Open to different experiences	1 2 3 4 5 6 7 8 9 10	Closed to different experiences
Spontaneous	1 2 3 4 5 6 7 8 9 10	Guarded
Autonomous	1 2 3 4 5 6 7 8 9 10	Dependent
Objective	1 2 3 4 5 6 7 8 9 10	Subjective
More creative	1 2 3 4 5 6 7 8 9 10	Less creative
Democratic	1 2 3 4 5 6 7 8 9 10	Autocratic
Great ability to love others	1 2 3 4 5 6 7 8 9 10	Limited ability to love others

The values on the left of this scale are characteristics of people operating at the self-realization level. Thus, if you total your points on all the scales, a score of 49 or less indicates greater tendencies toward self-realization. A score of 51 or more indicates lesser tendencies toward self-realization.

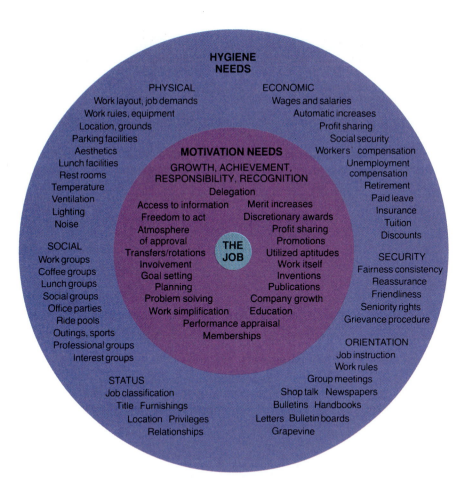

HYGIENE NEEDS

PHYSICAL
Work layout, job demands
Work rules, equipment
Location, grounds
Parking facilities
Aesthetics
Lunch facilities
Rest rooms
Temperature
Ventilation
Lighting
Noise

SOCIAL
Work groups
Coffee groups
Lunch groups
Social groups
Office parties
Ride pools
Outings, sports
Professional groups
Interest groups

STATUS
Job classification
Title Furnishings
Location Privileges
Relationships

ECONOMIC
Wages and salaries
Automatic increases
Profit sharing
Social security
Workers' compensation
Unemployment compensation
Retirement
Paid leave
Insurance
Tuition
Discounts

SECURITY
Fairness consistency
Reassurance
Friendliness
Seniority rights
Grievance procedure

ORIENTATION
Job instruction
Work rules
Group meetings
Shop talk Newspapers
Bulletins Handbooks
Letters Bulletin boards
Grapevine

MOTIVATION NEEDS
GROWTH, ACHIEVEMENT, RESPONSIBILITY, RECOGNITION
Delegation
Access to information   Merit increases
Freedom to act   Discretionary awards
Atmosphere   Profit sharing
of approval   Promotions
Transfers/rotations   Utilized aptitudes
Involvement   Work itself
Goal setting   Inventions
Planning   Publications
Problem solving   Company growth
Work simplification   Education
Performance appraisal
Memberships

THE JOB

Figure 10.3
Herzberg's motivation and hygiene needs.
Source: Adapted from M. Scott Myers, "Who Are Your Motivated Workers?" Harvard Business Review, *January/ February 1964, p. 86.*

oriented). Examples include company policy, administration, supervision, work conditions, salary, relationships with peers, personal life, relationships with subordinates, status, and security.

Herzberg says, "Hygiene factors do not motivate employees to perform." Does this mean they are not important? No! While hygiene needs may not motivate performance, they do cause people to be upset when they are unfulfilled. We must satisfy hygiene needs of employees or they will get frustrated and quit, work slowly, be absent, form a union, or express their displeasure in other ways. On the other hand, when we do satisfy employees' hygiene needs, we cannot necessarily expect them to show their gratefulness by working hard. In a sense we only come out even, because we have merely prevented unhappiness; we have not created a desire to perform.

As you study Fig. 10.3, you will see many ways that organizations motivate their people. A skeptic

usually remarks, "I know that money is motivating. That is the reason a lot of people work." Before you concur too strongly with these skeptical supervisors, think about what would happen if an organization doubled the salary (or status, or working conditions) of its employees. Would they work twice as hard? Probably not. Would they be 50% more productive? Probably not. Would they work any harder? Probably, but only for a few weeks. People surely want to satisfy their hygiene needs. And organizations have done a very good job of providing these satisfactions. But if we are to motivate today's employees, we must appeal to their motivational needs.

Motivational needs. While hygiene factors are peripheral to the work, **motivational needs** are associated directly with the work itself (that is, they are job-content oriented). Figure 10.3 contains examples of these needs, including the work

What People Want from Their Work

Motivation, in reality, is an exchange process. The organization wants employees to apply their physical and mental efforts toward reaching the objectives of the department. For this, the organization must give their workers what they want. However, many managers try to give employees what they think they want from their work without really trying to find out their real aspirations. A survey conducted by the Labor Relations Institute of New York some years back, and repeated many times since then, reveals the differences between what employees actually want from their work and what managers think they want. Rankings of ten things employees wanted from their work are listed here. The left column shows how the employees ranked these items, and the right column shows how managers ranked them.

Employees' Rankings		Managers' Rankings
1	Full appreciation for work done	8
2	Feeling of being "in" on things	9
3	Sympathetic help on personal problems	10
4	Job security	2
5	Good wages	1
6	Interesting work	5
7	Promotion and growth in the organization	3
8	Personal loyalty to employees	6
9	Good working conditions	4
10	Tactful disciplining	7

Note the vast differences on the first three items. What employees ranked 1, 2, 3, the managers ranked 8, 9, and 10. Do you see why we have motivational problems?

itself: individual growth, recognition, advancement, responsibility, achievement, and individual development. According to Herzberg's research, and hundreds of others that have replicated his studies, people are moved to perform by the satisfaction of these higher-level needs.

PRACTICAL APPLICATIONS OF THEORIES

Theory is necessary because it gives us a good understanding of why things happen. But knowing theory does not automatically guarantee that we can practice it. So, we will now dwell on the practical ways to apply these theories. After a dis-

cussion of the role of money in motivation, we will examine the techniques of job enrichment, management by objectives, quality circles, and quality of work life.

The Role of Money in Employee Motivation

Compare the following comments of two managers.

> "I just don't understand people today. We try to pay according to performance, but they just don't seem to be interested in money. Many seem to do their jobs poorly even when they know it will be reflected in their paychecks."

"That's not true of our employees. Money is all they want to talk about. In fact, a lot of our people say they enjoy working for us, but they quit to take higher-paying jobs."

Such comments underline the confusion over money as a motivator. To motivate, money must fulfill some of the needs that we discussed earlier. From experience and research, we see that money can in some way apply to both higher- and lower-level needs.

Surely, money is necessary to help satisfy the basic needs of life. While we cannot eat, drink, or clothe ourselves in money, we use it to purchase food, water, clothing, and shelter. Money also helps to satisfy security needs. We save it, invest it, build retirement programs with it, and buy insurance with it. All these purchases help to satisfy our need for security and safety.

In our culture, money is also a great help in satisfying social needs. We may have friends without much money. But, money makes it easier to socialize with others at the movies, parties, or clubs. We also use it to entertain in our homes, join fancy clubs, and travel with family and friends.

But as a once-popular song put it, "Money talks, but it can't dance and it can't sing." Few people would say that money equals respect and dignity. Still, money can be a sign of respect. Salaries represent the worth of an individual to the organization. Therefore, high salaries and good pay increases show that the organization respects the individual's contribution. And this can be used to communicate to others outside the company how much their organization respects them. "If you really want to show me how much you appreciate my work, put it in my paycheck."

So we see that money satisfies need levels from the tangible to the intangible. We feel insecure when we do not have enough money for life's basics. And we may feel a lack of respect when our companies do not pay us what they are paying our peers or what we feel we deserve.

Because money applies to so many different need levels, it would appear to be an excellent motivator. But practice suggests that money does not have nearly the motivational impact it once had. Compared to 20 or 30 years ago, real wages and incomes are much higher. Yet, employees do not seem to be as motivated by wages. As a speaker in a recent training session put it, "If we could solve our motivational problems with money, they would be solved. Employees receive much more pay today than they did in 'the good old days.' Yet, we have more apathy, absenteeism, theft, and general unconcern for the work output than ever before."

In fact, we probably rely too much on money. Although monetary incentive plans were quite effective 40 or 50 years ago, most are not producing the desired results today.

Job Enrichment

While pay is an attempt to reward zestful employees, job enrichment is an effort to motivate via the work itself. **Job enrichment** is the process of changing the job so that the work will appeal to employees' higher-level needs. Its aim is to make the work itself more meaningful. If people get enjoyment and need fulfillment from doing their tasks, the job will motivate them to work.

First, job enrichment is not asking people to produce more, or sell more, or get through their work more quickly. This is merely speeding up, working harder at what you are doing. Second, it is not **job enlargement,** merely adding another meaningless task to an already meaningless job. Washing knives and forks is not a lot more fulfilling than washing just knives. Some managers assume they are enriching subordinates' work lives by adding other duties, but the duties must make the job more whole or more meaningful in order to be enriching. Third, rotating meaningless tasks does not help, at least not very much. To say that you can wash knives in the morning, but you get to wash forks in the afternoon will cause few, if any, employees to shout and sing. Fourth, job enrichment does not mean taking away all the hard parts and making the task more routine. Such a change takes fulfillment out of the job rather than putting it in.

Job enrichment means checking less frequently on your employees, giving them more responsibility, and making them more accountable for their work.

Then what is job enrichment? Here are a few pointers. Remove some of the controls. If you have been checking on employees every hour, start checking only every two hours, then every three. Place more responsibility on people. Make people accountable for their work. If they do not do it, the work does not get done. If there are problems, the employee should correct them, not the supervisor. An older employee relates an example, "I've had this scheduling job for years. It is tough; hard to get everything right. There are always conflicts. The boss got a new assistant. I guess she wants to impress someone, so she has started double-checking everything I turn in. Now, when I get the schedule down to two or three conflicts, I turn it in. She finds the problems, then takes whatever time is necessary to straighten them out. It was fun doing this at first, watching her scurry around. But I've lost a little respect and the scheduling is not as satisfying. I don't get the satisfaction of knowing that I did a good job."

There are many other ways to broaden and enrich a task. Give an employee a complete natural work unit and more authority to make decisions. Rather than instructing a secretary to "fill in Part A of Form 1098," let him complete the entire

Does New Role of Father Reduce Motivation?

In the 1960s, the role of parents was well established. Typically, the role of the mother was to raise the children, and the father's responsibility was to provide financial support for the family and be a caretaker for the mother. While this is surely oversimplifying the situation, these father-mother roles were quite recognizable in the 1960s.

However, the changing roles of mothers in society have also brought about a changing role for fathers. A father, today, is more likely to share the domestic role with the mother, especially the role of child care. Simultaneously, the mother is more likely to take some responsibility for "bringing home the bread."

Some psychologists say the father's increased role in child care has significantly reduced the motivation to succeed in business. A study by American Telephone & Telegraph Co. of ten major industries found that the younger employees had less motivation and interest in getting ahead, and they were less concerned about their organization than were their older counterparts.

Reporting at the American Psychological Association conference in 1983, Professor Philip Cowen said that fathers who were more involved in the family were more likely to feel better about themselves and have wives that were less depressed, regardless of whether the mother worked. Cowen further said that industries should adapt their working hours so that fathers can assume more of the child care role.

Other studies also indicate that younger managers have less drive for leadership and accomplishment than their counterparts did 20 years ago, but some of these studies attribute the difference to the "generation gap" rather than changing roles. What do you think?

Do you think that the increased role of a father in child care reduces the father's desire to succeed in the company? Why?

___A. Yes   ___B. No

Do you think that companies should try to adapt their working hours to family needs, regardless of whether it affects productivity at work? Respond on a scale from 7 to 1, with 7 indicating companies should "try hard to adapt" and 1 indicating they should adapt "no more than at present." Why?

Try hard to adapt   7 6 5 4 3 2 1   No more than at present

Honda Plants in the United States

Honda built its first manufacturing facility in the United States in Marysville, Ohio — a $35 million motorcycle plant. The first motorcycle came off the sparkling new assembly line in 1979. A couple of years later, Honda started building a $250 million car plant, and the first Honda Accord car was produced in 1982.

One reason Honda located in Marysville is that they wanted to find a relatively homogeneous work group without previous assembly-line experience. Unlike most American auto companies, Honda trains their people in all aspects of the work, not to do just a narrow job. Honda management also spends a lot of time communicating with people in the plant. They have short meetings every morning to talk about any problems that might have arisen the previous day. And the top executives spend a lot of time in the field. An official says that none of top management's desks is very comfortable. This goes back to an early tradition established by Mr. Honda. He believed that managers would more likely be out and available to employees if their desks and offices were not too comfortable.

So far, the employees and the community have responded well to the new Honda plants. "We could not ask for any finer or any fairer relationship than with Honda," said Marysville's mayor, Tom Nuckles.

The big question is, "Can the Japanese be as successful producing products in the United States as they were in Japan?" Although it is too early to tell whether they will be successful, the early signs look good. As one of the plant coordinators admitted, when dealers find out that a Honda product was produced in the United States, "they will be looking for a flaw." Management says it is up to the employees to make sure that the cars produced here are of the same outstanding quality as those produced in Japan.

project and carry it through. Rather than having the receptionist refer every call to the boss, train her to answer many of the callers' questions. Then try to give employees direct feedback on how well they are doing. If there are computer printouts on costs, scrap, hours, and the like, teach the employees to read them. Seeing direct feedback themselves is more powerful than having a leader interpret progress, or lack of it, to them. Occasionally, introduce new and harder tasks to employees. They really want to do more, not less. Learning is a form of growth; it awakens and refreshes us. Finally, it is very enticing to become known as a person who is an expert. So give people specific areas of responsibility. When things go well, everyone will know who gets the credit.

Most readers have work experience. Can you think of some changes that would cause a job to be more exciting? Figure 10.4 contains a checklist that can be used to evaluate the meaningfulness of work.

Management by Objectives

Like job enrichment, **management by objectives,** often called **MBO,** is a program that tries to increase motivation by appealing to higher-level needs. Basically, management by objectives involves a supervisor and subordinate agreeing upon what the subordinate is to accomplish in the immediate future, say 3 to 6 months. Rather than describing activities of a job, MBO concentrates on the results of the job. For example, the traditional job description of a service department manager might include such things as supervising service employees, maintaining accurate service records, training employees, establishing relationships with customers, and the like. Under MBO, the service manager might have four to seven specific objectives to accomplish such as: (1) design a new maintenance contract program by June 14, (2) reduce the absentee rate in the department from 4% to 2% within the next 6 months, (3) select at least

PLANNING: Can the individual or group . . .	no	sometimes	yes
1. Set goals and standards of performance?	___	___	___
2. State the product quality and quantity commitments?	___	___	___
3. Organize the work layout and influence personnel assignments?	___	___	___
4. Name customers and state delivery dates for products and services?	___	___	___
5. State the sources of their materials and problems in obtaining them?	___	___	___
6. List direct and overhead costs, selling price, and other profit and loss information?	___	___	___
DOING: Does the job . . .			
1. Utilize peoples' talents and require their attention?	___	___	___
2. Enable people to see the relationship of their work to other operations?	___	___	___
3. Provide access to all the information they need to do their work?	___	___	___
4. Have a satisfactory work cycle—neither too long nor too short?	___	___	___
5. Give people feedback on how well they are doing?	___	___	___
6. Enable them to see how they contribute to the usefulness of the product or service to the customer?	___	___	___
CONTROLLING: Can the individual or group . . .			
1. State customer quality requirements and reasons for these standards?	___	___	___
2. Keep their own records of quality and quantity?	___	___	___
3. Check quality and quantity of work and revise procedures?	___	___	___
4. Evaluate and modify work layout on their own initiative?	___	___	___
5. Identify and correct unsafe working conditions?	___	___	___
6. Obtain information from people outside the group as a means of evaluating performance?	___	___	___

Figure 10.4
Sample items from supervisory worksheet for analyzing meaningfulness of work. *Source: Adapted from M. Scott Myers, "Every Employee a Manager,"* California Management Review, *1968, pp. 9–20.*

four employees to attend technical training schools within the year, and (4) handle 3000 projected service calls during the year within 24 hours after each call is placed. Once they agree on the objectives, the supervisor more or less gets out of the way and lets the employee work toward the objectives in his or her own way. At the end of the period, the supervisor and employee get together to measure progress. If the employee has reached the objectives, they set others for the next period and repeat the process. If the employee came up short of some objectives, they try to find out why and improve during the next period. Figure 10.5 diagrams the concept of MBO.

MBO has several sweet-sounding benefits. It gives employees specific targets (objectives) to work toward. It goes beyond the specifics of tasks they are supposed to perform to what they should be accomplishing. And once objectives are set,

employees can monitor their own progress on a daily or weekly basis. They get feedback on whether they are ahead or behind or on schedule. Such feedback on progress helps to satisfy higher level needs of growth, improvement, and autonomy. It also allows the employees to work more on their own because they know where they are and where they are going. Supervisors do not have to look over their shoulders all the time, checking on progress. Research also shows that when people are involved to some degree in setting their own objectives, they are more committed to reaching them. The objectives are no longer something that the impersonal organization requires of them; they are, at least partly, their own ideas. In these ways, MBO appeals to higher-level needs.

MBO has not been equally successful in all organizations. In fact, research reports numerous failures and partial successes of MBO in organizations. Organizations that have maintained successful MBO programs tend to:

1. State in specific, measurable terms four to seven objectives for each manager's job.

2. Ask each subordinate manager or employee to report his or her objectives to superiors in writing. Both superior and subordinate must come to agreement on the objectives.

3. Include methods to measure results and steps that are necessary to accomplish the objectives.

4. Systematically gather data on the progress toward the objectives and regularly report this to subordinates.

5. Engage managers and subordinates in supportive, problem-solving discussions to improve performance when progress falls behind.

6. Concentrate on using MBO at management levels.

Quality Circles

A **quality circle (QC)** is a group of workers in the same area who meet together voluntarily on a regular basis to try to solve problems and reduce costs in their departments. The early 1980s saw U.S. organizations placing a tremendous emphasis on using quality circles to motivate their employees to produce better-quality products and services.

Authorities estimated that more than 400 organizations had some type of quality control system in 1983.

In fact, authorities estimated that more than 400 organizations had some type of quality circle system in 1983.

Dr. W. E. Deming, an American consultant, introduced QCs in Japan, probably around 1961. QCs spread throughout most of Japanese industry; and in 1974, Lockheed introduced them into the United States. After Lockheed reported savings of $2.8 million in the first 2 years of using QCs, other companies became interested. Companies provide many instances of how their circles have benefited them, for example:

Keithley Instruments, Inc., a manufacturer of electronics measuring equipment, using the quality circle concept in the form of product-oriented work teams, reports that:

- Inventory costs were reduced $550,000 from 1981 to 1982.

Figure 10.5
The concept of MBO.
Employee A is told exactly what to do and how to do it. He is too closely supervised. Employee B is neither told what to do nor how to do it. She is too loosely supervised. Employee C and supervisor agree on what to do, and Employee C has some latitude as to how he will do it. This is management by objectives.

- Inventory turnover was increased from 1.8 to 2.14 per year.
- Increase in productivity was 21 percent.
- Improvement in the company's quality audit rating went from the low 80s to 95.5%.

How quality circles typically operate. While there is variation among circle operations, most follow a pattern that includes five themes:

1. *Regular meetings.* Circles typically have between five and ten members, and they meet on a regular basis. Effective QCs set a schedule and stick by it. Usually, they meet once a week, for an average of 45 minutes to an hour per meeting. Most meetings occur on company time, but some occur before work, during lunch, or after work.

2. *Problems within their departments.* QCs tackle problems within their areas of expertise, usually within their departments. They try to solve only those problems they have control over. Many of the problems they deal with, especially when a circle is new, may seem insignificant. But effective circles do not try to tell other departments how they should operate, nor do they try to tell the president how to run the company.

3. *Participation by all members.* Circle leaders encourage participation by all members. When deciding what problems to work on and when searching for solutions, effective leaders encourage ideas from all members.

4. *Training.* Circles receive a lot of training. Experts, usually from outside the company, train the leaders on topics ranging from leadership to statistical techniques. Leaders then train their circle members. Training may be a part of the circle meetings for 15 to 20 weeks.

5. *Management presentation.* When QCs identify significant problems and solutions, they may present these to a group of higher-level managers. This is called a "management presentation." Using charts, visuals, slides, and other analytical devices, circle members try to persuade management that they have found a way to solve a problem. Of course, the circle members must understand that management has the final say on whether the solution will be adopted.

Organization of quality circles. In addition to the QC members and leader, circle structures typically include facilitators, coordinators, and a steering committee. The facilitator helps the leader coordinate the circle activities, provides training when needed, and aids the circle in whatever way is necessary. The coordinator oversees the overall company program, and policies are set by the steering committee. Figure 10.6 diagrams a typical organization structure of a QC program.

Potential problems with quality circles. Since U.S. culture differs from Japanese culture, many authorities have warned that we simply cannot adapt circles easily into our work force. And while there have been many successes, there is also evidence that some circles also have problems. In fact, after about a year's operation, it is not uncommon for a circle to show signs of burnout. Some members stop attending meetings, both members and leaders get frustrated and lose patience with the process, the group runs out of problems, and upper management loses interest. Our work force is also much less stable than Japan's. Turnover and layoffs make it hard to maintain continuity in circle meetings.

Dr. Matthew Goodfellow of University Research Center studied quality circle programs in twenty-nine companies and found that in twenty-one companies the quality circles produced measurable results totaling less than their cost. Westinghouse, which established about 1000 circles at 200 locations, has been disappointed, primarily because of poor union cooperation. And North American Phillips Corp. in Jefferson City, Tennessee, developed a quality circle program that did not succeed. Again, failure to gain union commitment, as well as lack of preparation for the circles, probably led to the failure. While there are many reported successes with circles, managers should be aware that they require large investments in time and energy to make them successful.

Quality of Work Life Programs

In an effort to improve both employee satisfaction and productivity, General Motors in 1973 incorporated **quality of work life (QWL)** activities into its collective bargaining agreement with the United Auto Workers. Work teams of sixteen persons at GM's Cadillac plant in Livonia, Michigan,

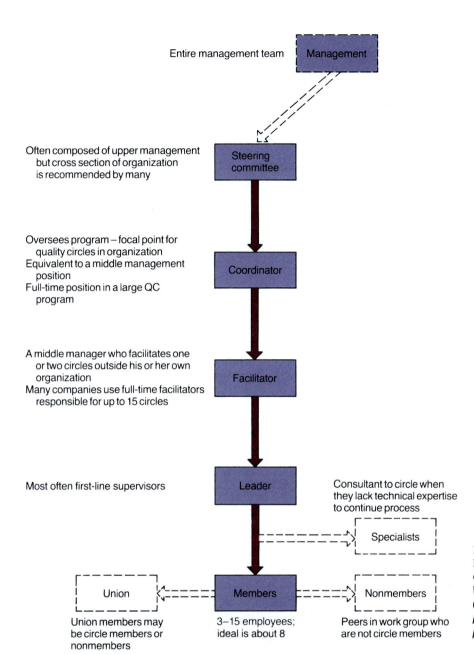

Entire management team — Management

Often composed of upper management but cross section of organization is recommended by many — Steering committee

Oversees program – focal point for quality circles in organization
Equivalent to a middle management position
Full-time position in a large QC program
— Coordinator

A middle manager who facilitates one or two circles outside his or her own organization
Many companies use full-time facilitators responsible for up to 15 circles
— Facilitator

Most often first-line supervisors — Leader

Consultant to circle when they lack technical expertise to continue process — Specialists

Union
Union members may be circle members or nonmembers

Members
3–15 employees; ideal is about 8

Nonmembers
Peers in work group who are not circle members

Figure 10.6
Example of a quality circle structure. *Source: William L. and Harriet Mohr, Quality Circles, Reading, Mass.: Addison-Wesley Publishing Co., 1983, p. 78.*

QWL activities saved General Motors $440,000 in 1982.

set their own work rules, production levels, and were responsible for quality of their output. Suggestions from the workers saved GM $440,000 in 1982, and outside auditors rated their engines as the best or among the best produced by the company. Because of the success at General Motors, many other corporations have introduced some type of QWL program into its management.

Quality of work life programs are efforts by companies and employees to increase employee participation, democratic processes, and improved working conditions in the company. The programs usually consist of employee problem-solving groups and gain-sharing plans. Employees, through group discussion and other means, try to develop ideas that will improve productivity and employee contentment. And when these programs result in improved productivity, the company usually shares the savings through some type of bonus system for the employees and managers.

Results of quality of work life programs. As you might expect, some QWL programs are successful and some are not. In a coal mining company, QWL programs have introduced additional job training, supervisory training, some pay changes, and better communications between shifts. These efforts resulted in slight productivity increases. An auto parts factory gained significant productivity increases by making the following changes through their QWL program:

- Time-off bonus incentives.
- Increased training.
- A safety program.
- A plant newsletter.

Other examples of changes by QWL programs in companies include: (1) four-day work weeks, (2) communication programs, (3) better equipment, (4) improved parking facilities, (5) staff meetings, (6) management development activities, (7) attitude surveys, (8) job assignment systems, and the like. Many of these changes improve the working life of employees; some improve both working life and productivity; and others improve neither.

Conditions for success. Companies that have improved both productivity and employee satisfaction with their QWL programs meet the following conditions:

- There is an apparent need for change.
- There is a strong commitment from higher management.
- There is sufficient time and budget to effect changes.
- The firms have a reputation for being well managed.
- Employee-management trust is high.
- Changes occur only after adequate planning and preparation.

When these conditions are not met, the company likely will be disappointed in the results of its QWL programs.

When these conditions are present, however, a QWL program can have very positive benefits for both employees and the company. The production department of a large chemical plant remained dissatisfied with its production performance even after repeated efforts to increase it. They formed a QWL program and held many meetings with hourly workers and other appropriate groups throughout the company. After much discussion and a long time lapse, employees, working with their supervisors, created many new work plans and projects for improvement. As a result, production rose from 90% of capacity to 106%, the packaging department produced 125% of its goal, the lab consistently met its turnaround target of 3 hours, and cooperation and employee morale increased significantly. Figure 10.7 lists the problem-solving process used in QC and QWL groups.

MOTIVATING EMPLOYEES THROUGH EFFECTIVE SUPERVISION

In addition to the suggestions for applying motivational theories, managers can increase employee motivation through more effective day-to-day supervision. Here are some guidelines for improving motivation through effective supervision.

Increasing Authority Delegation

Authority delegation includes (1) assigning work to people, (2) getting out of their way while they perform it, and (3) checking when the job is finished. As individuals become proficient at their current jobs, managers can encourage them to take on even more responsibilities. Some employees may resist this process at first, but both theory and practice suggest that they really want to progress to more responsible tasks.

Communicating Expectations

It is surprising how many employees do not know what is expected of them, that is, do not understand their goals. A research experiment with second-grade school children illustrates the power of

1. Identify a list of problems.
2. Select one problem to solve.
3. Clarify the problem.
4. Identify and evaluate causes.
5. Identify and evaluate solutions.
6. Decide on a solution.
7. Develop an implementation plan.
8. Present the plan to management.
9. Implement the plan.
10. Monitor the solution.
11. Think ahead.

Figure 10.7
The problem-solving process. *Source: William L. and Harriet Mohr,* Quality Circles, *Reading, Mass: Addison-Wesley Publishing Co., 1983, p. 82.*

expectations. Researchers tested the children at the beginning of the year. One of the tests was an intelligence test. At the end of the semester, researchers compared the teacher's grades to the test scores. Sure enough, the kids with higher intelligence scores also had higher grades. This does not surprise you, right? But the reported intelligence test scores were not that at all: They were the kids' locker numbers, which had been randomly assigned.

The kids with higher locker numbers responded to teacher expectations. Suppose you were the teacher. A student with a locker number of 120 turns in ten arithmetic problems and gets only five right. You are disappointed. You ask the child, "What is wrong? Why did you miss five? What can I do to help you?" But suppose locker number 65 turns in five correct problems. You say, "That's good! You got five right. Now don't get discouraged." You expect more from the higher locker numbers and you get more.

If you expect employees to be at work on time every day, tell them. If you expect employees to finish a job in a specific time, let them know. Goals are important and should be made known.

Giving Earned Recognition and Praise

Employees want to please their superiors, and they want them to appreciate what they do for them. In a survey, a researcher asked supervisors,

BUSINESS BULLETIN

Flextime and Job Sharing

Two trends have emerged in recent years to try to accommodate more of employees' special needs: flextime and job sharing.

Flextime means letting employees have some flexibility in choosing their working hours. Typically, employees have a choice about what hours they will work, within limits set by the company. For instance, employees might be able to choose to come to work between the hours of 6:00 to 9:00 A.M. Of course, they would have to work their normal number of hours.

To the employer, flextime often reduces tardiness, absenteeism, and time lost due to sick leave. It can create some scheduling and record keeping problems, however. For the employee, flextime provides an opportunity to gain some control over the work day and to accomplish errands and keep doctor's appointments, for example, that must be done during usual working hours.

Job sharing allows two employees, each of whom works part-time, to share a job. Typically, one employee will work in the morning and another employee will work in the afternoon. Firms encourage job sharing to accommodate parents who want to work part, but not all, of the day. By doing this, companies have been able to acquire better-qualified people than they could otherwise find.

Both flextime and job sharing are attempts to attract and retain a more highly motivated work force.

"How many of you give your employees a pat on the back when they do a good job?" Eighty-two percent said they did. But when subordinates were asked the same question, only 12% said they received a pat on the back for good work. A simple but sincere "thank you" is a powerful motivator.

After attending a seminar on motivation, a supervisor was determined to put some of the ideas into practice. She called one of her maintenance helpers over. The helper, probably thinking that he was going to be criticized, was a little frightened and slowly walked over, shoulders slumped and head slightly bowed. The supervisor placed her hand on the helper's shoulder and commented, "I want to thank you for the job you did on the machine yesterday. We really needed you and you sure came through." The helper gradu-

With one balloon marking each of a succession of accident-free days, a unique ceremony recognizes work well done.

BUSINESS BULLETIN

The One Minute Manager

Kenneth Blanchard and Spencer Johnson are the authors of a small book called *The One Minute Manager*. They believe that the quickest way to increase productivity, profits, job satisfaction, and personal prosperity is to follow their three-step management method: one minute goal setting, one minute praising, and one minute reprimanding. (The authors contend that not one of these three processes takes more than one minute to do; indeed, so manic about minutes are they, the book scarcely takes more than a minute to read.)

One-minute goal setting works well when you:

- Agree on your goals.
- See what good behavior looks like.
- Write out each of your goals on a single sheet of paper, using fewer than 250 words.
- Read and reread each goal.
- Take a minute every once in a while to look at your performance.
- See whether your behavior matches your goal.

One-minute praising works well when you:

- Tell people up front that you are going to let them know how they are doing.
- Praise people immediately.
- Tell people specifically what they did right.
- Tell people how good you feel about what they did right, and how it helps the organization and the other people who work there.

ally straightened, and when he walked back to his work place, he was almost beaming.

Giving Feedback on Progress

An experiment divided employees into two groups. Group A was told to work as well as they could and to finish as quickly as they could. During the week, they were never told how well they were doing. Group B received different instructions: They discussed and set specific weekly targets and were also issued weekly progress reports, so they could easily tell if they were ahead or behind. Group A, working on the same kind of tasks, knew nothing of Group B's arrangement. As you probably have guessed, Group B outperformed Group A by about 40%. Employees seek specific, tangible feedback on how well they are doing.

Involving Employees in Decision Making

People like to feel that they have some degree of control over their destinies. Although they may resist management's first efforts, employees do want to be more involved in their work. They want to use their intelligence and experience as well as their muscles. If employees are not in the habit of offering suggestions, managers should take it easy at first. Managers might tell them something like, "I want to allow you more involvement in your work. In the next three months, I will gradually broaden your responsibility, and I will

- Stop for a moment of silence to let them feel how good you feel.
- Encourage them to do more of the same.
- Shake hands or touch people in a way that makes it clear that you support their success in the organization.

One-minute reprimanding works well when you:

- Tell people beforehand that you are going to let them know how they are doing and in no uncertain terms.
- Reprimand people immediately.
- Tell people specifically what they did wrong.
- Tell people how you feel about what they did wrong—in no uncertain terms.
- Stop for a few seconds of uncomfortable silence to let them feel how you feel.
- Then, shake hands or touch them in a way that lets them know you are honestly on their side.
- Remind them how much you value them.
- Reaffirm that you think well of them but not of their performance in this instance.
- Realize that when the reprimand is over, it's over.

Applying these practices to daily management, the authors say, will result in healthier, happier, more productive lives for managers and minions.

Source: Kenneth Blanchard and Spencer Johnson, *The One Minute Manager,* New York: William Morrow and Co., Inc., 1982, pp. 34, 44, and 59.

expect more inputs from you." Patience is necessary. Five or six months should be allowed for employees to change. When people are involved in decisions that affect their work, they are much more likely to accept, and become committed to, those decisions. By contrast, people who are not involved in decision making often resist decisions involving them.

Encouraging Learning and Growing

Learning is a powerful motivator. Almost any educational program improves morale and productivity. But a training program need not be big and fancy to be effective. Supervisors should look around to see what training employees can benefit from.

Managers can make suggestions for improvement and teach employees new skills. More communication on the department's objectives involves employees, as does additional information about products and services. Supervisors can share with employees criteria the organization evaluates for promotions. It is a good idea to pick out something new to teach employees each week and do it!

Giving Salary Increases on Merit

Most supervisors are not honest in their employee reviews. They do not tell employees their weaknesses and how to improve. Sometimes a manager has to say to an employee something like, "Frankly, I'm disappointed that you have not been able to do your job as expected. Here is what I expect of you during the next three months. If you perform properly, I will be eager to give you a good salary recommendation. What can I do to help?" Even though the employee may get angry, such an approach will be appreciated by most people.

Stimulating Creativity in Employees

Since the 1960s, a number of firms have been buying works of fine art to display in their corporate corridors and offices. Though the art may be bought because the chief executive officer is a collector, it does seem to stimulate employees to be more creative. The Business Committee for the Arts estimates that more than 500 corporations now have art collections. Atlantic Richfield Company, for instance, has a 9000-piece collection of contemporary works with which they ornament their offices throughout the world.

Aside from such purely atmospheric concessions to stimulating creativity, a number of firms are hiring creativity consultants who provide consultations, seminars, and publications to stimulate creativity and innovation in business and industry. Roger von Oech, founder and president of Creative Think, specializes in unlocking the minds of his clients so they may become more receptive to new ideas. He has identified ten mental attitudes that keep people thinking the same old things:

- Believing there is only one right answer.
- Being forever logical.
- Always following the rules.
- Being practical.
- Avoiding ambiguity.
- Believing to err is bad.
- Believing play is frivolous.
- Shunning a topic if it's not in your area.

A painting from Atlantic Richfield's large contemporary art collection adorns a new West Coast office.

- Not wanting to appear foolish.
- Believing you're not creative.

By overcoming these attitudes, von Oech believes, business people will find it far easier to generate new ideas and be creative. John Opel, CEO of IBM, says that to its motto "Think," IBM has appended the word "differently." "Too many people in business are binary," he laments. "It's either left or right, on or off" — right or wrong.

SUMMARY

Motivation is the use of physical or mental effort, resulting from unfilled needs. A need is a tension or state of discomfort that exists within people. The two major theories of motivation are Maslow's need hierarchy and Herzberg's motivation-hygiene theory. Maslow identified five needs, existing in a hierarchy, that people strive to satisfy: physiological, safety, social, esteem, and self-realization. Herzberg said we can divide needs into two categories: hygiene and motivational. Hygiene needs represent factors peripheral to the job itself. Although they will not motivate people to higher performance, they will cause people to be unhappy if they are not fulfilled. Motivational needs are associated directly with the work itself and include the need for growth, recognition, praise, advancement, and the like.

We use money, job enrichment, management by objectives, quality circles, quality of work life programs, flextime, job sharing, and management practices to implement these theories. Research shows that money can help to satisfy employees' needs, but to motivate, it must be directly related to employees' unfulfilled needs. Job enrichment is the process of changing the job so that the work will be more appealing to employees. Management by objectives tries to accomplish similar goals by asking managers and employees to agree on what each employee is to accomplish in the near future. Both quality circles and quality of work life programs encourage employee participation in decision making and problem solving. Flextime allows employees discretion about the hours they will work, and job sharing makes it possible for two part-time employees to fill one job.

Managers can help motivate employees by the way they supervise them. Suggested practices for improving employee motivation are to increase authority delegation, communicate what you expect from employees, give praise and recognition when earned, give feedback on progress, involve employees in decision making, encourage learning and growing, base salary increases on merit, and encourage innovativeness in employees.

MIND YOUR BUSINESS

Instructions. In the list below, mark a Y (yes) beside those items you believe people are motivated to work for and N (no) beside those items you believe people are not, or are no longer, motivated to work for.

____ 1. Lighting
____ 2. Employee handbooks
____ 3. Praise
____ 4. Coffee groups
____ 5. Promotions
____ 6. Goal setting
____ 7. Job title
____ 8. Delegation
____ 9. Fringe benefits
____ 10. Company newspapers
____ 11. Unemployment compensation
____ 12. Increased knowledge
____ 13. Recognition
____ 14. Office furnishings
____ 15. Work layout
____ 16. Feedback
____ 17. Bulletin boards
____ 18. Bowling teams
____ 19. Sense of accomplishment
____ 20. Work status
____ 21. Christmas turkey
____ 22. Social security
____ 23. Merit increases
____ 24. Paid leave
____ 25. Access to information
____ 26. Freedom to fail
____ 27. Challenge
____ 28. Seniority rights

_____ 29. Office parties

_____ 30. Wages and salaries

_____ 31. Company growth

_____ 32. Sympathetic help

See answers at the back of the book.

KEY TERMS

REVIEW QUESTIONS

1. Define motivation. Define needs. How are they related?

2. Describe Maslow's need hierarchy theory of motivation.

3. In Herzberg's motivation-hygiene theory, distinguish between hygiene needs and motivational needs. Give some examples of each.

4. Does money motivate employees to perform better? Explain.

5. What is job enrichment? Give some examples. How does it differ from job enlargement? Identify some factors that are not enriching to jobs.

6. What is management by objectives? What are the problems with MBO? Benefits?

7. Define quality circles. How do quality circles typically operate? Identify potential problems with them.

8. Define quality of work life programs. Discuss the results of QWL programs and identify the conditions for success.

9. Describe flextime and job sharing.

10. List and describe some practical ways supervisors can motivate their employees.

11. Discuss the impact of feedback on employee performance.

CASES

Case 10.1: New Leader of a Demoralized Marketing Department

To say that the marketing department of Hybrith Company, a manufacturer of auto parts, was demoralized is an understatement. The morale decline started about a year ago when their sales began falling off. Their previous manager had not kept up the sales organization, and with increasing competition, their sales began to slide. She was terminated because of declining sales.

Morton Williams, a long-time and well-liked employee in the department, got the job as marketing manager. Williams soon became an unimaginative paper shuffler, and sales declined further. Muddled and confused, the morale of the entire department worsened. Reacting to pressure from top management, Williams resigned after a few months and went back to his previous job.

Today was the big day. Mervin Hopson, the president, had called the staff together to introduce their new marketing manager, Susan Blanchard. After a brief introduction, Hopson turned the meeting over to Blanchard.

"Men and women," Blanchard began, "I want to get better acquainted with you as quickly as possible. Together, we have to work Hybrith back to the top. I am new to Hybrith and unknown to you, so I would like to give you an idea about my way of working, my style, so to speak."

Blanchard continued, "There is an old legend about a small Greek village that was constantly under attack. Their problem was leadership. One year, a stranger by the name of Gordias came into the village and provided leadership when they were attacked. The people supported him, and they were successful in warding off their attackers. Gordias was wise, and in his old age, he tied a large knot around the yoke of a chariot at the edge of the village. Gordias said, 'This knot, which is the most complex knot in the universe, will be your symbol of strength. Until someone who can untie this knot comes along, you will never have to worry.'

"The village remained safe for years until one day Alexander the Great marched by. Upon seeing the knot and hearing the legend, Alexander took out his sword and slashed through the knot. His army then stormed the village, which put up no defense against the attack." Blanchard finished with, "Symbols of strength will not stop us. Together, we will slash our competition and move on."

Questions

1. Do you think this approach would motivate you?

2. Do you think this was an effective approach?

3. What would you suggest that Blanchard do to improve her first impression?

Case 10.2: Where Do You Draw the Line on Sympathetic Help?

Betty Hart has been supervisor for three years. She has nineteen people in her department and is respected for being a very good supervisor.

One of her employees, William Wentz, is 24 years old and his wife is expecting their first child. Wentz has been in the department for a year and is an above-average worker. During the last couple of months, he has been bringing many of his personal problems to Hart. He has asked her advice about purchasing a car, how to prepare for the baby's arrival, whether he should take out more life insurance, how to humor his wife during her pregnancy, and many other such personal questions. It has come to the point where Wentz seems to want to talk about his personal situation every chance he gets. Hart suspected that Wentz needed to feel appreciated, and she was careful to listen and pay a lot of attention to him at first.

Now, Hart feels uncomfortable in her role as counselor. She worries that other employees might think she is spending too much time with Wentz. She also thinks that Wentz is leaning too much on her, asking her to make decisions that he really should be making. Wentz shows a lot of promise, and Hart wants to do what she can to help him.

At a recent meeting with her boss, she summed up her feelings, "I want to help Wentz, but I think I must discourage him from bringing all of his personal problems to me. I would like to do this without hurting his feelings."

Questions

1. Does a supervisor have a responsibility to talk with employees about their off-the-job, personal problems? Why?

2. If you were Hart, what would you do?

After completing this chapter, you should be able to:

■ Describe three things unions do for their members.

■ Identify three types of unions.

■ Discuss the implications for business and labor of the four most significant labor laws of this half-century.

■ Discuss the pros and cons of right-to-work laws.

■ Outline and identify the steps in the collective bargaining process.

■ List key factors typically covered in labor-management contracts.

■ Diagram and explain a typical method for handling employee grievances.

■ Speculate on the future of union-management relations.

11

MANAGEMENT
AND LABOR

The early 1980s were hard times for unions. The country was in an economic recession, unemployment was high, and sentiment shifted away from unions. Still, some of the largest unions and some of the largest companies were squaring off with each other. The Teamsters, by a 45 to 41 vote, won the right to represent characters like Mickey Mouse, Donald Duck, and Goofy at Disney World in Florida. The Communication Workers of America struck American Telephone & Telegraph Company for both pay increases and job security. The United Auto Workers, which had given up more than $4 billion in wage and benefit concessions, increased their expectations of getting additional benefits as the auto industry began showing profits.

Arguments about the value of unions, such as the one that follows, will no doubt continue to be part of management-labor relations for many more years.

"Would you join a union if we had one?"

"No."

"Why not?"

"Because I don't need them. I want to do my best. If you do your work and give an honest day's labor, management will treat you fairly."

"But unions can get you more money. My cousin belongs to a union, and his pay scale is much higher than ours."

"But he lives in a large city where the cost of living is much higher than it is for us."

"Why do you think management cares about us? All they want from us is production. If they could find a robot to do our work, we'd be out of here in a second."

"Well, I don't think so. Look at the pension plan they have set up for us, and you can't knock our benefits either."

"But who is going to protect you if you get a supervisor you don't like?"

"I'll just go to the big boss. He said anyone can stop by to see him if we're having a problem. Anyway, I couldn't go on a strike against this company; I've worked for them for over 12 years."

"Maybe you couldn't, but I could. I've been here for 2 years, and I can't see any hope for advancement unless we bring some pressure to bear on management. All they seem to be interested in is cutting costs, and that might mean my job."

"I know what you're saying, but I'll take my chances without the union. I'm voting against them."

"Well, I'm voting for them."

This argument between a procompany and a prounion employee poses some good questions concerning labor-management relations. **Labor unions** were formed so that workers could increase their bargaining power. They felt that, with larger numbers, employees would have more say in their jobs and gain a larger piece of the reward pie. Now, we have two large structures in many organizations: union and management. The competition and cooperation of these two groups have brought about a body of labor law to govern their relationship. The contracts between labor and management have become so entangled that many labor specialists work full time on ensuring that the company does not accidentally or purposefully violate the agreement.

Labor relations are also important to nonunion companies. Responding to indirect pressures, many managers have set up procedures for dealing with employees much like those of unionized companies. And more than one manager has said, "We purposefully keep our salaries higher than those of unionized companies to show our employees how much better off they are without a union." Because they are so important in business, this chapter focuses on labor relations by discussing unions, labor legislation, collective bargaining, and grievance procedures.

UNIONS

Unions are highly visible in today's industrial world, but just a few years ago, unions were struggling to become accepted. Amidst antiunion sentiment, big business power, and government indifference, employees banded together to present a counterforce to the all-powerful owners. In the last 50 years, unions have emerged as a powerful force.

The Birth of Unions

The early 1800s marked the beginning of union activity in the United States. Printers, carpenters, shoemakers, and other skilled trades grouped to-

Though an early force in the union movement, the Knights of Labor lost much of their influence after 1886, when a rally in Chicago's Haymarket Square exploded into a riot.

gether to bargain collectively with their respective employers. Goals of these early unions were higher wages and better working conditions. Following the introduction of factories, many employees were forced to work long hours under hazardous conditions with little pay. This prompted the development of larger unions to deal with the growing power of large management. The **Knights of Labor** exercised its influence during the 1870s and grew to more than

700,000 members by 1885. But its ambitions outreached its resources by the late 1880s, and it began to fade. The next year, however, during a labor rally in Chicago's Haymarket Square, someone threw a bomb, killing a number of policemen and workers. The riot that resulted did as much as anything to turn public opinion against the labor movement in general and the Knights of Labor in particular, whose influence quickly began to wane.

In the early 1900s, the International Workers of the World (IWW, or Wobblies), a group modeled after the Knights of Labor, grew by seeking to organize all industrial workers into one huge union. The Wobblies, however, had difficulty holding onto their members, perhaps partly because of the violent activities of some of its leadership. With the one exception of the Knights of Labor, unions had only nominal influence on management until the 1930s. Unions were unable to muster much support for several reasons:

1. Most manufacturing companies were small and did not have enough employees to make organization worthwhile.

2. Employees feared economic recession and retaliatory actions by business owners.

3. Employers made it hard for union leaders to get work by circulating a **blacklist** of activists.

4. At hiring, companies required employees to sign a **yellow-dog contract,** an agreement that they would not join a union. (The implication was that the employees would be "yellow dogs" if they joined.)

5. Because owners received sympathy from the courts, they were able to stop strikes under a **conspiracy doctrine,** a doctrine stating that it was an illegal act of conspiracy for unions to bring economic pressure on employers.

6. Many companies merely refused to deal with the unions.

Nevertheless, several unions originated during these years. The most significant was the **American Federation of Labor (AFL),** which was formed in 1886 and flourished under the leadership of Samuel Gompers. By the 1930s, the AFL was a major force in the work world. In 1935, a group of unhappy members, under the leadership of John L. Lewis, split off to form the **Congress of Industrial Organizations (CIO).** The two organizations competed with each other for many years before rejoining in 1955 to create the AFL-CIO and become the largest federation of unions in the United States, with a membership of about 16 million.

What Unions Do for Their Members

Just what do unions do for their membership? In trying to improve the lot of workers, they perform three major functions: collective bargaining, political lobbying, and employee care and fringe benefits.

Collective bargaining. By far the most important union function is collective representation of employees to management. Individually, workers exert almost no power over an owner's ability to withhold wages, terminate or discipline employees, and otherwise make life miserable. So unions balance management power with organized collective bargaining. Union representatives meet with management to negotiate wages, fringe benefits, working conditions, discipline, safety, work hours, job design, and the like. These agreed-upon conditions form the labor contract and become binding to both labor and management. During the contract period, unions monitor its implementation and provide a channel of appeal.

Political lobbying. A second union function is to lobby with politicians, legislators, government agencies, and the public to gain advantages favorable to their membership. Unions give financial support, offer organizational expertise, and volunteer individual effort to their legal and public causes.

Employee care and fringe benefits. Third, unions offer avenues for their members to satisfy security, social, recognition, and leadership needs. Some unions offer fringe benefits very similar to company fringes, and some organize consumer watchdog groups to protect their membership in the marketplace. Larger unions offer such services as medical and dental assistance, scholarships for employees' children, vacation retreats, recreational facilities, hobby groups, and strike benefits. Union leaders say that members become more closely identified with their peers, which leads to more recognition and a sense of belonging. Finally, the organization structure provides some employees with leadership opportunities that would not be available through company involvement.

Types of Unions

Four types of unions have developed: craft unions, industrial unions, independent unions, and associations.

Craft unions. Craft unions such as the International Brotherhood of Electrical Workers, restrict their membership to employees of a certain trade (craft) regardless of company affiliation, and they represent the unique interests of similar employees. Within a community, there might be a craft union for carpenters, another for meat cutters, and still another for painters. Each union has members who work for competing firms. Local

CROSS FIRE

Should There Be a Lower Minimum Wage for Teenagers?

For years, the business community and labor leaders have been divided over whether Congress should lower the minimum wage for teenagers. The basic arguments for lowering the minimum wage are:

1. Employers would hire more teenagers at the lower wage rates, thereby reducing unemployment among teenagers. Robert Thompson, Chairman of the Board, U.S. Chamber of Commerce, estimates that a lower wage could create several hundred thousand jobs.

2. The program should be limited to newly hired teenagers so as not to reduce the wages of teenagers currently working year round.

3. As a concession to labor, the plan would only take effect during the summer months.

4. Adding workers under reduced wage plans would be creating new jobs; therefore, it would not jeopardize the jobs of older people in the work force.

Arguments against plans to reduce minimum wages for teenagers include:

1. Subminimum wages do not provide new jobs; they only displace current workers. Thus, such a program would simply mean a wage cut for many people currently employed at the minimum wage level.

2. Many employers such as mom-and-pop stores are already exempt from minimum wage standards.

3. There is already a provision for full-time students to be paid 85% of the minimum wage, and Labor Department studies show that this has caused no appreciable increase in the number of jobs available.

What is your position?

Do you believe that lowering the minimum wage for teenage employees in the summer will create new jobs or displace current workers at a lower wage rate?

____ A. Create new jobs   ____ B. Displace current workers

How do you feel about lowering the minimum wage rate for teenage employees?

____ A. It should be lowered significantly.   ____ B. It should be lowered only slightly.

____ C. It should not be lowered.

TABLE 11.1 ■ PRINCIPAL U.S. LABOR UNIONS AND EMPLOYEE ASSOCIATIONS, 1980

Labor Union	Membership
International Brotherhood of Teamsters, Chauffeurs, Warehousemen, and Helpers of America	1,891,000
International Union, United Automobile, Aerospace and Agricultural Implement Workers of America	1,357,000
United Food and Commercial Workers Union	1,300,000
United Steelworkers of America	1,238,000
American Federation of State, County and Municipal Employees	1,238,000
International Brotherhood of Electrical Workers	1,041,000
International Association of Machinists and Aerospace Workers	745,000
Service Employees' International Union	650,000
Laborers' International Union of North America	608,000
Communications Workers of America	551,000
American Federation of Teachers	502,000
Amalgamated Clothing and Textile Workers of America	455,000
Hotel and Restaurant Employees and Bartenders International Union	400,000
United Association of Journeymen and Apprentices of the Plumbing and Pipefitting Industry of the United States and Canada	352,000
International Ladies' Garment Workers Union	323,000
American Federation of Musicians	299,000
American Federation of Government Employees	255,000
American Postal Workers Union	251,000
United Mine Workers of America	245,000
International Union of Electrical, Radio and Machine Workers	233,000
National Association of Letter Carriers	230,000
United Paperworkers International Union	219,000
Retail, Wholesale, and Department Store Union	215,000
National Association of Government Employees	200,000

craft unions have considerable power relative to their national unions, which they use primarily as a servicing agency.

Industrial unions. Unlike craft unions, **industrial unions** cut across trade lines to represent a wide variety of occupations. Industrials criticize the crafts for being elitist, worrying only about the highly skilled laborers, and ignoring the masses. But in reality, few crafts or industrials exist in pure form. Some crafts accept a mix of trades, and industrials may be organized around a particular trade. The United Mine Workers, made famous by John L. Lewis, illustrates the overlap. Although it is a mine workers' union, its membership includes several types of industrial workers.

Independent unions. A third group, **independent unions,** are not associated with any national organization. Being local in nature, many independents take their total membership from one company or include members from companies within a narrow region. Independents retain complete control and concentrate on the specific needs of their communities; they also do all the bargaining, watchdogging, and public relations. The Teamsters Union, one of the largest independents, was originally affiliated with the AFL-CIO, but the association ruptured because of disagreements over ethical standards.

Associations. Some groups, employees in the public sector and white-collar, professional em-

TABLE 11.1 ■ (continued)

Labor Union	Membership
United Transportation Union	190,000
International Association of Bridge and Structural Iron Workers	184,000
American Nurses Association	180,000
Brotherhood of Railway, Airline, and Steamship Clerks, Freight Handlers, Express and Station Employees	180,000
International Association of Firefighters	178,000
International Brotherhood of Painters and Allied Trades of the United States and Canada	164,000
Amalgamated Transit Union	162,000
United Electrical, Radio, and Machine Workers of America	162,000
Bakery, Confectionary, and Tobacco Workers International Unions of America	160,000
Oil, Chemical, and Atomic Workers International Union	154,000
Sheet Metal Workers International Association	154,000
United Rubber, Cork, Linoleum, and Plastic Workers of America	151,000
Fraternal Order of Police	150,000
International Brotherhood of Boilermakers, Iron Ship Builders, Blacksmiths, Forgers, and Helpers	145,000
International Union of Bricklayers and Allied Craftsmen	135,000
Transport Workers Union of America	130,000
National Alliance of Postal and Federal Employees	125,000
International Printing and Graphic Communications Union	122,000
International Woodworkers of America	112,000
Office and Professional Employees International Union	107,000
California State Employees Association	105,000
Brotherhood of Maintenance of Way Employees	102,000

Source: U.S. Department of Labor, Bureau of Labor Statistics.

Although they do not refer to themselves as unions, associations behave much like unions and represent their members collectively to higher management.

ployees, form **associations** that tend to operate much like unions. Although they typically do not refer to themselves as unions, they behave much like unions and they represent their members collectively to higher management. Some examples include American Federation of State, County, and Municipal Employees (AFSCME) and 9to5, the

National Association of Working Women. See Table 11.1 for a list of principal labor unions and employee associations.

LABOR LEGISLATION

The greatest single influence on union strength has been labor legislation. Laws have changed from preventing collective bargaining to guaranteeing it. We can relate union strength directly to key legislation.

Although a few labor laws of minor impact existed earlier, the **Railway Labor Act of 1926** was the first significant piece of legislation. This act gave railroad employees the right to organize and bargain collectively and established an independent mediation board to assist unions and managers in settling their differences. The **Norris-La Guardia Act of 1932** made the controversial yellow-dog contract illegal and severely reduced the conditions under which courts could issue injunctions preventing work stoppages. But the landmark law that gave unions a big boost was the Wagner Act of 1935.

The National Labor Relations Act (Wagner Act), 1935

The **National Labor Relations Act (Wagner Act),** giving workers the legal rights to organize and join unions of their choice, made the follow-

ing five practices unlawful for employers:

1. Employers may not interfere with an employee's right to join a labor organization or engage in union activities.

2. Employers may not interfere with an employee's right to recruit new members on their own free time.

3. Employers may not dominate or interfere with any labor organization or contribute to its support in any way.

4. Employers may not hire, fire, or discriminate against employees because of their attitudes toward unions.

TAKING STOCK

Rights and Respect for Office Workers

In 1973, Karen Nussbaum, at the time a clerk-typist at the Harvard Graduate School of Education, founded an organization of female clerical workers known as 9to5. Starting with only ten women, the group, by 1983, had more than 12,000 members in 22 chapters across the country. On their tenth anniversary, 9to5 was able to proclaim the following victories:

1973	First edition of the *9to5 News* leads to the first Bill of Rights for office workers.
1973	Formation of Local 925 of the Service Employees' International Union, a union for office workers.
1975	9to5 forces investigations into employment practices of major banks and insurance companies, leading to hiring, training, and promotion programs for women.
1975–1978	9to5 National Association of Working Women becomes a national organization.
1976–1978	First working women's convention brought together by 9to5.
1976–1978	9to5 targets three book publishers and files three sex discrimination suits resulting in $1.5 million in back pay for women employees, job-posting procedures, tuition reimbursement for training, and written job descriptions for all employees.
1979–1980	9to5 targets a large national bank and wins a 10% across-the-board pay increase for nonmanagement employees and a job-posting program.
1979–1980	SEIU District 925, a national union for office workers, is established.
1979–1980	9to5 won an age discrimination suit resulting in $¼ million in back pay for dismissed "over 40" employees.
1981	Pressured by 9to5, a large insurance company granted 10.5% pay increase to nonmanagement personnel, established a complaint-review process, granted $19,000 in back pay to word processing personnel, and donated $100,000 to area child-care centers.
1982–1983	9to5 hosted the International Conference on Office Automation.
1982–1983	9to5 published "The Human Factor," the first consumer guide to office automation.
1982–1983	Tenth Anniversary of 9to5.

5. Employers may not refuse to bargain collectively with union representatives.

The Wagner Act also established the **National Labor Relations Board (NLRB)** and gave the board the power to determine which workers are in a bargaining unit, to conduct secret union elections, and to prosecute those who commit unfair labor practices.

It has been said that, "The Wagner Act was labor's Magna Carta." For the first time, employees who wished to organize were legally protected, and union growth started a surge that lasted for 10 years.

The Fair Labor Standards Act, 1938

Aimed at ensuring minimum pay levels, the **Fair Labor Standards Act (Minimum Wage Law)** made it illegal for most companies to pay wages below a fixed level. The minimum wage began at 25¢ per hour in 1938, but quickly moved upward. Since 1946, Congress has upped the minimum wage 625%, while the cost of living has climbed only 277%. (See Fig. 11.1.) Although the law first covered only industries engaged in interstate commerce, it has been broadened until the vast majority of today's workers are covered. While this is not a union law *per se*, it helped unions by applying pressures for higher pay.

Despite these victories, there were, at the tenth anniversary celebration of 9to5, some "horror stories" told as well:

- An employer in Minneapolis still refers to his secretary as his "squaw."
- A woman reported that she still has "to take the seeds out of her boss's watermelon and the stems off his grapes."
- Another woman, who had to take time off from work to care for a sick child, was told by her boss she "had to choose between her family and her job."

9to5 Tenth Anniversary Poster.

Source: By permission of 9to5 Organization for Women Office Workers.

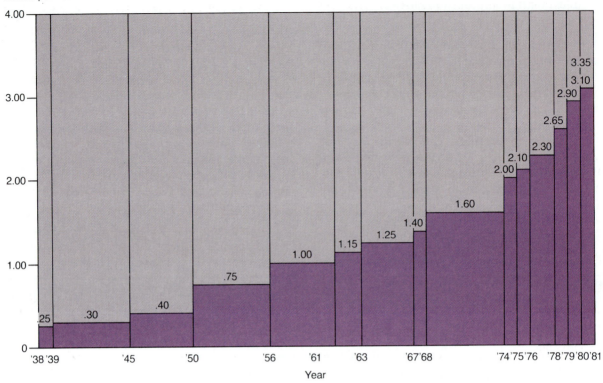

Dollars per hour

Figure 11.1
Federal minimum wage per hour over the years. *Source: U.S. Department of Labor.*

The Labor-Management Relations Act (Taft-Hartley Act), 1947

Many people thought the Wagner Act had swung the pendulum of power too much in favor of the unions. Reacting to this feeling, Senators Taft and Hartley authorized the **Labor-Management Relations Act (Taft-Hartley Act)** to more nearly equalize management and labor. Labor strongly opposed the law. When the law finally emerged from Congress, President Truman vetoed it, and Congress squared off in another confrontation. They finally mustered the support to override the president's veto. In amending and supplementing the Wagner Act, the Taft-Hartley Act defined unfair labor practices of both employers and unions.

Unfair employer practices. As of 1947, the following activities by employers were defined as unfair and therefore illegal:

1. Employers may not interfere, restrain, or coerce employees in their exercise of the right to organize freely.

2. Employers may not dominate or interfere with the information or administration of any labor organization, or contribute financial or other support for it.

3. Employers may not discriminate in hiring, tenure, or in conditions of employment for the purpose of encouraging or discouraging membership in any labor organization.

4. Employers may not discharge or otherwise discriminate against employees who filed charges or gave testimony under this act.

5. Employers may not refuse to bargain collectively with the duly chosen representative of the company's employees.

Unfair union practices. The Taft-Hartley Act also defined many union practices as unfair and illegal, for example:

1. Unions may not restrain or coerce employers in the exercise of their rights under the Wagner Act.

2. Unions may not restrain or coerce an employer in the selection of parties to bargain on management's behalf.

3. Unions may not persuade an employer to discriminate against any employees.

4. Unions may not refuse to bargain collectively with an employer.

5. Unions may not participate in secondary boycotts and jurisdictional disputes.

6. Unions may not attempt to force recognition of a union when another union is already certified as the employees' representative.

7. Unions may not charge excessive initiation fees.

8. Unions may not require wage payments for services not performed (a practice frequently referred to as **featherbedding**).

The act also permitted employers to express their feelings more freely about labor matters as long as they did not threaten employees. What's more, companies could fire employees who engaged in illegal strikes. To smooth jangled nerves, the act provided for an 80-day cooling-off period before a strike becomes legal (a provision that is also used by the president of the United States

Organized labor's opposition to the Taft-Hartley Act centered on restrictions the bill placed on union practices.

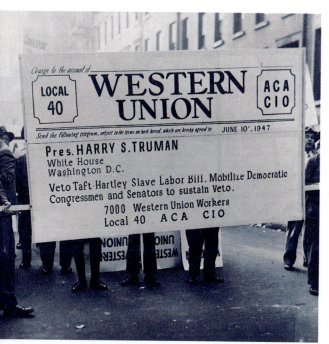

when he feels the nation's safety or health is being put in danger by a strike). During the first 60 days, management and labor unions are permitted to reach an agreement on their own. During the next 20 days, the NLRB conducts a secret ballot among workers to see if they will accept their employer's final offer.

Landrum-Griffin Act (1959)

After a few years of experience with the Taft-Hartley Act, several abuses began to leak through legal loopholes. Many felt a need to protect the rights of individual employees through better supervision of money in union welfare and pension funds and by curbing racketeering by union officers and company managers. Because of these concerns, Congress passed the Labor-Management Reporting and Disclosure Act in 1959, more widely known as the **Landrum-Griffin Act.** Most provisions of this complicated act try to regulate internal union affairs with a bill of rights and detailed reporting requirements.

Union members' bill of rights. A major section of the Landrum-Griffin Act identifies specific rights of all union members, including the right to:

- Nominate candidates for union offices.
- Vote in union elections.
- Attend union meetings.
- Participate in union meetings.
- Vote on union business.
- Examine union records and accounts.

If members were denied these rights, they could seek relief in federal courts.

Reporting regulations. The act also spelled out specific procedures for both union officers and company managers to protect employees' money in welfare and pension funds. Unions are required to submit annual financial statements to the Secretary of Labor. They must also report any loans to union officers in excess of $250 and all conflicts of interest by union officers. Company managers must report money spent and any agreements made between the company and labor consultants in their attempts at persuading employees to exercise their bargaining rights. While these laws did not eliminate all the undesirable conflict in union-management struggles, they illustrate the increasing concern for the individual caught between two bureaucratic forces.

Right-to-Work Laws

Section 14-B of the Taft-Hartley Act allows states to pass laws prohibiting the union shop. A **union shop,** sometimes called a **closed shop,** means that, if workers vote to have a union, all employees must join the union, and future employees who come to work for the company must eventually join the union. An **open shop** means that individual employees may choose not to join the union. Obviously, unions prefer states that permit union shops, and the repeal of Section 14-B has long been a goal of organized labor. Unions maintain that all employees benefit from their activities and benefits. Thus it is unfair for employees to come to work, receive the same pay, fringe benefits, and other union-won privileges without sharing the costs by paying union dues. However, many states, arguing that it is morally improper to require workers to join unions to get and hold a job, have passed laws making the union shop illegal.

By 1980, twenty-one states had passed right-to-work laws.

Some arguments provide for an **agency shop** where all employees pay dues to the union whether they join or not. By 1980, twenty-one states had such laws, which are referred to as **right-to-work laws.** The vast majority of these states are nonindustrial and heavily agricultural. The industrial states, where the bulk of union members reside, are nowhere close to passing right-to-work laws.

COLLECTIVE BARGAINING

Most labor legislation aims at refining collective bargaining, the key ingredient in labor-management relations. **Collective bargaining** is the process of negotiating the labor contract, which spells out the working conditions and relationships between employees and employer in a unionized company. Union representatives speak for their membership in an adversary struggle with company representatives. Because the labor contract legally binds both parties for at least a year (more commonly, three years), detailed procedures are followed in preparing and negotiating the contract. There are also well-defined alternatives for handling bargaining deadlocks.

Preparing for Negotiation

The thoroughness of preparations varies with company size and union strength. Where the company is small or union strength is nominal, preparations may be skimpy, but in larger companies or where unions are powerful, they are extensive. Both parties begin preparing for the next negotiation immediately after they agree to the current contract.

Company personnel specialists chart the day-to-day disturbances in employee relations by studying grievances, turnover, layoffs, overtime, transfers, and all disciplinary problems. The company continuously studies the contract for mistakes and unforeseen occurrences, while remaining alert to rumors about what the union will ask for in the next negotiation, and what they will settle for. Company fact-finding groups survey prevailing wage rates in the community and record setlements of similar companies in the industry. Experts also study business literature on economic conditions and analyze industry and company forecasts to build their case for the company's limitations in meeting union demands.

In matching company preparations, union officials also study the contract continuously and analyze grievances, turnover, and related disciplinary problems for clues as to what they can do to serve employee needs. Union experts also gather their version of economic conditions, community wage rates, industry trends, and the company's financial health. Many unions periodically poll their membership to find out what members would like to see changed in the current contract and what they would like to bargain for in the upcoming contract. Even though both sides prepare for negotiations by analyzing similar information, no one is surprised when wide gaps occur in data interpretation.

As the end of the current contract period nears, both union and management begin shaping their bargaining strategy by preparing lists and cost estimates of preliminary demands. Before negotiations begin, companies may try to gain public

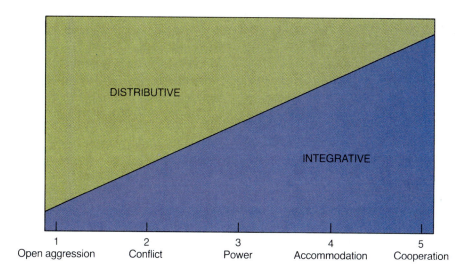

| 1 | 2 | 3 | 4 | 5 |
| Open aggression | Conflict | Power | Accommodation | Cooperation |

Figure 11.2
Bargaining strategies.

favor by publicizing their positions through newsletters and press releases. Unions also seek public support by inviting the press to their meetings and circulating information to their memberships.

Negotiating the Contract

After the spring training of preparations, the season begins as both sides battle for an advantage in the negotiation contest. Management's team usually consists of three to five members, including such specialists as lawyers, economists, engineers, and personnel experts. The union team is usually larger because it includes local officers, **shop stewards** (elected union officials who represent union members' interests), committee regional and national representatives, and (more and more frequently) legal counsel. Both sides approach the bargaining table to fight for specific issues with cloak-and-dagger strategies.

Bargaining strategies. The strategies range from open hostility to enlightened cooperation (see Figure 11.2). **Distributive bargaining** describes confrontations in which one party wins points at the direct expense of the other. **Integrative bargaining** assumes that both union and company officials work cooperatively. The distributive extreme is open aggression: a hungry, hostile management attempts to choke the union, while the equally aggressive union fights to take over all management's prerogatives. Conflict strat-

egies are used in those situations in which management tries to get rid of the union, and the union fights for the right to represent employees. More common is power bargaining: union and management struggle to win as many concessions from the other as possible. Accommodation strategies reflect a more realistic live-and-let-live attitude. Company officials might prefer not to deal with a union, but they accept their role as a fact of life.

> **Cooperative bargaining strategies assume that both sides are working for the betterment of employees and the company, but collective strategies are rarely seen.**

Union leaders are more educated to management's pressures and try to analyze the issues from both perspectives. Cooperative strategies assume that both sides are working jointly for the betterment of employees and the company. Bargaining strategies appear to be more cooperative than in the past. American Can shares with their union just about any piece of information that the union wants, including income, capital plans, and profit margins on customer contracts. And the United Steelworkers union is experimenting with agreements that have no seniority provisions or grievance procedures. About 4% of union contracts have cooperation between labor and man-

The signing of a new contract satisfactory to both labor and management is the goal of collective bargaining. (Seated from left are United Auto Workers executives Owen Bieber and Douglas Fraser and General Motors Chairman Roger Smith in March, 1982.)

agement built into the provisions. The steps of negotiating a contract appear in Fig. 11.3.

The union contract. If the bargaining is successful, the result is a **union contract** (or agreement): a legal document spelling out the conditions of employment. Both employees and management are bound by this contract for the specified period, usually one to three years. However, for all practical purposes, collective bargaining is now a year-round activity. Tony Verdream, vice president for American Can, says, "Changes are occurring too rapidly to wait three years." A few contracts, called evergreen pacts, are subject to near-constant revisions. While these are still few in number, labor experts predict that they will become more common in the future.

Since the contracts are usually quite complex, both union and management make special efforts to be sure the terms are communicated to employees and supervisors. Many companies hold training programs for their supervisors, identifying what they can and cannot do under the contract terms. Union leaders communicate in writing and through meetings what employees can expect under the new contract and what to do if their rights are violated. Table 11.2 summarizes some of the factors generally covered in the labor-management contract.

Bargaining Deadlocks

Few negotiations progress smoothly through all the bargaining steps. On some issues, neither party is willing to budge. After contracts are rati-

fied, disagreements sometimes arise over interpretations. When the deadlocks seem insoluble, management and labor face alternatives of conciliation and mediation, strikes, lockouts, boycotts, arbitration, and government intervention.

Conciliation and mediation. When the two teams stall during negotiations, they can invite an independent third party to help them reconcile their differences. A **conciliator** serves as a catalyst to nudge both parties into movement. Usually, calling in a conciliator is a face-saving technique.

Both management and labor can adopt the conciliator's suggestions without appearing to give in. A **mediator** plays a stronger role by offering compromise solutions, but neither side is bound by the mediator's suggestions. In practice, the conciliator and mediator roles usually overlap.

Mediators are often helpful in bringing two sides of a labor dispute together after they reach an impasse and just quit talking with each other. When the National Basketball Association (NBA) and its referees could not reach agreement on a new contract at the beginning of the 1983 season,

Figure 11.3
The process of collective bargaining.

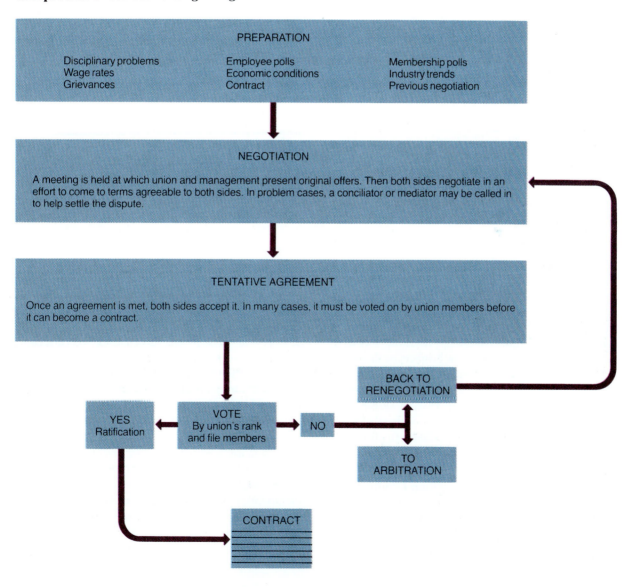

TABLE 11.2 ■ SOME FACTORS COVERED IN LABOR-MANAGEMENT CONTRACTS

Wages and Working Conditions	Employee Benefits	Promotions and Transfers	Discipline Policies
Wage rates for regular hours	Sick-leave benefits	Policies on promotions	Discipline procedures
How overtime is allocated and paid	Vacations, how they are accumulated and scheduled	Policies on transfers	Grievance procedures for employees
Shift differentials, if any	Pension program and retirement	Job evaluations	Employee rights
Cost of living adjustments (COLA)	Medical and life insurance	Employee performance	Management rights
Time for breaks, lunch periods, starting and stopping times	Unemployment benefits		
Work environment and other working conditions	Holidays and other days off		

the NBA locked out the referees and would not allow them to officiate games. Negotiations between NBA representatives and the referees' union, the National Association of Basketball Referees, sputtered along for a while and then broke off. Both sides refused to talk with each other until federal mediator Ed McMahon was able to bring them together. Two days and two nights of intensive negotiations resulted in a three-year agreement.

Union strategies. **Strikes,** outright refusals of the employees to continue working, have been declining in recent years. In 1983 there were only 81 work stoppages involving 1000 or more workers, while in 1974 there were 424 strikes involving 1000 or more workers. **Wildcat strikes,** which employees sometimes engage in on their own, are walkouts not duly sanctioned by the union. Employees may also resort to a halfway measure called a **slowdown.** During slowdown strikes, employees show up but work at a decidedly slower pace, causing significant production drops. Sometimes, during a strike, some employees may choose to continue to come to work, or persons not previously working for the company may take jobs left vacant by union members on strike. Unions contemptuously refer to such employees as **strikebreakers** or **scabs.**

A strike may occur at any time, but 90% happen during contract negotiations.

A strike may occur at any time, but 90% happen during contract negotiations. The Bureau of Labor Statistics estimates that less than 4% of contract negotiations result in strikes, but strikes are usually quite expensive to management, employees, and the surrounding community.

During strikes, the union may **picket** the employer by placing employees around the work premises with signs and placards announcing that the employees are on strike against the company. Friction sometimes develops when a number of employees form picket lines across entrances to discourage others from coming to work or prevent the delivery of goods and supplies.

Less intense than strikes are boycotts, which result when union members refuse to buy a company's product. If the union membership is nationwide, this can have a serious economic effect on the firm. Boycotts against the company with which the union is in disagreement are called **primary boycotts,** and most are legal. Attempts by unions to include third parties such as suppliers and customers to quit buying from a particular company are called **secondary boycotts,** and they are illegal in most states. In the 1970s the agricultural workers in California, with sympathy from Attorney General Robert Kennedy, conducted a successful boycott against lettuce. By encouraging people to stop buying lettuce, workers were able to pressure producers into giving higher wages.

More recently in western Pennsylvania, steelworkers and other unions urged members to withdraw their deposits from the Mellon Bank. Union leaders claimed that Mellon had invested too heavily in foreign industry while neglecting locally depressed businesses, thus depriving people of jobs at home. Currently, the AFL-CIO is telling its almost 14 million members to quit buying products from firms it accuses of antiunion activities. Some of the firms on the AFL-CIO's boycott list are Coors brewery, Procter & Gamble, R. J. Reynolds, Faberge, and Equitable Life Assurance Society.

Management strategies. Since companies are aware that they could find themselves beset by a strike, some develop strike contingency plans.

Lockouts are seldom used because of lost revenue to the company.

During strikes or boycotts, companies have the alternative of continuing operations as best they can (Phelps Dodge, despite a strike and scattered violence, kept their facility open by using replacements and nonstriking workers) or of taking more severe action such as a **lockout.** (The Metropolitan Opera Company a few years ago locked out — that is, refused to allow to come to work — their orchestra employees, members of Local 802.) Because of lost revenue to the company, lockouts are seldom used. What's more, there is evidence that

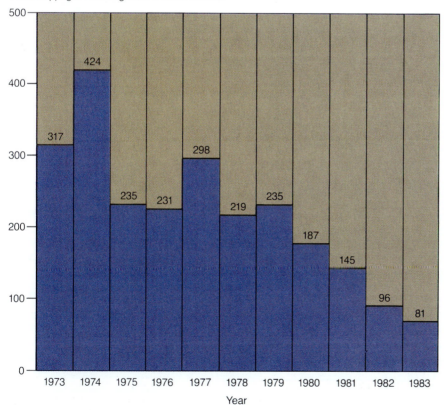

Work stoppages involving 1000 or more workers

Figure 11.4
How strikes have declined in recent years.
Source: U.S. Department of Labor.

they build bad public relations and could possibly result in lawsuits against the firm.

Managers of competing companies may also form **employers' associations** to help them combat or negotiate with unions. Sometimes the associations collect money from members to help a company if its employees strike.

Arbitration. **Arbitration,** the last means of dissolving a deadlock, means that the two dissonant parties bring in an independent expert to make judgments that are binding to both sides. Both union and management must agree upon the arbitrator. The arbitrator begins by holding hearings on the positions and supporting evidence of each side. Operating something like a judge, the arbitrator asks questions, listens to witnesses, and studies the documents to get a fair picture. After the hearings, the adjudicator writes the decision, called the arbitration award, which is binding to both parties. Losers have taken their cases to the courts, but the arbitration decision has always been upheld. Contract interpretation is the most common dispute that goes to arbitration, and employee discipline is second.

Arbitration may be voluntary or imposed. **Voluntary arbitration** occurs when both sides agree to use the services of an impartial third

BUSINESS BULLETIN

Anatomy of a Negotiation

After 3 weeks of being on strike, management and union negotiators have not been able to reach agreement. The basic differences in their positions are as follows:

Issue	Management Position	Union Position
Wage increase	5%	15%
Increase in fringe benefits	3%	10%
Work week	40 hours	36 hours
Benefits for laid-off workers	30% of base pay for a 3-month period	60% of base pay for a 6-month period
Paid vacation:		
10 years	3 weeks	4 weeks
5 years	2 weeks	3 weeks
2 years	1 week	2 weeks

After a few more meetings, both management and labor agreed they were making scant progress and decided to call in a mediator. The mediator, after meeting with them several times, offered the following compromise proposal:

Wage increase	8%		Paid vacation:	
Increase in fringe benefits	5%		10 years	4 weeks
Work week	40 hours		5 years	3 weeks
Benefits for laid-off workers	50% for 3 months		2 years	2 weeks

Union and management officials agreed to this proposal. They took the proposal to the union members for a vote, and the agreement was ratified by a vote of 72% for, 28% against.

Worker Ownership of Companies

In the past few years, there have been several instances where workers took over the ownership of their company. Employee ownership, as you might expect, creates new relationships between managers and employees. And these new relationships apparently are having a profound impact upon the company's operations and profits.

In 1981, the employees of Hyatt Clark, a manufacturer of bearings, bought the company from General Motors. Since then, the employees have cut costs, including their own wages, and reduced the break-even point from $12 million in sales to below $6.5 million. Productivity has increased, and scrappage is down by a third.

The Hyatt Clark Company holds frequent meetings between managers and workers. Manufacturing superintendents hold problem-solving sessions each week and keep employees informed about the company's finances. Officers' salaries are posted in a public place. Experts believe these efforts are paying off. A money-loser when owned by GM, the company broke even in the second half of 1982 and expects to make a profit in 1983. The accompanying table shows the current list of companies that are 100% employee owned. Other companies are expected to be added to the list in the near future.

Employee-Owned Companies	Headquarters	Number of Employees
Weirton (steel)	Weirton, West Virginia	7000
Southern Medical Services (nursing homes)	Birmingham, Alabama	3500
The Okonite Company (cable manufacturing)	Ramsey, New Jersey	1850
Hyatt Clark Industries (roller bearings)	Clark, New Jersey	1400
Katz Communications (broadcasting, ad sales)	New York	1100
Bates Fabrics (bedspreads, construction textiles)	Lewiston, Maine	950
South Bend Lathe (machine tools)	South Bend, Indiana	230

Source: "When Workers Take Over the Plant," *U.S. News & World Report*, April 18, 1983, pp. 89–90.

party to help them settle their dispute. In some cases, the federal government may force the disputing parties to seek arbitration; this is **compulsory arbitration.** The government usually does not intervene unless it thinks national security is at stake.

HANDLING EMPLOYEE GRIEVANCES

Labor contracts provide specific **grievance** steps for employees who feel supervisors have violated their rights. Many nonunion companies also have formal grievance procedures. Effective managers attempt to prevent grievances because they are

costly and disruptive, but even under the best of conditions, an occasional grievance will work its way through the formal channels.

The grievance procedure varies according to the union contract and company size, but a typical procedure contains a sequence of steps from the original filing to the ultimate arbitration. Many grievances are settled before they get to arbitration, and middle-sized and smaller companies have fewer steps. The general purpose is to move successively upward in both union and management structure until there is a settlement. Figure 11.5 shows the possible steps in grievance procedures. Most contracts specify that aggrieved employees communicate their complaints in writing. If the supervisor has open communications, the

ARBITRATION PROCESSES

National and international union officials	←→	President or high-level corporate officer
Local union officer or union grievance committee	←→	Plant manager (top level)
Local union business agent or chief shop steward	←→	Industrial relations officer or plant midmanager
Shop steward or aggrieved employee	←→	Plant supervisor

VARIOUS LEVELS OF GRIEVANCE PROCEDURES

Employee or union officials   vs.   Company officials

Figure 11.5
Levels in the settling of a grievance.

disagreement may be settled at this point; otherwise, the grievance enters the formal machinery. Typically, when employees file grievances, they meet with their supervisor and shop steward.

CURRENT AND FUTURE STATUS OF UNIONS

Unions today are facing their toughest challenge. Union membership as a percentage of the work force has declined from 28.4% in 1965 to about 20% in 1983. (Figure 11.6 shows the increasing percentage of workers who do not belong to unions since 1965.) Further, unions won only 30% of certification elections in 1981, down from 60% in 1965. (Figure 11.7 pictures this declining trend.) And there is evidence that union members are not as united among themselves as they once were. For instance, 44% of union families voted for Ronald Reagan in 1980, compared to the average of about 35% that normally vote for the Republican candidates. For another example, on August 12, 1983, the International Association of Machinists and Aerospace Workers walked out on Continental Air Lines. But just a few days after the strike began, Continental reported that 50% of the 1200 employees were reporting back to work. As Don Thomas, president of United Steel Workers Local

1219 in Braddock, Pennsylvania, explains it, "There's no spirit of 'we're all in it together' any more. There are no John L. Lewises, no spirit of solidarity."

There may be several reasons why unions are not as powerful as they once were. The recent economic recession surely had something to do with it. When workers are worried about losing their jobs, they are less likely to band together for higher wages or benefits. What is more, unions are being confronted by increasing skepticism from potential new members as the spread of concessionary bargaining raises questions about the value of union membership. Second, the nature of the work force has been changing. There are relatively fewer blue-collar jobs available, as the composition of workers changes to service, professional, and informational employees. Typically, the so-called white-collar workers have been less supportive of unions than have blue-collar workers. Third, robotics and office automation have begun to erode the strength of labor unions and service unions alike. Fourth, much of industry is moving to the South and Midwest, and unions have typically been weaker in these areas than in the North and West. Finally, there is some evidence that management is trying harder to keep unions out or to get rid of those that are already in. This attitude seemed to be condoned

Percentage

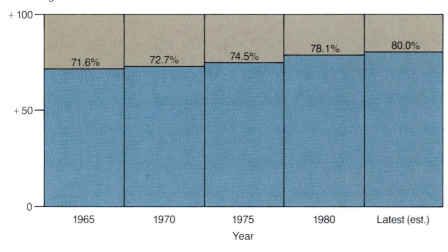

Figure 11.6
**Percentage of workers
who do not belong to
unions.** *Source: U.S.
Department of Labor.*

by Ronald Reagan's breaking of the Professional Air Traffic Controllers Organization (PATCO) in 1981.

Union leaders argue that there is a conspiracy by big business to eliminate them. Labor has recently suffered setbacks in Congress, rebuffs from factories, and defeats at the voting booths. Many leaders say there is a conspiracy of business and right-wing forces to destroy their movement.

Social, economic, and business issues will determine the role of unions in the future. Unions will no doubt continue to exist, but their status will surely be determined by how well they can react to current, changing conditions.

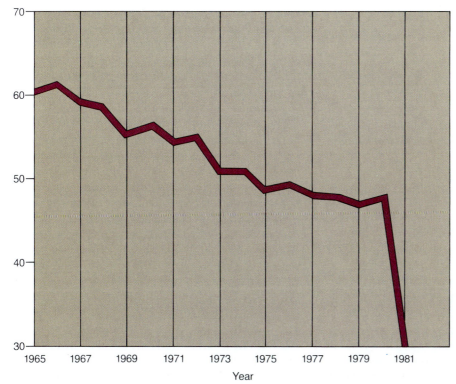

Figure 11.7
**Percentage of elections
won by unions.** *Source:
National Labor Relations
Board.*

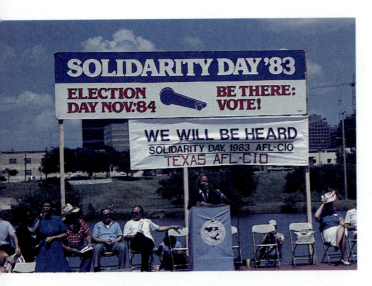

This Solidarity Day rally in 1983 is emblematic of renewed union efforts to reverse their declining influence in the work force.

In Support of Unions

Most union leaders believe that their role in equalizing management and employees remains essential. Union supporters feel that, even with existing legislation, companies could take advantage of their employees should unions fail to exist. Those in support of today's unions mention the following benefits of unions:

1. Unions, acting as a bargaining agent for employees, helped overcome abuses of corporate power.

2. Unions give employees a collective voice in negotiating working conditions with management.

3. Unions do much to upgrade pay levels, improve safety, and increase job security for employees.

4. Unions protect future earnings by negotiating automatic cost-of-living allowances (COLA) built into their pay contracts.

5. Unions increase the quality of working life for employees by pressuring for more democratic and pleasant working environments.

6. Unions provide a balance of power between employees and large businesses.

Criticism of Unions

Many people feel that unions have tilted the balance of power too far in employees' favor. Four major criticisms of today's unions are:

1. Unions, with their seniority rules, provisions for rewards, and rigid pay levels, stifle flexibility and creativity in a company.

2. Unions are too costly. The costs of strikes, luxury wage and benefit packages, and the time and staff needed to deal with unions may be too high in today's competitive markets.

3. Unions overprotect underachieving employees. As stated by critic H. L. Mencken, "Unionism seldom, if ever, uses such power as it has to insure better work; almost always it devotes a large part of that power to safeguarding back work."

4. Unions are unnecessary. "A progressive, well-managed company — one that can make it in today's competitive world — will watch out for and provide for its employees," stated a corporation president. "Failure to do so would be poor management."

SUMMARY

Labor relations cover the activities of preventing and settling management/employee differences in both unionized and nonunionized companies. Unions have emerged as a powerful force since the 1930s. The AFL-CIO is the largest federation of unions in the United States.

Unions grew in size and influence because of legal changes insuring their rights to organize and bargain collectively. Unions serve their membership with the following functions: collective representation, political lobbying, and need satisfaction. National organizations employ full-time administrators and specialists such as lawyers, engineers, and tacticians. Locals have the day-to-day responsibility of protecting members' contractual rights; their officers include president, vice-president, secretary-treasurer, business representative, and stewards. Unions can be classified as craft, industrial, or independent.

The first major labor law was the Railway Labor Act of 1926, which gave railroad employees the right to organize and bargain collectively. The

Wagner Act of 1935 established the National Labor Relations Board and obliged the federal government to protect employees in the process of organizing. In 1948, the Fair Labor Standards Act helped labor by establishing minimum wages. The Labor-Management Relations Act of 1947 streamlined collective bargaining by pointing out unfair employer and union practices. The 1959 Landrum-Griffin Act regulated internal union affairs with a members' bill of rights and detailed reporting requirements. Under Section 14-B of the Taft-Hartley Act, twenty-one states have passed laws making the union shop illegal.

Collective bargaining is the process of negotiating the labor contract and identifying working relationships between employees and employer. Both union and company representatives begin detailed preparations immediately after a contract has been negotiated. Negotiating usually centers around management rights, union rights, working conditions, contract coverage, contract duration, fringe benefits, and of course, wage rates. Distributive bargaining strategies describe win-lose confrontations. Integrative strategies assume both union and company officials work together toward improving relationships. Bargaining deadlocks may be handled by conciliation, mediation, strikes, lockouts, boycotts, arbitration, and government intervention.

Most contracts identify specific grievance steps for employees who feel their rights have been violated. Employees begin by submitting grievances in writing. Depending on the situation and the size of the company, a typical grievance moves through several steps: (1) steward and aggrieved employee meet with supervisor, (2) business agent meets with industrial-relations personnel, (3) local union officers meet with plant superintendent, (4) international officers meet with president, and (5) arbitration.

In recent years, unions have lost both elections and membership. Undoubtedly, unions will continue to exist, but they are not likely to maintain the strength and success they had earlier.

MIND YOUR BUSINESS

Instructions. In many cases, there is an adversary relationship between labor and management.

Which of the following do you think favor unions? Management?

A = favors unions   B = favors management
C = favors neither

____ 1. The National Labor Relations Act (Wagner Act) of 1935

____ 2. The Labor-Management Relations Act (Taft-Hartley Act) of 1947

____ 3. Union shop

____ 4. Right-to-work laws

____ 5. Collective bargaining

____ 6. A mediator

____ 7. The right of "lockout"

____ 8. The right to strike

____ 9. Arbitration

____ 10. Grievance procedures

See answers at the back of the book.

KEY TERMS

labor union, 266

Knights of Labor, 267

blacklist, 268

yellow-dog contract, 268

conspiracy doctrine, 268

American Federation of Labor (AFL), 268

Congress of Industrial Organizations (CIO), 268

craft unions, 269

industrial unions, 270

independent unions, 270

associations, 271

Railway Labor Act of 1926, 271

Norris-LaGuardia Act of 1932, 272

National Labor Relations Act (Wagner Act), 1935, 272

National Labor Relations Board (NLRB), 273

Fair Labor Standards Act (Minimum Wage Law), 1938, 273

Labor-Management Relations Act (Taft-Hartley Act), 1947, 274

REVIEW QUESTIONS

1. What are unions? Sketch their beginnings in the United States. Outline the role of the AFL and the CIO in early union development.

2. What do unions do for their members?

3. Distinguish between craft unions, industrials, independents, and employee associations.

4. Outline the major provisions of the following acts: Wagner Act, Fair Labor Standards Act, Taft-Hartley Act, and Landrum-Griffin Act.

5. What are right-to-work laws?

6. Define collective bargaining. Identify four reasons why companies might lose a collective bargaining election.

7. How do union and management teams prepare for bargaining a contract?

8. Briefly identify major bargaining strategies between unions and managements. What is concession bargaining? Define givebacks, getbacks.

9. Give examples of items that union contracts usually cover.

10. What alternatives are available for working through bargaining deadlocks? Explain each alternative.

11. What are the typical steps in the grievance procedure for employees who feel they have been wronged under the contract?

12. Assess the current status of unions in the United States.

CASES

Case 11.1: Orientation toward Unions or Management?

Two employees, Helen and Wilbert, were discussing their feelings toward their union. Helen said that she did not think they needed the union. She said, "If employees do their best, if they are successful in their jobs, and if they complete their work properly and on time, management would take care of them. They do not need the union to do their bidding for them." Wilbert disagreed. He said, "I know many employees who are working hard, doing a good job, but they are not particularly recognized. And I know that all of us would have lower salaries, fewer fringes, and less vacation time if we did not have a union."

Helen responded, "You know, the difference between us is that I want to do the work. I want to be left alone, and I want to carry on my own battles. If I disagree with my supervisor, I'll work it out with him face-to-face. If I can't get it worked out, I'll leave. But you like a lot of extra attention and sympathy. You want the company to pat you on the head and treat us as a family. But we're not family. I have a job to do. I do it and they reward me."

Wilbert agreed, "We *are* different. I do want more attachment to my work than just doing a job and getting rewarded for it. I want to improve our conditions for all of us, employees and management. Your problem is that you do not care about anyone else but yourself. You are a good worker, highly motivated, and management will probably treat you well so long as they have the hidden pressure of the union. But without the union, you would see that management would just treat you like a workhorse."

Questions

1. With which employee do you tend to agree? Why?

2. Do you think that prounion employees have different personality traits than procompany employees? Explain.

Case 11.2: Codetermination

For 25 years, the labor force in West Germany has had a minority voice in company plans. For the past 6 years, they have been seeking parity (equal representation) under the concept of codetermination, whereby workers will be represented on corporate supervisory boards. Workers have been demanding an equal, or controlling, voice in company operations. Business leaders have been happy with minority representation of the past 25 years, but they are intensely opposed to increasing the unions' board power. Managers fear that parity would put them in a position of demanding the union for their jobs. West German workers have had a voice in management, and unions and management have worked together quite well, managing to avoid major strikes. At present, because of a combination of apathetic workers and government fears that parity would lengthen a recession, laborers' demand for equal voice has been turned back.

Questions

1. What are your feelings about having unions share equally in the management of companies? How is this similar to union-management relations in the United States?

2. If unions were to share equally with management in controlling companies, what changes do you think would occur?

3. How do you feel about the balance of union-management power in the United States? Which side has the most power? Why? Which side should have the most power? Why? What changes do you think should be made, if any?

THE MANAGING OF BUSINESS

The following list includes a variety of activities, personality characteristics, career goals and objectives, and skills and aptitudes. All have special relevance to careers in business management. Put a check mark in front of those statements that apply to you.

____ I like to plan and direct the activities of others.

____ I do not object to defending my position to others once I have spoken my mind.

____ I plan to take as many courses as possible in business administration.

____ I have served successfully as president of a club or other organization.

____ I feel I could withstand the pressures of negotiating a multimillion dollar contract.

____ I have the ability to lead others.

____ I would like to take a course in organizational psychology to learn how people function in large companies.

____ I am often able to persuade others to adopt my plans and way of thinking.

____ I have the ability to get the most out of those who work with me.

____ Job security is less important to me than having the opportunity to be a leader.

____ I have planned and directed programs for a school, church, or community organization.

____ It is important to me to gain prestige and the recognition of others.

____ When I am with others, they tend to see me as their leader.

____ I have served as captain of a school team.

____ I look forward to a job in which I have the responsibility to make the final decision.

____ I have the ability to represent a company as a public speaker.

____ I want a job in which I closely supervise the work of others.

____ People have told me that I have good organizational skills.

____ It is important to me to find a career in which I can develop creative solutions to problems.

____ I want a job in which I have as much control of my duties as possible.

____ People see me as a logical, decisive, commonsense thinker.

____ I have a lot of confidence in myself and look forward to a job with heavy responsibilities.

____ I enjoy influencing the opinions and decisions of others.

____ I have strong social skills, so that in a group I tend to be the center of attention.

____ I have been told that I am an effective communicator and write clearly.

There is no single set of personality characteristics, skills, and aptitudes that fits a particular job. Generally speaking, the more activities and self-descriptors you checked in this list, the more satisfaction you may find in this major and its related jobs.

Job Title	Job Description	Suggested Education and Training	Personality Traits	Average Pay	Outlook through 1990
Human resources manager	Personnel (or human resources) managers supervise the hiring and firing of company employees. Personnel policies and regulations are planned and carried out by them, as is the preparation of employee performance evaluations. Workmen's compensation, employee benefits, salaries and wages, labor negotiations and training fall under the personnel manager's jurisdiction.	A college degree is required for most beginning positions in this field. Prospective personnel managers have a wide choice of undergraduate majors, for a number of disciplines provide a suitable background. Some employers look for individuals who have majored in personnel administration or industrial and labor relations, while others prefer college graduates with a general business background. Still other employers feel that a well-rounded liberal arts education is best; many personnel managers have degrees in psychology, sociology, counseling, or education. A master's in business administration (M.B.A.) also provides suitable preparation for a job in the field.	Human resources managers need supervisory abilities and must be able to accept responsibility. Integrity, fair-mindedness, and a persuasive congenial personality are all important qualities.	Starting salaries range between $20,000 and $50,000 a year, depending upon a person's experience.	Great demand
Employment interviewer	Employment interviewers help people evaluate themselves and their work potential. They help clients identify their interests and abilities; make them aware of career opportunities and alternatives; help them set goals; and assist them in planning the steps they need to take to reach their goals.	All states require interviewers in public employment offices to meet civil service or merit system requirements. However, state standards setting minimum education and experience vary widely. The majority of interviewers in state employment agencies have a bachelor's degree plus additional courses in guidance and counseling. Experience in counseling, interviewing, and job placement also may be required, particularly in the case of those without advanced degrees.	Persons aspiring to be employment interviewers should have a strong interest in helping others make and carry out vocational decisions. They should be able to work independently and to keep detailed records.	Average starting salaries are likely to be between $13,500 and $19,000 a year.	Moderate demand

Job Title	Job Description	Suggested Education and Training	Personality Traits	Average Pay	Outlook through 1990
Credit manager	A credit manager has final authority to accept or reject a credit application. In extending credit to a business (commercial credit), the credit manager analyzes detailed financial reports, interviews a company representative, and reviews credit agency reports. The manager also checks at banks where the company has deposits or previously was granted credit. In extending credit to individuals (consumer credit), the credit manager must rely more on personal interviews and credit bureau and bank reports.	A college degree is becoming increasingly important for entry level jobs in credit management. Employers usually seek persons who have a degree in business administration, but they may also hire graduates holding liberal arts degrees. Courses in accounting, economics, finance, computer programming, statistics, and psychology all are valuable in preparing for a career in credit management.	Credit managers should be able to analyze detailed information and draw valid conclusions based on this analysis. Because it is necessary to maintain good customer relationships, a pleasant personality and the ability to speak and write effectively also are characteristics of the successful credit manager.	Credit manager trainees who have a college degree earn annual salaries that range from about $13,000 to $15,000. Salaries of experienced credit managers average about $22,000 to $27,000 annually.	Moderate demand
Blue-collar worker supervisor	Blue-collar worker supervisors direct the activities of other employees and ensure that millions of dollars worth of equipment and materials are used properly and efficiently. They make work schedules and keep production and employee records, plan employees' activities and must allow for absent workers and machine breakdowns. Supervisors train new employees, explain company plans and policies, recommend wage increases or promotions, and issue warnings or recommend that poor performers be disciplined or fired.	Completion of high school often is the minimum educational requirement, and 1 or 2 years of college or technical school can be very helpful. Most supervisors rise through the ranks—they are promoted from jobs where they operated a machine or worked on an assembly line. This gives them the advantage of knowing how jobs should be done and what problems may arise and provides them with insight into management policies and employee attitudes. Although few supervisors are college graduates, a growing number of employers are hiring trainees with a college or technical school background.	When choosing supervisors, employers generally look for experience, skill, and leadership qualities. Employers place emphasis on the ability to motivate employees, maintain high morale, command respect, and get along with people.	Average annual earnings of blue-collar worker supervisors are about $23,000. Supervisors usually are salaried, and their salaries generally are determined by the wage rates of the highest paid workers they supervise. For example, some companies keep wages of supervisors about 10 to 30% higher than those of their subordinates.	Moderate demand

Job Title	Job Description	Suggested Education and Training	Personality Traits	Average Pay	Outlook through 1990
Labor relations specialist	Labor relations specialists advise management on union-management relations. When a collective bargaining agreement is up for negotiation, they provide background information for management's negotiation position, a job that requires familiarity with sources of economic and wage data as well as extensive knowledge of labor law and collective bargaining trends. Labor relations specialists might work with the union on seniority rights under the layoff procedure set forth in the contract or meet with the union steward about a grievance.	Courses in labor law, collective bargaining, labor economics, labor history, and industrial psychology provide a valuable background. Graduate study in industrial or labor relations may be required. A law degree seldom is required for entry level jobs, but most of the people responsible for contract negotiations are lawyers, and a combination of industrial relations courses and a law degree is highly desirable. Although a growing number of people enter the labor relations field directly, some begin in personnel work and move into a labor relations job.	Labor relations specialists should speak and write effectively and be able to work with people of all levels of education and experience. They also must be able to see both the employee's and the employer's points of view. What's more, they should be able to work as part of a team.	Average salaries for labor relations specialists employed by state governments range from $13,700 to $18,500. Specialists with supervisory responsibilities average from $19,500 to $27,000.	Moderate demand
Community recreation director	Recreation directors manage recreation programs. They are responsible for the operation of playgrounds and community centers, as well as for program planning, budget, and personnel.	A college degree with a major in parks and recreation is increasingly important for those seeking full-time career positions in this field. A bachelor's degree and experience are minimum requirements for directors. However, increasing numbers are obtaining master's degrees in parks and recreation as well as in related disciplines. Many persons with backgrounds in other disciplines including social work, forestry, and resource management, pursue graduate degrees in recreation.	Persons planning recreation careers must be good at motivating people and sensitive to their needs. Good health and physical stamina are required. Activity planning calls for creativity and resourcefulness. Willingness to accept responsibility and the ability to exercise judgment are important qualities since recreation personnel often work alone.	The average salary for recreation directors in public park and recreation agencies is about $25,000 and ranges as high as $50,000.	Moderate demand

Job Title	Job Description	Suggested Education and Training	Personality Traits	Average Pay	Outlook through 1990
City manager	Although duties vary by city size, city managers generally administer and coordinate the day-to-day operations of the city. They are responsible for functions such as tax collection and disbursement, law enforcement, and public works. They also hire department heads and their staffs and prepare the annual budget to be approved by elected officials. In addition, they study current problems, such as housing, traffic congestion, or crime, and report their findings to the elected council.	A master's degree, preferably in public or business administration, is essential for those seeking a career in city management. Although some applicants with only a bachelor's degree may find employment, strong competition for positions, even among master's degree recipients, makes the graduate degree a requirement for most entry level jobs. In some cases, employers may hire a person with a graduate or professional degree in a field related to public administration, such as political science, planning, or law.	Persons who plan a career in city management should like to work with detail and to be a part of a team. They must have sound judgment, self-confidence, and the ability to perform well under stress. To handle emergencies, city managers must quickly isolate problems, identify their causes, and provide a number of possible solutions. City managers should be tactful and able to communicate and work well with people.	Salaries of city managers vary according to experience, job responsibility, and city size. The average annual salary for all managers is more than $34,000. Average annual salaries of city managers ranged from about $28,000 in small cities of 5,000 to 10,000 inhabitants to about $49,000 in medium-sized cities of 50,000 to 100,000 inhabitants.	Moderate demand
Medical record administrator	Medical record administrators direct the activities of the medical record department and develop systems for documenting, storing, and retrieving medical information. They supervise the medical record staff, which processes and analyzes records and reports on patients' illnesses and treatment. They train the medical record staff for specialized jobs, compile medical statistics for state or national health agencies, and assist the medical staff in evaluations of patient care or research studies. Medical record administrators serving as department heads are a part of the hospital management staff and participate fully in management activities.	Preparation for a career in this field is available through college and university programs that lead to a bachelor's degree in medical record administration. Medical schools offer many of these programs. Since concentration in medical record administration begins in the third or fourth year of study, transfer from a community or junior college is possible. One-year certificate programs are open to those who already have a bachelor's degree and required courses in the liberal arts and biological sciences.	Medical record administrators must be accurate and interested in detail, and must be able to speak and write clearly. Because medical records are confidential, medical record administrators must be discreet in processing and releasing information. Supervisors must be able to organize, analyze, and direct work procedures and to work effectively with other hospital personnel.	The average starting salary for medical record administrators in hospitals is about $20,000 a year. Experienced record administrators in hospitals average about $23,600 a year, with some earning well over $30,000.	Stable demand

Job Title	Job Description	Suggested Education and Training	Personality Traits	Average Pay	Outlook through 1990
Bank officer	Practically every bank has a president who directs operations; one or more vice presidents who act as general managers or who are in charge of bank departments; and a comptroller or cashier responsible for all bank property. Loan officers may handle installment, commercial, real estate, or agricultural loans. Bank officers in trust management require knowledge of financial planning and investments. Operations officers direct the workflow and update systems. A correspondent bank officer is responsible for relations with other banks; a branch manager, for all functions of a branch office; and an international officer, for advising customers with financial dealings abroad.	Bank officer and management positions are filled by management trainees, and by promoting outstanding bank clerks or tellers. College graduation usually is required for management trainees. A business administration major in finance or a liberal arts curriculum, including accounting, economics, commercial law, political science, and statistics, serves as excellent preparation for officer trainee positions. A Master of Business Administration (MBA) in addition to a social science bachelor's degree, which some employers prefer, may provide an even stronger educational foundation.	Persons interested in becoming bank officers should like to work independently and to analyze detailed information. The ability to communicate, both orally and in writing, is important. They also need tact and good judgment to counsel customers and supervise employees.	Officer trainees at the bachelor's level generally earn between $1200 and $1600 a month. Those with master's degrees generally start at between $1400 and $2100 a month. Graduates with an MBA are usually offered starting salaries of $1500 to $2800 a month.	Great demand
Hotel manager	Hotel managers are responsible for operating their establishments profitably, and satisfying hotel guests. They determine room rates and credit policy, direct the operation of the food service operation, and manage the housekeeping, accounting, security, and maintenance departments of the hotel. Handling problems and coping with the unexpected are important parts of the job.	Experience generally is the most important consideration in selecting managers. However, employers increasingly are emphasizing college education. A bachelor's degree in hotel and restaurant administration provides particularly strong preparation for a career in hotel management. Included in many college programs in hotel management are courses in hotel administration, accounting, economics, data processing, housekeeping, food service management and catering, and hotel maintenance engineering.	Managers should have initiative, self-discipline, and the ability to organize and direct the work of others. They must be able to solve problems and concentrate on details.	Hotel manager trainees who are graduates of specialized college programs may start at around $15,500 a year. Experienced managers may earn several times as much as beginners. For example, salaries of hotel general managers range from about $20,000 to $80,000 a year.	Moderate demand

THE
MARKETING
OF BUSINESS

LEARNING OBJECTIVES

After completing this chapter, you will be able to:

■   Identify eight marketing functions.

■   Explain the marketing concept.

■   Describe the four elements of the marketing mix.

■   Define market target.

■   Explain four types of market segmentation.

■   Identify marketing research and describe its
    purposes.

■   Discuss buying motives and how our culture
    influences buying decisions.

■   Diagram and explain a consumer decision model.

12

THE MARKETING
PROCESS

John Sculley, newly hired president of Apple Computer, Inc., is a highly regarded consumer goods marketer who, just a short time ago, was working in that capacity at Pepsi Co, Inc. Apple's recruitment of Sculley is just one of many signs that marketing is becoming the new number 1 priority of corporations. In the past, Apple, like a number of other companies, has concentrated more on developing new technologies than on understanding the intricacies of the marketing process, and has suffered for its oversight. According to James McManus, head of a marketing consulting firm, "Today, companies realize that their raw material, labor, and physical-resource costs are all screwed down and that the only option for dramatic improvement will come from doing a better marketing job."

An excellent example of the marketing process is southern fried chicken. Years ago, fried chicken was popular primarily in the South. Today, however, so many people nationwide like fried chicken that restaurants specializing in this product ring up $4 billion annually in sales. Can you imagine the marketing phenomenon that happened over the years to allow people to casually drive up to a national chain restaurant like Kentucky Fried Chicken and order "chicken and biscuits to go"?

Marketing includes all the activities of getting products or services from the producer to the consumer. It starts with finding out what consumers want or need, and then assessing whether the product can be made or sold at a profit. A **market** is any segment of the overall population that will be interested in purchasing a particular product or service.

This chapter helps explain the marketing process by describing marketing functions, the marketing concept, the marketing mix, market targets, marketing research, and buyer behavior.

MARKETING FUNCTIONS

Businesses perform marketing functions to create **utility**—the ability of a product or service to satisfy needs and wants—for consumers.

Eight Marketing Functions

To deliver fried chicken or any other product or service to consumers in a desirable form, businesses must perform eight marketing functions. These functions are:

1. *Buying.* Typically, businesses buy many items to get a product to the consumer. Restaurants must buy chicken before they can cook it, and they must purchase hundreds of other items, ranging from spices to tableware.

2. *Selling.* Businesses must also sell. Chicken producers sell their chicken to large restaurants, who in turn, sell the finished product to consumers.

3. *Storing.* For chicken to be available when consumers want it, someone must store it until they are ready to buy it. For most fast food items, the storage may be for only a short period. McDonald's, for instance, keeps french fries only a few minutes after they cook them, but businesses may store products such as clothes for a longer period.

4. *Transporting.* Very few consumers go to a poultry farm to buy chickens for fried chicken. Businesses transport the product to consumers so that most of them only drive a mile or two to get the product they want. In fact, Kentucky Fried Chicken, the largest chicken restaurant, had 6640 outlets in 1983. And they were only 1 of 192 chains that specialized in fried chicken.

5. *Financing.* Chicken producers typically borrow money to build facilities, buy feed, and raise the chickens. Transportation also requires financing; and restaurants typically engage in high finance to be able to provide consumers with what they want.

6. *Risk bearing.* Many people in the marketing process have to take risks, sometimes high risks. Suppose the producers produce more product than consumers buy, or perhaps they prepare a new item that consumers do not like, and therefore do not buy. In such cases, people lose money — perhaps a lot of it.

7. *Securing information.* Chicken restaurants find out what kind of product consumers want and how they want it prepared. They also try to find out how many people will buy their food, where they should locate, and how they should promote. Church's Fried Chicken, number 2 behind Kentucky Fried Chicken, has many outlets in black neighborhoods because research showed blacks on the average ate seven times more chicken than whites.

8. *Standardization and grading.* Finally, the marketing process standardizes and grades products. The chicken legs consumers eat are easily identifiable because the leg has become a standard serving. Likewise, government inspectors grade foods for quality and safety.

Whether purchases be product or service, businesses perform these marketing functions to bring them to us. In some cases, the functions may be minor; in other cases, they may be major, but all the functions are important and necessary.

Utility Creation

Marketing, through these eight functions, adds to consumer satisfaction by creating four forms of utility. Moving goods from site or production to a place that is convenient to consumers is called **place utility. Time utility** is getting the goods or services to people when they want them. The legal arrangement that transfers the title from seller to purchaser at the time of the purchase is **possession utility.** The fourth type of utility, combining materials and labor to create the finished product, is called **form utility.**

THE MARKETING CONCEPT

Since the industrial revolution, marketing has evolved from a production to a consumer orientation.

Production-Oriented Marketing

At the beginning of the industrial revolution, companies concentrated on production. Producers believed that consumers would open their arms and pocketbooks to buy whatever they produced. In the early 1900s, the Pillsbury Company's philosophy said, in part, "Our basic function is to mill high-quality flour, and of course [and almost incidentally], we must hire salesmen to sell it." This production orientation worked for a while because people had been unable to satisfy all of their demands. Eventually, however, inventories built up as firms began producing more than enough to satisfy consumer demands. This led companies to think more about selling their products and services.

Sales-Oriented Marketing

Since businesses had a lot of inventory, they decided they should try harder to get consumers to buy what they had. The good, quality product no longer sold itself. Many marketers believed that a good sales force could sell almost anything. After a few years, though, customers began to resist the sales effort. Customers wanted some input into what was produced and what services were to be created for them. Wagon manufacturers went broke building and promoting "superior" wagons when the customers really wanted faster, more efficient transportation means—the automobile. Later, developers of fancy, downtown hotels lost money because the public wanted convenient motels on the outskirts.

Consumer-Oriented Marketing

While there are still companies that emphasize product or sales, many have adopted a more consumer-oriented marketing concept. The purpose of the **marketing concept** is to find out what consumers want and then to produce it for them at a profit. The marketing concept rests on the importance of customers to a firm and states that: (1) all company policies and activities should be aimed at satisfying customer needs, and (2) profit-

able sales volume is a better company goal than maximum sales volume. Companies use research to identify customer needs, and then work backward to develop and deliver a product that satisfies those needs.

More specifically, the marketing concept emphasizes the following:

1. Research departments try to find out what consumers really want.

2. Marketing research departments communicate to production departments what the consumers need.

3. Distribution channels are evolved to deliver consumer products at the place and time desired by customers (see Chapter 14).

4. Marketing activities are integrated and coordinated with all the firm's functions—financing, production, engineering, design, and personnel—to yield an overall approach to consumer satisfaction.

CROSS FIRE

Do Most Firms Practice the Marketing Concept?

Some people debate whether the majority of today's firms actually practice the marketing concept.

People who contend that most firms do practice the marketing concept point to all the research that firms conduct before they introduce a new product or service into the market. For example, P&G tests most of its products for months and even years before they enter the market. Further, there is evidence that firms adjust quickly to market demands. For instance, when people became interested in small home computers, existing, as well as many new, firms began designing these products to fit customers' needs. And many argue that if a firm does not pay close attention to what customers really want, their competitors will bankrupt them.

On the other side, some argue that companies would not make as many mistakes if they were sincere about customers' needs. They cite the auto industry for continuing to build and promote large, expensive cars when consumers clearly wanted more economical autos. Further, they say firms would not have to spend so much money promoting their products and services if they truly fulfilled a need. Finally, critics point to cases where companies apparently try to deceive the public by misrepresenting their products or services.

Do you think that the majority of today's firms practice the marketing concept? Why?

___ Yes   ___ No

This consumer orientation broadens company missions. For example, Revlon defines its business as "the creation of hope" rather than the production of cosmetics. Oil companies see themselves as being in the "energy business." Xerox is in the "automated office business," and IBM is "a problem solver."

In sum, the marketing concept changes the orientation from "take what we produce and sell it" to "find out what they want and make it." All roads lead to consumer satisfaction. If all marketers fully practiced the marketing concept, there would be little cause for consumer criticism. However, legislators have passed hundreds of laws, consumer protection agencies have sprouted nationwide, and communication media are engaging in consumer education programs. But the greatest potential for reducing consumer complaints is an expanded version of the marketing concept referred to as **enlightened marketing.** Enlightened marketing emphasizes long-run improvement for the entire system; according to marketing authority Professor Philip Kotler, it embodies five principles:

1. *Consumer-oriented marketing.* Under enlightened marketing, consumer orientation goes beyond trying to discover what the customer wants; it means looking at the world through consumers' eyes.

2. *Innovative marketing.* The marketing system can be justly criticized for adding a development here and a change there without creating integrative systems for more efficient distribution. Marketers need to research the depth of people's need and put together systems that serve both company and society interests.

3. *Value marketing.* Value marketing emphasizes promotional programs that put real values into products rather than creating imagined benefits. It exchanges hard-sell, gimmicky, emotional appeals that deliver transparent excitement for better products, more educational promotion, and increased customer services.

4. *Sense-of-mission marketing.* Kotler believes that companies should devote more energy toward developing social goals to give a company and its customers a sense of dignity and fulfillment that comes from pursuing a worthwhile destiny. Sales growth, market

Practicing "enlightened marketing" even before the term was coined, Seagram has run ads promoting moderate consumption of its products since 1934.

share, and investment returns are still important, but they are too narrow to be the ultimate goals.

5. *Societal marketing.* Marketers should develop wide appeals that balance three sometimes conflicting forces: consumer needs, company profits, and societal benefits. The indiscriminate satisfaction of customer needs and company profits places too weighty a burden on society's efficient use of natural resources such as clean water, fresh air, and healthy foods.

Enlightened marketing is really a broad interpretation of the marketing concept. It would be naive to expect its adoption by companies who ignore the marketing concept. Enlightened firms must replace short-run, selfish interests with long-run systems interests, and legislators need to clarify problems and establish guidelines for enlightened marketing practices. But the greatest force rests in consumers' hands; there is little doubt that the marketing system responds with lightning speed to consumer purchasing habits. In fact, today, all types of companies — airlines like Eastern, financial concerns like Visa, and high-tech firms like Hewlett-Packard — are trying hard to shape their products and services to changing consumer needs. Kroger Co., for example, interviews 250,000 consumers a year to define their demands more precisely.

Companies that do not respond to changes in their consumers' tastes and desires run the risk of failure. For years, Safeway Stores catered to the family of four where 85% of the shopping was done by women. However, the market changed to smaller households, two-income households, and more and younger men in the grocery stores. Safeway had to change to accommodate what they called the "jogging generation." They began to stay open longer, added bakeries, delis, pharmacies, and placed automated teller machines in many stores. Their new motto, "Fresh and Full at 5," stresses their appeal to consumers who have eclectic tastes and little shopping time. A spokesperson for Safeway says, "Marketing is our prime focus. In the past, we ran our business by giving the consumers what we thought they wanted. Now we've got to find out what they want and then develop the products."

THE MARKETING MIX

To operate a marketing program effectively, firms have to balance all the factors involved in reaching their market segment. The total package of these elements is the **marketing mix,** often referred to as the 4 Ps of marketing (see Fig. 12.1):

- Product planning.
- Pricing decisions.
- Placement channels (distribution).
- Promotional strategies.

Product Planning

Product planning includes deciding what products to produce; and it also covers package design, trademarks, guarantees, new product development, and product mix. Procter and Gamble (P&G), a company that likes to bring out new products, introduced six varieties of chocolate chip cookies under the brand name Duncan Hines in their Kansas City test market in 1983. In a few weeks, they had 25% of the area's packaged cookie market. A year earlier, PepsiCo, Inc., through its Frito-Lay subsidiary, had similar success with its Grandma's cookies. But since most new products are not successful, companies usually spend a lot of money in research and development (R&D) before deciding to enter the market.

Pricing Decisions

Pricing decisions aim at setting prices and credit policies that are reasonable to the consumer while

Figure 12.1
Variables in the marketing mix.

affording the firm a profit, Bissell, Inc., sells a disposable toothbrush (with paste already applied) for 39 cents. You use it once and throw it away. However, many discount stores sell regular toothbrushes for 39 cents; and for another 39 cents, you could get a tube of toothpaste. Although the product would seem to be overpriced, Bissell says that its tests have been very successful. A lot of people apparently like to keep their mouths fresh by brushing frequently, and they worry that the brush they have in their drawer is gathering germs. "Pricing decisions are critical," says a marketing manager. "If we get them too high we lose the market, if we get them too low we lose our shirt." (Chapter 13 discusses product planning and pricing in more detail.)

Placement Channels (Distribution)

Placement channels describe the routes and stops that products make from production to consumption. Firms try to select the channel that will get the product to the user in the most efficient manner. Some companies promote their channel usage. For example, Fuller Brush will sell their products only through a direct channel, from the manufacturer to the consumer, via door-to-door sales. (Chapter 14 discusses distribution channels in more detail.)

Promotional Strategies

Promotional strategies indicate the advertising, selling, and promotional programs designed to educate and persuade consumers to use products and services. Procter & Gamble introduced its new chocolate chip cookies by advertising heavily in the area, offering coupons for cents off the price, and even by mailing cookies to homes. Shortly after the campaign started, customers began pouring into the stores looking for the new cookies. (Chapter 15 discusses promotion in more detail.)

TARGETING A MARKET

Yuppies, YAPs, and yumpies are the latest labels to describe an important group for marketers. (Yuppies are young urban professionals; YAPs are young aspiring professionals; and Yumpies are young upwardly mobile professionals.) The labels describe fast-track middle managers and profes-

sionals in their 20s to early 40s. Their work uniforms include pinstripe suits (no polyester, please) and wingtips or dark pumps. Yuppies, according to marketers, have an insatiable appetite for designer clothes, computers, video recorders, pasta makers, phone-answering devices, espresso machines, pagers, and other gadgets.

Marketing strategy entails identifying customer groups that a business can effectively serve and tailoring its product offerings, prices, distribution, and promotional efforts and services toward those particular market segments. A good strategy recognizes that a business cannot be all things to all groups of people and that successful marketing programs appeal to specific groups of potential customers. Lloyd E. Reuss, general manager of General Motors Corp.'s Buick motor division, agrees: "We've treated the car market as a mass one, but I'm now convinced that concept is dead." Reuss now believes in target marketing — specific products and ads aimed at specific groups.

Market Segmentation

Market segmentation is the process of dividing markets into groups with similar characteristics. "We have to take the whole and divide it into smaller circles and squares, until we can get an idea of the nature of our audience," is the way a marketing manager explained it. He added, "Rather than trying to produce a swimsuit for the total market, we divide our customers into segments such as youth, older people, jet setters, and pregnant women. Then we can design and promote our products differently for each group." Campbell Soup, which recently reversed a market share decline, believes that they have to build and promote different products for different market segments. R. Gordon McGovern, Campbell's CEO, says, "My 83-year-old doesn't eat like my son, and my daughters eat differently from their parents, and," he adds, "we eat differently from the people around the corner." Campbell's is trying to gear their products and ads to specific groups. For example, they sell their spicy Ranchero Beans only in the South and Southwest.

Of the many bases for segmenting markets, the most popular are:

Geographic segmentation. This approach develops a loyal group of consumers in a known geographical territory. Coors Beer for many years concentrated on markets in the West, primarily California. This allowed the company to develop

FUNNY BUSINESS

Source: The Wall Street Journal — Permission, Cartoon Features Syndicate.

"The following show is aimed at the 18–35 age group. If you don't fit into that category, you're not *supposed* to like it."

its distribution and promotional programs for the tastes and life-styles of one particular region.

Demographic segmentation. Perhaps the most common segment, demographic segmentation groups customers according to common characteristics such as age, sex, race, or income. Many companies still gear their products and ads to the 18-to-35 year olds who dominated the marketplace of the 1970s, but it is the 25-to-45 year olds

Figure 12.2
A psychographic segmentation. *Source: Arnold Mitchell,* The Nine American Lifestyles. *New York: Macmillan Publishing Company, 1983.*

1. *Survivors.* The depressed and poor. They tend toward decaffeinated coffee and gelatin desserts and do not have much fun in their lives. About 4% of the population.

2. *Sustainers.* Better off than survivors, but still anxious, combative, and often feeling left out. They eat breakfast out a lot, make overseas phone calls, and read condensed books. About 7% of the population.

3. *Belongers.* Traditionalists who follow the rules. Gardening and daytime television are popular with these people. Many own cats, tend to live in the same place for more than ten years, and are against extramarital sex. About 35% of the population.

4. *Emulators.* The young and ambitious. They tend to lead hollow lives. They play poker, collect tropical fish, and like to go to parties. About 10% of the population.

5. *Achievers.* Diverse, gifted, hard working. These are people who have built the system and still run it. They like

California wines, own racing bicycles, tend to be Republican, and are committed to the free enterprise system. About 23% of the population.

6. *I-Am-Me.* Students and younger people. They are typically into waterskiing and cashew nuts. Surprisingly, they have a good deal of confidence in the military. About 5% of the population.

7. *Experientials.* Sophisticated and politically effective. They prefer natural to synthetic products, enjoy backpacking and chess, take a holistic view of health, and embrace left-leaning political views. About 7% of the population.

8. *Societally conscious.* Very similar to experientials. About 9% of the population.

9. *Integrateds.* Truly trustworthy and likable. They are quick with laughter and generous with tears. Alas, only about 2% of the population.

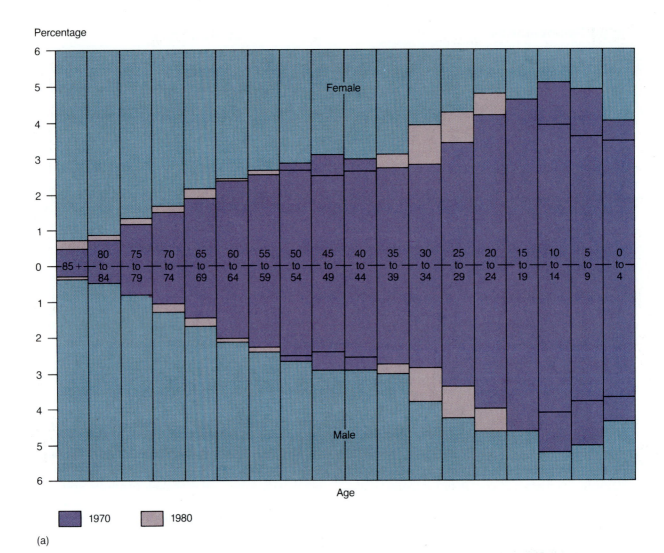

Percentage

Female

85+ | 80 to 84 | 75 to 79 | 70 to 74 | 65 to 69 | 60 to 64 | 55 to 59 | 50 to 54 | 45 to 49 | 40 to 44 | 35 to 39 | 30 to 34 | 25 to 29 | 20 to 24 | 15 to 19 | 10 to 14 | 5 to 9 | 0 to 4

Male

Age

■ 1970   □ 1980

(a)

Figure 12.3
Segments of our population.
(a) Distribution of population by age and sex, April 1, 1970 and April 1, 1980.
(b) Distribution of population by region, 1950–1980. (c) Distribution of population by urban
and rural areas, 1900–1980. *Source: U.S. Department of Commerce.*

who today have the power and the size. Petticord Swimwear sells a line of swimwear specifically for women between the ages of 25 and 45. Realizing that most women in this age group do not look like Cheryl Tiegs, Petticord's suits have a mitered pattern for a slimming effect, and they include ruffles and torso wraps for softening.

Psychographic segmentation. This rather recent method of segmentation identifies groups of people by personality, life-style, or values. A recent study by sociologist Arnold Mitchell identifies nine life-style categories. The study's 800

questions focused on values people hold and life-styles they pursue. Figure 12.2 identifies Mitchell's psychographic segmentations.

Product segmentation. Product segmentation identifies existing best-selling products and services and promotes them. When Mercedes Benz introduced its Model 190E (sedan) to the United States, it was relying on an existing reputation and demand for its products.

Figure 12.3 identifies some segments of the United States population and shows how they have been changing.

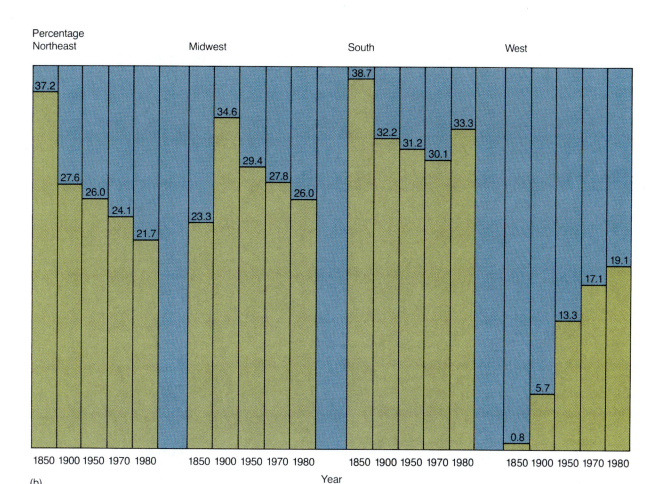

Percentage

Northeast — Midwest — South — West

Northeast: 1850 37.2, 1900 27.6, 1950 26.0, 1970 24.1, 1980 21.7
Midwest: 1850 23.3, 1900 34.6, 1950 29.4, 1970 27.8, 1980 26.0
South: 1850 38.7, 1900 32.2, 1950 31.2, 1970 30.1, 1980 33.3
West: 1850 0.8, 1900 5.7, 1950 13.3, 1970 17.1, 1980 19.1

(b)

Year

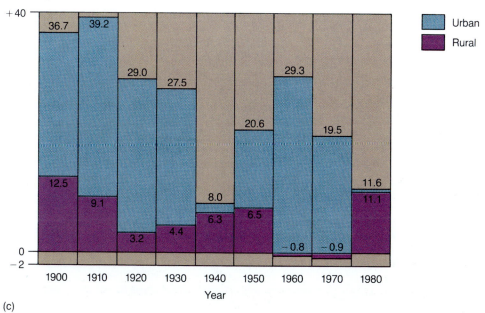

Percentage

Urban
Rural

Urban: 1900 36.7, 1910 39.2, 1920 29.0, 1930 27.5, 1940 8.0, 1950 20.6, 1960 29.3, 1970 19.5, 1980 11.6
Rural: 1900 12.5, 1910 9.1, 1920 3.2, 1930 4.4, 1940 6.3, 1950 6.5, 1960 −0.8, 1970 −0.9, 1980 11.1

Year

(c)

Market segment	Family income level			
	Less than $12,000	$12,000 to 17,999	$18,000 to 26,000	More than $26,000
Youth		▓	▓	
Teenage		▓	▓	
Young adult				
Middle age				
Mature				
Senior citizen				

**Figure 12.4
An example of a market grid.**

▓ = Market target

Choosing a Market Target

Out of numerous alternatives, marketers select well-defined marketing targets for their products. We define a **market target** as the characteristics of the specialized consumer group the firm is trying to reach. Market targets can be defined and isolated by developing a **market grid** of the total market. Figure 12.4 illustrates a record-producing company that aims its promotion at the teenage and youth markets in families whose income ranges from $12,000 to $26,000. In this way, the firm segments and precisely pinpoints its marketing target. From the market grid, managers can develop a profile of their customers. Figure 12.5 shows how Chevrolet has profiled buyers of Corvettes. In developing their marketing program, Corvette promoters know that they have appeal to younger car buyers, mostly male, a large percentage of whom are single and of higher-than-average income and education.

Chrysler is also trying to target its markets more precisely. Because pickup truck drivers are concentrated in Texas and Louisiana and like to listen to country and western music, Chrysler buys radio time on C&W stations in these areas to promote its trucks. "It's like a rifle taking aim at a direct target versus a shotgun that's fired in a 360-degree arc," says Campana, Chrysler's vice-president of marketing.

MARKETING RESEARCH

Why on earth would a company test a toilet bowl cleanser for as much as two years before deciding whether to produce it full scale? That is what Procter & Gamble did with its Brigade cleaner. Up to seven years may lapse between the time a new product is proposed and its nationwide distribution. Vice-president of marketing at Hershey's, Gary W. McQuaid, says, "Developing a new prod-

**Figure 12.5
Profile of Corvette buyers.**

Age	30	Quite a bit younger than the average age of all new car buyers, which is about 40.
Sex	Male	About 80% of purchasers are male.
Marital status	43% single	Since only 20% of the total new-car buyers are single, Corvette appeals to singles.
Income	More than $23,000	Considerably higher than the median income of all new-car buyers.
Education	College and above	Higher than average for new-car buyers.

uct is like shooting a duck. You can't shoot it where it is; you've got to shoot it where it's going to be." One reason companies take so long is they want to be sure, or as sure as they can be, that the product will be a success because it takes so much money to bring the product to national distribution. Procter & Gamble spent almost $100 million to roll out Citrus Hill orange juice, and outlays of $50 million are typical to bring new products to national distribution. Still, there is an urgency to get products from proposal to distribution more quickly. Aiming too far into the future is just too risky. Market testing is only one type of **market research,** the systematic gathering, recording, and analysis of data about products and services.

What Marketing Research Does

Basically, marketing research tries to provide answers to a firm's questions about such concerns as consumer likes and dislikes and the cost and effectiveness of various marketing activities. Specifically, research tries to answer such questions as:

- Who are our customers and what are they like?

- Why do people buy or refrain from buying our products or services?

- How do potential customers respond to our quality, prices, distribution methods, and promotions?

- Why do our customers want what we are not providing?

- How do we compare to our competitors?

Although it is not an exact science, firms that conduct good market research are better able to satisfy consumers' needs. Management Analysis Center, Inc. (MAC), an international consulting firm, helped a community hospital find ways to increase its occupancy rate through marketing research. They mailed surveys to 800 consumers in the hospital's area to find what kinds of care potential hospital users liked. Additionally, MAC surveyed 80 area doctors by telephone to find out what they preferred in hospitals. After analyzing the information, the hospital focused on improv-

ing its capabilities to better provide what patients and doctors wanted.

How to Conduct Market Research

Research, in reality, provides information, and conducting research is really looking for information. There are many ways and places to look.

Information from internal records. Records often contain a wealth of information. Companies might check through records to see who buys from them, how often they buy, and what types of goods or services they buy. Also, companies look at credit records, which frequently contain data on customers' jobs, income levels, marital status, and so on.

Also companies ask their employees questions about customers. They may hear a lot of minor gripes and complaints, which can give cues on what customers like and dislike.

Secondary research. Although information gathered internally is usually very good, firms may not be able to find out everything they want to know. Secondary research (which is done before undertaking any primary research) is information that has already been gathered and published in books, magazines, trade publications, government reports, and the like. For instance, if a company sells major appliances, it might keep a check on the housing starts in the area. While secondary research can provide a lot of information, it may not always relate as specifically to production as companies would like.

Primary research. Primary research is collecting data for the first time, usually by the user or by research firms hired by the user. While this research is often helpful and specific, it can also be quite expensive. A group of seventy-three corporations paid $2 million for the research to identify the psychographic information mentioned in Fig. 12.6.

Mail surveys and personal interviews are common ways of collecting primary data. Of course, test marketing products also provides good primary data. A somewhat creative approach to personal interviewing, which firms seem to be relying upon more, is the **focus group,** where a group of people, usually community leaders, are led by a skilled professional to

Middle class	Lower class
1. Pointed to the future.	1. Pointed to the present and past.
2. Viewpoint embraces a long expanse in time.	2. Lives and thinks in short expanse of time.
3. More urban identification.	3. More rural in identification.
4. Stresses rationality.	4. Essentially nonrational.
5. Has well-structured sense of the universe.	5. Has vague, unclear, and unstructured sense of the world.
6. Horizons vastly extended or not limited.	6. Horizons sharply defined and limited.
7. Greater sense of choice making.	7. Limited sense of choice making.
8. Self-confident, willing to take risks.	8. Very much concerned with security.
9. Thinking is immaterial and abstract.	9. Thinking is concrete and perceptive.
10. Sees self as tied to national happenings.	10. World revolves around family and self.

Figure 12.6
Psychological differences between middle- and lower-class buyers. *Source: Pierre D. Martineau, "Social Classes and Spending Behavior,"* Journal of Marketing, *Vol. 23 (October 1958), p. 129.*

discuss some topic in which researchers are interested. The group typically does not know the identity of the firm doing the research, and executives might even watch the discussion through one-way mirrors or via videotape. A newspaper of the Knight-Ridder Chain used focus groups to help it develop a supplement for its paper. The paper hired a moderator who invited about two dozen community leaders, in two groups of twelve, to discuss types of information they would like the local media to provide about local business conditions. The participants did not know that the paper was involved; they were told that a local communication medium was interested in finding ways to improve their service by offering more information on local business. From the discussion, the paper designed a "Business Monday" supplement, which proved to be quite successful.*

BUYER BEHAVIOR

Why do we buy products and services? This question is the subject of much research for marketers, and it often haunts the customer. Research shows us how we spend our money. In 1983, buying everything from toy rockets to his-and-her dirigibles, we spent more than $2 trillion on goods and services. Although taking a smaller percentage bite than in the past, food still claims the largest expenditure in the family budget. We are also spending less on clothes and home expenses (with the exception of utilities) than in the past. By contrast, housing, utilities, and health costs have increased and form a larger percentage of our expenditures.

But the record of our expenses does not answer the questions of why we buy a Ford instead of a Chevrolet. Nor do the records nail down all the reasons for our spending patterns. We try to give some insight into these questions by examining buying motives and cultural influences.

Surveying a market population by telephone is one method of generating primary research data.

---

* Enrichment Chapter C, "The Use of Statistical Methods," provides more information on research methods.

Why People Buy

Basically, we buy to fulfill some need. When needs are aroused to our conscious levels, we classify them as motives because they activate our behavior. Thus, we say that our motives cause us to buy, and we can classify these as rational motives and emotional motives. **Consumer behavior** is that aspect of marketing that studies people's motives for purchasing certain products.

Rational buying motives. Rational motives are objective; they are based on the logic of why we should or should not buy a particular item. For example, a person may buy a new small car because her old gas guzzler was in need of repairs. Though the small car is not as prestigious or quite as comfortable, it is much more economical. It will save her a lot in gas and repair bills, and it is dependable. Decisions on price and quality are examples of rational motives.

1. *Price*. If we find two items of equal quality that perform the same function, a rational decision would be to buy the lower-priced item. That is why many people search for after-holiday sales and the less-popular brand names. Marketers appeal to this rational motive by advertising specials offering coupons for discounts and by cutting service and packaging frills in favor of lowering the price.

2. *Quality*. Some people search for quality to be sure that they are getting their money's worth. The item's construction and materials, the quality of workmanship, and its durability become important in buying decisions where quality is a motive.

Emotional buying motives. From our own fickle experiences, we know that not all of our purchases are rational. Fancy labels do not mean that jeans will last longer, but they create a lot of attention, and many people like that. **Emotional motives** are rarely logical or rational; they are subjective, and we may not be able to explain them with logical soundness. There are many emotional buying motives; we offer a few as illustrations.

1. *Status*. We see people in sports, politics, entertainment, and government who get a lot of publicity. From media reports, it looks as though they live storybook lives. We may

Seeking to emulate the status of the famous may motivate the purchase of a luxury fur or an item from a celebrity-endorsed line of clothing.

envy them and try to capture some of their glow. We often see these people wearing expensive items such as Gucci shoes, Piaget watches, and Lucchase boots. While people may not actually need or be able to afford a Mercedes, sable mink, or hand-tailored Italian suits, some buy them in reaching for the status of the stars.

2. *Getting a bargain.* Some buyers simply cannot refuse to take advantage of a bargain. Although their closets are filled with shoes, many of which they seldom wear, they just have to buy a new pair of shoes at the "ridiculous sale price." The feeling of getting a good buy or taking advantage of the seller is a powerful enough motive to stimulate the purchase.

3. *Reducing depression.* Have you ever wondered why so many people crowd into the stores on overcast, rainy, winter weekend days? Psychologists tell us that many people buy to help them overcome boredom and depression. Feeling bad? Go out and buy a new suit. Frank Sinatra once said, "When I feel down, I go buy a half-dozen new suits, and I feel better." If it works for Frank, it might work for us. While the purchase might give us a temporary boost, it is not likely to do anything to help remove the underlying causes of our dreary feelings.

4. *Fear.* We buy some things out of fear. The encyclopedia salesperson tells us that our kids may grow up ignorant if we do not buy the books. Insurance companies appeal to our fear of dying, and manufacturers of hair-care products often take advantage of our fears of being rejected by the opposite sex. Manipulation of the fear of losing our health, being unable to take care of our families, losing our social status, or being rejected is the powerful motive behind much of our buyer behavior.

How Our Culture Influences Buying Decisions

How the buying motives affect us also depends on cultural influences. Cultural influences vary between and within societies. For example, the color green represents coolness and outdoor feelings in the United States, but it connotes sickness and disease in Malaysia. Blue is warm and feminine in Holland but cold and masculine in Sweden.

Social class. We can understand a lot about cultural influences in the United States by looking at characteristics of different social classes. Six class levels have been identified.

1. *Upper-upper class.* Prominent families with third- and fourth-generation wealth compose this class: Blue bloods, professionals, merchants, and financiers abound. They often use their wealth to travel extensively. The upper-upper class represents 1.5% of our population.

2. *Lower-upper class.* This class consists of the new rich: top executives, successful doctors, lawyers, and founders of large businesses who are not yet accepted by the upper-upper class. These people represent 1.5% of our population.

3. *Upper-middle class.* Reasonably successful business and professional people, middle managers, and owners of medium-sized companies are grouped here. They are status-oriented, family conscious, and associate with each other. Ten percent of our population is included in the upper-middle class.

4. *Lower-middle class.* This class consists of white-collar office workers, salespeople, small business owners, and skilled blue-collar workers. This class is conservative, respected, and strives for self-betterment; it represents 33% of our population.

5. *Upper-lower class.* Here are these semiskilled and blue-collar factory workers with reasonably high incomes. They often hold a short-run view of life and their surroundings. Thirty-eight percent of our population resides in this class.

6. *Lower-lower class.* This group encompasses the unskilled, unemployed welfare recipients and slum dwellers who are often apathetic or rebellious. This class comprises 16% of our population.

Class membership in these groups is dictated by education, family background, occupation, and earnings. Their purchasing habits differ. Even in the same income bracket, families in different social classes spend their incomes differently; they are attracted by different products and promotional methods. Pierre Martineau distinguishes ten psychological differences that affect buying patterns between the middle- and lower-class families. These appear in Fig. 12.6.

Reference groups. Each of us has certain reference groups, groups that we relate to because of special interests, that affect our buying decisions. We may identify with groups through our work, hobbies, geographical location, or other means. For instance, the National Rifleman's Association may serve as a reference group for sportspeople who like hunting. The Sierra Club may be an identity for many environmentalists.

Family influences. All of us are influenced, at least to some extent, by our family habits, traditions, and values. Pork may not sell well in traditional Jewish communities, but New York style delicatessens may thrive. The market for alcoholic beverages, because of the influence of Mormon families, is much less than average in Utah. Chinese neighborhoods have unique grocery needs.

In these and other cases, family influences help determine our tastes and buying decisions.

Consumer Decision Model

Analysts have developed **consumer decision models** to help analyze the influences on the buyer. Figure 12.7 is an adaptation of several decision models. Buyers receive information about products through promotion, advertising, sales presentations, and word of mouth.

Driven by aroused motive, consumers select a goal or goals they think will lead to need satisfaction. Then the potential customer usually faces several alternative actions (buying decisions) that can meet the goal. Eventually, one alternative may lead to purchasing a product. If the purchase does indeed satisfy the consumer's needs, this becomes reinforcing feedback. Dissatisfaction, however, is likely to move us backward to the selected goal, and we begin anew our search for alternatives that lead to need satisfaction.

**Figure 12.7
Example of a consumer decision model.**

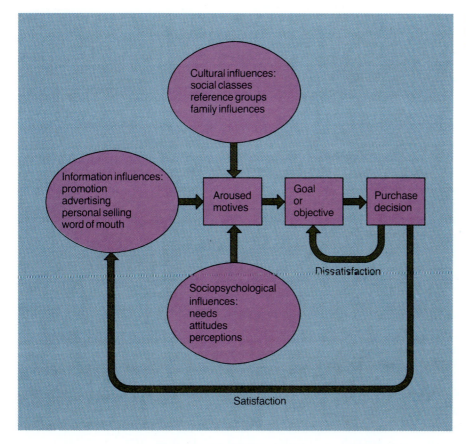

For example, suppose new-car commercials perk your need for status and recognition to the point of arousing a buying motive, and you select for yourself the goal of purchasing a new car. To satisfy your goal, you face many alternatives in price, luxury, size, weight, color, and model. Finally, you decide that a new two-tone blue convertible with a luxury interior, racing stripes, and enlarged tires fits your image of status and recognition. So you sign on the dotted line, which commits you to 36 equal payments. If this action satisfies your needs, you will remember it favorably on your next purchase decision. But if the action leaves you dissatisfied, you will seek additional alternatives, such as a trade-in as soon as you can afford it.

SUMMARY

The real purpose of production is consumption, and marketing engages in eight functions to move goods or services from production to consumers. At the turn of the century, manufacturers stressed production quality, efficiency, and improvement of the production process. Later, as firms found they were building excess inventory, they developed a more aggressive marketing program. Finally, a consumer orientation emerged as the marketing concept: firms find out what customers want and try to deliver it.

At the same time that the marketing concept gained prominence, consumers began demanding more consideration in product planning and distribution. In developing marketing plans, managers consider market segments and mixes. Segmentation divides markets into smaller groupings of people with similar characteristics. Three popular means of market segmentation are geographic location, age, and expenditure patterns. After segmentation, planners identify a specific market target — the specialized characteristics of the consumer group the firm is trying to reach. The total package of variables balanced in a program is called the marketing mix and consists of: (1) product planning, (2) pricing decisions, (3) distribution channels, and (4) promotional strategies. Marketing research is the process of recording and analyzing information about customers' reactions to firms' products and services. The study of buyer behavior identifies both rational and emotional motives for buying, both of which are sub-

ject to cultural influences. Consumer decision models help to explain the interrelatedness of buying variables.

MIND YOUR BUSINESS

Instructions. Answer each of the following questions by writing Y for yes or N for no in the blanks at the left.

____ 1. Are grading and standardizing products and services considered part of the marketing process?

____ 2. Does the marketing concept emphasize the notion of "Take what we produce and sell it"?

____ 3. Are pricing decisions considered part of the marketing mix?

____ 4. Is promotion considered part of the marketing mix?

____ 5. Does market segmentation mean "store products until there is a need for them"?

____ 6. Does marketing research try to find out what customers want that the firm is not providing them?

____ 7. Do people buy for purely rational motives?

____ 8. Does our culture influence our buying decisions?

____ 9. Do lower social classes have different buying habits from higher social classes?

____ 10. Is concern for getting the best price an emotional buying motive?

See answers at the back of the book.

KEY TERMS

marketing, 300
market, 300
utility, 300
place utility, 301
time utility, 301
possession utility, 301
form utility, 301
marketing concept, 302
enlightened marketing, 303

REVIEW QUESTIONS

1. Discuss the eight major functions of the marketing process.

2. What is the marketing concept? What is the opposite of the marketing concept?

3. Briefly describe production-, sales-, and consumer-oriented marketing.

4. What is the marketing mix? Describe the four Ps of marketing.

5. What is involved in choosing a target market? Identify four means of market segmentation. What would be the target market of detergents? Sports cars? Vacation tours?

6. What is the relationship between target markets and market segmentation?

7. What is marketing research? Describe several ways of conducting marketing research.

8. What is consumer behavior? Why is it practiced?

9. Describe rational motives and emotional motives involved in buying a new car.

10. How does culture affect buying decisions? What are the three major cultural influences with regard to purchase decisions?

11. Describe the consumer decision model.

CASES

Case 12.1: The Marketing Process

Martina Cross is director of marketing for a new radio station, KROX. They feature hard rock music exclusively. Their goal is to become the most popular hard rock station within a large, metropolitan area. Having just started her new job, Martina is most concerned with reaching the potential audience.

Questions

1. Which of the basic functions of marketing will be her first and greatest concern?

2. In what ways will the station create utility?

3. Which of the four Ps of the marketing mix will receive the most of Martina's attention at the beginning?

4. Prepare a marketing grid for Martina. Which qualities of the potential audience will she be most interested in? Detail her target market.

5. What motives will the listeners of KROX be using as they decide which radio station to listen to? What cultural influences will be involved?

Case 12.2: The Problem of Customer Wants

Jose Wiley is director of marketing for a small greeting card company. So far, store accounts have gone very well, and they have a proper supply of inventory. However, the company has a serious problem. Stores seem to be running out of some cards, while being overstocked with others. The loss of sales, especially for most big holidays, is hurting both the company and the stores it supplies. Jose needs to solve the problem of providing the stores with a more appropriate selection of greeting cards.

Questions

1. If you were Jose, using only topics presented within the chapter, how would you solve the problem? Propose some cultural influences that may be causing the shortages of the proper cards.

2. How could Jose more fully utilize the marketing concept?

3. Prepare a target market profile for the following occasions: Thanksgiving, Hanukkah, Easter, and graduation.

4. Discuss changes in target market and influences in purchasing decisions for card retail stores located in each of the following: (a) Inner city, (b) Wealthy suburban community, (c) Heavily ethnic neighborhood, and (d) Small rural neighborhood.

After completing this chapter, you will be able to:

■ Describe the steps involved in the strategic marketing process.

■ Explain how market planners go about evaluating the corporate strategic plan and tying their own plan to it.

■ Relate how strategic marketers formulate a target market strategy.

■ Discuss the major types of objectives found in a strategic marketing plan and the characteristics that good objectives must possess.

■ Describe how a position strategy is developed, with primary attention given to the product, price, distribution, and promotion aspects of the strategy.

■ Discuss how implementation and control of this plan is carried out.

B

STRATEGIC

MARKETING

In the late 1970s, high school rings and yearbooks accounted for two-thirds of The Jostens Company's sales. But because of changes in their environment — student population was expected to decline almost 3% annually — the company had to develop a new strategy for dealing with this environment or face declining sales and profits. To counter the trend of their diminishing market, Jostens refocused their marketing effort to appeal to junior high students and to students in the sun belt. They projected sun belt enrollments to remain relatively stable; most of the student decline was in the north. Jostens also advertised more in executive periodicals to reach graduates who might not have purchased a ring when they graduated. And they made an attempt to get into traditional jewelry markets. These were strategic responses to environmental shifts.

Today virtually all large organizations have strategic plans. Many medium-size firms also have them. A strategic plan sets forth long-range objectives that the firm intends to pursue. Typical examples include return on investment, growth, and market share. These objectives help the organization compare its own performance with that of the competition.

The two primary considerations in every strategic plan are marketing and finance.

In contrast to many other types of plans, a strategic plan is external in orientation. It focuses on helping the organization get ahead of the competition. There are two primary considerations in every strategic plan: marketing and finance. Both have one thing in common: the firm lacks total control over them. For example, a company can design the most up-to-date products possible and market them via a vigorous promotion campaign; however, it cannot make people buy the new goods. Likewise, when a firm has to go to the bank to raise money, it can negotiate with the banker; but in the final analysis, it will end up paying the going rate for money. So unlike areas such as production or personnel, where the organization has a great deal of control regarding what to do and when to do it, in marketing and finance the firm is in the position of having to respond to the market.

At the heart of every strategic plan is the marketing area. Even finance is secondary when one stops to consider the fact that banks will lend a firm money if they feel it is a good risk. For this reason, many organizations today spend a great deal of time developing the strategic marketing part of their overall plan. They know that if they are successful in the marketplace, they will be able to attain their desired goals of return on investment, growth, and market share.

The **strategic marketing plan** has six basic steps or phases: (1) evaluation of the corporate strategic plan, (2) analysis of the product-market situation, (3) formulation of a target market strategy, (4) setting objectives, (5) development of a positioning strategy, and (6) the implementation and control of the marketing plan. We will examine each of these six steps in detail.

EVALUATION OF THE CORPORATE STRATEGIC PLAN

Strategic marketing activities must be tied to the organization's overall plan. Thus the process begins with a review of the corporation's strategic plan. In this evaluation, the company's basic mission must be examined. This requires the planners to answer the question: What business is the firm in? Figure B.1 provides a statement of purpose or basic mission for a family-owned regional firm. Notice that the purpose spells out what the company does and where the firm intends to be heading. This statement is very well developed and offers important direction for the marketing plan. Particularly, it focuses on two key marketing-related areas: new business direction and new product development. With information like this,

it is possible for the marketing people to link their plan into that of the strategic plan.

Large firms that have many different divisions and product lines offer even more guidelines than those proffered in Figure B.1. However, too much input can be detrimental to the formulation of a viable strategic marketing plan. For this reason, it is common for marketing people to merely seek out the overall, general direction of the firm and tie their plan to that focus. In this process, the planners will try very hard to stay within the basic expertise of the firm. For example, if we are dealing with IBM, the marketing people will develop a plan that draws on the company's two major strengths: strong research and development and effective service. In the case of Sears Roebuck, the strategic marketing people will develop a plan that concentrates on the firm's ability to offer a wide array of consumer goods at very reasonable prices. Marketing does not lead the strategic plan; it meshes with it.

Consolidated Distributors is a family-owned regional distributor of industrial lubricants and solvents. It prides itself on product knowledge, customer counsel, and promptness in filling orders. Within the Northeast region that it serves, it is recognized and respected as a company that is competitive and will stand behind its products.

The principals recognize that the market served is shrinking—customers are slowly but steadily relocating to the Sunbelt. Remaining customers are not modernizing and are losing their competitive positions. Further, the principals themselves are aging and new family members may or may not wish to pursue the business. The principals note a weakness in their middle management.

The principals are watching closely the development of industrial "robots." While unsure about the extent of their application, they feel that robots will replace at least 40 percent of the workers on production lines by the year 2000. They believe that robots will require special care and a new line of lubricant products.

Based on the company's existing position, and the expectation that the cost of their products will generally go up faster than prices overall (because many of the products are petroleum based), the principals have established the following goals:

1. Expand Consolidated's territory to the Sunbelt states, starting with those areas where old customers have relocated.
2. Seek alternative products that will meet the requirements of existing customers but that are not petroleum-based or contain a minimum quantity of petroleum and, thus, are not totally subject to the turbulence of the petro markets.
3. Study closely the further development of robots and develop a complete product line to serve this growing market.
4. Build middle management by selective hiring, primarily to coincide with expansion into the Sunbelt region.
5. Prepare the company so that it can be taken over either by junior family members or so that it will be attractive as an acquisition by a company with stock traded on the New York or American Stock Exchanges.

Figure B.1
An example of basic mission. *Source: Bruce M. Bradway, Robert E. Pritchard, Mary Anne Frenzel,* Strategic Marketing: A Handbook for Managers, Business Owners & Entrepreneurs, *© 1982, Addison-Wesley, Reading, Massachusetts. P. 4. Reprinted with permission.*

ANALYSIS OF THE PRODUCT-MARKET SITUATION

The first real action step in strategic marketing is the analysis of the situation. In this step, marketing people scan the environment for the purpose of identifying customers and competitors. Customers represent opportunities; competitors represent threats. The firm wants to take advantage of these opportunities but not at the price of costly retaliation by the competition. During this phase, marketing people also draw conclusions regarding the likelihood of customers buying the firm's current and proposed products and the strategies likely to be employed in these markets by the competition.

If a firm makes a serious marketing error, it usually does so as a result of incorrect product-market situation analysis. For example, in 1981, Adam Osborne introduced the first portable personal computer. He was convinced that people would be willing to pay $1800 for a machine that they could take to the office, bring home, and carry on trips. The convenience of having a computer so close at hand, he believed, would be recognized by millions. For the first couple of years, his machine sold well. For example, in 1982, the firm grossed $100 million. Unfortunately, in that same year, the company just managed to break even. Why? Because fifty other firms also were in the personal computer (PC) market and many of them were offering portable PCs that had larger video screens (making it easier to see what was being displayed) and software that was IBM-compatible (meaning that if the firm already had the IBM PC, staff could take the work they did on the road and at home, and throw it into an office computer to finish the job). Osborne overlooked the large number of competitors that would enter the market with better-quality machines. Additionally, the firm seemed to lack a general understanding of how to plan. Confronted with complaints that its screen was too small and the machine was not IBM-compatible, Osborne announced that it would soon be coming out with a machine to correct these problems. Result? Customers who were thinking of buying an Osborne decided to wait and see what the new machine looked like. Cash flow dried up, machines sat col-

lecting dust on dealers' shelves, and the firm filed Chapter 11 bankruptcy in late 1983.

IBM refused to say a word about their PC Jr. before it was released, realizing that if customers believed the PC Jr. was a better buy than their PC, sales of the latter would dry up.

Meanwhile, IBM continued to dominate the market because it did understand the product-market situation. As its PC gained market share, the firm let it be known that it had a smaller version that would sell for less money than the original and would be called the PC Jr. When would this machine hit the market? What would it look like? What would it be able to do? IBM refused to say, realizing that if customers believed the PC Jr. was a better buy than their PC, sales of the latter would dry up until the PC Jr. was released. Instead, IBM kept everyone in the dark. The firm knew better than to follow Osborn's example.

The two specific types of product-market analysis conducted during this phase relate to customers and competitors. Some of the typical questions that the marketing staff attempt to answer in their **customer analysis** of new products include: How many of these units will we sell in a year's time? What is the annual growth of this market likely to be over the next 5 years? What kinds of people are likely to buy this product (income level, education level, geographic region, occupation, etc.)? Where are they likely to want to go to buy it? How much would they be willing to pay for it? Responses to such questions are used to construct a detailed customer analysis.

Key competitor analysis questions focus on the activities, present and projected, of other firms in the market. Some of the most common queries include: How many firms are there in this market and how many more can be expected within the next 2 to 3 years? What share of the market does each of these current competitors now have, and how will this change, given the expected entry (or exit) of additional firms? What is the financial strength of each competitor? What other strengths, crucial to success in this market, do each of the competitors have? What market strategy is each likely to pursue during the next 2 to 3 years in terms of product, price, distribution, and promotion?

Target marketing means deciding which

specific products should be marketed and

what particular groups of people should be

pursued.

These questions give the market planning team the general type of information it needs in order to proceed. Now planners must decide which specific products should be marketed and what particular groups of customers should be pursued. This is done with target marketing.

FORMULATION OF A TARGET MARKET STRATEGY

In formulating a **target market** strategy, planners answer the question: To whom do we want to sell our product(s)? In some cases, although these are rare, the answer is: Just about everyone. For example, to whom does McDonald's want to

---

Tractor Firms Make Strategic Changes

The recession in tractor-making firms has caused them to have to make changes in their planning and way of doing things. In the desolate International Harvester Co.'s tractor plant in Rock Island, plant manager Pete Babcock says, "You could shoot a cannon in here and not harm anyone. Things have got to change."

When the recession began, companies reacted by shutting down plants and laying off people. Now, the industry is making fundamental, strategic changes in the way they are doing things. Some changes include:

1. *Offering few models rather than many models.* Typically, manufacturers have offered the widest possible array of tractors, combines, planters, and plows. Now, most companies are sharply reducing their product lines and specializing in fewer models and fewer products. Allis-Chalmers has dropped some of its plows, farm implements, and one of its larger tractor models. Instead, the company is focusing on its smaller, more profitable machines. Massey, likewise, has abandoned its top-line tractor.

2. *Considering joint ventures.* Some firms are considering entering into joint ventures to compete in the marketplace. John Deere Co. has such a commanding lead in the market now that competitors may join ranks in joint venture programs to compete with Deere.

3. *Relying on outside suppliers.* Increasingly, firms are buying their parts and supplies from outside suppliers. Harvester, for example, tries to take advantage of the well-known Harvester name by buying Avco implements and marketing them under the red paint and I-H symbol of the Harvester company.

Source: "Tractor Firms Are Changing Old Practices," *The Wall Street Journal*, Oct. 28, 1983, p. 31.

sell hamburgers? Their potential market is just about everybody from 6-year-old kids to teen-agers to adults. On the other hand, most firms do not have products that appeal to everyone. Consider automobiles. To whom does General Motors want to sell a Cadillac? Realistically, the market is people who are looking for status, want a good quality car, and can afford to pay more than the average buyer. Chevrolet comes closer to McDonald's strategy than does Cadillac, although it too realizes that not everyone will be interested in buying its car. At the other extreme is Rolls Royce, which targets itself toward a very narrow, exclusive segment of the auto market. While the quality and reliability of the car is very high, so is the price. So what we have here are three different cars that attempt to capture specific niches in the overall automobile market.

Most target strategies are similar to our auto example; they focus on a limited market niche. Consider the PC market. There are a number of different niches here. One is for business PCs that have bubble memory and color graphics. The cost of these machines can range up toward $10,000. Companies that need a good, efficient, rugged PC are attracted to this type of machine. The average executive or homeowner does not need anything this sophisticated. The IBM PC, Apple II, and simi-lar machines suffice. Then there are the very limited home computers that offer word processing and some calculation power. These typically cost $1000 or less and are particularly attractive to families who want computers that can be used by their children for educational assignments or can help them balance their budgets or do financial forecasts. Commodore and Coleco offer products for this market niche. Finally, there are the portable PCs that are so useful to executives who want to conduct financial analysis or write memos or reports while away from the office. Depending on the desired size of the machine (the smaller ones cost more), there are a number of competitors in this market niche including Compaq, Corona, Gavilan, and Zorba.

Unfortunately, it is not very easy to identify specific niches in these markets because there is a great deal of blurring caused by machines that offer characteristics desired by customers in more than one niche. For example, the Compaq portable is really not so much a portable as it is a comportable, meaning that it can be moved from place to place but it is fairly bulky. On the other hand, Compaq is IBM-compatible and many firms like it better than the IBM. Its price is also less than that of the IBM PC. So while its original niche was in the portable computer market, it has also invaded the

BUSINESS BULLETIN

Find a Market Niche

Rather than trying to conquer the world with marketing, it is better to find a small niche and then branch out. As entrepreneurship professor Frederick Wiersema says, ''Pick your area. Than try to preempt others from coming in. Once you have control, you can branch out.''

The software firm Finreport Systems Inc. did just that. Massachusetts has 110 general acute care hospitals. The president of Finreport was a former assistant controller of a large Massachusetts hospital. He believed that existing software was aimed at a more widespread market, so he set out to develop file programs, management programs, and a programming language just for these 110 hospitals. Because his product fit the niche so uniquely, he got 90% of the market, which totals $3 to $4 million annually. Now, Finreport is branching out into New York to attempt the same thing.

Source: ''Gaining Market Share,'' Venture, Aug., 1983, pp. 81–84.

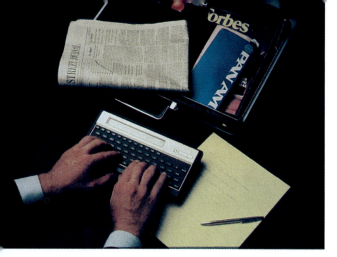

By offering both self-sufficiency and the capability of interacting with larger systems, portable computers appeal to customers in several market niches.

desk-top market. On the other end of the portable market niche are lightweight, liquid crystal, calculator/typewriters that offer the user many of the same features as do portable PCs. They can be used to write memos and make financial calculations. They have memory capacity and, when hooked up to a printer, can provide a copy of the material that has been put into memory. They do have limited capabilities and are currently fairly expensive ($700 to $1000), but they can fit easily into a small attache case and operate off batteries so executives can even use them while on a plane or in a taxi. As their prices come down and their capabilities increase, we are likely to see some of the demand for portable PCs being taken away by these smaller, lighter machines, especially among those who want the machines for word processing only.

SETTING OBJECTIVES

Market objectives are goals toward which the strategic plan is geared. Large firms today place **return on investment (ROI)** (profits/assets) very high on this list and with good reason. By measuring the amount of profit they are able to achieve with the assets they have committed to this product line, they are able to judge their effectiveness in the marketplace. After all, even though a large firm makes $10 million from one of its product

lines, this may not be a very significant accomplishment; we need to know how much money they put into plant, equipment, marketing effort, etc., in order to judge their overall success. This is one of the primary reasons why ROI is so important to these firms. A second reason is that the computation allows the firm to compare its effectiveness with that of other major competitors quickly. Rather than looking at profit, the company can compare ROI. Small firms, on the other hand, tend to be much more interested in profit as a strategic objective. They know that if they compete with larger firms, they will have to offer lower prices or extra service. So they cannot hope to match the giants in terms of ROI.

Market share is another major objective of many strategic marketing plans. Consider the big TV networks: ABC, NBC, and CBS. Every week, the Nielsen ratings indicate which shows were the most popular and which did not do well. Based on these ratings, the networks renew or cancel their offerings. Market share is important on a week-to-week basis in this industry. Another group that pays close attention to market share is the automobile industry. Every week, the number of cars sold by the big four American producers (General Motors, Ford, Chrysler, and American Motors) is reported in the financial press. Executives at these firms closely monitor how well their companies are doing against the competition.

Protecting your market share is often harder than building a market.

Protecting market share is often harder than building a market. If a company has a good idea and a unique product or service, they might start with 100% of the market. But when others see the company's results, successful competitors will move in.

Firms try to preserve their market shares in a variety of ways, including:

- Creating a unique character for the company.
- Advertising to build a specific image.
- Creating and holding onto customer representative (dealer) networks.

- Protecting the product's or service's distinctiveness by going to court if necessary.

Growth is a third major objective. Every strategic marketing plan is designed to help product lines grow (or at least stop them from shrinking). Naturally, since products go through life cycles, there comes a time when growth stabilizes and then begins to decline. This is when new product offerings are brought on to the market and promoted as substitutes. At the same time, the marketing plan encourages those who are buying the old product to continue doing so. Since this latter strategy is often only a holding action, it is common to find businesses reducing the amount of promotion they are putting behind their fading product lines and attempting to milk as much profit from them as possible. These products have become "cash cows" and as long as they remain, the marketing strategy will be one of minimum promotional expenditures and maximum ROI.

ROI, market share, and growth are the three most common strategic marketing objectives.

While ROI, market share, and growth are the three most common strategic marketing objectives, there are others ranging from promotion

CROSS FIRE

Tracking Strategic Changes at CBS

CBS, by comparison to ABC and NBC, has earned unimpressive profits in recent years. And they have made two strategic changes to try to better themselves.

In mid-1982, CBS economists told their market planners that the recession would soon be over. Thus, the network wanted to sell fewer commercials up front, that is, before the fall season began. They wanted to hold off and sell commercials later — scatter sales, as they are called — hoping to get higher prices. However, scatter sales went soft and CBS had lots of prime time on its hands with few commercials to cover them; this ploy cost them about $50 million in revenues. This year, CBS went strong for the up-front market.

CBS also had a policy of demographic guarantees. That is, they would guarantee their client that certain programs would deliver viewers with specified demographic characteristics — say women between the ages of 18 and 49. If the viewers did not fit these characteristics, CBS would offer clients free commercials, called "make-goods," to get the desired number of viewers. CBS has offered such guarantees for several years, but the network's previously stable demographics suddenly turned widely unstable. And although many of their programs rated well, they could not predict the demographics of the audience very well. So they had to offer a lot of make-goods. Last year, they changed their policy, but clients were soon hollering, so hooked were they on the guarantees. Today, CBS is again offering their clients demographic guarantees.

Do you think the effort to sell more up-front commercial time will prove to be a good idea for CBS? Why?

___ Yes   ___ No

Do you think the change back to demographic guarantees was a sound decision? Why?

___ Yes   ___ No

efforts to sales force activities. Yet all objectives will have five common characteristics:

1. They help the organization achieve effective overall results.

2. Each is consistent with the other objectives being pursued.

3. Each provides a clear guide to accomplishment; progress can be measured clearly.

4. Each is realistic; it can be accomplished within the time, cost, quality, and quantity parameters assigned.

5. The individuals responsible for each objective know their tasks, and if there is joint responsibility, this is spelled out clearly.

Multiple brands manufactured by a single firm allow growth through different market segments.

DEVELOPMENT OF A POSITIONING STRATEGY

A **positioning strategy** fine tunes the marketing plan. At this point, the planners determine how product, price, distribution, and promotion strategies can be combined to market the company's goods and services effectively.

Product Strategy

Product strategy is the core of strategic planning for the organization. This strategy plays the central role in shaping the company's marketing effort. One group of authors explained its significance by noting that:

> In the 1980s, one of the most important "Ps" in the marketing mix could well be positioning. For most packaged goods—and for many other products and services as well—positioning (product, service, or corporate stance) will probably be more critical to success than product, pricing, promotion, packaging, place, or any other element in the marketing mix. You can make many mistakes in other areas and survive, if your position is right. For many products and services, if it's wrong, nothing on earth will assure success for your product or service.*

In its product strategy, the firm decides what it will offer to the customers. This decision will cut

---

* Bruce M. Bradway, Robert E. Pritchard, Mary Anne Frenzel, *Strategic Marketing: A Handbook for Managers, Business Owners & Entrepreneurs*, © 1982, Addison-Wesley, Reading, Massachusetts. P. 41. Reprinted by permission.

across every functional area of operations: distribution, advertising, pricing, sales force activities, etc. The firm's objective is to place a brand in that part of the market where it will have the most favorable reception vis à vis the competition. (See Chapter 13 for additional information on brands.)

There are a number of reasons why firms introduce multiple brands. One of the most common is to offset competitive threats to their single brand. A second reason is to seek growth through different market segments. When a firm offers something that is similar to its present product, to some degree it cannibalizes on this product line. For example, if a company selling 1 million digital watches a year comes out with a liquid crystal watch, some of those who would have bought their digital may now buy their liquid crystal offering. Is the new product line a wise decision? The answer may well be yes because those who were attracted to the liquid crystal may well have bought a similar watch from the competition. Multiple brand strategy is a little like flooding the zone in football. By sending two or more pass receivers into the same area, the quarterback hopes that if one of them is too well guarded by the defense, the other(s) will be open for the catch.

Sometimes a product needs to be repositioned. This is particularly true when a competitor has entered the market, positioned its product next to the firm's, and begun to erode the latter's market share. What else can the firm do but move to another market niche? Another reason for repositioning is when consumer preferences have undergone a change and the firm needs to alter its product niche to keep up with the customers. A third reason is when new customer preference clusters with promising opportunities have been discovered, and the firm wants to take advantage of this newly discovered market. One of the most interesting examples is provided by General Foods, which repositioned Jell-O by promoting it as a base for salads. A similar strategy was used by the 3M Company when it introduced a new line of colored, invisible, waterproof, and write-on Scotch tapes that could be used for gift wrapping. A third example is provided by the orange juice industry that used to advertise its product as an excellent breakfast drink but has now adopted the jingle, "Orange Juice — it's not just for breakfast anymore." This ad campaign has been particularly successful in getting people to drink more orange juice. In other cases, firms have attempted to reposition their product for new users. For example, Miller Beer's promotional campaign built around the slogan "If you've got the time, we've got the beer" was tremendously successful in attracting new customers to their product. Finally, there are times when a company will want to reposition its product for new uses. Nylon is an excellent illustration. When DuPont first introduced the product, it was used to make parachutes. Then

---

If new uses had not been found for nylon, it would have disappeared from the market years ago.

---

it was used for varied types of hosiery such as stretch stockings and stretch socks. Today, it is used in tires, textured yarns, and carpeting. If new uses had not been found for nylon, it would have disappeared from the market years ago. Thanks to research and development and repositioning strategies, it has remained with us for decades.

Price Strategy

Price strategies vary, depending on whether or not the product is new. New product pricing strategies tend to be of two types: skimming or penetration. As you will learn in Chapter 13, **skimming pricing** is a strategy of establishing a high initial price for a product, with the intent of "skimming the cream" off this segment of the market. Quite often, a new product that has required a lot of research and development or will soon encounter strong competition will be introduced with a skimming strategy. One of the best examples has been video game cassettes. When these cassettes first hit the market, it was not uncommon to pay $20 to $60 for them. However, as other firms began to offer games and the market started to soften, the manufacturers realized that they could not keep their prices high. Strong competition, coupled with limited market demand, dictated lower prices.

Penetration pricing is the strategy of entering a market with a low initial price so as to capture as large a share of the market as possible. There are two typical reasons for this approach. One is to discourage competition. The other is that customers will be indifferent or negative toward the product if it is offered at a high price. One of the most recent examples is Coleco's Adam, a home computer. Originally offered at $700, including a printer, the company's objective was to deeply penetrate the home computer market.

Established product pricing follows a different approach. The most common approaches are to maintain price, reduce price, or increase price. Firms that maintain price tend to have strong buyer loyalty. For example, in very few cases does IBM discount its products to the general public. If you want an IBM, you have to pay the established price.

Distribution Strategy

Distribution strategies are concerned with the channels employed in making goods and services available to customers. (Chapter 14 covers channels in more detail.) The most common types of distribution are exclusive, selective, and intensive. Exclusive distribution means that one particular retailer in a given area is granted the right to carry the product. It is not uncommon to find Hart, Schaffner & Marx suits distributed through only one store in a town. Manufacturers looking to have their goods distributed through national chains often agree to give exclusive rights to just one chain in return for the latter's promise to vigorously market the product.

An intensive distribution strategy makes a product available at as many outlets as possible. Convenience goods are often marketed this way. If a retailer is willing to carry them, the manufacturer is prepared to use outlets. Consider all the items you see near the supermarket checkout counter, from razor blades to magazines. These are all marketed via an intensive distribution strategy.

Selective distribution is a strategy in which some, but not all, outlets in a locale are given the right to distribute the product. The best example is found in the marketing of shopping goods like refrigerators, ovens, ranges, and TVs. Retailers do not want to carry a product that can be purchased at every other competitor; they want some degree of exclusivity. So it is common to find manufacturers limiting their choice of outlets. Additionally, some manufacturers do not want just any retailer selling their product line. They may want to rely only on salespeople who know or are specifically trained in their product's features. When Head skis first hit the market, the company would market only through select stores and insisted that only skiers be allowed to sell the product.

We have explained the way in which a great many distribution strategies are carried out. However, there are other combination approaches. Most of these fit under the heading of multiple-channel strategies, which refer to situations in which two or more different channels are employed for the distribution of goods or services. The most common example of a multiple-channel strategy is the complementary channel. Complementary channels exist when each channel handles a different noncompeting product or non-competing marketing segment. For example, except for some cosmetic changes, American Tourister sells the same type of luggage to discount stores that it sells to retailers.

Promotion Strategy

Promotion strategies are used to inform customers about product offerings or persuade them to purchase the goods or services. (See Chapter 15 for information on promotion.) There are three basic types of promotion strategies: advertising, personal selling, and sales promotion. Advertising strategies are geared toward choosing the most effective media for conveying the message(s) and writing the most effective advertising copy. Countless rules and guidelines can be cited regarding how to carry out these strategies. Those drawing up the strategic marketing plan will know which are of most value to the organization and implement them accordingly. Personal selling strategies are designed to ensure the greatest amount of efficiency and effectiveness from the sales force. All other forms of promotion, including demonstrations, contests, sampling, cents off, etc., are collectively known as sales promotion strategies.

IMPLEMENTATION AND CONTROL OF THE PLAN

The last step in the strategic marketing process is implementing and controlling the plan. Whenever something goes wrong, it is usually because some part of the plan was incorrect. Perhaps the competition came out with a new and unexpected product. Or the company raised its prices but no one else followed. Or thanks to superior research and development, competitors were able to reduce their costs and consequently their selling prices dramatically.

The firm must continually assess how well it is doing and be prepared to take necessary correc-

Effective strategic marketing plans require constant input and assessment from the sales and marketing staff.

A Successful Strategy for Gerber

Gerber's share of the baby food market has grown to an all-time high of 71%. They did it by "selling more to the same mothers." Gerber has long dominated the baby food market (they had a 69% share in 1978), but the declining birth rate made it hard for them to continue growing.

Gerber tried to improve its sales by venturing into other markets. They tried to market adult foods, but they failed. They even dipped into investing in mail-order insurance and day-care centers, but these were at best modest successes. Then they decided to go back to what they knew best, selling baby foods and related products to mothers. In 1983, their profits totaled $39 million, up 63% from 1978.

Gerber's planners do not expect their 71% share to increase very much, but they think the market will expand at about 3% a year as babies eat more prepared foods. In 1976, the average baby ate twenty-seven cases of baby food before going on solids. This eventually dropped to twenty-two cases as mothers used more infant formulas and prolonged breast feeding. Now, planners believe that the market will expand slowly, and Gerber hopes to sell a little more each year to a few more mothers.

Source: "Gerber: Concentrating on Babies Again for Slow Steady Growth," *Business Week,* Aug. 22, 1983.

Perhaps the most important thing to keep in mind is that few plans work as intended; without fine tuning, desired ROI, market share, and growth are usually not possible.

tive action. Perhaps the most important thing to keep in mind is that few plans work as intended. Even the most successful plan must be changed in some way. Without this fine tuning, desired ROI, market share, and growth are usually not possible. Additionally, since most markets are in a state of flux, strategic marketing efforts must be periodically evaluated. The longer the plan's time horizon, the more likely it is that things will not work out as anticipated. Yet this need not be fatal to the firm's effort, just as long as it is willing to revise its plans and adjust to these external conditions. Successful strategic marketing is less a matter of willingness to plan as it is a matter of willingness to change.

SUMMARY

Strategic marketing is a six-step process. Its purpose is to help the organization achieve desired ROI, capture market share, and attain growth. The first step in this process is an evaluation of the corporate strategic plan. The reason for this evaluation is to ensure that the strategic marketing plan is properly linked to the overall efforts of the organization.

The second step is an analysis of the product-market situation. At this point, marketing people scan the environment for the purpose of identifying customers and competitors. Some of the most important questions that are raised at this point include: What do people want from our product? Who is likely to buy it? What forms of competition will we encounter both now and over the next 3 to 5 years?

The third step in this process is the formulation of a target market strategy. At this point, the objective is to identify the desired market niche. Specifically, the company wants to know as much as it can learn about the customer: How much does the individual earn? Where does the person live? What is the individual's background? Where does the person go to buy the company's product? How much is the individual willing to pay? Answers to these types of questions help the company clearly pinpoint its target group.

The fourth step in this process is setting objectives. The three most common strategic marketing objectives relate to ROI, market share, and growth. These objectives also have common characteristics, including helping the organization to achieve effective overall results, being consistent with each other, providing a clear guide to accomplishment, and being realistic.

The fifth step in this process is the development of a positioning strategy. The purpose of this step is to fine tune the marketing plan. This is when the planners determine how product, price, distribution, and promotion strategies can be combined so as to market the company's goods and services effectively. Each of these four is developed in sufficient detail to ensure effective implementation of the plan.

The sixth and last step in the strategic marketing process is the implementation and control of the plan. Quite often, something in the plan goes wrong. Even under the best conditions, plans need fine tuning. The most important thing for the management to remember is that a willingness to change direction and alter the plan is often the factor that turns failure into success.

MIND YOUR BUSINESS

Instructions. Check your knowledge of strategic marketing by designating the following statements as true (T) or false (F).

___ 1. The two primary considerations for strategic planning are marketing and finance.

___ 2. The organization's overall plan must be tied to its strategic marketing plan.

___ 3. The product-market analysis focuses on internal production capabilities.

___ 4. It is often hard to identify specific market niches of products or services.

___ 5. Return on investment is an example of a marketing objective.

___ 6. Price strategy is the core strategy for planning for the organization.

___ 7. Companies introduce multiple brands to counter competitive threats and to seek growth in different market segments.

___ 8. When a competitor enters the market and erodes market share, it may be necessary to reposition the product.

___ 9. Pricing strategies are usually different for new and established products.

___ 10. Distribution strategies are concerned with getting the product promoted in the right physical locations.

See answers at the back of the book.

KEY TERMS

strategic marketing plan, 320
customer analysis, 322
key competitor analysis, 322
target market, 323
market objectives, 325
return on investment (ROI), 325
positioning strategy, 327
product strategy, 327
price strategy, 328
skimming pricing, 328
penetration pricing, 328
distribution strategy, 328
promotion strategy, 329

REVIEW QUESTIONS

1. Strategic marketing activities must be tied to the organization's overall plan. What does this statement mean?

2. What is a statement of purpose or a basic mission? What does it contain? What is its relevance to strategic marketing?

3. In conducting a customer analysis, what types of questions are commonly asked? What does the organization hope to learn from the answers?

4. In conducting a key competitor analysis, what types of questions are commonly asked? What

does the organization hope to learn from the answers?

5. When formulating a target market, what specific types of questions does the market planner hope to answer? Identify two and discuss each.

6. In a strategic marketing plan, what are three of the most common objectives? Identify and describe each.

7. What are some common characteristics possessed by all good objectives? Identify and describe four.

8. What is the objective of the market planner when developing a position strategy? Explain.

9. How do each of the following help the market planner develop a positioning strategy: product strategy, price strategy, distribution strategy, promotion strategy?

10. When would a company be likely to use a skimming pricing strategy? A penetration pricing strategy? When would it be likely to price above the average market price? With the average? Below the average? Give an example of each of your answers.

11. What is the most important thing a company should keep in mind regarding control of the marketing plan? Be complete in your answer.

CASES

Case B.1: Gil's Challenge

Until recently, Gil McCarthy was in charge of the East Coast marketing division for a large computer firm. Gil was highly regarded as a marketing expert, and much of the company's success has been attributed to his advertising and sales promotion ideas.

Last month Gil was offered a job by a home computer manufacturing firm. This company is located in California and in the process of developing a computer that appeals to children and family members. The machine will do word processing, mathematical calculations, and spread sheets. The company is also developing educational material for use with the machine. Current plans call for programs to help people read faster, spell better,

and learn basic high school and college courses such as math, physics, and chemistry. The firm hopes to bypass the competitive market niche being dominated by the IBM PC and Apple II and go head-to-head with Coleco's Adam. Initial estimates by the firm reveal that there are approximately 15 million homes in this market niche. At an average price of $500, this translates to $9 billion just for the hardware. Software packages are expected to sell for about $25 each.

Gil has decided to accept the new offer to become head of the company's entire marketing division. His first job will be to develop an effective strategic marketing plan to get the new product off the ground. The president of the firm has indicated that he would like to see the company capture 4% of this market within the first year and 18% within the first 3 years. Although Gil has not made any promises to the president, he believes that these market share estimates are indeed realistic.

Questions

1. In your own words, what does a strategic marketing plan involve? Provide a thumbnail sketch.

2. What specific analysis will Gil have to conduct in making an evaluation of the product-market situation? Be complete in your answer.

3. What recommendations would you give to Gil regarding implementing and controlling the plan? Be as realistic as possible.

Base B.2: A New Way to Travel

The Claiborne Company's research and development department recently patented a new process that can be used in making a long-lasting auto tire. This tire, if production estimates are correct, can be manufactured for less than $35 and will have a life span of between 45,000 and 50,000 miles. Although Claiborne is best known for its consumer products, the firm believes that this new product is too important to sell to another company. The firm wants to develop and sell these new tires personally.

Last week there was a meeting of top management staff in the boardroom. During the meeting, the head of R&D gave a brief report on the proposed tire. There were a half dozen samples for the managers to look at. There were also four tires that had been road-tested. "It took us two months, but we drove a car up and down the state, changing drivers every four hours," reported the head of R&D, "We put 1000 miles a day on this car for almost 50 days. When we got to 47,477 miles, we decided to stop. The right rear tire was too worn to continue. The other three, however, could probably have gone another 1500 to 3500 miles, depending on road conditions."

The management staff all believe that Claiborne will make a great deal of money if it develops this tire. The biggest challenge will be convincing the public that this tire is better than anything else on the market. This will require a very effective marketing plan.

The head of marketing, Janice Ramirez, believes that the company's product is so superior to anything on the road that it will literally sell itself. "We've already conducted preliminary analysis on the product quality and marketing approaches of Goodrich, Goodyear, and the other top tire manufacturers," she told the group, "and there is no reason why we can't bring out this tire and dominate the market. It's all a matter of effective marketing. We've never tried selling a product of this nature before, but we do know what strategic marketing is all about. On that score, we have a lot of experience. I'm really looking forward to promoting and selling this tire."

The chairman of the board was delighted with her comments. "We've allocated $20 million to developing a strategic marketing plan and introducing the tire to the general public," he told her. "You've got 90 days to get everything going. Let's see your stuff."

As they left the boardroom, Janice was all smiles. "I can't wait to see the competition's faces when we make our first announcement," she told her assistant.

Questions

1. How should the company go about formulating a target market strategy? Explain.

2. In what way will Janice use product, price, distribution, and promotion to develop a position strategy? Be complete in your answer.

3. What is the biggest threat that Janice's company has to look out for? Explain.

After completing this chapter, you will be able to:

■ **Define a product.**

■ **Classify products into consumer and industrial goods.**

■ **Identify seven levels in the product hierarchy.**

■ **Describe four stages of the product life cycle.**

■ **Identify six steps in new-product development.**

■ **Explain the functions of product brands, packaging, and labeling.**

■ **Explain alternative pricing policies for new products.**

■ **Describe product pricing strategies.**

13

PRODUCT
PLANNING AND
PRICING

Remember TV dinners? Most customers have quit buying these low-quality, frozen dinners in tin trays. But consumers still spend $1.6 billion a year for frozen entrees, purchased primarily in supermarkets. Frozen food giants dominate this highly competitive market, the major brands being Nestle's Stouffer, Pillsbury's Green Giant, and Campbell's Swanson and Mrs. Paul's Kitchens.

How does a smaller company like Van de Kamp compete in product and pricing with these larger firms? President Steven H. Porkress, in the 1970s, believing that most frozen fish dinners were undistinguished, introduced a high-quality, light-tasting line of batter-fried fish. Today, they hold 16% of this market. A competitor said, "Van de Kamp's was smart. They spotted a category that had a history of quality problems and filled a void."

In the 1980s, Porkress decided to introduce another higher-quality and higher-priced line of frozen dinners — Mexican Classics. Later, the company added Chinese Classics and Italian Classics. To compete with the giants, the company is offering better meats, spicier foods, and unusual flavors. They are also charging higher prices. Van de Kamp management believes that these high-quality ethnic frozen foods, even though they are higher priced, will be the right recipe for success in this crowded market.

Product planning and product pricing are two critical management decisions. How do companies decide what products or services customers want? And how do they price their product or service? This chapter addresses how managers make these decisions.

PRODUCT PLANNING

Decisions about products depend on many factors, including: What do customers want? What do owners like to make? How much money is available? Do we have the technology? Do employees have the skills? How creative is the company? This section classifies different types of products, examines the product life cycle, describes the steps in new product development, reports methods of product identification, and discusses the importance of product differentiation.

What Is a Product?

Your first thought might be, "Why waste time with the definition of a product?" We know what they are: cameras, airplanes, shoes, candies, breakfast cereals, watches, pianos, electric shavers, rakes, and helium-filled balloons. You might even add sophistication to your answer and say that services are also products: razor haircuts, shoe shines, auto repairs, counseling, legal advice, and medical checkups. But these products and services exist beyond their physical characteristics. A hand-painted tie is certainly more than a neck napkin, platform shoes do more than cover feet, movies provide more than celluloid experiences, and cars are surely more than mere transportation. Thus, marketers identify three aspects of a product. The **tangible product** is the physical item or visible service a company offers to a buyer. You can touch fine underwear, smell freshly ground coffee, and taste juicy steak, to name a few examples. The **extended product** is a broader conception that includes packaging, services, financing arrangements, delivery alternatives, branding, labeling, and other things that customers value. The **generic product** comprises the intangible social and mental benefits that satisfy needs beyond the product's tangible functions. Perfumes are sex appeal, razor cuts are uptown, and steaks are status food.

Product Classifications

We can group products from chocolate-coated crickets to Smith and Wesson pistols into different classifications, according to consumer attitudes toward them. Since the products have varied features and appeal, special strategies are necessary for selling each. The two major groupings are consumer and industrial goods.

Consumer goods. Items purchased by the ultimate buyer are called **consumer goods.** We classify goods according to consumer buying habits into convenience, shopping, and specialty categories. **Convenience goods** are purchased quickly and often with minimal effort. Examples are magazines, milk, beer, cigarettes, candy, and most other items near checkout counters or in vending machines. Because they are inexpensive, conveniently located, often duplicated, and often bought on impulse, companies try to establish brand loyalties for convenience goods. **Shopping goods,** in contrast, generate much effort in comparing prices, quality, style, design, and service. Shopping goods include dresses, suits, shoes, and furniture. Buyers seek more product information because cost is greater. They meticulously go from store to store, noting prices, quality, and services. Shopping goods usually locate centrally because traveling a long distance deters shoppers. Brands are influential, certainly more so than they are for convenience goods; physical attributes of pricing and styling receive more attention. For **specialty goods,** the consumer knows exactly what he or she wants and makes every effort to find it. Examples are expensive cameras, shotguns, art objects, and some brands of clothing. The consumer acquires exhaustive information about the product and may travel miles to make a purchase. There are fewer retail outlets for higher-priced, brand-designated specialty goods. But price, effort, and shopping distance are secondary to distinguishing characteristics and particular brand preferences.

All products do not fit neatly into one of these three categories. What is a shopping good for one person might be a specialty good for another. Many items fit somewhere in between. Some buyers scrutinize all twelve eggs in a dozen, while others pick up the front carton.

Industrial goods. **Industrial goods** are items that companies purchase to make something else, which they will then sell. Unlike consumer goods, we classify industrial goods on the basis of use rather than buying habits. Raw materials include farm and natural products such as wheat, corn, cotton, lumber, silver, and coal. These become part of final products. Supplies are necessary for daily operations, but they do not become part of the finished product. Supplies include paper, typewriter ribbons, light bulbs, lubrication oil, brooms, and pencil sharpeners. Installations cover capital equipment that is instrumental in producing the final product, such as machinery, trucks, and production lines. Fabricated parts are partial or complete items that become part of the final product. Flour for cake mix, tires for automobiles, and leather for shoes are end products for some firms; for others these items are used to make the final product.

Convenience goods are purchased quickly, almost impulsively; offering such goods with other quick services is one outlet.

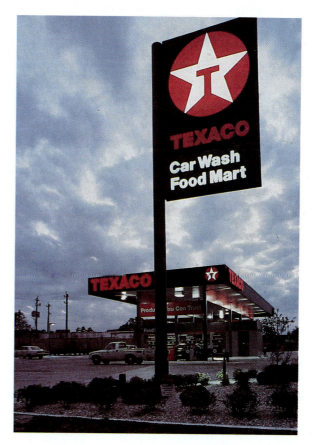

Product Hierarchy

Each product or service can also be related in hierarchical fashion to many other products. Professor Philip Kotler, in his *Marketing Management* text, identifies seven levels of the **product hierarchy.** Definitions and illustrations of this hierarchy are as follows:

1. *Item.* The distinct unit, product, or service that we can identify by size, shape, color, etc.: a personal computer.

2. *Brand.* The name that we associate with items in this line of products: IBM, Apple, Commodore.

3. *Product type.* The range of items that share similar characteristics: personal computers.

4. *Product line.* A group of products that are closely related and serve similar functions: microprocessors.

5. *Product class.* A larger group of products that serve the same basic functions: computers.

6. *Product family.* All the product families that tend to perform similar functions: information processing equipment.

7. *Need family.* The core needs that this line of product appeals to: efficiency, status, fulfillment.

Product Life Cycle

Like physical organisms, products pass through several distinct life stages, each of which produces unique problems and opportunities, calling for special strategies. Figure 13.1 depicts a **product life cycle,** the total sales from a product over a period of time. Both sales and profits move along a growth pattern of early struggle, rapid growth, stabilization, and decline. Of course, all products

**Figure 13.1
Characteristics of each stage of the product life cycle.**

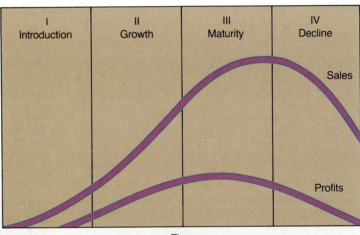

Characteristic	Stage I	Stage II	Stage III	Stage IV
Sales	Low	Rising fast	Level	Declining
Promotional costs	High	Rising	Stable	Minimum
Profits	Lowest	Average	Too high peaks and declines	Average or below average
Cash	Starved	Hungry	Rich	Fair
Price	High	Declining	Lower and stable	Low, but may rise

do not follow this precise movement and some will continue to recycle through the steps, but it is a good model for developing marketing strategies.

Introduction. During its introduction, the product is new to the public, and sales falter while the company loses money. Customers have established purchasing habits and do not quickly change. The company meanwhile takes time to gear up to production capacity and devise distribution channels. Since the public is unfamiliar with the product, promotional expenditures are often very high. The company has to indicate the market with information to potential consumers and middlemen on product benefits. Prices are also high because of heavy development costs; sales overhead has to be spread over few products; production bugaboos mysteriously appear; and high promotion costs have to be borne. When Texas Instruments brought out their first hand-held calculator, prices were very high, running more than $100 for many models. Losses are common during the introduction period while the company gambles that its product will eventually be accepted. Mead Corporation spent more than $27 million over 6 years on its computerized information service, Lexis (which provides legal information), before finally making money in 1977. Three years later, Mead introduced Nexis (which provides general news) and expected it to be profitable by 1984.

Growth. If the product is accepted, it usually enters a rapid growth stage. Persuaded by advertising, word of mouth, and acceptance by opinion leaders, many individuals give the product a try. Because of greater sales, promotion costs per product sold become much less significant. Prices remain high in the beginning of the growth stage to recoup heavy introduction losses. During later growth, prices decline to fend off competitors who enter the field in a mad rush. Improvements are usually developed, and the firm vigorously penetrates its market targets. Because profits are rising, it is to the firm's advantage to prolong the growth period as much as possible.

The personal computer industry was in a growth stage during the early 1980s. IBM, Apple, and Radio Shack were holding strong; but many

Like most products in the introduction stage, Mead Data Central's Nexis, which provides computerized access to these publications, required time and extensive investment to establish itself as a profitable venture.

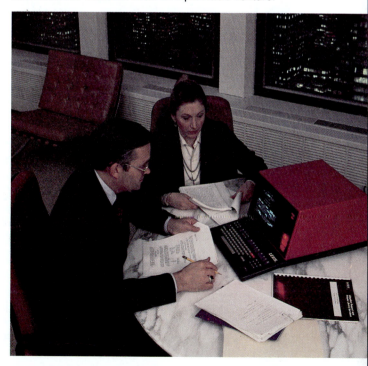

new competitors — Compaq Computer, Kaypro, Convergent Technologies — were flailing away at the market with differing strategies. Some old standbys like Osborne Computer bit the dust. Companies spent millions, $500 million in 1983 alone, on advertising and promotion. And prices began dropping as much as 20 to 40%, as specials and advertised sales became more widespread.

Maturity. Growth rates stabilize and eventually decline during maturity. Competition is intense, and pressure to reduce prices persuades some producers to get out. The maturity stage usually lasts longer than the introduction or growth stages. Customer loyalty to certain brands be-comes well established, and sales are limited to repeat purchases by satisfied customers. Most competitors, fearing counteractions, spend about the same amount on promotions. They search for new messages, catchy phrases, and bright per-sonalities. American Home Products Corporation is trying to establish a bond between some of its products and the persons advertising them. In 1983, it hired actress Patricia Neal to promote its well-known Anacin. The company believes that Neal, who recovered from a series of strokes, is associated with fighting pain. Another product, newer and not so well known, is Youth Garde, a beauty lotion. For good reason, American Home has hired actress Catherine Deneuve to promote this lotion.

TAKING STOCK

Time for NutraSweet

Aspartame is a natural sweetener that the Food and Drug Administration has recently approved for inclusion in consumer products. Although at $90 a pound, it costs thirty times as much as saccharine, it has the potential for taking much of saccharine's market share because the FDA still considers saccharine a potential health hazard. What's more, consumers, if not disturbed by the threat of saccharine's possibly causing cancer, dislike its bitter aftertaste.

Aspartame, better known by its brand name, NutraSweet, was already being used in hundreds of products in twenty-two countries by 1983. It has been approved for such American products as cereals, desserts, and table-top sweeteners. But the major market potential is the diet soft-drink area, which accounts for 23% of all soft-drink sales.

This sweetener, serendipitously discovered in 1966 by a researcher for G. D. Searle Company, might be the salvation for this old-line company that has had a lot of problems. In 1982, Searle sold $74 million worth of NutraSweet and they estimate that sales will go as high as $900 million by 1984 and account for about half of the company's total sales by 1985.

Searle's aspartame patent does not run out until 1992; and while there are competing sweeteners in the lab, they are years away from the marketplace. Robert Shapiro, president of Searle's aspartame operation, says, "The real test is are American consumers going to like this product? All implications are that the answer is emphatically yes."

Recent research, however, suggests that NutraSweet may chemically break down in warm climates to form methanol, a toxic substance. Equally disturbing are the reports of dizziness, menstrual irregularity, and convulsions suffered by people who have heavily used the product. Whether NutraSweet is the cause of these inauspicious side effects or not may take some time to discern. Meanwhile, Searle's NutraSweet is savoring sweet success.

Attempts are frequently made to increase product sales by adding slight improvements, developing new uses of the product, and concentrating on different market segments.

Prices during the maturity stage are lower and relatively stable among competitors. After hand-held calculators entered the maturity stage, customers could buy one for less than $20 that would perform many more functions than the earlier, higher-priced models. Furthermore, attempts are frequently made to increase sales by adding slight improvements, developing new uses of the product, and concentrating on different market segments. This stage may experience cyclical spurts and declines as improvements take hold, quickly become imitated, and are improved again.

Decline. In the decline stage, the product fades as something new takes its place. Fewer firms produce the product. Businesses withdraw from smaller market segments and reduce promotion costs as they begin to accept the product's fate. Automobiles outpaced horse carriages, color television bedazzled black and white, and denims faded to prewashes. Companies differ in handling this period: some scurry off in a rush; others cling to a dead horse. Firms with strong brand loyalties are able to eke out a profit for some time, while less identified products drop quickly out of existence.

Some products move through the life cycle rapidly, others more slowly. CB radios for automobiles, now in the decline stage, enjoyed only 2 or 3 years in the maturity stage, whereas Coke has served many years in the maturity stage. Remember hula hoops? They spun through the cycle about as quickly as they spun around the torsos of those who bought them.

Some experts claim that the product life cycle concept is not much help because prediction is extremely difficult. But most say it is useful because the general model aids management in preparing competitive marketing strategies and planning for anticipated stages. Several products have been able to extend the maturity stage by making adjustments. Jell-O found new users for its products in salad molds and all types of diets. Jell-O also gained new users—especially among youth—with colorful displays and dressed-up advertising and packaging designs. Yet the basic product has remained unchanged for many years.

Marketers modify products to try to extend their life cycles in some of the following ways:

- Longer warranties
- Change the color
- Trademarks
- Change design
- Change advertising media
- Alter accessories
- Add accessories
- Change the size
- Change the package
- Different advertising
- Alter taste
- Lower price
- Relate to other products
- Extend credit

Stages in New Product Development

Because products eventually decline, companies are interested in creating new products. Researchers have identified six stages of product development or modification. At each stage, management decides whether to maintain or abandon the idea.

1. *New idea generation.* Every new product begins as an idea. Ideas flow from research departments, managers, salespeople, employees, customers, and the average person on the street. General Foods receives more than 80,000 spontaneous letters from consumers each year. To encourage idea generation, companies have to establish ways of stimulating and rewarding ingenious ideas.

2. *Screening.* While generation multiplies ideas, screening reduces them. Screening is the first decision stage and can be very costly. Some-

Prototypes of a new product (such as this interactive home videotex service) are often tested by experts as part of its development.

for safety, a new tea mix is tasted, and the fragrance of a new perfume is sniffed. Experts also look at the functional design, packaging, and possible brand or labeling aspects of their new product.

5. *Test marketing.* Next comes the adrenalin-producing, market-testing phase. For the first time, the company tests the idea by asking a selected group of consumers to pay money for it. The real test, then, comes when a company produces a limited number of the product, chooses a representative sample for its test market, and observes how the product sells. If sales justify their hopes, managers stand ready to jump into full-scale production. Some larger firms introduce products at a rapid rate. From mid-1982 to mid-1983, Procter & Gamble unveiled eleven test products. And at one point in 1983, they had twenty-two products in the testing phase.

6. *Commercialization.* Even with testing, new product failure is astonishingly high. Two out of three products still fail, about the same percentage as in the 1960s. For that small handful of products that do survive to this point, managers busily project sales, expand facilities, recruit needed labor, and search for capital to gear up for mass production and distribution.

In late 1983, after years of development and testing, Hattori Seiko Company entered the commercialization stage with the first wristwatch-type computer system. The system can calculate, retain memo data, carry out basic programs, and print out data. The watch unit, along with providing time, has a calendar, an alarm, and a chronograph. The price: $230.

Martin Friedman of the ad agency Dancer Fitzgerald Sample estimates a new brand must log first-year sales of at least $25 million to be considered a success. Only about 1% of new products that he tracts meets this qualification. Manufacturers, however, give themselves higher marks. In a recent Association of National Advertisers survey of 138 major marketers, 92 claim that at least 50% of their new products meet "key business objectives."

Not every new product traverses all these stages. A few managers prefer to reduce expenses by shortcutting one or more of the development steps. Some skip testing for fear they will tip off their competitors. The development cycle varies

times managers lack vision to see an idea's potential, or a company sends a bad idea into the analysis or production stage. Production managers or committees screen out ideas that do not fit company objectives, skills, and capabilities, or that would flop in the marketplace.

3. *Market research.* Market research is the systematic gathering of data regarding the market of a potential product. The information may include any or all of the following: (1) past sales of similar or competing products, (2) sales and industry trends of similar or competing products, (3) consumer tastes and buying motives of current products on the market, and (4) testing of new product features.

4. *Limited development.* The very few products that survive business analysis enter development on a limited scale. Products move from the idea stage or crude model phase to an actual, concrete product. A few sample products called prototypes are created for expert examination. For example, ski poles are tested

from a few weeks to several years. Figure 13.2 diagrams the product decay curve for new product ideas.

Product Liability

Rely, a superabsorbent tampon, was taken off the market in 1980 after it had been linked to toxic-shock, a sometimes fatal reaction to the product. Although different experts argued about whether or not the company was liable for the product, the manufacturer did, without admitting guilt, agree to settlements with some families of victims. In 1982, someone put cyanide poisoning into Extra-Strength Tylenol capsules in Chicago, resulting in several deaths. Though Johnson and Johnson, the parent company of the makers of Tylenol, still have lawsuits against them totaling $40.1 million claiming negligence, evidence may eventually prove that the company was not negligent. Still, product liability is becoming an increasingly important issue.

Just to what extent is a producer responsible for injury or damage caused by a product's use? Traditionally, most states have said that a manufacturer generally was not liable for defective products. However, this has changed in the past 10 years; today, courts are holding manufacturers and sellers responsible for injury or damage due to a product determined to be defective or unsafe, when the product was used as intended. Even if the product functions as intended, the producer may still be responsible if it appears that they overlooked problems in the design and testing of the item. And if misleading advertising causes damage or injury, this, in most cases, is a liable activity.

Product Rejuvenation

Because of the feeble chances of scoring a hit with a new product, many companies try to breathe new life into dying brands. Chester Kane, president of Kane, Bortee & Associates, a new-product consulting group, says, "There are dozens of older brands lying around that have been neglected over the years. Companies must discover ways to make them viable for today's consumer." Gillette is trying just that. Its Right Guard deodorant, which in the mid-1960s enjoyed 25% of the market, has today plummeted to a mere 8% of the market share. For the past 2 years, Gillette's marketing, R&D, manufacturing, sales, and finance departments have been meeting monthly to discuss a strategy for rejuvenating Right Guard. So far, they have settled on a boldly striped container and a huge $28 million ad campaign.

Figure 13.2
Product decay curve for new product ideas.
Source: Management of New Products, *New York: Booz, Allen, and Hamilton, 1968, p. 2.*

Product Identification

Because so many items vie for consumer attention, producers must create a means of identifying their products among countless others that share the shelves in shopping centers. Companies go to tremendous trouble to create worldwide identities; even a kindergartener can distinguish Coke from other soft drinks, spot a Sunkist at a fruitstand, or spy the distant red roof of Kentucky Fried Chicken. Indeed, identification decisions may be as important to product development as the actual product. Companies rely primarily on three means to identify and maintain product recognition: brands, packaging, and labeling.

Brands. A brand name can be a name, song, symbol, design, or combination thereof to distinguish a product from other similar offerings. The **brand name** is the words or letters that identify the product. Xerox, Scotch tape, Coke, Kleenex, and Band-Aid are brand names. In fact, these particular names are so well known that they are rather close to becoming generic designations; that is, many people say Xerox when what they actually mean is photocopy, or Kleenex when they mean tissue (see Fig. 13.3).

The brand name becomes a **trademark** when the company gains legal protection as the only user. This allows companies to spend millions on promotion without worrying that someone else is copying the brand and taking advantage of promotional buildups. There are some 500,000 active trademarks registered at the U.S. Patent Office. And 25,000 new ones are added every year. Companies use brands to reach the following objectives:

1. *Standardization in the eyes of the customer.* From a customer: "I know that all Smucker's jellies are cooked to certain specifications. When I buy Smucker's, I know it will taste like Smucker's."

2. *Build brand loyalty.* From a marketing manager: "If we can get customers to identify and become loyal to our brand, we don't have to worry quite as much when the competition lowers its price." Familiar brands of aspirin like Bayer typically sell at higher prices than lesser-known brands such as Certified.

3. *Quick recognition.* From an advertising agency: "We try to develop instant recognition through sight and sound." For this reason, brand names are usually short, catchy, and easy to say. How many of the brand names can you match to the product in Fig. 13.4?

**Figure 13.3
Brand names — preserved and spoilt.** *Source: "The Name of the Game," Donna Sammons, Inc., September 1983, p. 89.*

Many companies have successfully preserved their trademarks, despite the fact that their brand names have become virtually synonymous with an entire product category and are often incorrectly applied to products made by other manufacturers.

Band-Aid (Johnson & Johnson)	**Q-tips, Vaseline** (Chesebrough Ponds Inc.)
Coke (The Coca-Cola Co.)	**Ritz crackers** (Nabisco Brands Inc.)
Formica (American Cyanamid Co.)	**Scotch tape** (3M)
Jeep (Jeep Corp.)	**Styrofoam** (Dow Chemical Co.)
Jell-O (General Foods Corp.)	**Technicolor** (Technicolor Inc.)
Kleenex (Kimberly-Clark Corp.)	**Teflon, Orion** (E. I. Du Pont de Nemours & Co.)
Magic Marker (Berol Corp.)	**Windbreaker** (Men's Wear International Inc.)
Ping-Pong (Parker Bros.)	**Xerox** (Xerox Corp.)

Some of the most common nouns in the English language started out as brand names before going generic.

aspirin	escalator	shredded wheat
cellophane	kerosene	thermos
celluloid	lanolin	yo-yo
cola	milk of magnesia	zipper

Brand name	Product	Brand name	Product
Swiss Miss	_____	Mellow Yellow	_____
Gulden's	_____	Keebler	_____
Oscar Mayer	_____	Kretchmer	_____
Mueller's	_____	Era	_____
Mattel	_____	Trojans	_____
Jif	_____	Craftsman	_____
Jhirmack	_____	Technics	_____
Reunite	_____	L'Air du Temps	_____
Glidden	_____	Commodore	_____
Kohler	_____	L'Eggs	_____

Figure 13.4
How many of these brand names can you match to the product?

A **family brand** covers several products of the same company such as Hunt foods and Johnson & Johnson baby products. This helps reduce promotional costs by spreading expenses over a variety of products, and new products are cradled by promotion of previous products. **Individual brands** cover only one product, and a single company may have several. Individual brands can be used when a company chooses to market dissimilar products or goods of varying quality and cost. A company can separate its discount product from its more prestigious item via individual brands. **National brands** or manufacturer's brands are identified by the company that makes the product, and they are usually promoted nationally or worldwide. But large wholesalers and retailers put their own **private brand** on products they sell. The wholesaler or retailer buys the manufacturer's product and places its brand on them to develop store loyalty. More typically, the manufacturer produces the item to retailer specifications and identifies it as the retailer's product. Sears, Roebuck and J.C. Penney are two organizations that have developed their own brands. National brands of washing machines can be found in many stores, but you can buy a Kenmore only at Sears.

Packaging. The package does more than protect the product; it announces the contents with color, shape, and design. The package is considered a part of the product by producers. Package development may require many months, and more than $20 billion is spent annually on packaging, which makes it approximately as large as the automobile industry.

Since Henry Heinz meant for ketchup to be poured when he first introduced it in 1876, he packaged it in a tall, narrow-necked bottle. But in the 1960s, when consumers complained about how hard it was to get the ketchup out of the bottle, Heinz introduced a short, squat, wide-mouthed, 12-ounce bottle. It was not popular; the bottle never made it. People still wanted to pour ketchup over their food. But Heinz is trying again. They have agreed to buy from American Can Company six-layer, plastic, squeezable bottles for their ketchup. American Can says it is the perfect ketchup bottle. Consumers will be the judge of that.

About 65% of consumers' buying decisions are made at the store; thus product packaging is very important. The package must catch the consumer's attention and, as they say in the trade, "walk off the shelf." L'Eggs pantyhose, for instance, hit upon a very novel and successful idea when they packaged their hose in an egg-shaped plastic container with the brand name L'Eggs.

Philip Morris, the nation's biggest tobacco company, has launched a new brand of cigarettes called Players, packaged in an elegant black box. By deciding on black, the company is breaking a long-standing taboo against using what, for the tobacco industry especially, is regarded as a morose color. "The American brands are finally waking up to elegance in packaging," says Jerry Nestos of England's Dunhill cigarettes. Or, as one ad executive remarked, "They're creating extra value through the beautiful black box."

Still another innovation in packaging occurred when the Tylenol tampering case signifi-

The lean, black box of Players cigarettes broke industry rules of packaging to distinguish itself from its competitors.

cantly altered packaging habits for over-the-counter medications. The Food and Drug Administration now requires that all capsules and liquid medications be placed in tamper-resistant containers. The package for Tylenol has triple safety seals: outer boxes with all flaps glued shut, plastic bands sealing bottle caps to necks, and inner foil seals over the mouths.

Even more recently food companies are packaging products in "retort pouches," sometimes called "flexible cans." The retort pouch is made of aluminum and polypropylene. After pouring food into these pouches, machines seal them airtight and heat them at very high temperatures. Kraft currently markets such products as sweet-and-sour pork, beef burgundy, and chicken milanese in retort pouches. The consumer can store the products on the shelf rather than in a refrigerator and simply pop them into a microwave for a few minutes when preparing them for serving.

Because packaging changes are very expensive to develop and easy to copy once developed, many packages remain the same for years. Since 1892, toothpaste has been sold in a tube, and the 6.5-ounce Coke bottle has been around since 1915.

Labeling. Labels are usually an integral part of the package and perform promotion and informing functions. Because promotional programs confused consumers with their vague use of "giant, king-sized, family-sized, and economy-sized," the **Fair Packaging and Labeling Act** was passed in 1966 to require that descriptions and package size be easily comparable among competitors. Several industries developed voluntary packaging and labeling standards: Toothpaste companies reduced their variety of sizes from fifty-seven to five. Federal legislation requires many clothing, drug, and food packagers to label fabric, chemicals, calorie count, and ingredients accurately. For example, the label on McCormick's Pure Vanilla Extract lists the ingredients as: vanilla bean extractives in water, alcohol 35%, and corn syrup. The label on Target's enriched skin care lotion is a little more complex, listing such ingredients as water, glycerin, mineral oil, stearic acid, glycol stearate, and twenty additional items.

Product Differentiation

Product differentiation includes all the ways that producers try to make their product different from others on the market. Differences may appear in product design, quality, packaging, labeling, pricing, or promotion. To differentiate themselves, McDonald's restaurants have a distinctive golden arch, what's more, they emphasize the freshness of their hamburgers and fries and the speed of their service. Even a city dweller can tell the difference between John Deere and International Harvester products at a distance: John Deere's tractors are green; International Harvester's are red. At one point, Irwin Publishing Company published all of their textbooks in a blue color. On a bookshelf with hundreds of books, the Irwin publications stood out.

Through product differentiation, sellers can develop recognition and loyalty for their products. Often, promotional programs contain a theme that highlights a product's distinctiveness from those of competitors. When Bounty paper towels wanted to stress that their product was more absorbent than competitors, their advertising showed pictures of their paper towel absorbing more liquid than others. And they often repeated the catchy phrase, "the quicker picker upper."

PRODUCT PRICING

After product development, managers face the pricing decision. Economic theorists have long argued the ramifications of pricing and price changes. Marketing managers treat pricing as a decision commensurate with product planning, distribution channels, and promotion. One study of 135 successful firms ranked pricing decisions sixth in importance behind research development, sales research and planning, sales management, advertising, and service. **Price** is the value given up in exchange for the item purchased.

So how should the price be set? To try to answer this question, we will examine some of the pricing policies of firms and then observe how the prices are quoted.

Pricing Policies

Even with an uncertain basis for understanding and justifying prices, managers have to establish policies for pricing decisions. Pricing policies must be set for new products, promotions, product lines, odd pricing, flexibility, and markup.

CROSS FIRE

Competition in the Coin-Operated Telephone?

The breakup of AT&T has caused a lot of uncertainty in the phone business. One of Ma Bell's few remaining strongholds, the coin-operated telephone, is also currently under seige. Robert Albertson, president of Tonk-a-Phones, Inc., is selling alternative pay phones called Tonk-a-Phones.

The phones are mechanically a little different from Bell phones. But the biggest difference is cost and possible benefits to owners. If, for example, someone owned an apartment house and installed a Bell phone, the owner would have to pay to have the line installed. When phone users dropped their coins into the phone to make calls, the Bell system would collect the money. However, with the Tonk-a-Phone, the customer would pay for the phone, the installation, and the hookup — a cost of about $650 — but the revenues and profits would go to the phone's owner. In other words, the apartment owner could make a profit off the phone much like he or she might make a profit off coin-operated washers and dryers in the complex.

As you might expect, local phone companies are fighting this approach. Phone companies argue that the pay phone is a public service and it could deteriorate under deregulation. And some companies have pulled the plug on business lines connected to non-Bell pay phones. President Albertson says that allowing his and other companies to sell pay phones where the owner keeps the revenue is just good free enterprise. And he adds that service will get better rather than deteriorate.

Do you favor the position taken by local phone companies or the position taken by Albertson of Tonk-a-Phone?

____ A. Local phone companies   ____ B. Tonk-a-Phone

Do you think the government will eventually force local phone companies to maintain business lines to non-Bell pay phones? Why?

____ Yes   ____ No

New products. One of the toughest pricing decisions concerns new products because the price has so much to do with their success or failure. And the lowest price is not necessarily the best price. Companies face two types of new product pricing decisions: penetration pricing or skimming pricing. With **penetration pricing,** the product usually comes out with a lower price than the firm maintains for the long run. A lower price may mean better market acceptance. After promotion establishes some brand loyalty, prices may be raised. The low price has the advantage of discouraging early competition, but brand loyalty must be strong if it is to overcome dissatisfaction with later price increases. Customers are particularly enraged by large price hikes.

The opposite policy is to set a **skimming price,** a high price, and capture just a small share of the market. This policy assumes that the firm will later have to reduce the price in the face of competition. Ballpoint pens first came out at about $20 each; the top seller now goes for around 19 cents. Mercedes Benz introduced its Model 190E to the U.S. market at a price of $24,000. This is more than double the $10,601 price tag for the same model sold in West Germany. Mercedes Benz, practicing a skimming philosophy, continues to price their products using a high-margin strategy because, as they say, it has produced "profits that have got to be phenomenal." Table 13.1 shows other German and U.S. automobile price comparisons. Market skimming prices hold several advantages. They allow the company to recover its investment more quickly and acknowledge that price reductions are better received than increases. The major problem with skimming is flocking competition, which may force the firm to drop its price before it planned to.

BUSINESS BULLETIN

"To Market, to Market . . ."

Of course, profits are important, but some authorities insist that gaining a sizable share of the market is more important than earning healthy profits, especially in the early years of a new business. After a customer base is secured, profits, these people believe, will follow naturally. Strategies to win market share vary from product to product, but some include:

1. *Underprice the competition.* Victor Kiam bought Remington Products in 1979 when it was unprofitable and had less than 20% of the electric shaver market. By slashing prices, he was able to nearly double the company's market share.

2. *Target your market.* Finreport Systems, Inc. decided to customize software to Massachusetts hospitals. The company now claims 90% of that market and is branching out into other states.

3. *Corner distribution network.* Micro Data Base Systems, Inc., is offering its software distributors discounts of up to 90% in order to ensure dealer loyalty.

4. *Cater to your customers.* Bioanalytical Systems retains 90% of the electrochemical detection market because their competitors cannot adequately explain the complicated product to their own users.

5. *Prevent erosion.* American Express Company, after 25 years of pursuing affluent businessmen, realized it needed a different kind of applicant to prevent its market share from slipping. The company now has an ad campaign geared to convincing "interesting women and younger men" to apply for the card.

Source: Adapted from "Gaining Market Share," *Venture,* August, 1983, p. 80.

TABLE 13.1 ■ EXAMPLE OF A SKIMMING STRATEGY

Make and Model	German Price	U.S. Price
Mercedes Benz 190E (sedan)	$10,601	$24,000
Mercedes Benz 300TD (stationwagon)	$13,157	$33,850
Mercedes Benz 380SL (sports car)	$23,620	$43,822
BMW 318i (sedan)	$ 8,483	$16,430
Audi 4000 (sedan)	$ 6,062	$10,205
Audi Coupe	$ 8,313	$13,105

Promotional pricing. **Promotional pricing** is similar to new-product pricing. It may be used to introduce a new product, regenerate interest in an old product, or focus on a good seller. Promotional prices are lower for the sake of advertising one product or another in the company's line. This approach is often used at retail levels; a store will price some items very low to entice customers into the store, hoping they will buy other items at regular prices. This strategy is based on the fact that customers can only remember a limited number of prices on widely advertised staples like coffee, sugar, and milk. The philosophy used is that keeping these prices low will develop customer loyalty. Although promotional pricing can have the advantage of drawing attention to a product, it may violate fair trade laws in some states. Also, the artificially lower price may become so fixed in the customer's mind as to prevent a company from ever raising it without undue resistance.

Product-line pricing. Most firms sell several products and their aim is to develop a pricing mix for their total merchandise that helps them achieve company goals. This approach is superior to pricing each product in isolation. **Price lining** identifies a limited number of prices for merchandise. A shoe manufacturer sells one style of shoe at $19.95, another type at $24.95, and a still fancier shoe at $49.95. There are no prices between these lines. This simplifies pricing decisions and adds

consistency because each product does not require the agony of a completely separate decision. The major problem is again the difficulty of adjusting established price lines in the face of consumer awareness. Price lines may be a prime factor in creating a company's image; to change it by adjusting several prices upward simultaneously hampers the entire product line's reputation.

Odd pricing. Some companies quote their merchandise at various prices for psychological purposes. **Odd pricing** (also called **psychological pricing**) is quoting just under the next highest dollar figure. For instance, $19.99 sounds like a savings compared to $20. There is an even more sophisticated concept: Since prices ending in .95, .98, or .99 are the custom, some retailers end prices with threes and sevens, such as $8.93 or $6.97, because they believe the customer thinks these are discount or bargain prices. There is little research to indicate just what impact odd pricing has on consumers, but it has become a tradition in the last few years. One of the original purposes of odd pricing was to force clerks to be conscious of giving correct change. But the additional record keeping, working with odd figures, and totaling the numbers might more than offset any advantage.

Flexible pricing. What is the policy on price flexibility? Will the product be sold at one price to all markets, or will variable pricing develop as the result of individual or retail bargaining? In U.S. retailing, one price is common because of mass markets and mass purchasing; the customer either takes or leaves the quoted price. For some items such as automobiles, furniture, and expensive jewelry, where customer outlay is great, prices may vary according to size of purchase, inventory level at the moment, or the customer's bargaining ability. Flexible pricing is more common in the large-scale consumption of industrial markets. Industrial customers usually make large purchases, but some buy smaller; some are longtime customers, others newly arrived. These factors affect the price. Flexible pricing allows the company more latitude; it can show concern and feeling for the consumer. But some purchasers will be angry when they find that another buyer negotiated a better price.

Gasoline wholesalers, as noted in this Exxon TV ad, have been providing cash discounts directly to customers of their retail outlets to discourage use of credit.

Markup pricing. **Markup pricing** adds a certain percentage to the actual cost of the product. This method is popular in retailing. For instance, a firm might decide to mark up its jeans 50%. Thus, if the store paid $16 for the jeans, they would sell them for $24 (50% × $16 = $8, and $16 + $8 = $24). Some restaurants mark up canned soft drinks as much as 100%.

Price Quotations

Describing prices is an art and depends upon many factors. Price quotations become part of the information about the product, a portion of the promotional package, and must be understood for intelligent, competitive purchasing.

List prices. Prices normally quoted to purchasers, listed in catalogs and on invoices, or shown on price tags in the store are list prices. This is the beginning stage of price identification and for many items remains the final purchase price.

Price discounts. When buying from wholesalers or manufacturers, purchasers sometimes pay a discounted price that is lower than the catalog price. Retailers are given **cash discounts** when the purchaser buys on terms and pays promptly. Terms such as 2/10, net 30 mean that the purchaser has 30 days to pay the bill but receives a 2% discount for paying within 10 days. These discounts normally occur between suppliers and manufacturers or between wholesalers and retailers. Such terms are not usually available for the ultimate consumer. The **trade discounts** are unique in that they are given to buyers who perform some of the functions the manufacturer normally performs. The list price might be 100%, but when the manufacturer sells to wholesalers, asking price may be 40% of the list price to pay for the wholesaler's services.

Transportation pricing. Part of the product's price rests in transportation. If the items are enormous and bulky, the transportation charges are likely to be considerable. For most volume purchases in retail outlets, the price reflects transportation costs. But for large, hard-to-handle items, various alternatives exist. **F.O.B.** factory or F.O.B. origin indicates that the buyer will pay all freight charges and the seller will load the merchandise, but the price reflects what the item costs at the manufacturer's location. This allows buyers the choice of how they cover their transportation. If they are a long distance from the origin, transportation costs may prohibit the purchase. Opposite to F.O.B. is **uniform delivered price** where the buyer pays the same price, which includes transportation, regardless of how far products are shipped. Buyers who are a long distance from the origin pay less freight cost per mile, but this is averaged out by purchasers located closer to the origin who pay a "phantom freight" — or higher freight cost per mile. Uniform delivered price is used mostly for small items or where a market is concentrated. **Zone pricing,** a modification of uniform delivered price, means producers divide their market into geographic zones and establish the same charge within each zone. Mail-order houses usually vary their price in different sections of the country to absorb relative freight charges. This flexibility makes transportation costs more equitable.

SUMMARY

Effective marketing departments concentrate on systematic product planning and pricing. All products can be classed into consumer goods or industrial goods. Consumer goods are purchased by the ultimate consumer, and producers buy industrial goods to make their products. Each product also can be related to other products in hierarchical fashion.

Product sales and profits follow an S-shaped life cycle growth pattern. After the introduction stage, products typically, if they are successes, begin to sell very rapidly — the growth stage. Next, in the maturity stage, growth rates decline. Finally, in the decline stage, sales and profits begin to drop off. Profits are usually highest toward the end of the growth stage and in the maturity stage. Advertising and promotion strategies also differ as the stages change.

As new products develop, they pass through stages of new-idea generation, screening, business analysis, limited development, test marketing, and commercialization. Courts are holding product manufacturers and sometimes sellers liable for damage or injury when the product was used as intended by the consumer.

Firms try to identify their products with brands — names, songs, symbols, designs, etc. — that distinguish the product from similar offerings. Brands help standardize the product, build consumer loyalty, and offer quick recognition.

In packaging, a $20 billion plus industry, firms protect the product and try to announce the contents with color, shape, and design. Product labels may help in promotion as well as in describing the contents of the product. Pricing policies serve as guidelines for consistency and work with other factors of the marketing mix. Policies usually address such concerns as pricing new products, promotional pricing, product-line pricing, odd pricing, flexible pricing, and markup pricing. Actual price quotations take the form of list prices, price discounts, and transportation considerations.

MIND YOUR BUSINESS

Instructions. Test your knowledge of product planning and pricing by designating the following statements true (T) or false (F).

___ 1. Marketing people consider packaging, services, and intangible aspects to be a part of the product.

___ 2. Magazines, candy, and milk are examples of specialty goods.

___ 3. Profits are highest during the introductory stage of the product life cycle.

___ 4. Price is usually highest during the maturity stage of the product life cycle.

___ 5. All new products pass through six stages of development.

___ 6. Both manufacturers and sellers of a product can be held liable for injury or damage when the product is used as intended.

___ 7. Strong brand loyalty allows producers to charge a higher price for their products.

___ 8. The sole purpose of packaging is to protect the product.

___ 9. Most managers follow the same policy when pricing new products.

___ 10. Product-line pricing and odd pricing are the same thing.

See answers at the back of the book.

KEY TERMS

REVIEW QUESTIONS

1. What, specifically, is a product? What is not a product?

2. Discuss the two major classifications of products. How do they differ?

3. Identify and give an example of the seven levels in a product hierarchy.

4. What are the four major aspects of a product life cycle? Explain how sales, promotional costs, profits, cash requirements, and prices vary at each stage.

5. Explain each of the stages in new product development.

6. Describe product liability. What are its implications for producers and sellers?

7. What are the four major methods used in product identification?

8. How do the pricing policies of new products differ from those of existing products?

9. What is product-line pricing?

10. Give some examples of odd pricing. Is it common in your area? If so, present some specific examples from your local newspaper.

11. The chapter presents three major types of price quotation. Discuss each and give some examples where each may be used.

CASES

Case 13.1: Price versus Taste

For the past 10 years, Dr. Pepper has been a major seller in the soft drink market, rising out of towns in the South and Midwest to compete in major markets across the country. Until recently, the giants—Coca-Cola and Pepsi, who control 55% of the soft drink market—ignored the small company based in Dallas. But now the big two are fighting back. Coca-Cola is particularly upset because about 25% of its bottlers have opted to distribute Dr. Pepper instead of its own cherry soda, Mr. Pibb. Still, W. W. Clements, the chairman of Dr. Pepper, believes that the company can double its profits and earnings every 4 years for the immediate future.

Questions

1. What is the importance of pricing for soft drink products?

2. How do soft drink manufacturers differentiate their products?

3. If you were going to develop a new soft drink, outline how you would go about it.

Case 13.2: The Pricing Decision

A mobile home manufacturer produces a single model, the Streamline. It sells this line through dealers at a retail price of $12,000. Because of the company's reputation for quality, dealers have been asking them to produce a higher-priced mobile home. The company decided to produce the line and is trying to decide what price range to target for.

It will take about $150,000 to get set up to produce the new line, and they can produce the product at about $8000 per unit. Their plant capacity allows them to produce only about 800 additional units per year; if they produced more, they would have to expand their plant. The company showed their new model at a mobile home fair, and visitors expressed a strong preference for the design over all other competitors.

Preliminary market testing suggests that retailers could sell the product at a retail price of about $16,000, about 10% above the major competitor's model. Managers in the firm are arguing about the pricing policy they should take. The marketing manager wants to price the model to their dealers at about $15,000. He says they have a good product and they should try to get as much profit as they can while their design is new. The general manager is afraid that this strategy would alienate some of the dealers, and she believes it is a good idea to maintain dealer loyalty. She argues for a price to dealers of about $13,000. This would allow the dealers to make a little more profit, and they could lower the price a bit if they needed to. While the manufacturer would not make as much profit per unit, the general manager believes that dealer loyalty is more important than quick profits.

Questions

1. Do you tend to agree with the marketing manager or the general manager? Why?

2. In general, do you think it is best to price high when you have a design advantage, or do you think you should price lower and try to build long-term commitment from dealers and consumers? Why?

3. What other things should be considered in the pricing decision?

After completing this chapter, you will be able to:

■   Diagram four marketing channel alternatives.

■   Identify five kinds of channel flows.

■   Explain four factors that managers should consider when making a channel selection.

■   Describe three kinds of direct marketing channels.

■   Explain the functions of middlemen.

■   Explain vertical marketing systems.

■   Comment on horizontal marketing, multichannel marketing, and channel conflicts.

■   Explain the objectives of physical distribution.

DISTRIBUTION
CHANNELS

"Whoever controls the channels of distribution controls the market," says James Lally, partner in a high-tech venture capital firm. In the first half of the 1980s, there were as many as 150 personal-computer manufacturers, each trying to get their 10% of the market. However, there were not enough dealers to handle the products from all these manufacturers.

With any mass consumer product, marketing and distribution becomes as important as research and development. As the sheer volume of personal computers began to clog the market, it was not enough to have a better product at a lower cost. Dealers could only handle, at most, three or four different brands and still know something about them. Although IBM was not the first to introduce a personal computer, they became the top seller in 1983. Of course IBM had a good product, but their mastery of distributing and marketing is what gave them their key advantage.

Today, instead of relying solely on their legendary direct-to-the-customer sales force, IBM is selling more and more small systems through new channels: industrial middlemen, independent retailers (ComputerLand, Sears), and its own retail outlets (IBM has more than forty stores and will build at least as many more by the end of 1983).

Getting the product from the producer to the user (that is, creating place utility) involves channels, middlemen, and physical distribution.

CHANNEL DECISIONS

A **distribution channel** is all the institutions that perform the activities necessary to move the product and its title from producer to consumer. Channel decisions are important to marketing managers because: (1) they affect all other decisions once the channel is fixed, and (2) they usually imply long-term commitments to a particular distribution method. Normally, it takes years to build a channel and, once built, it is not easy to alter.

Effective marketers evaluate channel alternatives to achieve the best results for their firm.

Channel Alternatives

The simplest channel flows goods from producer to consumer; this direct channel, or zero-stage channel, has no intermediaries. Some vacuum cleaners, encyclopedias, cosmetics, mail-order items, or roadside vegetable stands represent a direct channel. Less than 5% of consumer sales travel this route, but it is the most popular for industrial goods. For example, heavy machinery manufacturers have salespeople who visit user firms.

A one-stage channel contains one intermediary, usually a retailer in consumer goods. The most-used process is a two-stage channel from producer to wholesaler to retailer to consumer. Thousands of small and medium-sized manufacturers who produce limited lines feel that this channel best suits them. Smaller producers use the expertise and financial support of wholesalers to find their markets and take specialized distribution functions off their hands.

When there are a great number of smaller companies, they might use an agent, forming a three-stage channel. An agent does not take title to the goods but finds a wholesaler for them. The meat packing industry uses another three-stage channel, which goes from producer to wholesaler to jobber to retailer to consumer. A jobber orders from wholesalers, accumulates products, and distributes them to retailers not accommodated by the regular wholesaler. In the industrial market, the three-stage channel might be termed manufacturer to agent to wholesaler to industrial user. Figure 14.1 diagrams these channels.

Forms of Channel Flows

In addition to moving the physical product through channels to the consumer, a firm must also move title, payment, information, and promotion materials through the channels.

Physical flows. Physical flows refer to ways the physical products move from producer to user. For large items such as automobiles, manufacturers usually ship the cars via truck to dealers who then sell to the user.

Title flows. The actual passage of the title from one marketing institution to another is the title flow. In some cases, the manufacturer holds the title even though the product is in the hands of a retailer. In other cases, the title may pass to the dealer and then to the user when he or she buys from the dealer.

Payment flows. How does the payment get from the ultimate purchaser back to the pro-

ducer? This is called payment flow, and it may take several forms. For instance, when a customer buys an automobile, he or she might borrow money from a credit union. Thus, the payment flow would be from the customer to the credit union, to the dealer, to the manufacturer.

Information flows. Information flows describe the way information is exchanged between the marketing institutions in the channel.

Promotion flows. The promotion flow pictures how advertising, personal selling, and the like move through the channels. (Promotion is covered in more detail in the next chapter.) In some cases, the manufacturer might advertise to channel institutions or promote directly to the ultimate purchaser.

Channels for Services

Although not exactly the same, sellers of services must also create place utility for the user. Unless the service is provided at the right place, consumers will not buy the service. For example, banks provide a service. As people moved away

Direct	Producer				Consumer
One-stage	Producer			Retailer	Consumer
Two-stage	Producer	Wholesaler		Retailer	Consumer
Three-stage	Producer	Wholesaler	Jobber	Retailer	Consumer

**Figure 14.1
Examples of channel alternatives.**

from downtown areas, banks began to build branches in outlying neighborhoods so their service would be convenient.

Selecting Channels

Although it is hard to change channels, managers do not select only one channel and stay with it forever. As conditions change, they have to adjust.

Goods often travel through several channels simultaneously.

Often, their goods travel through several channels simultaneously. Newer or smaller companies nearly always rely upon middlemen. As companies grow and markets expand, they face a diversity of methods for moving their products. Channel selection involves characteristics of the consumer, product, company, and middlemen.

1. *Consumer.* Of foremost concern is the consumer. Channels will be long if there are large numbers of customers, if customers are geographically scattered, and if they purchase goods in small quantities. It becomes very costly for a producer to perform all the functions in a long channel, so he or she calls on channel intermediaries, specialists in transportation, storage, and handling who operate more efficiently. When consumers are clustered and buy in volume, channels shorten.

2. *Product characteristics.* Many product characteristics directly affect the channel-selecting decision. Perishable products, such as fresh fruits, live lobsters, and jelly rolls, dictate direct channels by their nature. Custom-made products usually go from manufacturer to user because of design specifications communicated between them. Items needing special service or maintenance, such as technical machines and equipment, typically have shorter channels. Companies producing goods of high unit value often hire their own salespeople to move these products; control is thus maintained over handling, and individual attention can be given in training. Standardized

As this ad suggests, the perishable nature of fresh fruits and vegetables helps dictate a rail distribution channel.

products require less individual attention and travel longer channels.

3. *Company characteristics.* Financially strong companies can more easily develop their own sales forces for shorter channels. Weaker companies rely on commission payments to intermediaries who are better able to absorb inventory costs and customer services such as credit. Middlemen can combine deliveries for several companies that produce only one product. If a company manufactures a large variety of products, it can market directly and spread distribution costs. Increased service and individual attention require more direct channels of middlemen willing to represent company policy to customers.

4. *Middlemen characteristics.* The middleman is involved in many ways: the number of locations, transportation methods, facilities, customer services, transactions, and cost of delivery. Middlemen must be able to perform these functions more cheaply than the manufacturer. Producers also consider middlemen's attitudes toward sharing part of the advertising burden. Will they allow the company to train their salespeople? How interested are they in the company's product? What standing does the company's product assume in relation to other items they handle? Most important, will they do a good job with the company's product?

DIRECT MARKETING

Direct marketing is moving the product from producer to consumer through direct channels. Although most producers use multistage channels, direct marketing is increasing. The most common forms are mail-order, telephone, and door-to-door. Television marketing is on the way.

Mail-Order Marketing

In 1983, direct marketers bombarded consumers with nearly 6 billion copies of 5000 catalogs. But unlike the thick, general-purpose, traditional Sears and Montgomery Ward catalogs, most of today's models are sleek and specialized.

The *Epicurean Delights* catalog from Neiman Marcus is thirty-two pages of food as an art form.

A chile wreath, plum pudding, Italian flat bread, and chocolate popcorn are among the items you can order. The *Aztech* catalog from Aztech Electronics, Inc., in Springfield, Missouri, lists over 150 electronic items, ranging from stereos to Mickey Mouse telephones. Another catalog offers nothing but weather vanes and sundials—14, four-color pages of them, and another offers only nuts—pecans, peanuts, and mixed varieties.

The more traditional department stores have also gone to specialty catalogs. Spiegel, the nation's fourth-largest mail-order retailer, offered its first speciality catalog in the spring of 1983. A test issue, specializing in lingerie, went to 300,000 homes. The result: 7500 orders, averaging $80 each. Sears, Roebuck has issued twenty-four specialty catalogs, and Bloomingdale's issued fourteen in 1983 alone.

Specialty-catalog publishers use computers to advantage. If a customer buys a bathing suit at Saks Fifth Avenue, she is likely, in a short time, to receive a catalog of bathing suits. The computer tracks purchases, puts customers' names on the proper lists, and addresses the labels. Soon, the catalog is in the mail. Some companies also purchase mailing lists from other sources. Sears bought names of pregnant women from doctors and hospitals to mail catalogs for infants.

Companies also shower tons of direct-mail pieces on consumers each year. Some direct mail may promote a particular item such as a book or a training workshop. Other direct-mail pieces fold out in several directions and actually resemble small catalogs.

Why the increased emphasis on this form of direct marketing? There are several reasons. As John Shea, vice-president of Spiegel, puts it, "You don't want to waste time running from store to store on Saturday to find they don't have your color or size." Direct marketing is easy for the consumer, who simply flips through the catalogs at leisure, perhaps while visiting with a friend, and makes an order—either by returning the order blank or calling an 800 number and charging items. Another reason direct marketing is becoming more important is the larger number of women working at paid jobs who have less time to shop. Third, people buy from catalogs when there is no local store in the area: Most people do not live near a Bloomingdale's or a Saks. The catalog creates a form of place utility. Finally, marketing through direct mail is sometimes cheaper. The specialty catalogs aim for a well-defined target market and reach a lot of people at a low cost per person. According to the Direct Mail/Marketing Association, the use of direct marketing methods will become even more important in the future.

Telephone Marketing

In a recent report issued by the Distribution Research and Education Foundation (DREF), the ratio of field salespeople to inside telephone salespeople is shifting. By 1990, the report concludes, telephone salespeople will amount to 50% of the average wholesale distributor's sales force. In 1980, the figure was 30%. At Louisiana Oil & Tire Co., all ten of the traveling salespeople were brought inside and put at a bank of phones. Since then, the company's phone bill has increased by $6000 a month, but other sales expenses have declined by $15,000 a month. More important, says Gregory Martin, sales manager, is that sales have doubled.

Firms shied away from telephone marketing for awhile, and public sentiment was also against it. In fact, some groups, claiming that it was an invasion of privacy, proposed laws to ban or limit it. However, firms are finding they can establish the same rapport over the phone as they did with eyeball-to-eyeball selling.

"Telemarketing isn't just how to talk on the phone," says a telephone consultant. It may take 3 to 6 months before a program starts to pay off. Success depends upon: (1) an analysis of which accounts can best be sold by telephone and which accounts require hand-holding, (2) knowledge of company policies and product lines, (3) extensive training in telephone techniques, and (4) a good personality. The phone seller must be enthusiastic

TAKING STOCK

Trouble in the Direct-Marketing Industry?

During the first six months of 1983, Mary Kay Cosmetics' stock price plunged 65% in value. The main problem at Mary Kay, and for the whole direct marketing industry, is the inability to attract new recruits.

Much of the success of Mary Kay and similar direct sales companies comes from hiring new recruits. The new recruits typically have good sales for awhile; then sales drop off, and many of the recruits quit. So, without a successful recruiting program, direct marketing firms like Mary Kay, Avon Products, Inc., Dart & Kraft, and Tupperware face stagnant sales. A sales director for Mary Kay in Dallas says that she is attracting only about five recruits a month, compared to ten a month a year ago.

There may be several reasons why these direct-marketing efforts are having trouble. More women are working full-time; thus fewer are available to work in direct marketing. Also, because of divorce and changing life-styles, the extended family of relatives and friends is not as stable as it was to provide day-care. And direct sales jobs are less attractive during economic recoveries when more salaried jobs become available.

However, according to a spokesperson, Mary Kay is planning "to fly right in the face of the problem" by quadrupling the 1984 recruiting budget. The firm planned to take all of its 1984 promotional and advertising budget and pour it into recruiting. Part of the money will provide greater financial incentives to people who bring new recruits on board. No doubt, this effort will help; but a long-term problem for direct-marketing companies is the increasing number of steadier jobs available in other fields for women.

Source: Dean Rotbart and Laurie P. Cohen, "The Party at Mary Kay Isn't Quite So Lively, as Recruiting Falls Off," *The Wall Street Journal*, Friday, Oct. 28, 1983, pp. 1, 12.

enough to create interest and thick-skinned enough to handle dozens of rejections per day.

Door-to-Door Marketing

Perhaps the oldest form of direct marketing is door-to-door, or on-the-premise, selling. Here, a manufacturer's representative visits customers at their homes. Historically, we have associated this form of direct marketing with World Book Encyclopedias, Fuller Brush, Avon cosmetics, and Tupperware parties. All these companies have used this channel to great advantage. More recently, Amway and Mary Kay Cosmetics have made millions of dollars through door-to-door sales.

Currently, **multilevel marketing,** a process that uses levels of people with each person moving a small amount of product, is in vogue for door-to-door selling. In multilevel selling, salespeople get commissions for the products they sell. And if they hire others to sell products for them, they also get a small commission on what the people they hired sell. When people they hired hire someone else, the salespeople get a part of their commission also. Thus, there is a strong incentive to hire people to sell under your supervision and to encourage them to hire people to sell under them.

Salespeople for Mary Kay Cosmetics, called "beauty consultants," pay $20.75 for their beauty kits, and they sell them for $41.50—a 100% markup. However, the big incentive comes from recruiting other consultants. If a consultant recruits eight others, Mary Kay pays the original consultant 8% of the sales of all of his or her recruits. If the original consultant finds as many as twelve recruits, he or she achieves the title of "director," and gets 9 to 12% of recruits' sales. If a director and her recruits exceed $72,000 in sales in a 6-month period, the director gets the use of a pink Cadillac.

Although multilevel marketing has been around since 1944, it did not achieve acceptability until 1979. In that year, the Federal Trade Commission challenged Amway Corporation, saying their multilevel marketing operation was illegal. Amway won. Now, this rapidly growing field has about 1000 companies with annual sales between $5 and $7 billion. Rick Walsh, copublisher of *Multilevel Marketing News* magazine, says, "It is the fastest growing merchandising industry in the

U.S." One consultant says that several of the Fortune 500 companies are looking into it.

Television Marketing

After years of study, companies are beginning to offer sales and services through a combination of a telephone line, television set, and computer. Videotex systems offer consumers home access to shopping, banking, and a wide variety of computer information. Viewtron, a system developed by the Knight-Ridder newspaper chain, allows subscribers to shop electronically at more than 100 South Florida retailers. A purchaser simply looks through the color pages of an electronic catalog, displayed on the TV screen, and presses buttons to order something. The fee to the subscriber is $12 per month plus $1 in telephone charges for each hour of use. Initially, the subscriber must purchase a special terminal made by AT&T, called Spectre; the cost is $600.

To boost their catalog sales, J. C. Penney has already made arrangements with Knight-Ridder to link into the Viewtron system. Viewtron users, in addition to shopping, can also view the national news or get scores from a local little league, plus lots of other information. They can check the money in their bank accounts, transfer funds from one account to another, and pay bills.

Experts predict the revenues from television marketing will range between $4 and $30 billion by 1990.

Knight-Ridder plans to sweep the country with this technology if Viewtron does well in its test in the Miami area. Other firms, including Field Enterprises, The Times Mirror Co., and Chemical Bank, are poised in the wings ready to go. And in early 1984, three corporate powerhouses—IBM, Sears, and CBS—announced a joint venture to develop a nationwide commercial videotex service for households with personal and home computers. Albert Gillen, president of Knight-Ridder's Viewtron, called the venture "a vote of confidence in the videotex market." No one knows what the television marketing industry will amount to, of course; but experts predict that revenues will range between $4 and $30 billion by 1990.

Combined Methods of Direct Marketing

Some firms apparently are combining direct marketing methods. Telephone salespeople may make calls to prospects and follow up with direct mail. Or before a company tries to sell via telephone, they may send direct mail to a client, which might include the salesperson's picture along with catalogs and brochures.

And more companies now provide salespeople with computer terminals. From the terminal, the salesperson can get a wealth of information, such as inventory available, price, order status,

Knight-Ridder's Viewtron offers a number of services, as is shown by these photos of a terminal screen.

Electronic Shopping

Electronic shop-at-home services, where customers look at video screens and make their purchases by punching keyboards, is another form of direct marketing. Publishers, banks, and retailers are about to begin selling services that enable people to make purchases, check bank balances, and even buy and sell stocks — all without leaving home or talking to a human. The consulting firm of Booz, Allen, and Hamilton ran a two-year test on electronic shopping and concluded that electronic retail sales will total $50 billion by 1995.

Others are not so euphoric. An executive for a large video shopping system says, "The number of people who are going to change their behavior because of a technological change is small. To say that technology is going to make dinosaurs of retail stores is a little silly."

Although most are expecting electronic sales to grow, it does have some drawbacks:

1. Many shoppers enjoy the social interaction of a purchase. Video purchasing eliminates this.
2. Although video technology may present pretty good descriptions and in some cases images of the product customers are about to buy, it is not like seeing the product.
3. The systems require capital investments. For example, Knight-Ridder's system, called Viewtron, uses a special terminal that costs $600.
4. It is harder to shop around for the best deal.

The biggest problem, however, as James Holly, head of the Times Mirror system, laments, is that "the cost of providing this service to the consumer far exceeds what you can get from subscribers." So, despite the optimism of some, electronic shopping still has a few glitches.

Source: "Electronic Shopping Is Called Imminent, but Doubts Persist," *The Wall Street Journal,* June 23, 1983, and "Coming Fast: Services Through the TV Set," *Fortune,* November 14, 1983, pp. 5–56.

characteristics of the customer, previous customer activity, and perhaps the customer's nickname. With a handy terminal, a telephone salesperson can provide a lot more information to the client and get it there quicker.

FUNCTIONS OF CHANNEL MIDDLEMEN

Marketing channels are the province of **middlemen,** those institutions that handle goods between the producer and ultimate consumer. Middlemen are very important since well over 90% of goods move through their hands. Often the comment arises, "Middlemen drive up the prices. Why do we need them?" Middlemen aid in distributing products by performing the following functions:

1. They undertake many storage costs, assume the risk of price changes in storage, and provide a convenient means of storage.
2. They assume some of the financing burden by selling on credit and financing inventories while they hold items in storage.
3. They transport items.
4. They gain efficiency through volume transactions.

Figure 14.2
How your meat dollar is spread between rancher and middleman. *Source: U.S. Department of Agriculture.*

Rancher gets 58¢   Retailer keeps 28¢   Packer/   Wholesaler
                                                transporters   keeps 6¢
                                                keep 8¢

5. They gather information from the market-place.

6. They search out and communicate with prospective buyers.

Such services cost money. According to the U.S. Department of Agriculture, the rancher gets only 58 cents of a dollar from sale of beef; the remaining 42 cents goes to middlemen to perform the functions just described. Figure 14.2 shows how the middlemen divide the 42 cents. Studies show that middlemen are often responsible for 40 to 59% of the markup. But, does eliminating the middlemen reduce the cost to the purchaser? Not necessarily.

If producers eliminated middlemen, then producers would have to perform these channel functions. If Wrigley chewing gum were not sold through channel middlemen, the company would have to establish its own gum stores throughout the country, or else they would have to sell door-to-door or via direct mail. Either of these methods would no doubt drive up the price of gum. If General Motors decided to eliminate middlemen, they would have to build more storage facilities, buy delivery trucks, hire more laborers, build or buy dealerships, and add to their sales force. Middlemen are specialists in what they do, and they typically can perform these functions more efficiently than a producer. Two major channel institutions are wholesalers and retailers.

Wholesalers

Wholesalers market products between producers and retailers or between producers and other wholesalers. They ordinarily do not sell directly to the ultimate consumer. Over 300,000 wholesale establishments exist with sales totaling over $500 billion annually. Some manufacturers with huge volumes operate their own wholesale facilities. Others have branch outlets and sales offices far from the central office to provide many wholesale functions. Some smaller firms developing new territories use independently owned public warehouses as storage facilities. Independent wholesalers operate as a separate business entity and account for some 55% of the wholesale establishments and almost 70% of the wholesale sales in this country. Two categories of independent wholesalers are merchant wholesalers and agent wholesalers.

Merchant wholesalers actually take title to the goods. **Full-function merchant wholesalers** offer a full complement of functions to the producer: They store goods, maintain a sales force, make deliveries, and extend credit. Costs may go as high as 20% of sales. They are especially helpful to small retailers who carry inexpensive items such as hardware, drugs, and some groceries. **Specialist wholesalers,** known as rack jobbers, emerged with supermarket development to provide their own racks, stock merchandise, and deliver to retail outlets. **Limited-function merchant wholesalers** do not offer a full array of wholesale functions. **Cash-and-carry wholesalers** developed during the depression to try to reduce costs. Retailers pick up goods at wholesale warehouses and pay cash for the items. Several specialists have emerged among merchant wholesalers.

Agent wholesalers never take title to their goods, although they may assume possession. They are usually more specialized than merchant wholesalers, with an emphasis on bringing together buyers and sellers. Three major categories of agent wholesalers include brokers, selling agents, and manufacturers' agents.

Brokers bring buyers and sellers together; they represent either the buyer or seller, but not both, and collect a fee from their client. Brokers perform very few services because they operate on a less stable basis. They are effective in industries with a large number of small suppliers and purchasers, like real estate or frozen foods. **Selling agents** are usually responsible for the total marketing program of a firm with full authority over pricing and promotions. They may have exclusive rights to a company's products. They exist as independent marketing departments and provide their expertise to the small manufacturer. Selling agents thrive in textile, coal, and lumber industries. **Manufacturer's agents** are independent salespeople working on a commission. They may represent several companies. This agent develops efficiency by combining a list of many noncompeting items and spreading the distribution costs over several of these items.

Retailers

A **retailer** sells the product directly to the end user. About 97% of all consumer sales take place in retail stores. The general store became the first

---

CROSS FIRE

Do Middlemen Increase the Price?

Even though the argument is old, experts and politicians still continue to debate whether middlemen drive up prices unnecessarily. Of course, middlemen do charge for their services and this is reflected in the price to the consumer. But can middlemen perform their services more efficiently than producers or consumers?

Middlemen often perform many functions such as storing, risk taking, transporting, and the like. Some marketing channels have several middlemen. Frequently, the producer may get only about half of the actual price of an item for his or her efforts. Many argue that the producer takes the greater risks and should receive more rewards. Channel specialists counter that they also take risks, and in fact, they are reducing producer risks with their expertise and willingness to share risks.

Recently, we have seen greater use of direct marketing, from direct sales to television marketing. Does this mean that we are discovering that producers can deliver the product more efficiently than middlemen? We also see growth in factory outlets where consumers perform many of the middlemen functions by going directly to the factory. Will this become a major way to distribute products and services?

Do you think that middlemen, in general, charge too much for their services? Why?

____ Yes   No

Do you think we will see greater or less use of middlemen in the next 10 years? Why?

____ A. Much greater use   ____ C. Less use

____ B. Greater use   ____ D. Much less use

Do you believe that middlemen, in general, cause the prices of goods and services to be higher than they otherwise would be?

____ A. Much higher   ____ C. Somewhat lower

____ B. Somewhat higher   ____ D. Much lower

important retail institution although it was preceded by traveling peddlers who sold their wares or remedies across the country. The general store included truly one-stop shopping, handling everything from beans, drugs, and candy, to feed, rakes, cloth, and guns. A few survive today, primarily in rural areas. A few major examples of retail outlets consist of department stores, specialty shops, chain stores, and discount stores.

Somewhat like their general-store ancestors, the **department store** handles everything. Macy's in New York City has over 400,000 items in 168 departments to serve 150,000 customers per day. Most shopping centers include department stores. Some of the most famous are Marshall Field, Rich's, and Neiman Marcus. **Specialty shops,** or limited-line stores, stand opposite department stores and zero in on a special marketing segment. They offer great choice but within a limited category of products. Specialty shops concentrate on shoes, cameras, sporting goods,

Sears, Roebuck is currently the largest retail outlet in the world; their sales exceed the gross national product of many countries.

cheeses, stationery, or books, to name a few. **Chain stores** consist of two or more commonly owned and managed stores handling similar products. They try to gain the advantages of volume sales. Even though chain stores make up only 10% of all stores, they account for about one-third of retail sales. Chains dominate in variety stores (80% of sales), department stores (75%), and shoe stores (50%). The Mitsui was a chain store operated in Japan as early as the 1600s. Sears, Roebuck is currently the largest retail outlet in the world; its sales exceed the gross national product of many countries. After World War II, a number of **discount stores** emerged when marketers believed that customers would gladly sacrifice some store services in order to pay less for goods. So discount stores opened with reduced prices but no delivery services or credit, and with fewer sales clerks. As discount stores attracted attention and grew to over 10% of all retail stores, they added some of the previously cut features and services such as carpet and credit, moving toward full service. They now tend to deemphasize the discount trademark and carry as many services as possible.

Catalog showrooms allow customers to come to a showroom where they can see sample items of the products advertised in the catalog displayed. After selecting the products they wish to buy, customers wait only a few moments while store employees retrieve the product from a backroom warehouse. Safeway, Kroger, and A&P are examples of **supermarkets** — large departmentalized stores that offer a wide variety of food and food-related products. Supermarkets have, in recent years, expanded into other items such as delicatessens, computer sales, books, and even clothing items. Smaller stores located at easy-access locations that offer basic food and food-related items are called **convenience stores.** Examples include 7-Eleven and Quik-Trip. Finally, **factory outlets** offer merchandise to the consumer directly from the factory. Customers can buy items such as furniture, food, and housewares directly from factory-owned outlets usually for a cheaper price.

A few changes are occurring in the retailing system. There has been a decentralization from downtown and movement toward suburban centers, commensurate with population shifts. To counter this, downtown construction in such cities as Minneapolis, Houston, and Kansas City is again attracting retailers. Some predict that moves to shopping centers may be slowing and even turning around.

The clear-cut lines of retail distinction are being muddied by the concept of **scrambled merchandising** — stores adding products they normally do not carry: Drugstores sell milk, gasoline stations offer food, and food stores carry automobile accessories.

Retail trade has become concentrated in a few large-scale retailers. Countering this trend is the growth of specialty and subspecialty shops.

Specialty shops, like the Bell System's Phone Stores, offer a wide choice within a limited product category.

Vertical Marketing Systems

Traditionally, channel members emerge and negotiate agreements without an overall plan. However, **vertical marketing systems (VMS),** well-planned and coordinated distribution networks, have emerged to become a force in the channels. In fact, they are the most common means of distribution in the consumer goods area. Three types of VMS are popular.

Corporate VMS. **Corporate vertical marketing systems** combine stages of production and distribution under single ownership. Kroger, the supermarket, owns thirty-three manufacturing plants and a fleet of trucks. They make over 15% of all the prepared food they sell through their supermarkets. Sears owns many of the producers that supply its stores, and Sherwin-Williams operates thousands of retail outlets.

Administered VMS. Members in an **administered vertical marketing system** are able to achieve cooperation in the production and distribution stages because of the strength of one of its members. Because they are so large and powerful, companies like General Electric and Procter & Gamble can get unusual cooperation from channel members on such issues as shelf space, pricing policies, promotion, and the like.

Contractual VMS. In a **contractual vertical marketing system,** independent firms are able to achieve cooperation at different production and distribution levels via contractual agreements. Sometimes a wholesaler will make an agreement with a group of retailers to cooperate on promotion, pricing, and the like. These are called **wholesaler-sponsored voluntary chains.** Other times, a group of retailers will get together and organize themselves to form **retailer cooperatives.** Franchising agreements also link together various production and distribution stages.

Horizontal Marketing Systems

Horizontal marketing systems (HMS) occur when two or more companies agree to pool their efforts to take advantage of a marketing opportunity. Neither organization may have the know-how, capital, or connections to get the product to the user efficiently. However, between them, they might be able to do it. When Pillsbury Company developed its refrigerated doughs for biscuits and cookies, they realized that they did not know enough about the special, refrigerated displays that these products required. Since Kraft Foods had experience with refrigerated displays in marketing their cheeses, Pillsbury reached an agreement with Kraft to distribute their product.

Multichannel Marketing

Some companies try to reach the same or different markets with more than one channel system, called **multichannel marketing.** J. C. Penney operates three types of retail outlets: department stores, mass-merchandising stores, and specialty stores. Levi Strauss & Company sells its jeans through traditional department stores, specialty stores, Sears, and J. C. Penney's, and the prices may not be the same in each of these outlets.

Channel Conflict

As you might expect, there is often conflict between channel units. When Levi Strauss began selling their jeans to Sears and J. C. Penney's, Macy's discontinued handling them. Gap Stores, Inc., another group of retail stores, severely reduced their Levi product line. Some producers who depend heavily upon dealers also sell directly to the consumer through catalogs or via telephone. Thus, customers might use a dealer to educate themselves about the product and then order the item directly from the manufacturer at a lower price. Of course, dealers bridle at such producer practices.

Producers also create conflicts with channel members when the producer disapproves of dealer practices. An auto manufacturer might drop a dealer if the dealer does not follow the manufacturer's guidelines on service and promotion.

PHYSICAL DISTRIBUTION

After the channels are set, marketers must move the product from the producer to the user. The objectives of physical distribution are to get the product to the right place at the right time at the least cost. Physical distribution is important because the cost of storing and handling the product may run as much as 20% or more of their net sales.

In selecting carriers, companies consider cost, speed, convenience, product safety, storage facilities, and reliability. Table 14.1 identifies the advantages and disadvantages of the major types of transportation.

Air is the fastest and, as you might expect, the most expensive. Rail is usually cheapest, but rail

TABLE 14.1 ■ ADVANTAGES AND DISADVANTAGES OF VARIOUS SHIPPING METHODS

Mode of Transportation	Speed	Cost	Product Safety	Convenience	Storage Requirements
Plane	Best	Most	Best	Fair	Few
Truck	Fair	Moderate	Poor	Best	Many
Ship	Poor	Low	Poor	Poor	Many
Train	Poor	Low	Poor	Poor	Many
Pipeline	Good	Moderate	Good	Poor	Many

TRAINING TRUCKS.

CSX Railroads' Nonstop
Piggyback Corridors
Put Freight Distribution
In High Gear

"Piggyback" combinations
exploit the relatively low cost
of rail and the convenience
and flexibility of trucking.

does not always go to the buyer's location. Many times, shippers use a combination of methods for convenience and reduced costs. But most shipments today go by truck, at least for some part of their journey.

Many shipments combine two or more means of physical distribution. For example, a canned goods factory may load crates into a trailer for Safeway. A crane lifts the trailer onto a railroad flatcar. After the train carries the Safeway trailer to a regional destination, the trailer will be unloaded, and a truck will haul the trailer to distribution stores. Such a combination is called **piggyback. Fishyback** is a similar combination of truck and water service, and **birdyback** combines air and ground travel service.

Containerization, packaging of products by the producer in large-bulk containers that can be moved easily by heavy equipment, is a new trend in physical distribution. This method reduces manual labor costs, provides flexibility in shipping methods, increases speed of delivery, and reduces damage.

SUMMARY

Effective channel management is necessary to get goods and services to the user effectively. A distribution channel consists of all of the institutions that perform activities that move the product and title from producer to user. Some channels are direct from producer to consumer, but the most popular is a two-stage channel including a wholesaler and retailer. In selecting channels, firms consider customer needs, product characteristics, company characteristics, and middlemen characteristics.

Direct marketing is moving the product directly from the producer to the user. The most common forms are mail-order, telephone marketing, and door-to-door sales.

Channel middlemen perform specific functions, including storing, financing, transporting, volume transactions, information gathering, and seeking prospective buyers. Usually, the middlemen, because they are specialists, can perform these functions more efficiently than the producer.

Wholesalers market products between producers and retailers or between producers and other wholesalers. There are many different types of wholesalers, each performing different middlemen functions. Retailers sell the product to the ultimate user. Vertical marketing occurs when firms plan and organize their distribution functions in systematic ways. Horizontal marketing occurs when two or more firms agree to combine their efforts to exploit an opportunity. Many firms use many different channels, and there is often conflict between channel members.

Physical distribution involves all of the activities needed to physically move the product from producer to user.

MIND YOUR BUSINESS

Instructions. Respond to the following questions by answering yes or no in the blanks at the left.

____ 1. Is the most widely used distribution channel a direct channel?

____ 2. Is the passage of title to goods part of the channel flow?

____ 3. Do characteristics of the product influence the channel-selecting decision?

____ 4. Are catalogs becoming more general than they were in the past?

____ 5. Is telephone marketing decreasing in volume?

____ 6. Do middlemen sell directly to the ultimate consumer?

____ 7. Do agent wholesalers take title to goods?

____ 8. Does the sale of most goods take place in retail stores?

____ 9. Do administered vertical marketing systems achieve cooperation in the marketing channels because of the strength of a member?

____ 10. Is distribution by plane the most convenient mode of physical distribution?

See answers at the back of the book.

KEY TERMS

REVIEW QUESTIONS

1. What is a distribution channel? Describe the alternative channels available to marketers.

2. Identify five forms of channel flows.

3. Briefly comment on the channel for services.

4. Explain four factors firms consider when making decisions on what channels to use.

5. Define direct marketing. Discuss three common forms of direct marketing.

6. Define middlemen. Describe the functions middlemen perform.

7. Define wholesalers. Identify the various types of wholesalers.

8. Define retailers. Identify the various types of retailers.

9. Define vertical marketing systems and describe three types.

10. What is horizontal marketing? Multichannel marketing?

11. Explain the nature of channel conflict.

12. What are the objectives of physical distribution?

CASES

Case 14.1: American Can's Direct Marketing Strategy

American Can, in addition to its packaging operations, is engaged in specialty retailing and financial services. They signed a letter of intent to purchase Michigan Bulb Company, a mail-order garden supply firm, in 1984. Management of American Can said they wanted to move more into the service side of the economy and particularly into specialty retailing. Their people think that is where continued growth in the economy will be.

American Can, under their specialty retailing sector, already owns Fingerhut and Figi's, a specialty food and gift marketer, and Musicland, the retail stores that sell records, albums, and tapes. Michigan Bulb, which sells 120 garden and nursery products through the mail, will join these firms as part of American Can's specialty retailing.

Questions

1. What are the advantages and disadvantages of American Can diversifying into specialty retailing?

2. Do you think American Can's strategy of getting into specialty retailing is wise? Why?

___ Yes   ___ No

3. Do you think American Can's purchase of Michigan Bulb Company will prove to be a wise decision? Why?

___ Yes   ___ No

Case 14.2: Practices of a Large Retailer

In 1982, Kroger purchased Dillon's supermarket chain and became the largest supermarket chain in the United States. Sales totaled about $14 billion that year.

Kroger does not hesitate to close down stores that are not profitable; in fact, they have already closed 1237 supermarkets. They operate 1199 food stores in 19 states, plus another 560 drugstores. Last year alone, Kroger closed 65 stores in its Market Basket division in Southern California.

Kroger is also going for large size and additional volume. They have added 12 million square feet of supermarket floor space in the last 10 years, and the average-size Kroger store is 11% bigger than Safeway and 38% bigger than A&P.

Kroger can also be tough on unions. In Pittsburgh, a local chain won wage rollbacks from its union. Kroger demanded the same from its union; when they balked, Kroger threatened to close seven stores and stop construction on five others. Earlier, Kroger's union had refused similar demands in another state, and they sold their twenty-one stores in that state.

Questions

1. Do you agree with Kroger's policy of closing stores that are not profitable? Why?

___ Yes   ___ No

2. What do you think about Kroger's emphasis on large-sized stores?

3. How do you feel about their strategies for dealing with the union? Why?

___ Strongly agree   ___ Agree

___ Disagree   ___ Strongly disagree

L E A R N i N G   O B J E C T I V E S

After completing this chapter, you will be able to:

■ Identify five objectives of promotion.

■ Identify how firms try to measure promotional effectiveness.

■ Explain how firms determine their promotional budgets.

■ List and describe the seven steps of personal selling.

■ Explain eight advertising strategies.

■ Analyze six common forms of advertising media.

■ Discuss three criticisms of advertising.

■ Describe six sales promotion techniques.

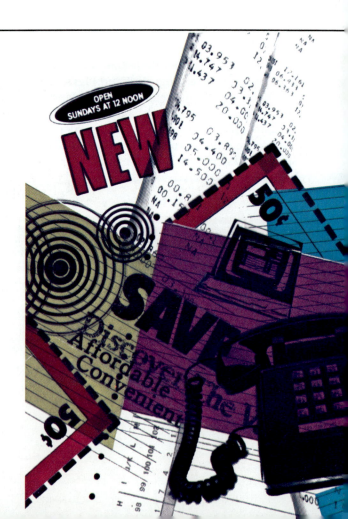

15

PROMOTION, ADVERTISING, AND PERSONAL SELLING

oft-drink producers are waging a promotion, advertising, and selling war to gain part of the soft-drink consumption market. Coca-Cola, introduced in 1886, was the first successful soft drink. And for many years, consumers could choose only Coke. Now Coca-Cola company offers Tab, Diet Coke, Caffeine-Free Coke, Caffeine-Free Diet Coke, and Caffeine-Free Tab. In addition, competitors offer a variety of other brands: Pepsi Free, Sugar-Free Pepsi, Dr. Pepper Free, Sugar-Free Dr. Pepper, Salt-Free Diet Rite Cola, Like, Pepsi Lite, and on and on. Figure 15.1 identifies the cola family tree.

According to a bottler, the soft-drink explosion happened because we live in a society where "people want a lot of different things." Because of the large market (Americans drank an average of 419.5, 12-ounce servings in 1982), the wide variety of products available, and differences in consumer preferences, the success or failure of a new cola depends heavily upon promotion, advertising, and selling techniques. As a promotional manager described it, "We try to instill in consumers' minds images that will make them want to buy the product."

To better understand how managers communicate their images to consumers, we examine in this chapter promotional mix, personal selling, advertising, promotional devices, and public relations.

PROMOTIONAL MIX

Promotion is any activity that encourages the purchase of a good or service. Managers must determine how much they are going to invest in promotion and what tools they will use. The **promotional mix,** or plan, utilizes personal selling, advertising, and sales promotion to deliver the message. Public relations and all types of publicity that attract customer attention to the product also become part of the mix. The mix depends upon the product, the life cycle stage, and how the product is sold. The more alike the products, the more promotions differentiate among them in the

early life cycle stages. Promotion is most important in the product's introduction and maturity stages. In introduction, the market is unaware of the product and therefore uninterested; promotion must overcome ignorance and generate interest. In the maturity stage, competition is stiff, and the promotion must show how a product is different or unique. Promotional mix policies are affected by promotional program objectives, implementation strategies, evaluation of program effectiveness, and the promotional budget.

The Objectives of Promotion

The key objectives of promotion are to:

Provide information. Promotion must inform the market about what is available, the characteristics of the product or service, and how to use it. For instance, Panasonic's ad for their voice-activated microcassette recorder tells customers that their product starts recording automatically when someone starts talking. And it also stops when they stop. Further, they claim, its playback is 30% faster than others; and because it has two tape speeds, owners can record for two hours on a one-hour microcassette.

Stimulate sales. Obviously, companies want to stimulate customers to buy their products and services. Promotion tries to get consumers to recognize, look for, examine, try, and purchase the product. In advertising their personal computer,

TeleVideo Systems, Inc., begins an ad with, "Here's what makes it irresistible. . . ." Then they stress the product's easy-to-use features to entice you to try it; and to stimulate you to purchase it, they close their ad with, "So why resist?"

Highlight values. Status-oriented advertising to highlight values makes sure customers are aware of what the company considers to be a real value. Canon, the first company to produce a low-priced personal copier, stressed the high-quality copy

that people could make conveniently in their homes. They also showed buyers how to produce color copies and described their removable cartridge, which made it unnecessary for the user to worry about adding fluids.

Differentiate between products. Somewhat related to highlighting values is product differentiation—letting consumers know how a product or service is different from that of competitors'. Few consumers can differentiate be-

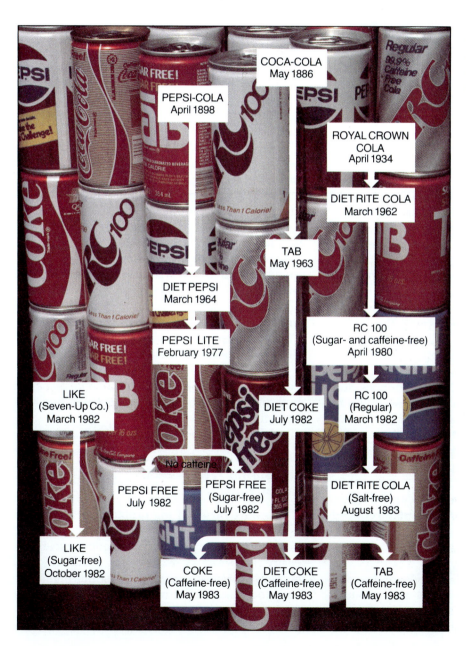

Figure 15.1
The cola family tree.
Source: Copyright Wichita Eagle-Beacon, reprinted with permission.

Eye-catching colors and the status of a designer's name can be effective in differentiating a product line from that of the competition.

tween the effectiveness of many similar products or services. Digital, trying to differentiate itself from IBM in the personal computer market, began offering a free, one-year, on-site maintenance contract to anyone who purchased a Digital personal computer through a retail outlet. Digital also announced a 30-day cash guarantee for all of its equipment. A spokesperson said they could have tried to differentiate by lowering the price; instead, they chose to add enhancements and customer protection. Similarly, since most consumers cannot distinguish between the effectiveness of many soaps, perfumes, shampoos, and the like, promoters try to make these different with color, shape, and packaging.

Stabilize sales.   Since consistent sales will help to smooth production output, some promotion attempts to create sales stabilization. In the middle of the summer, Gragg's Furs, an independent retail store, advertised their furs at prices reduced up to 40%.

Implementation Strategies

The promotional program pulls the product through the channels by stimulating ultimate consumer use. Customers shop for and request products and otherwise pressure retail outlets, who in turn pressure wholesale institutions to deliver the products. This **pull strategy** relies heavily upon advertising and public relations. Early in Elvis Presley's career, backers effectively used a pull strategy to sell his records. After he became known, he would appear on television and sing a number not yet released. Avid fans would look for the record, request it, sign waiting lists, and give their orders well in advance. This sent retail record stores scurrying to make sure they could pull the record through the channels from the producers.

The reverse, or **push strategy,** happens when producers work on channel members rather than the final user. With heavy emphasis on personal selling, producers try to make wholesalers and retailers aware of their product's benefits and how successful it will be. Producers stimulate interest in the channel with sales persuasion, dealer supports, trade discounts, and advertising allowances; channel members then take the incentive to convince the ultimate consumer of the product's value.

Federated Department Stores, Inc., is struggling with product differentiation. The store has added a lot of designer labels and discount items, and management fears that they are losing their unique identity. Their solution is to develop high-quality merchandise that carries a higher profit margin and is different from competitors'. For example, they brought out a line of sheets and towels under the brand name "Home Concept." Through their ads, they will try to promote the differences between their stores and others.

These strategies represent two ends of the continuum. Actually, most promotional plans use both pull and push pressures, although one may be highly featured.

Measuring Promotional Effectiveness

A haunting question for promotional experts is how well does the program work? Is it causing people to buy the product? Promotion research is costly and cannot isolate the variables well enough to be positive of the results. Still, managers have to measure effectiveness so they can decide whether or not to continue. The direct-sales approach is the most desired and addresses the question of how much the promotion increased sales. Suppose the company undertakes a $3 million advertising campaign over a 2-year period, and sales increase by 30%. Because of multiple variables, we will never know for sure how much sales would have increased without the program, or whether the direct-sales approach actually caused increased sales. Perhaps the price, competitors' actions, economic conditions, or change in consumer tastes had a greater impact than the promotional plan.

Other evaluation points use indirect methods. Some research tries to measure potential customer **readership;** how many people actually saw the promotion and were aware of it? Researchers test **recall** by interviewing or sending questionnaires to people to see what they can remember about the advertising program: the brand name, the price, how it is used. While research can measure these variables reliably, companies still do not know if recall and readership translate into sales. Customers can be informed and impressed with advertisements and still not purchase the product.

The Promotional Budget

There is no definitive answer to the question, "Just how much should we spend on promotion?" Several methods are used to determine

The most common way of allocating a promotional budget is percentage of sales.

budgets, and industries have developed guidelines for using each method. The most common way of allocating a promotional budget is percentage of sales. Managers may take last year's sales or next year's projections and designate promotion to be 5% of either figure. Others set aside a fixed sum for advertising, which does not vary directly with sales. Producers of high-cost items, such as cars or appliances, tend to use this fixed-sum method. Another promotional budget strategy is to keep up with the competition: Try to estimate what the competition is doing and match it. While this keeps competition from getting too far ahead, it is a passive strategy and probably does not relate to promotional objectives. The more recent task-objective method identifies program goals and estimates how much must be spent to accomplish these goals. Using this method, Pizza Hut spent several million dollars developing, testing, and promoting their very successful "5-minute" pizza. While this is more analytical and objective, it fails to project just how much must be spent to reach the objective. Suppose a promotional objec-

CROSS FIRE

Trade Promotions

Often, producers give wholesalers and retailers special discounts for promoting their products extra hard, to encourage them to provide desirable shelf space, and the like.

A supermarket may carry fifty different soft drinks. A single display at the front of the store can increase a product's sales by sixfold. So supermarkets may entertain bids from different producers to see who will give them the best price discount.

When a manufacturer gives a retailer a discount, the producer usually requires special treatment in return for the discount. For example, they might require the retailer to pass along some of the discount to customers, feature the product in local newspaper ads, or place the product in a special place within the store. Producers then follow up to see if the retailers kept their part of the deal.

Currently, there is a debate going on between manufacturers and retailers over trade discounts. Retailers say that manufacturers are trying to reduce their trade discounts and increase their profits at the expense of retailers. Manufacturers say that retailers often refuse to pass along the discounts to customers, and retailers have fattened their own profits at the expense of the manufacturer and the customer. Further, because competition is so fierce among producers, they may offer huge trade discounts without getting much benefit from them. Retailers tend to overstock during the discount period; thus, many months pass before they have to start buying at list price. Still, there will likely be little drop-off in this type of promotion in the near future. Do you believe trade promotions benefit the consumer? Why?

___ Yes   ___ No

Do you think manufacturers should increase or decrease the use of trade promotions? Why?

___ A. Increase   ___ B. Decrease

Source: Monci Jo Williams, "The No-Win Game of Price Promotion," *Fortune,* July 11, 1983, pp. 92–102.

tive is to increase sales by 10% during the year. We do not know how much to spend to generate this increase. Also, some promotional expenditures create proportionally larger shares of revenue than others.

While the last method is more objective and more active than the others, most decisions rely upon considerations of all these. The budget is still largely a matter of subjective judgment. It boils down to what someone in power thinks is appropriate.

PERSONAL SELLING

Nothing much happens in business until someone sells something. In our society, salespeople comprise more than 6 million employees, and selling costs average between 10 and 15 cents of each sales dollar. **Personal selling** occurs when a person interacts with one or more people with the purpose of promoting a good or a service.

Much of the stigma attached to the selling

profession originated with nineteenth-cen-

tury pitchmen who hawked novelties and

medicines on street corners and in bare

barns.

Much of the stigma attached to the selling profession originated with nineteenth-century pitchmen who hawked novelties and medicines on street corners and in bare barns. With magic, music, and jokes, they drummed up attention and attracted crowds for the pitch. They also used animals, monkeys, lizards, and burning money. One ingenious method developed by a pitchman called for a rope, the Bible, and a human skull. He would lay out these strange props and, with care and concentration, begin to rearrange them until a fascinated crowd gathered around him. This continued for a half hour or so after the crowd gathered until he felt his audience was ready. Then he launched into a lecture on his "medicines," never once mentioning the rope, skull, or Bible.

Pitchmen were able to hypnotize a crowd with oratory, giving their explications the intensity of a mystic. Many items they sold had no function, and some were harmful. The epitome of the pitchman was shown in the delightful musical *Music Man*. But there were a number of legitimate sales travelers or drummers in this era. Modern sales, composed primarily of professional salespeople, emerged in the late forties as the economy returned to normalcy after the war. As Arthur Miller's play *Death of a Salesman* depicts, we have turned the corner from the days of riding the smile and the flamboyant orator to the professional, knowledgeable salesperson who knows the product, consults buyers, helps with ordering, and advises on service calls.

Professional Selling

Professional salespeople know their companies, their products, competitors, customers, and themselves; they are professional communicators. Professional selling is an educational process. Salespeople have four primary responsibilities: creative selling, missionary selling, order receiving, and feedback.

Creative selling perhaps draws upon the energy of the old-time drummers in making the product come alive to the prospect. The purpose is to dramatize product appeal, product uses, and customer benefits. Professional salespeople stop short of the pitchman's final phrase, "If it doesn't cure you, prepare to meet your Maker!" But creative selling does appeal to intangible needs and buying motives. When selling to industrial users, a more logical approach is in order.

Missionary selling is indirect; it focuses on building goodwill and a positive company image. Follow-ups with customers, extra efforts to be sure they are satisfied, special attention to service, and technical and expert assistance on the continuing use of goods are classified as missionary selling.

Many wholesalers and retailers emphasize order receiving. Much catalog selling is order receiving in person or over the telephone. Salespeople who primarily receive orders also take positive action by identifying and inventorying stock and recommending order sizes. They can be especially helpful in smaller retail outlets by advising how much to order, how best to display the goods, and even recommending markups. In this way, missionary selling combines with order receiving.

Finally, professional salespeople are an excellent source of feedback for the company. Using their close relationship with the purchaser, they can relate feelings, emotions, and hunches on how the market is moving, which even well-designed research may not unearth. Although some salespeople tend to operate in one mode or another, most professional sellers employ all these activities.

Selling Steps

The actual selling process has been discussed and researched for some time. While authorities vary their models slightly, there are several identifiable activities or subprocesses in the personal-selling process. These activities — prospecting, qualifying, presentation, product demonstration, objections, closing, and follow-up — overlap, and some are omitted in certain situations.

Prospecting. Prospecting for customers, like panning for gold, means putting in time, sweat, and a lot of heart. **Cold canvassing** is going out prospecting without leads to interest people in the product. Likely prospect sources are current customers' friends, other vendors, social contacts, professional contacts, and systematic referral systems. Commercial real estate firms estimate that more than half their sales come from referrals after 2 years in the business.

Qualifying. Customers without the need or financial ability to purchase the product may be pursued fruitlessly. Insightful selling requires directed questions and an attentive listener to sense buying motives, purchasing ability, and need for the product. Many people wander into a furniture store to look around, compare prices, or "ooh and ah" over children's furniture though their children are grown. As one salesman quipped, "It is hard to tell the interested people from those with a few minutes to spare on the way to the airport."

Presentation. After qualification, the salesperson makes the presentation, emphasizing product advantages and uses, superiority to other products, research reports, customer satisfaction, and answering customers' questions. Some

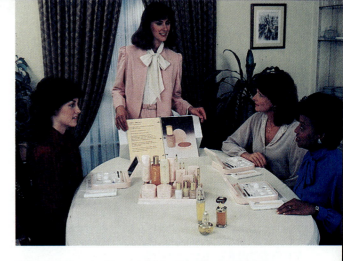

Sales representatives for Mary Kay Cosmetics bring their presentations into the homes of prospective customers.

"canned" approaches consist of a script that the salesperson memorizes, practicing wording, voice inflections, and effective pauses. Flexible presentations are favored and no doubt are the most effective because they tailor the presentation to the circumstance.

Product demonstration. When possible, sales approaches try to incorporate product demonstrations: a new car ride, a vacuum cleaner sweeping up dirt, or a cleaning fluid removing a spot. This visual approach often convinces the customer. Television commercials simulate demonstrations.

Objections. Responding to objections is a skillful art in personal selling. Objections should be viewed as clues to concern rather than obstacles to the selling process. Sometimes the more direct denials and arduous arguments fail to overcome the objection, but stressing the positive points, turning the objection into an advantage, and explaining the facts with a soft sell are persuasive.

Closing. Tension rises, adrenalin flows, and perspiration surfaces on closing the sale. This is the salesperson's last spurt and determines whether the sale will be consummated. As strange as it sounds, one mistake in closing is failing to ask for the order. At some point, the salesperson has to put his or her ego on the line and accept the possibility of a "no." Just before closing, the salesperson builds to a peak in trying to destroy any wavering doubts.

Follow-up. After the purchase, salespeople should follow up to reinforce the buying decision, increase customer satisfaction, and check on product usage. They can share the customer's excitement about the new purchase. Good repeat customers are invaluable and often provide leads to new customers.

ADVERTISING

Unlike personal selling, **advertising** is a paid nonpersonal appeal to customers. The power of advertising is debated and has many critics. Nonetheless, advertising keeps booming along, setting new records each year. In 1985, the money spent on advertising is expected to hover around $70 billion.

Product Advertising

The nonpersonal selling of a product is **product advertising.** Ads try to point out features of the product or a service. When Sharp Electronics Corporation, the leading seller of small copiers during the last 2 years, advertises its Sharp SF-755 model copier, it is engaging in product advertising. The same is true when Sears advertises its Budget Rent-A-Car and when Time, Inc., promotes *Sports Illustrated.* Product advertising concentrates on the personal attributes of the product, its brand, style, and type.

Institutional Advertising

Institutional advertising promotes a philosophy or a company image, such as Avis's successful motto, "We are second — we have to try harder." Other examples include, "Get your favorite NFL team shirt," the Dairy Association's promotions to get people to drink more milk, the state of Florida's ads to visit Florida on vacation, and the life insurance industry's efforts to educate consumers about life insurance. When engaging in institutional advertising, firms try to build an overall positive image of the company or of their industry.

Advertising Strategies

As the head of an ad agency commented, "We try to communicate, persuade, and reinforce customers to buy selected products and services. And

Although there is some doubt about its effectiveness, positioning, an advertising strategy that compares products to competitors, now makes up about 10% of all advertising.

in doing this, we are always looking for newer strategies, ones that work even better than what we have." These advertising strategies differ and have changed over time.

Positioning. **Positioning,** one of the newer strategies, compares products to competitors. "In the old days, we avoided naming competitors' products like they were painful plagues," said an elderly advertising executive. "But now," he added, "we put the competitor right up there beside our product so the customer can see the difference." Sometimes called **comparative advertising,** positioning tries to establish a relative market position for the product or service. Al-

A positioning ad

though there is still some doubt about its effectiveness, positioning now makes up about 10% of advertising. It is more widely used where a few brands dominate the market.

Pulsating. Another recent concept that does not claim many followers is **pulsating**—hitting the advertising hard for a period, then slacking off. Ipana was dropped as a brand name for toothpaste several years ago, but a couple of years ago, a company started using the Ipana label again without any advertising and found many sales still lingering from the advertising of earlier years. A beer distributor's research indicated that its advertising had a lingering effect. This distributor flooded the market with advertising for a few months, then stopped for several months, repeating the cycle in pulsating fashion.

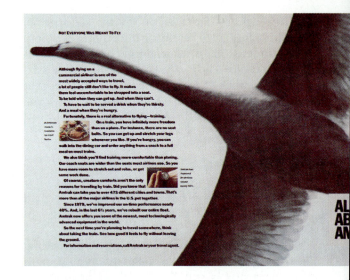

A persuasive ad

Persuasive advertising. **Persuasive advertising** tries to improve the competitive status of the product or service, and it is usually used when the product or service has been around for a while. An example of persuasive advertising is the Army Reserve's, "Join an army you don't have to leave home for," and, "Army reserve. Be all you can be." Another example is the state of Oklahoma's appeal to tourists, "Visit our green country."

Informative advertising. When the primary purpose of advertising is to provide information to the potential consumer, it is **informative advertising.** Many times, the ad asks viewers to write or call for additional information, perhaps a brochure or a catalog describing the products or service in more detail. Other times, informational ad-

An informative ad

Criteria for the ad were that it contain thinkers who are deceased, from a variety of disciplines and encompassing a chronological span from ancient to modern times. After the eight were chosen from among 15 to 20 well-researched possibilities, their accomplishments were rechecked with historical societies.

If you weren't able to identify all eight of the world's great thinkers, or would like to check your answers, please don't reach for the telephone. Corporate Advertising isn't staffed to handle 107,000 employee inquiries. (*Answer key:* Aristotle, DaVinci, Shakespeare, Newton, Jefferson, Darwin, Curie, and Einstein.)

Source: Reprinted with permission from the December 1983 issue of *Update,* the Allied Corporation employee publication.

vertising describes what a company can do or perhaps where their locations are. An ad on Xerox service centers says, in part, "Come to one of our Xerox Service Centers. We have eighty-two nationwide. And we're multiplying faster than software programs." The ad then lists twenty-one personal computers the service centers are equipped to work on and gives the addresses of its eighty-two service centers. Ernest Gray, an advertising consultant, considers informational advertising to be far superior to pointless boasts. Examples of messages that do not sell are: "The best your money can buy," "The best on the market," and "The top value around." A furniture ad makes this mistake with, "The finest furniture around." A competitor does better with an informational slogan, "Old-fashioned furniture at old-fashioned prices."

Reminder advertising. Reminder advertising tries to reinforce a message or an image from previous advertisements. Firms typically use this strategy when their product or service has been

A reminder ad

An advocacy ad

around for a long time and sales are beginning to drop. Sometimes coupons that allow you a discount on the price of the item accompany reminder advertising. An ad for Mazola margarine contained their oft-repeated slogan, "Made from 100% corn oil," and contained a clip-out coupon that customers could return for a 25-cent savings.

Advocacy advertising. In **advocacy advertising,** a firm takes a stand on a controversial issue or makes a proposal to solve some societal problem. Mobil Oil Company spends millions of dollars per year on advocacy advertising, most of which they aim at what is good about our private enterprise system. One of their recent ads included, "The U.S., with only one-twentieth of the world's population, accounts for fully one-fourth of its

Gross National Product." Another part of the ad read, "Well then, to the list of freedoms — of religion, of speech, of the press, and more — that make America *great*, let us add thanks for economic freedom: It makes America *work*."

Westinghouse provides another example of advocacy advertising with their emphasis on quality family entertainment on television. Their advocacy ads say they take the social responsibility of broadcasting very seriously. One ad says, in part, "We won't produce or distribute anything we wouldn't want our own families to watch." The ad goes on to say that they support the arts in Boston, crime prevention programs in Baltimore, and the Children's Hospital in Pittsburgh.

Pioneering advertising. The purpose of **pioneering advertising** is to stimulate demand for a new product or service. Last year, Coca-Cola launched their new product, Diet Coke, with Hollywood-style hype. The company rented Radio

A pioneering ad

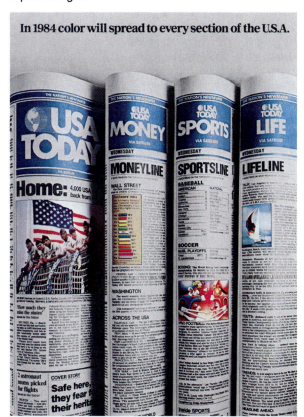

In 1984 color will spread to every section of the U.S.A.

Starting in July, 1984, color will come to the Life and Money sections of USA TODAY. That will make a total of 16 color pages, and give our advertisers the opportunity to run their color ads in all four sections.
© 1983 Gannett

We pay these guys, but we can't buy them.

A personality ad

City Music Hall and invited 4000 people to attend entertainment by the Rockettes and a forty-piece orchestra. Coca-Cola, after the event, took guests to a West Side pier where they feasted on hot dogs, ethnic delicacies, and, of course, Diet Coke. After the fireworks display, guests took home 4000 six-packs of the diet drink. Although this event cost $100,000, Coca-Cola spent at least an additional $50 million promoting the product across the country. As a result, Diet Coke was an instant success, moving to number 4 in soft drink sales shortly after its introduction.

Use of personalities. Using well-known personalities is another way companies try to build trusting images of their products and services. Some of these ads make a long-term commitment; some examples: Joe Namath signed a 10-year contract with Brut, O. J. Simpson and Arnold Palmer have become closely identified with Hertz Rent-A-Car, Bill Cosby and Coca-Cola, Bjorn Borg and the Concord Centurion Sportswatch, Bob Hope and Texaco Oil Company, and many years ago, Dinah Shore and Chevrolet.

However, there is some doubt about the effectiveness of using celebrities in ads. *Advertising Age* polled 1250 adults across the country. Fifty-four percent of the respondents said that using celebrities in ads made "no difference" in believability. Thirty-three percent said that a celebrity who plugs several products is actually less believable. And 64 percent said that they did not believe the celebrity spokesperson used the products or services they represented. The pollsters concluded that today's consumer is probably too sophisticated to place too much credence on advertised recommendations of hired celebrities.

How Advertisers Select Media

Advertisers have many choices on what media they are going to use to get their message to the public. In making their decisions, advertising managers consider three questions:

1. What is the size of the product's (or service's) market appeal?
2. How effective is the medium in reaching this market?
3. What does the medium cost?

A brief analysis of the more popular media for advertising follows.

Newspapers. Newspapers, receiving almost a third of all advertising revenues, are the most popular of all advertising media. In a 1982 survey that asked respondents to identify what they considered the "most believable" advertising media to be, 42% said newspapers had the most believable advertising. Twenty-six percent selected television, 11% chose radio, and 5% said direct mail.

Of course, experts perceive some newspapers to be better media than others. *Advertising Age* in 1983 polled 110 journalism faculty members from schools in 39 states. They concluded that the *New York Times*, which has a Sunday circulation of more than 1.5 million, was the country's number 1 newspaper. The *Washington Post* was second, the *Los Angeles Times* third, and *The Wall Street Journal* was fourth.

Firms like to advertise in newspapers because they are low-cost, require little lead time, and they can selectively penetrate market segments. The biggest negative: newspaper life is short, usually just a few minutes as readers scan the paper.

Television. Television advertising represents the fastest-growing media. Via television, commercials zoom to millions of viewers in a flash; their color and movement give an added glow to the message, and they can be repeated for lasting effect. However, the cost is prohibitive for many. Many commercials for sporting events, the highest priced of all, cost more than half a million dol-

---

In the 1983–1984 season, ABC TV's hunk-and-centerfold show "Dynasty" sold commercials at $179,000 for 30 seconds.

---

lars a minute (yes, that amounts to over $8000 per second). In the 1983–1984 season, ABC TV's hunk-and-centerfold show "Dynasty" sold commercials at $179,000 for 30 seconds. A half-minute on an average prime-time program went for $75,000. However, because of increased competition among the networks and from cable, executives are unable to raise the prices as much as they once did. Figure 15.2 shows the percentage change in TV commercial rates during the past 10 years.

Purchasers buy many of their commercials "up front," that is, before the season actually begins. Commercials sold after the season begins are called scatter sales. One of the largest up-front buyers, Ralston Purina, spends about $70 million annually advertising pet foods and cereals on network TV.

Also on the negative side, TV commercials carry only brief messages, and some research indicates that a lot of people leave the screen during the inevitable commercial break.

Direct mail. Chapter 14 covered direct mail as a distribution channel. But direct mail is also an advertising media. Companies can buy mailing lists from list brokers that identify market targets by zip code, profession, earnings, location, attendance at meetings, membership in organizations, family size, and the like. For instance, if an agency wanted to promote a training seminar to people in the Southwest, they could buy from a broker names of executives who had a title of mid-level manager or higher. If you wanted to, you could also specify that the list contain people who had attended at least one other training program during the last 3 years. Mailing lists sell between $175 and $300 for a list of 5000 names, which is usually a minimum order.

Often, direct mail advertising offers free samples or trial offers to would-be purchasers. According to Kobs and Brady Advertising in Chicago, 10 to 15% of the people who accept a trial offer will return the merchandise. Still, trial offers produce about twice as many orders as money-back guarantees.

Percentage

20 —

15 —

10 —

5 —

0 —

8.0   6.0   18.2   20.0   11.0   11.2   7.   8.   11.   .5   11.3

1974   1975   1976   1977   1978   1979   1980   1981   1982   1983   1984
                                                                (est.) (proj.)

Year

Figure 15.2
Percentage of increase in
TV commercial rates.
Source: McCann-Erickson.

While direct mail offers maximum selectivity and flexibility, it suffers from a negative image; many receivers ignore direct mail advertising, regarding it as "junk mail." Also, increased postage rates make mass mail-outs more costly than in the past.

Radio. Much like newspapers, radio stations blanket the country. There are more than 7000 and they send everything over the airwaves, from talk shows to news to hard rock. Radio broadcasting stations typically have a profile of their listeners, and this allows advertisers to make appeal to select market targets. The rates are reasonable, especially when compared to television, but like newspaper and television ads, the message appears for only a few seconds. The most effective stations for radio advertising develop a clear image of what they are. For example, The Great Empire, Inc., a chain of stations in the midwest, presents a country image by playing country music and building country images of their disk jockeys and station personnel. As they say, "We are country and we are selling it."

Magazine. Although there are a few general purpose magazines like *Reader's Digest, U.S. News, Time,* and *Newsweek,* most appeal to very specialized readers. There are magazines for practically every type of interest imaginable — from home computer users to hunters to gar-

deners. Because of this specialization, magazine advertising can appeal to special audiences. They also last longer than newspaper, television, and radio because people keep them around for days and maybe even weeks or years. Many people collect their special magazines, keeping them for 10 years or more. They do, however, require a long lead time; preparation sometimes takes several weeks before the publication goes to print. And elaborate ads in prestigious journals are quite expensive.

Of late, companies have begun creating their own publications that look and sound very much like magazines. They send the publications to potential buyers at no charge. These often slick and polished periodicals strive to convey the message that the corporate sponsor is concerned and helpful. Webb Co. of St. Paul, Minnesota, publishes for Farmers Insurance Group, Inc. a magazine called *Friendly Exchange.* Although *Friendly Exchange* goes to the 4 million policyholders of Farmers Insurance Group, the magazine rarely mentions the company or its policies. According to Jack Klobucar, communications director for Webb Co., the magazine "works almost subliminally."

This method of advertising is apparently effective. Younkers, an Iowa department store chain, mails *You,* a fashion magazine, to its 205,000 credit-card customers. A questionnaire survey of its readers concluded that not only did they keep the magazine around, many bought clothes fea-

TABLE 15.1 ■ ADVANTAGES AND DISADVANTAGES OF ADVERTISING MEDIA

Factor	Media					
	Television	Newspaper	Direct Mail	Radio	Magazines	Outdoor
Media cost	Most costly	Low	High per contact	Low	High	Low
Preparation cost	Most	Moderate	Low	Very low	High	Very high
Life span	Short	Short	Average	Short	Long	Longest
Lead time	Most	Little	Little	Little	Much	Much
Impact	Moderate	Highest	Low	Less	Moderate	Low to moderate
Selectivity	Slight	Slight	Excellent	Good	Excellent	Slight

tured in the publication. Not everyone is convinced, however. A Sears executive says that free magazines may benefit some groups such as insurance companies, but they probably would not benefit merchandisers that much.

Outdoor techniques. Billboards; inflatables; beetleboards; messages on buses, taxis, and subway trains; signs in the outfield at a ballpark; overhead streamers from a biplane; and T-shirt advertising are all examples of outdoor advertisements.

A few years ago, an enterprising entrepreneur made thousands of dollars by leasing space on the side of Volkswagen Beetles. About 6 years ago, Robert Vicino tried leasing space on the side of a hot-air balloon. On his first venture he floated over a cow pasture rather than over the busy highway he was aiming for. Now, however, he is apparently doing quite well by making inflatable advertising pieces in the shape of corporate products and characters. Resembling the helium-filled balloons used in a lot of parades, Vicino's company has produced giant soda pop and beer cans, liquor bottles, and cigarette packs that float over

---

As an outdoor advertisement, an inflatable, giant King Kong cost $35,000, and even though it collapsed when climbing the Empire State Building, it got the company a lot of publicity.

---

beaches, trade shows, and grand openings. You might remember, a couple of years ago, the inflatable giant King Kong that collapsed when mounted on the Empire State Building. This inflatable Kong cost $35,000, but it got the company a lot of publicity, even though it collapsed. Most inflatables cost the advertiser between $3000 and $10,000.

Outdoor advertising is very flexible and seems to be effective in metropolitan areas where there is a lot of traffic. These ads also last a relatively long time. However, the public sensitivity toward the cluttering effect of signs and billboards may limit the growth of outdoor advertising. Table 15.1 shows advantages and disadvantages of various advertising media.

Advertising Agencies

Typically, advertising agencies perform many advertising functions for companies. Employing about 160,000 people, ad agencies bill clients more than $28 billion annually for their services. Typically, the agencies collect a 15% commission on their billings. Agencies are under immense pressure to produce new clients and to keep current clients satisfied.

Agency-client relationships. A full-service agency typically offers five services to clients, including: (1) creative services—art, writing; (2) media services—media analysis, selection, and space purchasing; (3) research—surveys to help identify customer profiles and ad effectiveness; (4) merchandising advice—what mixes of products and services to offer and to what types of clients; and (5) campaign design and planning—overall theme, timing, and placement of ads.

Agency switching. With all the high pressure and the demands for creative freshness, both advertisers and agencies occasionally switch their loyalties. One advertising executive said, "You must always keep new accounts coming in the door. It is not a matter of whether you will lose an account, it is a matter of when you will lose the account." In any given year, hundreds of large accounts may change agencies.

And although it does not happen as often, the agency itself might drop an account to pick up a

Some large firms maintain an in-house agency to provide advertising services.

competing account. Young & Rubicam, Inc., did just that when they dropped Procter & Gamble to pick up $120 million in annual billings from Colgate-Palmolive Co. Understandably, P&G was miffed. A spokesperson said, ". . . our principal disappointment is that the agency has chosen to be employed by a direct competitor of P&G working on brands directly competitive to those it handled for us." Young & Rubicam said that Colgate approached them and they decided to go with them because "the best possibilities for long-term growth are with Colgate."

Criticisms of Advertising

Critics of advertising focus on truth, price, and material values.

Is advertising misleading? In a recent Harris poll, 85% of those questioned said they believed that TV advertising was misleading, and 80% felt the same way about newspaper and magazine ads. Of course, some commercials, like some ministers, are dishonest. And the Federal Trade Commission (FTC), the government watchdog, has taken on some of the largest companies. For instance, the FTC stopped Colgate-Palmolive commercials that said Rapid Shave creme enabled razors to scrape clean "tough, dry sandpaper." The sandpaper was really plastic sprinkled with sand. Campbell Soup Company had to stop showing ads that used marbles in bowls of soup to make solid ingredients rise to the top. Warner-Lambert Company had to stop claiming that Listerine mouthwash cured colds and sore throats. And the FTC stopped STP from claiming that its oil additive was equal to an engine tune-up.

Outright fraudulent practices can be caught and usually are, but sometimes it is hard to tell the difference between deception and trade puffery. Some advertisers argue that many products would go down the drain if promotions did not contain a little fluff because they claim purchasers do not make decisions strictly for functional reasons. Looking for subtle forms of deception such as half-truths and unsubstantiated claims requires enough effort.

But the FTC is also concerned about psychological manipulation. For instance, they are asking the advertising industry to defend itself on such questions as:

- Is it misleading to use adults to plug children's products because children tend to trust grown-ups?
- Is it misleading to link beautiful, clean, sunlit meadows with cigarette smoking?
- Is it misleading to imply that mouthwash, deodorant, shampoo, toothpaste, and chewing gum will make you sexy?

There may be some evidence, however, that the FTC is easing its rules requiring firms to support their ad claims. FTC Chairman James Miller began questioning some of the FTC rulings when he took office in 1981, and as a result, many firms are appealing the agency's new sympathies. In a recent ruling, the FTC ordered Bristol-Myers Co. and Sterling Drug, Inc., to drop ads saying tests show their Excedrin, Bufferin, and Bayer aspirin brands are better than others unless they have clinical studies to back up the claims. But the ruling said that the company might rely upon other kinds of scientific evidence. This changed a previous ruling that said that if an ad does not mention test data, superiority claims must be backed up by two clinical studies. In short, the FTC seems to be making it easier for sellers to make claims about their products' capabilities.

Just what is a reasonable accurate impression? The Supreme Court has tried to draw the fine line by saying, "Advertising as a whole must not create a misleading impression." It is not enough for each line, taken separately, to be literally true. The Supreme Court further adds that advertising must not conceal material facts or distract attention away from the true nature of the conditions. Because of the difficulty of this issue, more advertisers will probably find themselves trying to keep their wits as they struggle through stormy court cases. On the face of it, many modern commercials do seem to make claims that are at least somewhat exaggerated.

Does advertising increase the price? Critics charge that advertising costs run prices up higher than necessary. And economists add that since advertising does not create value, it fails to create new demand but merely switches buyers from one brand to another. Pointing to multimillion-dollar advertising budgets of larger companies, critics complain that as much as 40 to 60% of the price of products such as cosmetics, soaps, and toiletries result from advertising and packaging.

Likewise, stamps, games, contests, and other advertising gimmicks add significantly to the cost of the product without improving its tangible or psychological benefits. Companies spend millions of dollars packaging and promoting products to create brand loyalty. Yet studies indicate that most users cannot identify their favorite brand among all brands in blind tests.

On the other side, advertising serves a needed educational function by making consumers aware of prices, quality, and ingredients. With this information, consumers become better shoppers, selecting the most efficiently priced goods and leaving overpriced, poor-quality items to gather dust on the shelves. Some states prevent advertising of selected products or services. For instance, a few states prevent advertising by optometrists, and surveys show that eye examinations are more expensive in these states. There is little doubt that some advertising is wasteful, but the answer is surely not withdrawal of all advertising. Rather, businesses must plan promotional budgets more carefully. Also, consumers should be selective in their choices because unpurchased brands are quickly dropped.

Does advertising encourage excessive materialism? Critics accuse marketers of overstimulating demands for goods, especially those that return high profits, while ignoring more spiritual needs. Professor and author Vance Packard, in his best-selling book *The Hidden Persuaders,* accuses promoters of using psychiatry and social science findings to shape, mold, and alter our purchasing decisions beyond our ability to control them. Economist and social critic John Kenneth Galbraith adds that demand is managed through a network of communications, promotions, merchandising, selling, advertising, and related services.

Faultfinders add that our emphasis on materialism paints success as a large house in the suburbs, two cars in the garage, three color television sets, and a swimming pool in the backyard.

Achievers are disillusioned when they find that happiness did not accompany their material acquisitions. Others suffer emotional and physical damage through frustration because their best efforts get them only part way up the slippery treadmill. Some slide into an apathetic existence, feeling that they never had a chance.

This criticism probably exaggerates the power of promoters because consumers are not easily brainwashed. They receive information from many sources, including government, religion, education, and a host of social critics and protection groups. Media are quick to publicize information on malpractice and research findings that discount advertising claims, and competitors also watchdog improprieties that might hurt their industry's reputation. Advertising is only one ingredient in this wide information flow. Perhaps people are more easily persuaded to buy when a desire already exists, but dissatisfied buyers are not likely to repeat their purchases. They have too many other choices. The stark reality is that most new products fail. If companies were capable of manipulating the membranes of the brain with millions of promotional dollars, advertising managers would be able to reduce their failures substantially.

PROMOTIONAL DEVICES AND PUBLIC RELATIONS

In addition to advertising, sales promotion and public relations help firms create demand for their products and services.

Sales Promotion

Sales promotion devices, usually supplementing other forms of advertising, encourage the purchaser to buy now. A few popular sales promotion techniques include:

Trade shows, fairs, and conventions. Close to 100 million people attend trade shows, fairs, and conventions in any given year. Many industries organize trade fairs in conjunction with their conventions. They invite producers to display

A trade-show demonstration of new products — such as this industrial robot — is an effective sales promotion technique.

Samples. Samples contain free products, usually in a small quantity, given or mailed to the consumer. They are most widely used in calling attention to new products or pinpointing modifications of existing products. This approach expresses the belief that the product itself is the best communication available. Beecham Products mailed thousands of 1.4-ounce samples when introducing their fluoride Aqua-fresh toothpaste with a see-through tube.

Premiums. Premiums offer the buyer a gift or a prize, at little or no extra cost, as an incentive for purchasing a product or service. A local bank gave free toasters to people who opened a new account in excess of $500. For a period, manufacturers of the Maxell minifloppy disk offered a premium of four felt-tipped marking pens with the purchase of a box of ten disks. Zenith Corporation gave away Wordstar and Multiplan, two popular software packages, with the purchase of their Z-100 model personal computer.

Coupons. Unlike premiums, coupons actually offer a price reduction. Coupons are in effect bargains; buyers can clip them from newspapers,

their products so that potential buyers or middlemen can view a large number of competing products. At the American Society for Training Directors' (ASTD) annual meeting in Dallas in 1983, more than 100 producers of training equipment and material rented booths to display their latest products and services.

FUNNY BUSINESS

packages, or direct mail, and return them for a discount. Return rates average from 4% in newspapers to more than 20% for coupons on the package. An advertising supplement in a recent Sunday newspaper contained more than eighty-five coupons, some of which were: $1 to $2 refunds for sending proofs of purchase on Mazola corn oil, Hellmann's real mayonnaise, Skippy creamy peanut butter, and Mazola margarine. Last year, industry offered 119.5 billion coupons on practically everything — shoes, flying lessons, baby food, etc. Coupons are also changing. Burger King, on their TV ads, instructed buyers to say a few words about the advantages of the Whopper over the Big Mac. Customers who went to Burger King and did this received a free Whopper. What's more, coupons are turning up in the most unlikely places — shopping bags, cash register tapes, and phone books. Coke is even coming out with a coupon on its cans of soda that are sold through vending machines.

Contests. Some firms create interest with contests offering cash prizes, merchandise, or trips for winners. Among the more widely known contests are the Publishers Clearing House Sweepstakes and the Reader's Digest Sweepstakes, both of which offer hundreds of thousands of dollars in prizes and prize money to the lucky winners. However, many contests have come under legal fire because they did not offer the amount of prizes they said or they may have had contests where there were no winners.

Trading stamps. Trading stamps, a very old form of sales promotion, gives customers stamps on purchases, which can be redeemed for additional merchandise. Green Stamps, one of the most popular brands, were usually given at the rate of one stamp for a 10-cent purchase. The customer collected the stamps in books and then returned them for merchandise. Critics contend that stamps add to the price of the original purchase, and some states have made trading stamps illegal.

Point-of-purchase displays. Point-of-purchase (**POP**) consists of in-store promotions,

TAKING STOCK

How Gillette Got into Trouble with Premiums

In 1978, Gillette offered a premium of a lucite table lighter stand for Cricket disposable lighters at a nominal price. All customers had to do was send in 50 cents and two proof-of-purchase seals from Gillette's Cricket disposable lighters.

So what was the problem? Simply, Gillette, far from estimating the response, ran out of lucite table stands and left 180,000 customers holding the Cricket, so to speak. Steven Miner, a disgruntled customer and a law student, brought a class action case against Gillette, charging that the company continued to promote its offer extensively after supplies were running low. The suit also charged that Gillette made no effort to get new stands. A company spokesperson said that it would have taken several weeks to reactivate the molds and produce the lucite stands. They thought the delay and the additional costs would be prohibitive. So, Gillette refunded the 50 cents and sent a disposable Cricket lighter with a form letter explaining.

However, Miner's lawsuit says that Gillette owes 180,000 customers $7.95 for the stand they did not get and he is asking punitive damages. The premium industry is watching the outcome closely because it obviously has wide implications. Regardless of the outcome, one attorney in the case offered some good advice, "When you offer a premium, make damn sure you can fill the demand."

Source: Gary Levin, "The Accent Is on Having Enough Premiums," *Advertising Age*, Aug. 22, 1983, pp. 18–19.

using small cardboard displays, signs, loudspeakers, and the like, to call attention to a product. The POP often repeats a theme or trademark that has been widely advertised as a final reinforcer to encourage the product to jump into the shopper's basket. Business volume in the point-of-purchase topped $5.8 billion in 1982. According to a Consumer Buying Habits Study by POPAI/DuPont, consumers make almost two-thirds of their buying decisions in the store. Another study showed that one-third of all purchases in drug stores were unplanned. POP is most effective when tied into overall advertising and promotion schemes. When graphically tied to a TV commercial, for instance, POP can increase sales by more than 500%.

7-Up used POP effectively when they introduced their caffeine-free promotions. Reinforcing television that stressed that 7-Up did not have caffeine, the POP message said, "No caffeine. Never had it. Never will." After testing window banners, shelf talkers, and bottle hangers, 7-Up sent out 50 million pieces of POP. During the 12 months of this promotion, 7-Up was the only soft-drink company to increase market share.

Specialties. Giveaways of pins, bags, glasses, ashtrays, letter openers, and bottle openers sporting company names are specialty advertising. Tourists toting home Harrah's ashtrays from Lake Tahoe are participating in specialty promotions. Holiday Inn towels for sunbathing boast the trade name for neighbors to see.

Public Relations

Public relations represents any activity that increases public awareness of a company or a product or service that the company does not directly pay for. Usually, public relations is some form of legitimate news such as the company sponsoring a public event like a road race or a community fund drive. For instance, Pepsi sponsors a series of road races throughout the country.

Of course, firms get publicity whether they want it or not. When a utility company, for instance, announces a request for a rate increase, the news media cover it. But most firms have departments that strive to get them favorable publicity. One goal of the local publications department of the Kansas Gas and Electric Company is to have

BUSINESS BULLETIN

How Manufacturers Hanover Promotes Corporate Road Racing

Manufacturers Hanover Trust Co. has joined hands with the running boom to sponsor corporate challenge road races. According to a Hanover official, it costs only about $30,000 to sponsor a race, and, "It is the biggest bang for our buck in our whole marketing effort."

When people enter a MHT-sponsored race, their names and job titles go into the computer. Later, MHT officials go over the lists and screen out people who are already customers or too closely tied to other banking institutions; the remaining names are prospects. In a recent corporate challenge race in Houston, the company turned up twelve companies they consider to be active prospects. Additionally, the race was a morale booster for MHT's own people. Hanover has many subsidiaries scattered all over Houston, and the race brought them together, giving them pride in the company they work for.

Source: "What Makes Manny Hanny Run," *Business Week,* Aug. 29, 1983, p. 55.

at least one newspaper article or television story each month that is favorable to the utility industry. Dunkin' Donuts got an unusual amount of free publicity through human interest stories on the number of doughnuts consumed each month in their stores and on the "romance" of the doughnut: how the idea was born, the history of the hole in the middle, and how adults are now eating more doughnuts than children.

SUMMARY

Promoting the product to potential consumers includes personal selling, advertising, and miscellaneous sales promotion devices. Promotional objectives are to provide information, stimulate sales, highlight values, differentiate products, and stabilize sales. Pull strategies create forces within consumers to pull products through the channels, while push strategies stimulate middlemen to push products through to consumers. Promotional effectiveness is measured by several methods: direct sales, readership surveys, and recall interviews. Approaches to determining the promotional budget include percentage of sales, fixed sums, match competition, and task objective.

Professional salespeople know their companies, products, competitors, customers, and themselves. They engage in creative selling, missionary selling, order receiving, and information feedback. Steps in the selling process cover: (1) prospecting, (2) qualifying, (3) presentation, (4) product demonstration, (5) objections, (6) closing, and (7) follow-up.

Advertising, unlike personal selling, appeals to customers through impersonal media. Advertising is a paid nonpersonal appeal to customers. Two major forms of advertising are: (1) product advertising and (2) institutional advertising. Advertising strategies include: positioning, pulsating, persuasive advertising, informative advertising, reminder advertising, advocacy advertising, pioneering advertising, and use of personalities. In selecting media, advertisers choose from newspapers, television, direct mail, radio, magazines, and outdoor techniques. Many firms turn their advertising tasks over to advertising agencies. Critics of advertising say that advertising (1) is often misleading, (2) causes prices to be higher, and (3) encourages excessive materialism. Sales promotion devices and public relations efforts often supplement advertising programs.

MIND YOUR BUSINESS

Instructions. Designate each of the following questions true (T) or false (F).

___ 1. One key objective of promotional programs is to provide information.

___ 2. A pull promotional strategy tries to sell middlemen on the product's benefits.

___ 3. Percentage of sales is the most common way of determining the promotional budget.

___ 4. Missionary selling focuses on building goodwill and a positive company image.

___ 5. Closing the sale is the last step in personal selling.

___ 6. When using a positioning advertising strategy, a firm would very likely compare its product or service directly to competitors' products.

___ 7. Advocacy advertising offers a precise incentive for the customer to buy the product now.

___ 8. More money is spent on television advertising than in any other form of media.

___ 9. Advertising agencies typically receive a 15% commission on their billings.

___ 10. There is clear evidence that advertising increases the prices of products and services.

See answers at the back of the book.

KEY TERMS

promotion, 374
promotional mix, 374
pull strategy, 376
push strategy, 376

REVIEW QUESTIONS

1. What is meant by a promotional mix? Give some examples.
2. Discuss the five major objectives of promotion.
3. What is the difference between the push and the pull advertising strategy? Give at least one obvious example of each.
4. Give at least four different methods of figuring a promotional budget.
5. What is the difference between personal and professional selling?
6. Describe missionary selling and give an example.
7. The text presents seven major steps in personal selling. Discuss each step and give an example of each.
8. Distinguish between product and institutional advertising.
9. Describe eight advertising strategies and give examples other than those used in the text.
10. Describe the six major advertising media. Give advantages and disadvantages of each.
11. What do advertising agencies do for clients? Describe agency switching.
12. Analyze three criticisms of advertising.
13. Identify six sales promotion devices.
14. Explain public relations.

CASES

Case 15.1: Advertising by Doctors?

In January 1976, The Federal Trade Commission (FTC) filed an antitrust complaint against the American Medical Association (AMA) for illegally restraining competition by refusing to let doctors advertise and engage in price competition. The complaint reads that the AMA's position leads to fixing of prices, restraint of competition, and withholding of information pertinent to selection of a physician. The FTC claims that physician advertising could lead to lower prices and better information for patients about doctors' services.

But the AMA and most physicians are opposed to advertising, saying that advertising is unprofessional for them. Further, physicians say that pricing information can be provided simply by calling their offices. Physicians also think that the patient might be the loser in an advertising campaign because doctors cannot advertise competence and quality of work. One doctor said, "I don't believe people should shop for health care. It's dangerous to go to a physician because he charges less or more."

Questions

1. What advantages would there be to the patient if doctors were to engage in advertising? Disadvantages?
2. What are the advantages and disadvantages of advertising for the physician?
3. Do you think physicians should advertise or not? Justify your answer.

Case 15.2: Promotion or Communication?

The managers of a large company were debating over the approach the company should take in promoting their product lines. Several managers wanted to hire promotional specialists to develop promotional and advertising campaigns for making the products known to customers. Another smaller group wanted to hire total communicators seasoned in every facet of communications. They argued that it was not enough to have an advertising manager, sales promotion manager, or marketing manager. Rather, they needed a marketing communicator who thoroughly understood the internal aspects of the business, as well as promotion and all other types of communi-

cation, including writing and speaking. Such an approach could give consistency through service uniforms, company identification, interiors, trucks, and the like. These skilled personnel would be a great help with internal organizational communication and would make it mesh with the external promotional program.

Questions

1. What are the advantages of the total communication approach? Disadvantages?

2. Which approach do you think would be most effective? Why?

3. What impact does the total communication approach have on costs?

THE MARKETING OF BUSINESS

The following list includes a variety of activities, personality characteristics, career goals and objectives, and skills and aptitudes. All have special relevance to careers in business marketing. Put a check mark in front of those statements that apply to you.

____ I would like to plan a sales campaign for a company.

____ I would like to take a course in merchandising.

____ People have told me that I am good at selling.

____ Traveling frequently and being away from home for several days at a time would not bother me.

____ I would like to study people's buying habits.

____ I would enjoy taking an advertising course.

____ I would enjoy attending a trade exhibition and displaying merchandise.

____ I would like to compete with others in buying merchandise.

____ People have often asked me how to go about selling something that they own.

____ I have enjoyed working in a sales position.

____ I would like conducting market research.

____ I want to buy and sell commodities.

____ I have sold door to door or telephoned people to persuade them to buy something.

____ I would like to train a group of new salespersons.

____ I feel that I can create an attractive merchandise display in a retail store.

____ I have sold advertisements for a school or community group's newsletter or publication.

____ I would like to explain to others the services that a company performs.

____ I am confident that I can influence others to make their purchases from me.

____ I have strong social skills so that it is easy for me to meet all kinds of people.

____ I would enjoy marketing a new product.

____ I would enjoy doing competitive purchasing for a large industry.

____ In the past, I have been able to accept other people rejecting my suggesting a product to use and not feel badly about it.

____ I do not easily accept no for an answer.

____ I would welcome the challenge of meeting large sales quotas.

____ I don't turn people off when I try to convince them to do something.

____ I have strong social skills so that in a group I tend to be the center of attention.

____ I have been told by my teachers that I am a very effective communicator and write clearly.

There is no single set of personality characteristics, skills, and aptitudes that fits a particular job. Generally speaking, the more activities and self-descriptors you checked in this list, the more satisfaction you may find in this major and its related jobs.

Job Title	Job Description	Suggested Education and Training	Personality Traits	Average Pay	Outlook through 1990
Public relations representative	Public relations workers help businesses, governments, universities, and other organizations build and maintain a positive public reputation. They may handle press, community, or consumer relations, political campaigning, interest-group representation, fundraising, or employee recruitment. Understanding the attitudes and concerns of customers and employees and communicating this information for management to help formulate policy is also an important part of the job.	A college education combined with public relations experience is excellent preparation for public relations work. Although most beginners have a college degree in journalism, communications, or public relations, some employers prefer a background in a field related to the firm's business — science, finance, or engineering, for example.	Creativity, initiative, and the ability to express thoughts clearly and simply are important to the public relations worker. Fresh ideas are so vital in public relations that some experts spend all their time developing new ideas. People who choose public relations as a career need an outgoing personality, self-confidence, and an understanding of human psychology. They should have the enthusiasm to motivate people. The ability to be competitive but function as part of a team are important qualifications.	Starting salaries for college graduates beginning in public relations work generally range between $12,000 and $15,000. The median annual salary of top level public relations workers is $39,000.	Moderate demand
Radio-TV announcer	At radio stations, most announcers are disc jockeys. They introduce recorded music; present news, sports, weather, and commercials; interview guests, and report on community activities and other matters of interest to the audience. Announcers at television stations often specialize in a particular kind of programming, such as sports events, general news broadcasts, or weather reports.	Though formal training in a college or technical school is valuable, station officials pay particular attention to taped auditions that present samples of an applicant's delivery and, in television, appearance and style on commercials, news, interviews, and other copy.	Announcers must have a pleasant and well-controlled voice, good timing, and excellent pronunciation. Good judgment and the ability to react quickly in emergencies are important because announcers may be required to "ad-lib" all or part of a show. A neat, pleasing appearance is essential, of course, for television announcers and news broadcasters. The most successful announcers combine an appealing personality with poise to win the following of large audiences.	Announcers generally start at around $10,000 to $15,000 a year. Earnings among experienced announcers are much higher, and some well-known personalities in major metropolitan areas earn extremely high salaries.	Slight demand (Competition for beginning jobs as announcers will be very keen through the 1980s. The broadcasting field will attract many more seekers than there are jobs.)
Market researcher	Market researchers analyze the buying public and its wants and needs, thus providing the information on which these marketing decisions can be based. Researchers plan, design, implement, and analyze the results of surveys. Most marketing research starts with a collection of data and information about products or services and the people who are likely to buy the product or service.	Although a bachelor's degree usually is sufficient for trainees, graduate education is necessary for many specialized positions in market research. Graduate study usually is required for advancement, and a sizable number of market researchers have a master's degree in business administration or some other graduate degree in addition to a bachelor's degree in marketing.	Market researchers must be able to analyze problems objectively and apply various techniques to their solution. Creativity is essential in formulating new ideas. Patience and perseverance are necessary to complete long research projects. As advisers to management, market researchers should be skilled in both written and verbal communication.	Salaries of beginning market researchers range from about $13,000 to $19,000 a year. Persons with master's degrees in business administration usually start with salaries of about $22,700 a year.	Stable demand

Job Title	Job Description	Suggested Education and Training	Personality Traits	Average Pay	Outlook through 1990
Advertising copywriter	Companies hire advertising agencies to create the general idea for an advertising campaign, prepare the ads, and arrange for them to be printed, broadcast, or televised. Agencies produce almost all national newspaper, magazine, radio, and TV ads. Copywriters write the text of ads, called copy, and scripts for radio and TV ads.	A college degree in journalism, English, or another liberal arts major is the usual background of advertising copywriters. Certainly, copywriters must be able to write persuasively and should have an excellent command of English.	According to David Ogilvy, founder of the Ogilvy and Mather advertising agency, the hallmarks of a potentially successful copywriter include: 1) obsessive curiosity about products, people, and advertising; 2) a sense of humor; 3) a habit of hard work; 4) the ability to write interesting prose and natural dialogue; 4) the ability to think visually; and 5) the ambition to write better campaigns than anyone has ever written before.*	Starting salaries hover between $14,000 and $17,000. Experienced, successful copywriters may earn as much as $50,000.	Moderate demand
Advertising account executive	Advertising account executives are in charge of coordinating the advertising for each of the agency's clients, or accounts. Account executives determine the nature of the advertising to be produced for their clients, coordinate and review all the agency's activities involved in producing it, and maintain good relations between the agency and the client. Account executives usually handle one large account or several smaller accounts.	A 4-year degree in liberal arts or business is a good start to becoming an account executive. A master's degree in business administration or advertising is, of course, better preparation for the job. David Ogilvy says that if he wanted to become an account executive he would first spend a couple of years at Procter & Gamble in brand management, followed by a year in a consumer research company, learning what makes people tick.*	Hardworking and knowledgeable are the principal traits of a successful account executive. The ability to make good presentations to clients is an indispensable trait. Maintaining friendly relations with clients and colleagues at once is also necessary.	Salaries range between $16,000 and $60,000, depending on the person's depth of experience.	Stable demand
Product manager	The product manager oversees the marketing of a manufacturer's product or products and is responsible for meeting profit objectives. By determining and managing the strategies for distribution, market research, promotion and advertising, and pricing, product managers decide on the proper marketing mix for a product.	A college degree in liberal arts or business administration is the best beginning for becoming a product manager. Sales and marketing experience and familiarity with the product are hugely helpful.	Product managers should be creative enough to think of ways to effectively promote their products. They should have initiative and be good at planning and organizing. They also need good oral and written communications skills.	Starting salaries are typically around $16,000 for product managers, though a newly hired manager with experience not in product management but a related area may earn as much as $30,000. Experienced product managers may earn as much as $60,000.	Moderate demand

* David Ogilvy, *Ogilvy on Advertising*, Crown Publishers, Inc., New York, 1983, p. 32.

Job Title	Job Description	Suggested Education and Training	Personality Traits	Average Pay	Outlook through 1990
Buyer	The job of retail buyer often brings to mind the glamour of high fashion; indeed, many fashion buyers do lead exciting, fast-paced lives. Not every buyer, however, travels abroad or deals in fashion. All merchandise sold in a retail store — garden furniture, automobile tires, toys, aluminum pots, and canned soups — appears there on the decision of a buyer. Buyers seek goods that satisfy their stores' customers and sell at a profit. The kind and variety of goods they purchase depend on the store.	An increasing number of employers prefer applicants who have a college degree. Many colleges and universities offer associate degree or bachelor's degree programs in marketing and purchasing. Postsecondary training also is offered in vocational schools or technical institutes that prepare students for careers in fashion merchandising. While courses in merchandising or marketing may help in getting started in retailing, they are not essential. Most employers accept college graduates in any field of study and train them on the job.	Buyers should be good at planning and decision making and have an interest in merchandising. They need leadership ability and communications skills to supervise sales workers and assist buyers and to deal effectively with manufacturers' representatives and store executives. Because of the fast pace and pressure of their work, buyers need physical stamina and emotional stability.	Buyers for discount department stores and other mass merchandisers are among the most highly paid. On the average, buyers earn between $20,000 and $30,000.	Moderate demand
Manufacturers' sales worker	Practically all manufacturers employ sales workers. They sell mainly to other businesses — factories, banks, wholesalers, and retailers. They also sell to hospitals, schools, libraries, and other institutions. Manufacturers' sales workers visit prospective buyers in their territory to inform them about the products they sell, analyze the buyers' needs, suggest how their products can meet these needs, and take orders. They also prepare reports on sales prospects or credit ratings, plan schedules, make appointments, handle correspondence, and study products literature.	A college degree is increasingly desirable for this job. Manufacturers of nontechnical products usually seek graduates with degrees in liberal arts or business; manufacturers of technical products, degrees in science or engineering. Many companies have formal training programs that last 2 years or longer for beginning sales workers. Trainees may rotate among jobs in plants and offices to learn all phases of production, installation, and distribution of the product; or take formal classroom instruction at the plant, followed by on-the-job training in a branch office under the supervision of a field sales manager.	A pleasant personality and appearance and the ability to get along well with people are important. Because sales workers may have to walk, stand for long periods, or carry product samples, some physical stamina is necessary. As in most selling jobs, arithmetic skills are an asset.	Some manufacturers pay experienced sales workers a straight commission, based on the dollar amount of their sales; others pay a fixed salary. Most use a combination of salary and commission, salary and bonus, or salary, commission, and bonus. Salaries for inexperienced sales workers generally range between $14,900 and $17,400 a year. Experienced sales workers generally earn between $17,400 and $32,000 a year.	Stable demand

Job Title	Job Description	Suggested Education and Training	Personality Traits	Average Pay	Outlook through 1990
Retail trade sales worker	Whether selling furniture, electrical appliances, or clothing, a sales worker's primary job is to interest customers in merchandise—by describing its construction, demonstrating its use, and showing various models and colors. For some jobs, special knowledge or skills are needed. In addition to selling, most retail sales workers make out sales checks, receive cash payments, and give change and receipts. They also handle returns and exchanges of merchandise and keep their work areas neat. In small stores, they may help order merchandise, stock shelves or racks, mark price tags, take inventory, and prepare displays.	Employers generally prefer high school graduates for sales jobs, but also hire those with less education. Traditionally, capable sales workers without college degrees could advance to management positions. However, a college education is now becoming increasingly important for advancement. Large retail businesses generally prefer to hire college graduates as management trainees. Despite this trend, capable employees with less than a college degree should still be able to advance to administrative or supervisory work in large stores.	Employers prefer those who enjoy working with people and have the tact to deal with difficult customers. Among other desirable characteristics are an interest in sales work, a pleasant personality, a neat appearance, and the ability to communicate clearly.	Median earnings generally range from $9000 to $15,000 a year for full-time sales workers. Some sales workers receive salary plus commissions; others are paid only commissions.	Moderate demand

Job Title	Job Description	Suggested Education and Training	Personality Traits	Average Pay	Outlook through 1990
Wholesale trade sales worker	Sales workers in wholesale trade represent wholesalers who distribute from the factory to stores selling directly to the consumer. Sales workers visit buyers for retail, industrial, and commercial firms, and institutions such as schools and hospitals. They show samples, pictures, or catalogs that list items their company stocks and may show how their products can save money or improve productivity. Other services they perform are to: check the store's stock and order items needed before the next visit; keep sales records; forward orders to wholesale houses; prepare reports and expense accounts; plan schedules; list prospects; make appointments; study product literature; and collect money.	The background needed for sales jobs varies by product line and market. Complex products require technical backgrounds. Drug wholesalers, for example, seek people with a college degree in chemistry, biology, or pharmacy as trainees. Wholesalers provide training on characteristics of their products and how to sell them. For non-technical products such as food, sales ability and familiarity with manufacturers and brands are more important than knowledge about the product itself. Most wholesale sales workers get their jobs by working up the ladder or by transferring in with the appropriate background.	As with the retail sales worker, desirable personality traits include an interest in sales, an agreeable manner, neatness, and an enjoyment in being with and talking to people.	Compensation plans differ among firms. One plan is salary plus a commission based on sales; others are straight commission or straight salary. Some include a bonus. Beginning sales workers average around $19,000 a year. Experienced sales workers may earn as much as $55,000 a year.	Moderate demand

IV

THE FINANCING OF BUSINESS

After completing this chapter, you will be able to:

■ Describe four characteristics of money.

■ Explain how banks create money.

■ Describe electronic banking.

■ Identify seven banking trends.

■ Explain the organization of the Federal Reserve System.

■ Describe three ways the FRS increases or decreases the money supply.

■ Explain three services of the FRS.

■ Identify five financial institutions other than banks.

16

MONEY, BANKING, AND FINANCIAL INSTITUTIONS

All people know about money is that they don't have enough," the late congressman from Texas, Wright Patman, was supposed to have said. Whether people have a little or a lot, they do not seem to have enough. When one very wealthy person was asked, "How much money would it take to make you happy?" he supposedly responded, "Just a little bit more." What is it about money that fascinates people so? What does it do for people? It cannot buy health, and many people proclaim that it will not buy happiness either. We know that we need money to live in our society, but it is more than that. The writer William McFee wrote, "It is extraordinary how many emotional storms one may weather in safety if one is ballasted with ever so little gold." Another writer, Jean Giraudous, said, "To have money is to be virtuous, honest, beautiful and witty. And to be without is to be ugly and boring and stupid and useless."

Perhaps it is not money itself that is harmful or good, but people's attitudes toward it. What does money mean to you? In our society, we have to have it to live: Money buys food, clothing, shelter, as well as entertainment. Even though it is so necessary, it is remarkable how little people know about it.

Money is the essence of financing. Like people, firms need money to exist. Banks, with the aid of our Federal Reserve System, play a vital role in creating, protecting, and moving money through our system.

WHAT IS MONEY?

The government has taken great pains to develop a secret method of making money so that counterfeiters cannot easily reproduce it. Still, we know that paper and metal currency have only symbolic value. In truth, **money** is a medium of exchange; it exists in many forms with identifiable characteristics. Money performs unique and necessary functions in our business system. Money serves us in three primary ways.

A Medium of Exchange

Money is symbolic. Although inherently worthless, it gains meaning by representing something of value. The government has declared paper money to be legal tender acceptable for payment of debts and taxes. Money may also be used to purchase goods and services. People work for money only because with it they can pay the landlord rent, the grocer for food, the bartender for beer, or purchase any commodity they can afford. Money is valuable only so long as we agree to use it as a basis of exchange.

A Means of Storing Purchasing Power

Money is a convenient way of storing purchasing power. Butter sours, potatoes rot, and milk curdles; but we can exchange these for money and hold the money indefinitely. Of course, how well money stores depends upon inflation rates; if inflation is high, the value of money that we hold decreases correspondingly. Thus, as an actual practice, we typically buy something with our money—stocks, bonds, real estate, gold—that we hope increases in value more than the inflation rate.

A Measure of the Value of Things

Money is a yardstick by which we express the value of things. We express goods, services, and other items in terms of dollars and cents to communicate how much they are worth. When a retail jeweler advertises, "You can buy this quartz, digital, dual-chronography watch for only $195.98," we know exactly what the exchange means.

The Forms of Money

We designate many things as money. A quarter is money and a five-dollar bill is money, but so is a checking account, a savings account, and credit.

Paper and metal money. Most of U.S. currency is token money. Citizens resisted the use of coins and paper money for years because they lacked confidence in the government. The government issued greenbacks during the Civil War, but people did not like them. The first paper money was in the form of certificates that could be redeemed for gold. But the government withdrew gold certificates and gold coins in 1933 when the United States went off the gold standard. It became legal for citizens to own gold again in 1975, and we have rekindled a romance with gold. For a while, the government issued silver certificates, which were backed by actual silver on deposit. But it issued more certificates than there was silver. If everyone had tried to redeem their silver at the same time, many would have been left holding worthless paper. As people gained more confidence in the government, silver certificates were replaced by promissory notes from the U.S. government. Then we went to notes issued by the Federal Reserve system. These notes constitute about 90% of our paper money today. Federal Reserve banks promise to redeem their notes with money, but the money can be other Federal Reserve notes. The government has also taken most of the valuable metal from our coins. Both coins and paper

Whether represented by paper currency or electronic signals, money serves as a medium of exchange, a measure of value.

Figure 16.1
How banks pay interest on checking accounts.

1. Individual opens tandem checking and savings accounts at bank.
2. Depositor puts money in interest-paying savings account, keeps little or nothing in checking.
3. Checks to pay bills are written against checking account.
4. Bank automatically transfers money from savings to checking as needed to cover drafts.
5. Individual collects up to 5% interest on funds in savings account and pays any fees that may be required on either account.

money are only tokens—IOUs in which people have confidence.

Checking accounts. The most widely used form of money is **demand deposits,** that is, **checking account.** People deposit coins or paper money (or more likely checks drawn on other demand deposits) in the bank. To pay bills, people write checks instructing the bank to give their money to others. The payees deposit the checks in their bank accounts and write checks. Behind the scenes, banks merely keep records of these transactions. In this way, demand deposits serve the same function as paper money—IOUs on a larger scale.

Interest-paying checking (NOW) accounts. One recent change is the form of interest-paying checking accounts, technically known as **negotiable order of withdrawal (NOW) accounts.** Since 1933, by law, depositors have been unable to earn interest on idle funds in their checking accounts. But now, under the 1980 Depository Institutions Deregulation and Monetary Control Act, banks can offer interest on checking account money.

But, as Fig. 16.1 illustrates, the process is rather complicated. An individual has to open both a checking and a savings account. Most of the money is deposited in the savings account, which draws interest. Then checks are written on the checking account. As the checking account becomes overdrawn, the bank automatically transfers money from savings to checking to cover the overdraft. Interest is drawn on funds in savings accounts.

Most all large banks and many medium-size ones are offering this service. But depositors are not flocking to the new service. Why? For one

thing, most banks charge fees for the new service, some of which might outweigh the advantages. For another, interest on savings these days is quite low. And to the average customer, the automatic transfer plan seems complicated and confusing. In explaining why he did not feel a need to use it in his bank, a small bank owner said, "We have been covering overdrafts for our good customers for years on an informal basis. We often pay the check and talk with them about how they want to cover it." However, for the depositor who normally has several hundred dollars in a checking account, the new service can provide a good deal.

Savings accounts. **Time deposits,** popularly called **savings accounts,** are a modification of demand deposits. Depositors may have to give the bank a notice 30 days to 6 months in advance to withdraw their money. The bank pays the depositor interest on money in time deposits. Time deposits are sometimes referred to as "near money" because of the restrictions on withdrawals. Money deposited in money market accounts (see Chapter 18 for a discussion of these) may also be near monies. The depositor can typically get money from these accounts, often in just a day or so, but it is not quite as quick as writing a check at the bank. Some of the money market accounts do allow check writing, but the person who accepts the check may not agree to give credit for the payment for a few days, that is, until the process clears the account.

Credit. Credit has emerged as a popular form of money in recent years. Credit is money because the seller takes a customer's word, usually backed by collateral, that the customer will pay the debt later.

The Characteristics of Money

Whatever form money takes, it remains usable in our business world only while it is acceptable, stable, easy to handle, and difficult to counterfeit.

Acceptability. Because money has no intrinsic value, its worth comes from its acceptability. As a businessman commented, "I know that money itself is of no value; but I will accept it for merchandise, because I know my creditors will accept it from me." Historically, when governments have issued large amounts of paper money during rampant inflation, people have become disillusioned and refused to accept the currency as a method of payment. Mass rejection renders the money system useless.

Stability. Stability is also a criterion of a successful monetary system. A wide variation in what money will buy from month to month causes an undercurrent of skepticism. If a $10,000 auto in 1980 costs $20,000 in 1985, the value of a dollar has been reduced by half. Inflation rates soaring over 10% during parts of the 1980s caused an agonizing alarm over the value of money.

Convenience. Money must be convenient. Dividing it into smaller denominations lets us discriminate minutely on pricing. But it must not be so tiny that we are in constant danger of misplacing it or so bulky we cannot carry it.

Difficulty of counterfeiting. Money is of little value if it can be counterfeited easily. Most countries go to great lengths to make it hard to counterfeit paper money by including silk threads and using special plates in printing. Other forms of money, checking accounts, etc., require strict identification procedures to prevent fraud.

BUSINESS BULLETIN

A Cashless, Checkless Society

Computers have made it technically possible to go to an all-computerized monetary system, and some banks are already preparing to do so. A computerized system could theoretically produce a cashless, checkless society that works as follows.

A customer, armed with a magnetized identity card, enters a store and buys a basket of groceries. The clerk records the sale by pressing buttons connected to the customer's account at the bank. The bank's computer deducts the amount from the customer's account and adds it to the store's account. When the store's owner buys produce from wholesalers, pays its employees, or takes out profit for himself, the appropriate buttons are pushed to adjust the records accordingly.

By adding a microchip to the plastic card, a **smart card** is created, allowing information to be stored directly on the card — amount of deposit, withdrawal, balance, and the like — to be printed out later. J.C. Penney is already experimenting with chip cards, and General Electric runs several gas stations in Phoenix with them. A home banking experimental project is also going on in North Dakota.

Smart cards are hard to forge because it takes sophisticated, exotic equipment to read the cards. Casio Computer Co. has developed a smart card that not only could be used with electronic terminals but also would give the user a calculator keyboard.

Still another development, the **Drexon laser card,** is capable of storing millions of bits of data directly on the card. While it does not qualify as a smart card, it has the advantage of being able to store much more data directly on the card. Because the equipment to read and write on the card will be quite expensive, the market will probably not include normal banking customers.

COMMERCIAL BANKING

Commercial banks are the department stores of our financial system. "We are the middlemen in the monetary transactions among all segments of our society," is the way a banker described his bank.

Just like giant companies and small, mom-and-pop stores, commercial banks are privately owned businesses that operate to make a profit. And when they organize, they incorporate by requesting a charter, just like other corporations. Of the approximately 15,000 banks in the United States, about 30% receive their charters from the federal government. The remaining 70% get their charters from state governments. Federally char-

tered banks are called **national banks;** state-chartered banks are called **state banks.** Table 16.1 lists the ten largest commercial banks in the United States.

How Banks Facilitate Financing

The major purpose of commercial banks is to facilitate financial flows by holding and loaning money. About half of the money going into commercial banks enters in the form of demand deposits (checking accounts). Banks obtain other money from time deposits (savings accounts), profits, and loans from the Federal Reserve system or other banks. A bank's primary source of revenue comes from interest on money loaned out.

TABLE 16.1 ■ THE TEN LARGEST COMMERCIAL BANKS IN THE UNITED STATES (RANKED BY ASSETS)

Company	Rank 1982	Rank 1981	Assets $ Thousands	Deposits $ Thousands	Rank	Loans $ Thousands	Rank	Employees Number	Rank
Citicorp (New York)	1	2	129,997,000	76,538,000	2	87,692,000	1	60,600	2
BankAmerica Corp. (San Francisco)	2	1	122,220,806	94,341,795	1	75,846,022	2	85,266	1
Chase Manhattan Corp. (New York)	3	3	80,862,903	56,857,847	3	54,973,264	3	36,810	3
Manufacturers Hanover Corp. (New York)	4	4	64,040,552	43,824,670	4	45,293,124	4	27,870	5
J.P. Morgan & Co. (New York)	5	5	58,597,000	37,910,000	5	31,477,000	6	12,711	13
Chemical New York Corp.	6	7	48,274,842	27,998,414	8	30,597,660	7	19,535	7
Continental Illinois Corp. (Chicago)	7	6	42,899,424	28,175,021	7	33,339,165	5	12,930	12
First Interstate Bancorp. (Los Angeles)	8	8	40,884,296	30,542,067	6	23,394,941	9	31,903	4
Bankers Trust New York Corp.	9	9	40,427,059	24,492,559	11	21,098,591	11	11,906	14
Security Pacific Corp. (Los Angeles)	10	11	36,991,034	25,848,489	10	26,094,632	8	27,058	6

Source: "The Fortune Directory of the Largest U.S. Non-Industrial Corporations," Fortune, June 13, 1983, p. 158.

The Ups and Downs of Chase Manhattan Bank

About 10 years ago, the Chase Manhattan Bank, dominated by the Rockefellers, stood at the top of the banking pyramid of influence. But the mighty Chase suffered embarrassment and humiliation and eventually became fodder for jokes.

After Chase lost millions of dollars in bonds and kept poor records regarding these losses, the U.S. Comptroller of the Currency said the Chase was running out of control in 1975. Yet, a few years later, the bank took devastating losses in real estate, got better for awhile, and then lost millions more to a suspect government securities dealer — Drysdale Government Securities, Inc. To add to their already considerable embarrassment, Chase lost hundreds of millions more through participation in energy-related loans with Penn Square Bank in Oklahoma. Loss write-offs for these two ventures finally totaled $192 million.

Reacting to such pitfalls, Chase today operates under the tightest internal controls in American banking. Of course, the strict controls offer disadvantages. A lending officer says, "I know other banks can act faster than we can or at least without the difficulty. If we try to do something innovative, we must knock ourselves out to get it through internally."

Not content to sit on their hands, the Chase people are trying to return to glory with a definite marketing strategy — reduce the percentage of business with smaller individual and corporate customer accounts and increase their business with the top half of the individual and corporate markets. Time will tell whether their strategy will work for them.

Source: Priscilla S. Meyer, "Burdens of the Past," *Forbes*, July 18, 1983, pp. 32–34.

The loan rate for the very best grade of customer is called the **prime rate.** It is a common practice to loan money to good risks at prime rate. Others may have to pay two or three points above the prime rate. Between 1969 and mid-1976, the prime rate fluctuated between 4.5 and 12%. But since 1976, it rose steadily upward to an all-time high of over 21% in the late 1970s. In the early 1980s, the prime rate fluctuated between 17 and 10%. Figure 16.2 shows the prime rate movement from January 1982 to March 1984.

How Banks Protect Money

You may be wondering, "What happens if I discover that the bank has loaned my money to someone else?" Even worse, "What happens if the bank has loaned it to someone who goes bankrupt and cannot repay it?" Do not worry excessively; you are protected in four ways. (1) The bank has to

> **About 99% of all banks belong to the FDIC, a government-sponsored program that insures accounts up to $100,000.**

keep a certain percentage of cash reserve at all times; the reserve may range from 10 to 20%. (2) In the unlikely event that a lot of people try to withdraw their money at the same time, the bank could borrow short-term funds to cover the cash outlays. (3) About 99% of all banks belong to the **Federal Deposit Insurance Corporation (FDIC),** a government sponsored program that insures an account up to $100,000. That is, if the bank fails, a customer can recover deposits up to a maximum of $100,000. (4) The FDIC establishes guidelines that banks must follow to be insured.

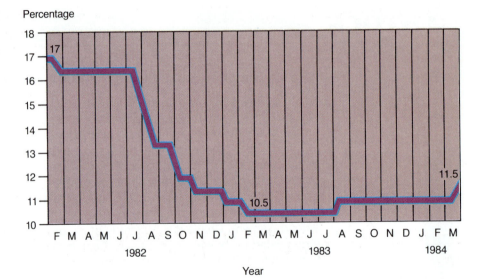

Percentage

**Figure 16.2
How the prime rate
changed from January
1982 to March 1984.**
*Source: Federal Reserve
Board.*

Year

The FDIC uses surprise audits to be sure that their guidelines are followed. A spokesperson for the FDIC says that 48 federally-insured banks failed in 1983, the most since 1939 when there were 60 failures. No depositor has ever lost money in a bank backed by the FDIC.

During the depression of 1932–1933, many people rushed to the banks to withdraw their money. But since much of the money was out on loan, the banks could not pay off and many had to close their doors. Thousands of people simply lost their deposits. Chastened by this adversity, the government created the FDIC in 1935.

How Banks Create Money

Banks create money by making loans on the money that people deposit in their checking and savings accounts. Here is the way it works. Suppose a person deposits $10,000 in a savings account (or checking account). The bank will loan most of the $10,000 but they have to keep a certain amount of reserve. If the bank loans out $8000, it has actually created money of $8000. The person or business who borrows the money will have $8000 to use or deposit in the bank. Thus, the original $10,000 now becomes $18,000. The depositor still has the $10,000 to draw interest on, show as part of net worth, or even withdraw. And the person or business that borrowed the $8000 can use it for investing, buying inventory, purchasing material, or whatever. But the money continues to expand. When the person who bor-

rowed the $8000 deposits it in a bank, the bank might be able to loan out as much as $6000 of that money. In this way, the money continues expanding until there is no more to lend.

A customer enters a personal identification number to initiate a debit-card electronic payment for a purchase at a Mobil service station in Norfolk, Virginia.

Electronic Banking

To lower the costs of processing the 30 billion-plus checks the U.S. banking system handles each year, banks are increasing their use of electronic means. It costs a bank between $150 and $200 per year to serve an average individual customer. Most analysts believe that banks must cut this by at least a third to cover the higher costs of deposits. One of the key challenges of banking is to move customers from traditional teller lines and brick-and-mortar services to electronic banking.

Automated teller machines (ATMs) allow people to get cash and make deposits by inserting a plastic card into specially equipped banking machines. A customer can place his or her card in the slot, the machine will quickly check the account balance; and if there is enough to cover the withdrawal, the machine will dispense the precise number of crisp, new bills. Today, about 40% of

CROSS FIRE

Are Banks Greedy?

At a time when banks are making large profits, many customers are unhappy with bank services. Thousands of borrowers say that banks are keeping interest rates too high. Cambridge Reports, a Massachusetts opinion research firm, in a 1982 survey, found that 50% of their respondents believed that banks' profit motives were at least partly the cause of high loan costs. Many consumers and some politicians are actively trying to pass laws setting limits on what borrowers must pay for loans.

Loans to foreign countries also do not set well with customers. People do not understand why banks charge hometown folks sky-high interest rates while at the same time making risky loans to foreign countries such as Mexico, Venezuela, and other developing countries.

Finally, many customers feel that they get poor service and too many hassles. For instance, people posing as Citibank employees bilked 485 customers out of thousands of dollars using the banks' ATMs. Citibank initially balked at paying the customers for the con-artist-imposed losses. But when the state attorney general filed suit, Citibank agreed to pay $135,000 to the 485 customers.

In their behalf, spokespeople for the banking industry say that much of the public outcry is based on the old-time distrustful feelings that borrowers naturally hold toward lenders. As John Collins, counsel for the House Banking Committee, puts it, "Bankers are in the business of having to say no to people. They have control over people's lives and people resent it." Bankers also quote economists who tend to agree that higher interest rates are the result of market forces, not bankers' profit motives. Regarding service, bankers say they have spent millions of dollars installing 24-hour teller machines, extending hours at their branch offices, and trying to make their services more friendly.

How do you rate the service provided by banks to their customers? Why?

___ A. Excellent   ___ D. Below average

___ B. Above average   ___ E. Poor

___ C. Average

Do you think banks tend to be greedy? Why?

___ A. Definitely, yes   ___ C. Probably, no

___ B. Probably, yes   ___ D. Definitely, no

the routine transactions at Wells Fargo banks are done by machine. They project the figure to reach 75% in the next few years. Customers of the Chase Manhattan Bank can withdraw cash from any of 2,000 ATMs located in 47 states. Citicorp estimates that a machine transaction costs 55 cents as compared to $1.27 for a teller transaction.

Electronic funds transfer systems (EFTS) also automate many transactions. Bank customers can, with their plastic cards, pay bills and make purchases automatically. A centralized computer system handles the transactions. Some merchants use a **point-of-sale (POS)** machine which allows customers to pay for purchases on the spot. A customer simply enters his or her plastic card, called a debit card, into the POS, which automatically transfers funds from the buyer's bank into the seller's account. In Norfolk, Virginia, customers can buy gas at Mobil service stations with plastic cards that deduct the cost from their checking accounts. And Florida shoppers can conduct banking business with robot tellers located outside public supermarkets. Within 10 years, many people predict, machines will handle the majority of consumer purchases; say goodbye to cash- and credit-card-filled wallets. See Fig. 16.3 for a diagram of this process.

Sears, offering investment, insurance, and real-estate services at their stores, is one of several new, nontraditional sources of financial services.

Trends in Banking

For years, banking has been a rich and powerful industry. With total assets soaring over $2 trillion, total deposits amounting to $1.5 trillion, and almost 300 billion accounts, banks have an enormous influence. But at a time when their size, profits, and growth over the past decades have been enough to make any board member proud, they are undergoing some pressure and public ridicule, and they are experiencing rapid change.

Increased competition. During the early and middle 1980s, the entire financial community became less regulated by the government. Savings and loan associations, money market funds, and others began offering the equivalent of checking accounts. And laws governing the amount of interest financial institutions could pay and charge became much less restrictive. Whereas in the past banks had a virtual monopoly on financial services, today they have to compete with other financial institutions for the customer's deposit.

Heavy profits. Even with the increased competition, banks are still experiencing profit growth. In 1972, the net, after-tax income of banks was $5.6 billion and that soared to $15.0 billion by 1982. They have been able to maintain this profit growth because of the difference between the interest they pay to depositors and the interest they charge to borrowers. In late 1983, banks were charging prime borrowers about 10.5%, but bank credit card plans returned 21% and new-car loans 16%. At the time, banks were paying less than 8% interest to their depositors. Further, they paid an effective income tax rate of only 2.3%, the lowest of all industries except railroads and paper.

Charges for services. Claiming that they can no longer provide free, or almost free, services for checking, savings, and other transactions, banks have started charging for more of their services. In other cases, they are raising prices on their services. Nearly 56% of all banks now charge fees, averaging $15 per year, on credit cards. This practice was almost unheard of before 1980. Some banks now charge as much as $75 a year for rental of large deposit boxes. And almost half of the banks charge at least $10 or more for a bounced

1. After sale is totaled, customer pulls a special plastic card through a "reading" machine attached to cash register, then punches a four-digit personal number onto a keypad.
2. Via a central processing center, the cash register electronically contacts a computer at customer's bank.
3. Bank computer is asked to transfer purchase amount from customer's bank account to merchant's account, even if at another bank. If customer's funds are sufficient, transfer is made.
4. Bank's computer notifies processing center that transaction has occurred.
5. Processing center relays word of transaction back to cash register, which prints receipt for customer. Entire process should take a few seconds.

METROBANK CARD

Figure 16.3
How purchases with plastic cards work.

check. Table 16.2 shows how average service charges surged between 1979 and 1983.

Broadening services. Banks are also adding more services. In addition to offering a full range of financial services, banks are handling more re-tirement accounts and serving as brokerage offices for people who want to buy stocks and bonds. A bank president commented about his local bank, "We would like to see the day when a customer could come to us for everything that in any way relates to finances."

BULLETIN

BUSINESS

How Visa Angered the Big Banks

Visa was created by financial institutions to market credit cards and to facilitate payments between businesses, banks, and cardholders. However, the current president of Visa, Dee Ward Hock, is planning to develop a worldwide network of automated teller machines (ATM) that would allow Visa cardholders to get cash from machines located far from the banks that issued the plastic cards.

Visa's automatic teller network is scheduled to have 8000 machines in dozens of countries by 1986. The initial purpose is to allow people to get cash from the machines, but eventually Hock would like to use the equipment to move a step closer to a cashless and checkless society.

Many larger banks are upset because they have competing ATM networks. These banks, most of which happen to be Visa participants, think it is unfair for Visa to compete with them via ATMs. For example, thirty-four banks, all Visa members, have invested up to $150,000 apiece to build an exclusive ATM system, based in Denver, called Plus System, Inc. More than 950 financial institutions take Plus cards. These banks are hardly happy with the idea of Visa's setting up competing machines in their territory.

Source: Arthur M. Louis, "Visa Stirs up the Big Banks—Again," *Fortune,* Oct. 3, 1983, pp. 196–203.

TABLE 16.2 ■ HOW AVERAGE SERVICE CHARGES INCREASED BETWEEN 1979 AND 1983

Service	Average Bank Fees		
	1979	1983	Percentage Change
Bounced check	$5.07	$ 9.46	86.6
Overdraft covered by bank	$4.72	$ 9.01	90.9
Annual rental for small safe-deposit box	$6.96	$11.37	63.4
Monthly checking fee	$1.17	$ 2.51	114.5
Cashing noncustomer's check	$ .40	$ 1.87	367.5
Balance inquiry	$1.20	$ 1.28	6.7
Credit card — annual fee*	—	$16.16	—

* Few if any banks charged such fees in 1979.

Source: Sheshunoff & Company.

Growth of interstate banking. In 1976, Congress agreed to let states nullify the federal ban on interstate banking. This gave states the right to decide for themselves whether they wanted to let out-of-state banks buy or start subsidiaries within their borders. Because of competition from other financial companies, many large banks are moving rapidly to increase their size by buying banks, particularly successful ones, in other states. Pittsburgh's Mellon Bank purchased Girard Bank in Philadelphia and another in Delaware. Bank of Boston merged with Casco-Northern Corp. of Maine and is making plans for further expansion. There are many other deals in process, some of which are quite large.

Increased mergers. Besides buying in other states, banks are also increasing their size by buying banks in their own states. A strategy of many banks seems to be, "Buy the biggest banks in the biggest markets you are not in, and then move to smaller local markets in the same area." Some experts believe that the optimal size of a bank for efficiency purposes is $15 billion in assets. Only

TABLE 16.3 ■ THE BIGGEST BANK MERGERS, 1982–1983

Price* (millions)	Announcement Date	Acquirer Headquarters	Assets** (billions)	Acquiree Headquarters	Assets** (billions)
$515	6/21/83	Mercantile Texas, Dallas	$10.2	Southwest Bancshares, Houston	$6.9
$334	5/9/83	Sun Banks of Florida, Orlando	$5.0	Flagship Banks, Miami	$3.1
$288	7/26/83	First City Bancorp of Texas, Houston	$16.6	Cullen/Frost Bankers, San Antonio	$3.0
$282	4/30/82	Interfirst, Dallas	$17.3	First United Bancorp, Fort Worth	$2.4
$275	8/9/83	First Chicago, Chicago	$35.9	American National, Chicago	$3.2
$269	7/14/83	CBT, Hartford	$5.1	Bank of New England, Boston	$5.1
$244	4/19/82	Pittsburgh National, Pittsburgh	$6.9	Provident National, Philadelphia	$3.3
$220	8/2/82	Mellon National, Pittsburgh	$18.4	Girard, Philadelphia	$4.8
$203	7/25/83	First National State Bancorp, Newark	$4.9	Fidelity Union Bancorp, Newark	$3.4
$175	2/25/83	Virginia National Bankshares, Norfolk	$3.9	First & Merchants, Richmond, Va.	$2.8

* Cash or stock being received by smaller of the two merger partners.
** Year-end prior to announcement.

Source: Merrill Lynch Capital Markets.